ARCHITECTS

OF

INTELLIGENCE

For Xiaoxiao, Elaine, Colin, and Tristan

ARCHITECTS
OF
INTELLIGENCE

THE TRUTH ABOUT AI FROM
THE PEOPLE BUILDING IT

MARTIN FORD

ARCHITECTS OF INTELLIGENCE

Acquisition Editors: Ben Renow-Clarke
Project Editor: Radhika Atitkar
Content Development Editor: Alex Sorrentino
Proofreader: Safis Editing
Presentation Designer: Sandip Tadge
Cover Designer: Clare Bowyer
Production Editor: Amit Ramadas
Marketing Manager: Rajveer Samra
Editorial Director: Dominic Shakeshaft

First published: November 2018

Production reference: 2201118

Published by Packt Publishing Ltd.
Livery Place
35 Livery Street
Birmingham B3 2PB, UK

ISBN 978-1-78913-151-2

www.packt.com

Contents

INTRODUCTION

MARTIN FORD

AUTHOR, FUTURIST

Artificial intelligence is rapidly transitioning from the realm of science fiction to the reality of our daily lives. Our devices understand what we say, speak to us, and translate between languages with ever-increasing fluency. AI-powered visual recognition algorithms are outperforming people and beginning to find applications in everything from self-driving cars to systems that diagnose cancer in medical images. Major media organizations increasingly rely on automated journalism to turn raw data into coherent news stories that are virtually indistinguishable from those written by human journalists.

The list goes on and on, and it is becoming evident that AI is poised to become one of the most important forces shaping our world. Unlike more specialized innovations, artificial intelligence is becoming a true general-purpose technology. In other words, it is evolving into a utility—not unlike electricity—that is likely to ultimately scale across every industry, every sector of our economy, and nearly every aspect of science, society and culture.

The demonstrated power of artificial intelligence has, in the last few years, led to massive media exposure and commentary. Countless news articles, books, documentary films and television programs breathlessly enumerate AI's accomplishments and herald the dawn of a new era. The result has been a sometimes incomprehensible mixture of careful, evidence-based analysis, together with hype, speculation and what might be characterized as outright fear-mongering. We are told that fully autonomous self-driving cars will be sharing our roads in just a few years—and that millions of jobs for truck, taxi and Uber drivers are on the verge of vaporizing. Evidence of racial and gender bias has been detected in certain machine learning algorithms, and concerns about how AI-powered technologies such as facial recognition will impact privacy seem well-founded. Warnings that robots will soon be weaponized, or that truly intelligent (or superintelligent) machines might someday represent an existential threat to humanity, are regularly reported in the media. A number of very prominent public figures—none of whom are actual AI experts—have weighed in. Elon Musk has used especially extreme rhetoric, declaring that AI research is "summoning the demon" and that "AI is more dangerous than nuclear weapons." Even less volatile individuals, including Henry Kissinger and the late Stephen Hawking, have issued dire warnings.

The purpose of this book is to illuminate the field of artificial intelligence—as well as the opportunities and risks associated with it—by having a series of deep, wide-ranging conversations with some of the world's most prominent AI research scientists and entrepreneurs. Many of these people have made seminal contributions that directly underlie the transformations we see all around us; others have founded companies that are pushing the frontiers of AI, robotics and machine learning.

Selecting a list of the most prominent and influential people working in a field is, of course, a subjective exercise, and without doubt there are many other people who have made, or are making, critical contributions to the advancement of AI. Nonetheless, I am confident that if you were to ask nearly anyone with a deep knowledge of the field to compose a list of the most important minds who have shaped contemporary research in artificial intelligence, you would receive a list of names that substantially overlaps with the individuals interviewed in this book. The men and women I have included here are truly the architects of machine intelligence—and, by extension, of the revolution it will soon unleash.

The conversations recorded here are generally open-ended, but are designed to address some of the most pressing questions that face us as artificial intelligence continues to advance: What specific AI approaches and technologies are most promising, and what kind of breakthroughs might we see in the coming years? Are true thinking machines—or human-level AI—a real possibility and how soon might such a breakthrough occur? What risks, or threats, associated with artificial intelligence should we be genuinely concerned about? And how should we address those concerns? Is there a role for government regulation? Will AI unleash massive economic and job market disruption, or are these concerns overhyped? Could superintelligent machines someday break free of our control and pose a genuine threat? Should we worry about an AI "arms race," or that other countries with authoritarian political systems, particularly China, may eventually take the lead?

It goes without saying that no one really knows the answers to these questions. No one can predict the future. However, the AI experts I've spoken to here do know more about the current state of the technology, as well as the innovations on the horizon, than virtually anyone else. They often have decades of experience and have been instrumental in creating the revolution that is now beginning to unfold. Therefore, their thoughts and opinions deserve to be given significant weight. In addition to my questions about the field of artificial intelligence and its future, I have also delved into the backgrounds, career trajectories and current research interests of each of these individuals, and I believe their diverse origins and varied paths to prominence will make for fascinating and inspiring reading.

Artificial intelligence is a broad field of study with a number of subdisciplines, and many of the researchers interviewed here have worked in multiple areas. Some also have deep experience in other fields, such as the study of human cognition. Nonetheless, what follows is a brief attempt to create a very rough road map showing how the individuals interviewed here relate to the most important recent innovations in AI research and to the challenges that lie ahead. More background information about each person is available in his or her biography, which is located immediately after the interview.

The vast majority of the dramatic advances we've seen over the past decade or so—everything from image and facial recognition, to language translation, to AlphaGo's conquest of the ancient game of Go—are powered by a technology known as deep learning, or deep neural networks. Artificial neural networks, in which software roughly emulates the structure and interaction of biological neurons in the brain, date back at least to the 1950s. Simple versions of these networks are able to perform rudimentary pattern recognition tasks, and in the early days generated significant enthusiasm among researchers. By the 1960s, however—at least in part as the direct result of criticism of the technology by Marvin Minsky, one of the early pioneers of AI—neural networks fell out of favor and were almost entirely dismissed as researchers embraced other approaches.

Over a roughly 20-year period beginning in the 1980s, a very small group of research scientists continued to believe in and advance the technology of neural networks. Foremost among these were Geoffrey Hinton, Yoshua Bengio and Yann LeCun. These three men not only made seminal contributions to the mathematical theory underlying deep learning, they also served as the technology's primary evangelists. Together they refined ways to construct much more sophisticated—or "deep"—networks with many layers of artificial neurons. A bit like the medieval monks who preserved and copied classical texts, Hinton, Bengio and LeCun ushered neural networks through their own dark age—until the decades-long exponential advance of computing power, together with a nearly incomprehensible increase in the amount of data available, eventually enabled a "deep learning renaissance." That progress became an outright revolution in 2012, when a team of Hinton's graduate students from the University of Toronto entered a major image recognition contest and decimated the competition using deep learning.

In the ensuing years, deep learning has become ubiquitous. Every major technology company—Google, Facebook, Microsoft, Amazon, Apple, as well as leading Chinese firms like Baidu and Tencent—have made huge investments in the technology and leveraged it across their businesses. The companies that design microprocessor and graphics (or GPU) chips, such as NVIDIA and Intel, have also seen their businesses transformed as they rush to build hardware optimized for neural networks. Deep learning—at least so far—is the primary technology that has powered the AI revolution.

This book includes conversations with the three deep learning pioneers, Hinton, LeCun and Bengio, as well as with several other very prominent researchers at the forefront of the technology. Andrew Ng, Fei-Fei Li, Jeff Dean and Demis Hassabis have all advanced neural networks in areas like web search, computer vision, self-driving cars and more general intelligence. They are also recognized leaders in teaching, managing research organizations, and entrepreneurship centered on deep learning technology.

The remaining conversations in this book are generally with people who might be characterized as deep learning agnostics, or perhaps even critics. All would acknowledge the remarkable achievements of deep neural networks over the past decade, but they would likely argue that deep learning is just "one tool in the toolbox" and that continued progress will require integrating ideas from other spheres of artificial intelligence. Some of these, including Barbara Grosz and David Ferrucci, have focused heavily on the problem of understanding natural language. Gary Marcus and Josh Tenenbaum have devoted large portions of their careers to studying human cognition. Others, including Oren Etzioni, Stuart Russell and Daphne Koller, are AI generalists or have focused on using probabilistic techniques. Especially distinguished among this last group is Judea Pearl, who in 2012 won the Turing Award—essentially the Nobel Prize of computer science—in large part for his work on probabilistic (or Bayesian) approaches in AI and machine learning.

Beyond this very rough division defined by their attitude toward deep learning, several of the researchers I spoke to have focused on more specific areas. Rodney Brooks, Daniela Rus and Cynthia Breazeal are all recognized leaders in robotics. Breazeal along with Rana El Kaliouby are pioneers in building systems that understand and respond to emotion, and therefore have the ability to interact socially with people. Bryan Johnson has founded a startup company, Kernel, which hopes to eventually use technology to enhance human cognition.

There are three general areas that I judged to be of such high interest that I delved into them in every conversation. The first of these concerns the potential impact of AI and robotics on the job market and the economy. My own view is that as artificial intelligence gradually proves capable of automating nearly any routine, predictable task—regardless of whether it is blue or white collar in nature—we will inevitably see rising inequality and quite possibly outright unemployment, at least among certain groups of workers. I laid out this argument in my 2015 book, *Rise of the Robots: Technology and the Threat of a Jobless Future.*

The individuals I spoke to offered a variety of viewpoints about this potential economic disruption and the type of policy solutions that might address it. In order to dive deeper into this topic, I turned to James Manyika, the Chairman of the McKinsey Global Institute. Manyika offers a unique perspective as an experienced AI and robotics researcher who has lately turned his efforts toward understanding the impact of these technologies on organizations and workplaces. The McKinsey Global Institute is a leader in conducting research into this area, and this conversation includes many important insights into the nature of the unfolding workplace disruption.

The second question I directed at everyone concerns the path toward human-level AI, or what is typically called Artificial General Intelligence (AGI). From the very beginning, AGI has been the holy grail of the field of artificial intelligence. I wanted to know what each person thought about the prospect for a true thinking machine, the hurdles that would need to be surmounted and the timeframe for when it might be achieved. Everyone had important insights, but I found three conversations to be especially interesting: Demis Hassabis discussed efforts underway at DeepMind, which is the largest and best funded initiative geared specifically toward AGI. David Ferrucci, who led the team that created IBM Watson, is now the CEO of Elemental Cognition, a startup that hopes to achieve more general intelligence by leveraging an understanding of language. Ray Kurzweil, who now directs a natural language-oriented project at Google, also had important ideas on this topic (as well as many others). Kurzweil is best known for his 2005 book, *The Singularity is Near*. In 2012, he published a book on machine intelligence, *How to Create a Mind*, which caught the attention of Larry Page and led to his employment at Google.

As part of these discussions, I saw an opportunity to ask this group of extraordinarily accomplished AI researchers to give me a guess for just when AGI might be realized. The question I asked was, "What year do you think human-level AI might be achieved, with a 50 percent probability?" Most of the participants preferred to provide their guesses anonymously. I have summarized the results of this very informal survey in a section at the end of this book. Two people were willing to guess on the record, and these will give you a preview of the wide range of opinions. Ray Kurzweil believes, as he has stated many times previously, that human-level AI will be achieved around 2029—or just eleven years from the time of this writing. Rodney Brooks, on the other hand, guessed the year 2200, or more than 180 years in the future. Suffice it to say that one of the most fascinating aspects of the conversations reported here is the starkly differing views on a wide range of important topics.

The third area of discussion involves the varied risks that will accompany progress in artificial intelligence in both the immediate future and over much longer time horizons. One threat that is already becoming evident is the vulnerability of interconnected, autonomous systems to cyber attack or hacking. As AI becomes ever more integrated into our economy and society, solving this problem will be one of the most critical challenges we face. Another immediate concern is the susceptibility of machine learning algorithms to bias, in some cases on the basis of race or gender. Many of the individuals I spoke with emphasized the importance of addressing this issue and told of research currently underway in this area. Several also sounded an optimistic note—suggesting that AI may someday prove to be a powerful tool to help combat systemic bias or discrimination.

A danger that many researchers are passionate about is the specter of fully autonomous weapons. Many people in the artificial intelligence community believe that AI-enabled robots or drones with the capability to kill, without a human "in the loop" to authorize any lethal action, could eventually be as dangerous and destabilizing as biological or chemical weapons. In July 2018, over 160 AI companies and 2,400 individual researchers from across the globe—including a number of the people interviewed here—signed an open pledge promising to never develop such weapons.[1] Several of the conversations in this book delve into the dangers presented by weaponized AI.

A much more futuristic and speculative danger is the so-called "AI alignment problem." This is the concern that a truly intelligent, or perhaps superintelligent, machine might escape our control, or make decisions that might have adverse consequences for humanity. This is the fear that elicits seemingly over-the-top statements from people like Elon Musk. Nearly everyone I spoke to weighed in on this issue. To ensure that I gave this concern adequate and balanced coverage, I spoke with Nick Bostrom of the Future of Humanity Institute at the University of Oxford. Bostrom is the author of the bestselling book *Superintelligence: Paths, Dangers, Strategies*, which makes a careful argument regarding the potential risks associated with machines that might be far smarter than any human being.

---

1 https://futureoflife.org/lethal-autonomous-weapons-pledge/

The conversations included here were conducted from February to August 2018 and virtually all of them occupied at least an hour, some substantially more. They were recorded, professionally transcribed, and then edited for clarity by the team at Packt. Finally, the edited text was provided to the person I spoke to, who then had the opportunity to revise it and expand it. Therefore, I have every confidence that the words recorded here accurately reflect the thoughts of the person I interviewed.

The AI experts I spoke to are highly varied in terms of their origins, locations, and affiliations. One thing that even a brief perusal of this book will make apparent is the outsized influence of Google in the AI community. Of the 23 people I interviewed, seven have current or former affiliations with Google or its parent, Alphabet. Other major concentrations of talent are found at MIT and Stanford. Geoff Hinton and Yoshua Bengio are based at the Universities of Toronto and Montreal respectively, and the Canadian government has leveraged the reputations of their research organizations into a strategic focus on deep learning. Nineteen of the 23 people I spoke to work in the United States. Of those 19, however, more than half were born outside the US. Countries of origin include Australia, China, Egypt, France, Israel, Rhodesia (now Zimbabwe), Romania, and the UK. I would say this is pretty dramatic evidence of the critical role that skilled immigration plays in the technological leadership of the US.

As I carried out the conversations in this book, I had in mind a variety of potential readers, ranging from professional computer scientists, to managers and investors, to virtually anyone with an interest in AI and its impact on society. One especially important audience, however, consists of young people who might consider a future career in artificial intelligence. There is currently a massive shortage of talent in the field, especially among those with skills in deep learning, and a career in AI or machine learning promises to be exciting, lucrative and consequential.

As the industry works to attract more talent into the field, there is widespread recognition that much more must be done to ensure that those new people are more diverse. If artificial intelligence is indeed poised to reshape our world, then it is crucial that the individuals who best understand the technology—and are therefore best positioned to influence its direction—be representative of society as a whole.

About a quarter of those interviewed in this book are women, and that number is likely significantly higher than what would be found across the entire field of AI or machine learning. A recent study found that women represent about 12 percent of

leading researchers in machine learning.[2] A number of the people I spoke to emphasized the need for greater representation for both women and members of minority groups.

As you will learn from her interview in this book, one of the foremost women working in artificial intelligence is especially passionate about the need to increase diversity in the field. Stanford University's Fei-Fei Li co-founded an organization now called AI4ALL[3] to provide AI-focused summer camps geared especially to underrepresented high school students. AI4ALL has received significant industry support, including a recent grant from Google, and has now scaled up to include summer programs at six universities across the United States. While much work remains to be done, there are good reasons to be optimistic that diversity among AI researchers will increase significantly in the coming years and decades.

While this book does not assume a technical background, you will encounter some of the concepts and terminology associated with the field. For those without previous exposure to AI, I believe this will afford an opportunity to learn about the technology directly from some of the foremost minds in the field. To help less experienced readers get started, a brief overview of the vocabulary of AI follows this introduction, and I recommend you take a few moments to read this material before beginning the interviews. Additionally, the interview with Stuart Russell, who is the co-author of the leading AI textbook, includes an explanation of many of the field's most important ideas.

It has been an extraordinary privilege for me to participate in the conversations in this book. I believe you will find everyone I spoke with to be thoughtful, articulate, and deeply committed to ensuring that the technology he or she is working to create will be leveraged for the benefit of humanity. What you will not so often find is broad-based consensus. This book is full of varied, and often sharply conflicting, insights, opinions, and predictions. The message should be clear: Artificial intelligence is a wide open field. The nature of the innovations that lie ahead, the rate at which they will occur, and the specific applications to which they will be applied are all shrouded in deep uncertainty. It is this combination of massive potential disruption together with fundamental uncertainty that makes it imperative that we begin to engage in a meaningful and inclusive conversation about the future of artificial intelligence and what it may mean for our way of life. I hope this book will make a contribution to that discussion.

---

2 https://www.wired.com/story/artificial-intelligence-researchers-gender-imbalance

3 http://ai-4-all.org/

A Brief Introduction to the Vocabulary of AI

The conversations in this book are wide-ranging and in some cases delve into the specific techniques used in AI. You don't need a technical background to understand this material, but in some cases you may encounter the terminology used in the field. What follows is a very brief guide to the most important terms you will encounter in the interviews. If you take a few moments to read through this material, you will have all you need to fully enjoy this book. If you do find that a particular section is more detailed or technical than you would prefer, I would advise you to simply skip ahead to the next section.

MACHINE LEARNING is the branch of AI that involves creating algorithms that can learn from data. Another way to put this is that machine learning algorithms are computer programs that essentially program themselves by looking at information. You still hear people say "computers only do what they are programmed to do..." but the rise of machine learning is making this less and less true. There are many types of machine learning algorithms, but the one that has recently proved most disruptive (and gets all the press) is deep learning.

DEEP LEARNING is a type of machine learning that uses deep (or many layered) **ARTIFICIAL NEURAL NETWORKS**—software that roughly emulates the way neurons operate in the brain. Deep learning has been the primary driver of the revolution in AI that we have seen in the last decade or so.

There are a few other terms that less technically inclined readers can translate as simply "stuff under the deep learning hood." Opening the hood and delving into the details of these terms is entirely optional: **BACKPROPAGATION** (or **BACKPROP**) is the learning algorithm used in deep learning systems. As a neural network is trained (see supervised learning below), information propagates back through the layers of neurons that make up the network and causes a recalibration of the settings (or weights) for the individual neurons. The result is that the entire network gradually homes in on the correct answer. Geoff Hinton co-authored the seminal academic paper on backpropagation in 1986. He explains backprop further in his interview. An even more obscure term is **GRADIENT DESCENT**. This refers to the specific mathematical technique that the backpropagation algorithm uses to the reduce error as the network is trained. You may also run into terms that refer to various types, or configurations, of neural networks, such as **RECURRENT** and **CONVOLUTIONAL** neural nets and **BOLTZMANN MACHINES**. The differences generally pertain to the ways the neurons are connected. The details are technical and beyond the scope of this book. Nonetheless, I did ask Yann LeCun, who invented the convolutional architecture that is widely used in computer vision applications, to take a shot at explaining this concept.

BAYESIAN is a term that can be generally be translated as "probabilistic" or "using the rules of probability." You may encounter terms like Bayesian machine learning or Bayesian networks; these refer to algorithms that use the rules of probability. The term derives from the name of the Reverend Thomas Bayes (1701 to 1761) who formulated a way to update the likelihood of an event based on new evidence. Bayesian methods are very popular with both computer scientists and with scientists who attempt to model human cognition. Judea Pearl, who is interviewed in this book, received the highest honor in computer science, the Turing Award, in part for his work on Bayesian techniques.

How AI Systems Learn

There are several ways that machine learning systems can be trained. Innovation in this area—finding better ways to teach AI systems—will be critical to future progress in the field.

SUPERVISED LEARNING involves providing carefully structured training data that has been categorized or labeled to a learning algorithm. For example, you could teach a deep learning system to recognize a dog in photographs by feeding it many thousands (or even millions) of images containing a dog. Each of these would be labeled "Dog." You would also need to provide a huge number of images without a dog, labeled "No Dog." Once the system has been trained, you can then input entirely new photographs, and the system will tell you either "Dog" or "No Dog"—and it might well be able to do this with a proficiency that exceeds that of a typical human being.

Supervised learning is by far the most common technique used in current AI systems, accounting for perhaps 95 percent of practical applications. Supervised learning powers language translation (trained with millions of documents pre-translated into two different languages) and AI radiology systems (trained with millions of medical images labeled either "Cancer" or "No Cancer"). One problem with supervised learning is that it requires massive amounts of labeled data. This explains why companies that control huge amounts of data, like Google, Amazon, and Facebook, have such a dominant position in deep learning technology.

REINFORCEMENT LEARNING essentially means learning through practice or trial and error. Rather than training an algorithm by providing the correct, labeled outcome, the learning system is set loose to find a solution for itself, and if it succeeds it is given a "reward." Imagine training your dog to sit, and if he succeeds, giving him a treat. Reinforcement learning has been an especially powerful way to build AI systems that play games. As you will learn from the interview with Demis Hassabis in this book, DeepMind is a strong proponent of reinforcement learning and relied on it to create the AlphaGo system.

The problem with reinforcement learning is that it requires a huge number of practice runs before the algorithm can succeed. For this reason, it is primarily used for games or for tasks that can be simulated on a computer at high speed. Reinforcement learning can be used in the development of self-driving cars—but not by having actual cars practice on real roads. Instead virtual cars are trained in simulated environments. Once the software has been trained it can be moved to real-world cars.

UNSUPERVISED LEARNING means teaching machines to learn directly from unstructured data coming from their environments. This is how human beings learn. Young children, for example, learn languages primarily by listening to their parents. Supervised learning and reinforcement learning also play a role, but the human brain has an astonishing ability to learn simply by observation and unsupervised interaction with the environment.

Unsupervised learning represents one of the most promising avenues for progress in AI. We can imagine systems that can learn by themselves without the need for huge volumes of labeled training data. However, it is also one of the most difficult challenges facing the field. A breakthrough that allowed machines to efficiently learn in a truly unsupervised way would likely be considered one of the biggest events in AI so far, and an important waypoint on the road to human-level AI.

ARTIFICIAL GENERAL INTELLIGENCE (AGI) refers to a true thinking machine. AGI is typically considered to be more or less synonymous with the terms **HUMAN-LEVEL AI** or **STRONG AI**. You've likely seen several examples of AGI—but they have all been in the realm of science fiction. HAL from *2001 A Space Odyssey*, the Enterprise's main computer (or Mr. Data) from *Star Trek*, C3PO from *Star Wars* and Agent Smith from *The Matrix* are all examples of AGI. Each of these fictional systems would be capable of passing the **TURING TEST**—in other words, these AI systems could carry out a conversation so that they would be indistinguishable from a human being. Alan Turing proposed this test in his 1950 paper, *Computing Machinery and Intelligence*, which arguably established artificial intelligence as a modern field of study. In other words, AGI has been the goal from the very beginning.

It seems likely that if we someday succeed in achieving AGI, that smart system will soon become even smarter. In other words, we will see the advent of **SUPERINTELLIGENCE**, or a machine that exceeds the general intellectual capability of any human being. This might happen simply as a result of more powerful hardware, but it could be greatly accelerated if an intelligent machine turns its energies toward designing even smarter versions of itself. This might lead to what has been called a "recursive improvement cycle" or a "fast intelligence take off." This is the scenario that has led to concern about the "control" or "alignment" problem—where a superintelligent system might act in ways that are not in the best interest of the human race.

I have judged the path to AGI and the prospect for superintelligence to be topics of such high interest that I have discussed these issues with everyone interviewed in this book.

MARTIN FORD *is a futurist and the author of two books: The* New York Times *Bestselling* Rise of the Robots: Technology and the Threat of a Jobless Future *(winner of the 2015 Financial Times/McKinsey Business Book of the Year Award and translated into more than 20 languages) and* The Lights in the Tunnel: Automation, Accelerating Technology *and the* Economy of the Future, *as well as the founder of a Silicon Valley-based software development firm. His TED Talk on the impact of AI and robotics on the economy and society, given on the main stage at the 2017 TED Conference, has been viewed more than 2 million times.*

Martin is also the consulting artificial intelligence expert for the new "Rise of the Robots Index" from Societe Generale, underlying the Lyxor Robotics & AI ETF, which is focused specifically on investing in companies that will be significant participants in the AI and robotics revolution. He holds a computer engineering degree from the University of Michigan, Ann Arbor and a graduate business degree from the University of California, Los Angeles.

He has written about future technology and its implications for publications including The New York Times, Fortune, Forbes, The Atlantic, The Washington Post, Harvard Business Review, The Guardian, *and* The Financial Times. *He has also appeared on numerous radio and television shows, including NPR, CNBC, CNN, MSNBC and PBS. Martin is a frequent keynote speaker on the subject of accelerating progress in robotics and artificial intelligence—and what these advances mean for the economy, job market and society of the future.*

Martin continues to focus on entrepreneurship and is actively engaged as a board member and investor at Genesis Systems, a startup company that has developed a revolutionary atmospheric water generation (AWG) technology. Genesis will soon deploy automated, self-powered systems that will generate water directly from the air at industrial scale in the world's most arid regions.

MARTIN FORD

> **❝** *Current AI—and the AI that we can foresee in reasonable future—does not, and will not, have a moral sense or moral understanding of what is right and what is wrong.*

YOSHUA BENGIO

SCIENTIFIC DIRECTOR, MONTREAL INSTITUTE FOR LEARNING ALGORITHMS AND PROFESSOR OF COMPUTER SCIENCE AND OPERATIONS RESEARCH, UNIVERSITY OF MONTREAL

Yoshua Bengio is a professor of computer science and operations research at the University of Montreal and is widely recognized as one of the pioneers of deep learning. Yoshua was instrumental in advancing neural network research, in particular "unsupervised" learning where neural networks can learn without relying on vast amounts of training data.

the

front of AI research, so I want to begin by asking
u think we'll see breakthroughs in over the next few
s on the road to AGI (artificial general intelligence)?

now exactly what we're going to see, but I can tell
lly hard problems in front of us and that we are far
from n⎯   ⎯archers are trying to understand what the issues are,
such as, why is ⎯   can't build machines that really understand the world
as well as we do? Is it just that we don't have enough training data, or is it
that we don't have enough computing power? Many of us think that we are also
missing the basic ingredients needed, such as the ability to understand causal
relationships in data—an ability that actually enables us to generalize and to
come up with the right answers in settings that are very different from those
we've been trained in.

A human can imagine themselves going through an experience that is completely
new to them. You might have never had a car accident, for example, but you can
imagine one and because of all the things you already know you're actually able
to roleplay and make the right decisions, at least in your head. Current machine
learning is based on supervised learning, where a computer essentially learns about
the statistics of the data that it sees, and it needs to be taken through that process by
hand. In other words, humans have to provide all of those labels, possibly hundreds
of millions of correct answers, that the computer can then learn from.

A lot of current research is in areas where we're not doing so well, such as
unsupervised learning. This is where the computer can be more autonomous in
the way that it acquires knowledge about the world. Another area of research is in
causality, where the computer can not only observe data, like images or videos, but
also act on it and see the effect of those actions in order to infer causal relationships
in the world. The kinds of things that DeepMind, OpenAI, or Berkeley are doing
with virtual agents, for example, are going in the right direction to answer those
types of questions, and we're also doing these kinds of things in Montreal.

MARTIN FORD: Are there any particular projects that you would point
to as being really at the forefront of deep learning right now? The obvious
one is AlphaZero, but what other projects really represent the leading edge
of this technology?

YOSHUA BENGIO: There are a number of interesting projects, but the ones that I think are likely in the long run to have a big impact are those that involve virtual worlds in which an agent is trying to solve problems and is trying to learn about their environment. We are working on this at MILA, and there are projects in the same area in progress at DeepMind, OpenAI, Berkeley, Facebook and Google Brain. It's the new frontier.

It's important to remember, though, that this is not short-term research. We're not working on a particular application of deep learning, instead we're looking into the future of how a learning agent makes sense of its environment and how a learning agent can learn to speak or to understand language, in particular what we call grounded language.

MARTIN FORD: Can you explain that term?

YOSHUA BENGIO: Sure, a lot of the previous effort in trying to make computers understand language has the computer just read lots and lots of text. That's nice and all, but it's hard for the computer to actually get the meaning of those words unless those sentences are associated with real things. You might link words to images or videos, for example, or for robots that might be objects in the real world.

There's a lot of research in grounded language learning now trying to build an understanding of language, even if it's a small subset of the language, where the computer actually understands what those words mean, and it can act in correspondence to those words. It's a very interesting direction that could have a practical impact on things like language understanding for dialog, personal assistants, and so on.

MARTIN FORD: So, the idea there is basically to turn an agent loose in a simulated environment and have it learn like a child?

YOSHUA BENGIO: Exactly, in fact, we want to take inspiration from child development scientists who are studying how a newborn goes through a series of stages in the first few months of life where they gradually acquire more understanding about the world. We don't completely understand which part of this is innate or really learned, and I think this understanding of what babies go through can help us design our own systems.

One idea I introduced a few years ago in machine learning that is very common in training animals is curriculum learning. The idea is that we don't just show all the training examples as one big pile in an arbitrary order. Instead, we go through examples in an order that makes sense for the learner. We start with easy things, and once the easy things are mastered, we can use those concepts as the building blocks for learning slightly more complicated things. That's why we go through school, and why when we are 6 years old we don't go straight to university. This kind of learning is becoming more important in training computers as well.

MARTIN FORD: Let's talk about the path to AGI. Obviously, you believe that unsupervised learning—essentially having a system learn like a person—is an important component of it. Is that enough to get to AGI, or are there other critical components and breakthroughs that have to happen for us to get there?

YOSHUA BENGIO: My friend Yann LeCun has a nice metaphor that describes this. We're currently climbing a hill, and we are all excited because we have made a lot of progress on climbing the hill, but as we approach the top of the hill, we can start to see a series of other hills rising in front of us. That is what we see now in the development of AGI, some of the limitations of our current approaches. When we were climbing the first hill, when we were discovering how to train deeper networks, for example, we didn't see the limitations of the systems we were building because we were just discovering how to go up a few steps.

As we reach this satisfying improvement that we are getting in our techniques—we reach the top of the first hill—we also see the limitations, and then we see another hill that we have to climb, and once we climb that one we'll see another one, and so on. It's impossible to tell how many more breakthroughs or significant advances are going to be needed before we reach human-level intelligence.

MARTIN FORD: How many hills are there? What's the timescale for AGI? Can you give me your best guess?

YOSHUA BENGIO: You won't be getting that from me, there's no point. It's useless to guess a date because we have no clue. All I can say is that it's not going to happen in the next few years.

YOSHUA BENGIO

MARTIN FORD: Do you think that deep learning or neural networks generally are really the way forward?

YOSHUA BENGIO: Yes, what we have discovered in terms of the scientific concepts that are behind deep learning and the years of progress made in this field, means that for the most part, many of the concepts behind deep learning and neural networks are here to stay. Simply put, they are incredibly powerful. In fact, they are probably going to help us better understand how animal and human brains learn complex things. As I said, though, they're not enough to get us to AGI. We're at a point where we can see some of the limitations in what we currently have, and we're going to improve and build on top of that.

MARTIN FORD: I know that the Allen Institute for AI is working on Project Mosaic, which is about building common sense into computers. Do you think that kind of thing is critical, or do you think that maybe common sense emerges as part of the learning process?

YOSHUA BENGIO: I'm sure common sense will emerge as part of the learning process. It won't come up because somebody sticks little bits of knowledge into your head, that's not how it works for humans.

MARTIN FORD: Is deep learning the primary way to get us to AGI, or do you think it's going to require some sort of a hybrid system?

YOSHUA BENGIO: Classical AI was purely symbolic, and there was no learning. It focused on a really interesting aspect of cognition, which is how we sequentially reason and combine pieces of information. Deep learning neural networks, on the other hand, have always been about focusing on a sort of bottom-up view of cognition, where we start with perception and we anchor the machine's understanding of the world in perception. From there, we build distributed representations and can capture the relationship between many variables.

I studied the relationships between such variables with my brother around 1999. That gave rise to a lot of the recent progress in natural language, such as word embeddings, or distributed representations for words and sentences. In these cases, a word is represented by a pattern of activity in your brain—or by a set of numbers. Those words that have a similar meaning are then associated with similar patterns of numbers.

What's going on now in the deep learning field is that people are building on top of these deep learning concepts and starting to try to solve the classical AI problems of reasoning and being able to understand, program, or plan. Researchers are trying to use the building blocks that we developed from perception and extend them towards these higher-level cognitive tasks (sometimes called System 2 by psychologists). I believe in part that's the way that we're going to move towards human-level AI. It's not that it's a hybrid system; it's like we're trying to solve some of the same problems that classical AI was trying to solve but using the building blocks coming from deep learning. It's a very different way of doing it, but the objectives are very similar.

MARTIN FORD: Your prediction, then, is that it's all going to be neural networks, but with different architectures?

YOSHUA BENGIO: Yes. Note that your brain is all neural networks. We have to come up with different architectures and different training frameworks that can do the kinds of things that classical AI was trying to do, like reasoning, inferring an explanation for what you're seeing and planning.

MARTIN FORD: Do you think it can all be done with learning and training or does there need to be some structure there?

YOSHUA BENGIO: There is structure there, it's just that it's not the kind of structure that we use to represent knowledge when we write an encyclopedia, or we write a mathematical formula. The kind of structure that we put in corresponds to the architecture of the neural net, and to fairly broad assumptions about the world and the kind of task that we're trying to solve. When we put in a special structure and architecture that allows the network to have an attention mechanism, it's putting in a lot of prior knowledge. It turns out that this is central to the success of things like machine translation.

You need that kind of tool in your toolbox in order to solve some of those problems, in the same way that if you deal with images, you need to have something like a convolutional neural network structure in order to do a good job. If you don't put in that structure, then performance is much worse. There are already a lot of domain-specific assumptions about the world and about the function you're trying to learn, that are implicit in the kind of architectures and training objectives that are used in deep learning. This is what most of the research papers today are about.

MARTIN FORD: What I was trying to get at with the question on structure was that, for example, a baby can recognize human faces right after it is born. Clearly, then, there is some structure in the human brain that allows the baby to do that. It's not just raw neurons working on pixels.

YOSHUA BENGIO: You're wrong! It is raw neurons working on pixels, except that there is a particular architecture in the baby's brain that recognizes something circular with two dots inside it.

MARTIN FORD: My point is that the structure pre-exists.

YOSHUA BENGIO: Of course it does, but all the things that we're designing in those neural networks also pre-exist. What deep learning researchers are doing is like the work of evolution, where we're putting in the prior knowledge in the form of both the architecture and the training procedure.

If we wanted, we could hardwire something that would allow the network to recognize a face, but it's useless for an AI because they can learn that very quickly. Instead, we put in the things that are really useful for solving the harder problems that we're trying to deal with.

Nobody is saying that there is no innate knowledge in humans, babies, and animals, in fact, most animals have only innate knowledge. An ant doesn't learn much, it's all like a big, fixed program, but as you go higher up in the intelligence hierarchy, the share of learning keeps increasing. What makes humans different from many other animals is how much we learn versus how much is innate at the start.

MARTIN FORD: Let's step back and define some of those concepts. In the 1980s, neural networks were a very marginalized subject and they were just one layer, so there was nothing deep about them. You were involved in transforming that into what we now call deep learning. Could you define, in relatively non-technical terms, what that is?

YOSHUA BENGIO: Deep learning is an approach to machine learning. While machine learning is trying to put knowledge into computers by allowing computers to learn from examples, deep learning is doing it in a way that is inspired by the brain.

Deep learning and machine learning are just a continuation of that earlier work on neural networks. They're called "deep" because they added the ability to train deeper networks, meaning they have more layers, and each layer represents a different level of representation. We hope that as the network gets deeper, it can represent more abstract things, and so far, that does seem to be the case.

MARTIN FORD: When you say layers, do you mean layers of abstraction? So, in terms of a visual image, the first layer would be pixels, then it would be edges, followed by corners, and then gradually you would get all the way up to objects?

YOSHUA BENGIO: Yes, that's correct.

MARTIN FORD: If I understand correctly, though, the computer still doesn't understand what that object is, right?

YOSHUA BENGIO: The computer has some understanding, it's not a black-and-white argument. A cat understands a door, but it doesn't understand it as well as you do. Different people have different levels of understanding of the many things around them, and science is about trying to deepen our understanding of those many things. These networks have a level of understanding of images if they've been trained on images, but that level is still not as abstract and as general as ours. One reason for this is that we interpret images in the context of our three-dimensional understanding of the world, obtained thanks to our stereo vision and our movements and actions in the world. This gives us a lot more than just a visual model: it also gives us a physical model of objects. The current level of computer understanding of images is still primitive but it's still good enough to be incredibly useful in many applications.

MARTIN FORD: Is it true that the thing that has really made deep learning possible is backpropagation? The idea that you can send the error information back through the layers, and adjust each layer based on the final outcome.

YOSHUA BENGIO: Indeed, backpropagation has been at the heart of the success of deep learning in recent years. It is a method to do credit assignment, that is, to figure out how internal neurons should change to make the bigger network behave properly. Backpropagation, at least in the context of neural networks, was discovered in the early 1980s, at the time when I started my own work. Yann LeCun independently discovered it around the same time as Geoffrey Hinton and David Rumelhart. It's an old idea, but we didn't practically succeed in training these deeper networks until around 2006, over a quarter of a century later.

Since then, we've been adding a number of other features to these networks, which are very exciting for our research into artificial intelligence, such as attention mechanisms, memory, and the ability to not just classify but also generate images.

MARTIN FORD: Do we know if the brain does something similar to backpropagation?

YOSHUA BENGIO: That's a good question. Neural nets are not trying to imitate the brain, but they are inspired by some of its computational characteristics, at least at an abstract level.

You have to realize that we don't yet have a full picture of how the brain works. There are many aspects of the brain that are not yet understood by neuroscientists. There are tons of observations about the brain, but we don't know how to connect the dots yet.

It may be that the work that we're doing in machine learning with neural nets could provide a testable hypothesis for brain science. That's one of the things that I'm interested in. In particular, backpropagation up to now has mostly been considered something that computers can do, but not realistic for brains.

The thing is, backpropagation is working incredibly well, and it suggests that maybe the brain is doing something similar—not exactly the same, but with the same function. As a result of that, I'm currently involved in some very interesting research in that direction.

MARTIN FORD: I know that there was an "AI Winter" where most people had dismissed deep learning, but a handful of people, like yourself, Geoffrey Hinton, and Yann LeCun, kept it alive. How did that then evolve to the point where we find ourselves today?

YOSHUA BENGIO: By the end of the '90s and through the early 2000s, neural networks were not trendy, and very few groups were involved with them. I had a strong intuition that by throwing out neural networks, we were throwing out something really important.

Part of that was because of something that we now call compositionality: The ability of these systems to represent very rich information about the data in a compositional way, where you compose many building blocks that correspond to the neurons and the layers. That led me to language models, early neural networks that model text using word embeddings. Each word is associated with a set of numbers corresponding to different attributes that are learned autonomously by the machine. It didn't really catch on at the time, but nowadays almost everything to do with modeling language from data uses these ideas.

The big question was how we could train deeper networks, and the breakthrough was made by Geoffrey Hinton and his work with Restricted Boltzmann Machines (RBMs). In my lab, we were working on autoencoders, which are very closely related to RBMs, and autoencoders have given rise to all kinds of models, such as generative adversarial networks. It turned out that by stacking these RBMs or autoencoders we are able to train deeper networks than we were able to before.

MARTIN FORD: Could you explain what an autoencoder is?

YOSHUA BENGIO: There are two parts to an autoencoder, an encoder and a decoder. The idea is that the encoder part takes an image, for example, and tries to represent it in a compressed way, such as a verbal description. The decoder then takes that representation and tries to recover the original image. The autoencoder is trained to do this compression and decompression so that it is as faithful as possible to the original.

Autoencoders have changed quite a bit since that original vision. Now, we think of them in terms of taking raw information, like an image, and transforming it into a more abstract space where the important, semantic aspect of it will be easier to read. That's the encoder part. The decoder works backwards, taking those high-level quantities—that you don't have to define by hand—and transforming them into an image. That was the early deep learning work.

Then a few years later, we discovered that we didn't need these approaches to train deep networks, we could just change the nonlinearity. One of my students was working with neuroscientists, and we thought that we should try rectified linear units (ReLUs)—we called them rectifiers in those days—because they were more biologically plausible, and this is an example of actually taking inspiration from the brain.

YOSHUA BENGIO

MARTIN FORD: What did you learn from all of that?

YOSHUA BENGIO: We had previously used a sigmoid function to train neural nets, but it turned out that by using ReLUs we could suddenly train very deep nets much more easily. That was another big change that occurred around 2010 or 2011.

There is a very large dataset—the ImageNet dataset—which is used in computer vision, and people in that field would only believe in our deep learning methods if we could show good results on that dataset. Geoffrey Hinton's group actually did it, following up on earlier work by Yann LeCun on convolutional networks—that is, neural networks which were specialized for images. In 2012, these new deep learning architectures with extra twists were used with huge success and showed a big improvement on existing methods. Within a couple of years, the whole computer vision community switched to these kinds of networks.

MARTIN FORD: So that's the point at which deep learning really took off?

YOSHUA BENGIO: It was a bit later. By 2014, things were lining up for a big acceleration in the community for the take-up of deep learning.

MARTIN FORD: That's when it transitioned from being centered in universities to being in the mainstream domain at places like Google, Facebook, and Baidu?

YOSHUA BENGIO: Exactly. The shift started slightly earlier, around 2010, with companies like Google, IBM, and Microsoft, who were working on neural networks for speech recognition. By 2012, Google had these neural networks on their Android smartphones. It was revolutionary for the fact that the same technology of deep learning could be used for both computer vision and speech recognition. It drove a lot of attention toward the field.

MARTIN FORD: Thinking back to when you first started in neural networks, are you surprised at the distance things have come and the fact that they've become so central to what large companies, like Google and Facebook, are doing now?

YOSHUA BENGIO: Of course, we didn't expect that. We've had a series of important and surprising breakthroughs with deep learning. I mentioned earlier that speech recognition came around 2010, and then computer vision around 2012. A couple of years later, in 2014 and 2015, we had breakthroughs in machine translation that ended up being used in Google Translate in 2016. 2016 was also the year we saw the breakthroughs with AlphaGo. All of these things, among a number of others, were really not expected.

I remember back in 2014 I looked at some of our results in caption generation, where the computer is trying to come up with a caption for an image, and I was amazed that we were able to do that. If you had asked me just one year earlier if we'd be able to do that in a year, I would have said no.

MARTIN FORD: Those captions are pretty remarkable. Sometimes they're way off the mark, but most of the time they're amazing.

YOSHUA BENGIO: Of course, they're way off sometimes! They're not trained on enough data, and there are also some fundamental advances in basic research that need to be made for those systems to really understand an image and really understand language. We're far away from achieving those advances, but the fact that they were able to reach the level of performance that they have was not something we expected.

MARTIN FORD: Let's talk about your career. What was your own path into the field of AI?

YOSHUA BENGIO: When I was young, I would read a lot of science fiction, and I'm sure that had an impact on me. It introduced me to topics such as AI and Asimov's Three Laws of Robotics, and I wanted to go to college and study physics and mathematics. That changed when my brother and I became interested in computers. We saved our money to buy an Apple IIe and then an Atari 800. Software was scarce in those days, so we learned to program them ourselves in BASIC.

I got so excited with programming that I went into computer engineering and then computer science for my Master's and PhD. While doing my Master's around 1985, I started reading some papers on early neural nets, including some of Geoffrey Hinton's papers, and it was like love at first sight. I quickly decided that this was the subject I wanted to do my research in.

MARTIN FORD: Is there any particular advice you'd give to someone who wants to get into the field of being a deep learning expert or researcher?

YOSHUA BENGIO: Just jump in the water and start swimming. There's a ton of information in the form of tutorials, videos, and open source libraries at all levels because there's so much interest in this field. And there is the book I co-authored, called *Deep Learning*, which helps newcomers into the field and is available for free online. I see many undergrad students training themselves by reading lots and lots of papers, trying to reproduce those papers, and then applying to get into the labs which are doing this kind of research. If you're interested in the area, there's no better time to start than now.

MARTIN FORD: In terms of your career, one thing I noticed is that of the key people in deep learning, you're the only one that remains entirely in the academic world. Most others are part-time at companies like Facebook or Google. What made you take that career pathway?

YOSHUA BENGIO: I've always valued academia and the freedom to work for the common good or the things that I believe would have more impact. I also value working with students both psychologically and in terms of the efficiency and productivity of my research. If I went into the industry, I would be leaving a lot of that behind.

I also wanted to stay in Montreal, and at that time, it was the case that going into the industry meant going to either California or New York. It was then that I thought that maybe we could build something in Montreal that could become a new Silicon Valley for AI. As a result, I decided to stay and create Mila, The Montreal Institute for Learning Algorithms.

Mila carries out basic research, and also plays a leadership role in the AI ecosystem in Montreal. This role involves working in partnership with the Vector Institute in Toronto, and Amii, in Edmonton, as part of the Canadian strategy to really push AI forward—in terms of science, in terms of the economy, and in terms of positive social impact.

MARTIN FORD: Since you mention it, let's talk more about AI and the economy, and some of the risks there. I have written a lot about the potential for artificial intelligence to bring on a new Industrial Revolution, and potentially to lead to a lot of job losses. How do you feel about that hypothesis, do you think that it is overhyped?

YOSHUA BENGIO: No, I don't think it's overhyped. The part that is less clear is whether this is going to happen over a decade or three decades. What I can say is that even if we stop basic research in AI and deep learning tomorrow, the science has advanced enough that there's already a huge amount of social and economic benefit to reap from it simply by engineering new services and new products from these ideas.

We also collect a huge amount of data that we don't use. For example, in healthcare, we're only using a tiny, tiny fraction of what is available, or of what will be available as even more gets digitized every day. Hardware companies are working hard to build deep learning chips that are soon going to be easily a thousand times faster or more energy-efficient than the ones we currently have. The fact that you could have these things everywhere around you, in cars and phones, is clearly going to change the world.

What will slow things down are things like social factors. It takes time to change the healthcare infrastructure, even if the technology is there. Society can't change infinitely fast, even if the technology is moving forward.

MARTIN FORD: If this technology change does lead to a lot of jobs being eliminated, do you think something like a basic income would be a good solution?

YOSHUA BENGIO: I think a basic income could work, but we have to take a scientific view on this to get rid of our moral priors that say if a person doesn't work, then they shouldn't have an income. I think it's crazy. I think we have to look at what's going to work best for the economy and what's going to work best for people's happiness, and we can do pilot experiments to answer those questions.

It's not like there's one clear answer, there are many ways that society could take care of the people who are going to be left behind and minimize the amount of misery arising from this Industrial Revolution. I'm going to go back to something that my friend Yann LeCun said: If we had had the foresight in the 19th century to see how the Industrial Revolution would unfold, maybe we could have avoided much of the misery that followed. If in the 19th century we had put in place the kind of social safety net that currently exists in most Western nations, instead of waiting until the 1940s and 1950s, then hundreds of millions of people would have led a much better and healthier life. The thing is, it's going to take probably much less than a century this time to unfold that story, and so the potential negative impacts could be even larger.

I think it's really important to start thinking about it right now and to start scientifically studying the options to minimize misery and optimize global well-being. I think it's possible to do it, and we shouldn't just rely on our old biases and religious beliefs in order to decide on the answer to these questions.

MARTIN FORD: I agree, but as you say, it could unfold fairly rapidly. It's going to be a staggering political problem, too.

YOSHUA BENGIO: Which is all the more reason to act quickly!

MARTIN FORD: A valid point. Beyond the economic impact, what are the other things we should worry about in terms of artificial intelligence?

YOSHUA BENGIO: I have been very active in speaking against killer robots.

MARTIN FORD: I noticed you signed a letter aimed at a university in Korea which seemed to be headed towards research on killer robots.

YOSHUA BENGIO: That's right, and this letter is working. In fact, KAIST, The Korea Advanced Institute of Science and Technology, has been telling us that they will avoid going into the development of military systems which don't have a human in the loop.

Let me go back to this question about a human in the loop because I think this is really important. People need to understand that current AI—and the AI that we can foresee in the reasonable future—does not, and will not, have a moral sense or moral understanding of what is right and what is wrong. I know there are differences across cultures, but these moral questions are important in people's lives.

It's true, not just for killer robots but all kinds of other things, like the work that a judge does deciding on the fate of a person—whether that person should return to prison or be freed into society. These are really difficult moral questions, where you have to understand human psychology, and you have to understand moral values. It's crazy to put those decisions in the hands of machines, which don't have that kind of understanding. It's not just crazy; it's wrong. We have to have social norms or laws, which make sure that computers in the foreseeable future don't get those kinds of responsibilities.

MARTIN FORD: I want to challenge you on that. I think a lot of people would say that you have a very idealistic view of human beings and the quality of their judgment.

YOSHUA BENGIO: Sure, but I'd rather have an imperfect human being as a judge than a machine that doesn't understand what it's doing.

MARTIN FORD: But think of an autonomous security robot that would be happy to take a bullet first and shoot second, whereas a human would never do that, and that could potentially save lives. In theory, an autonomous security robot would also not be racist, if it were programmed correctly. These are actually areas where it might have an advantage over a human being. Would you agree?

YOSHUA BENGIO: Well, it might be the case one day, but I can tell you we're not there yet. It's not just about precision, it's about understanding the human context, and computers have absolutely zero clues about that.

MARTIN FORD: Other than the military and weaponization aspects, is there anything else that we should be worried about with AI?

YOSHUA BENGIO: Yes, and this is something that hasn't been discussed much, but now may come more to the forefront because of what happened with Facebook and Cambridge Analytica. The use of AI in advertising or generally in influencing people is something that we should be really aware of as dangerous for democracy—and is morally wrong in some ways. We should make sure that our society prevents those things as much as possible.

In Canada, for example, advertising that is directed at children is forbidden. There's a good reason for that: We think that it's immoral to manipulate their minds when they are so vulnerable. In fact, though, every one of us is vulnerable, and if it weren't the case, then advertising wouldn't work.

The other thing is that advertising actually hurts market forces because it gives larger companies a tool to slow down smaller companies coming into their markets because those larger companies can use their brand. Nowadays they can use AI to target their message to people in a much more accurate way, and I think that's kind of scary, especially when it makes people do things that may be against their well-being. It could be the case in political advertising, for example, or advertising that could change your behavior and have an impact on your health. I think we should be really, really careful about how these tools are used to influence people in general.

MARTIN FORD: What about the warnings from people like Elon Musk and Stephen Hawking about an existential threat from super intelligent AI and getting into a recursive improvement loop? Are these things that we should be concerned about at this point?

YOSHUA BENGIO: I'm not concerned about these things, I think it's fine that some people study the question. My understanding of the current science as it is now, and as I can foresee it, is that those kinds of scenarios are not realistic. Those kinds of scenarios are not compatible with how we build AI right now. Things may be different in a few decades, I have no idea, but that is science fiction as far as I'm concerned. I think perhaps those fears are detracting from some of the most pressing issues that we could act on now.

We've talked about killer robots and we've talked about political advertising, but there are other concerns, like how data could be biased and reinforce discrimination, for example. These are things that governments and companies can act on now, and we do have some ways to mitigate some of these issues. The debate shouldn't focus so much on these very long-term potential risks, which I don't think are compatible with my understanding of AI, but we should pay attention to short-term things like killer robots.

MARTIN FORD: I want to ask you about the potential competition with China and other countries. You've talked a lot about, for example, having limitations on autonomous weapons and one obvious concern there is that some countries might ignore those rules. How worried should we be about that international competition?

YOSHUA BENGIO: Firstly, on the scientific side I don't have any concern. The more researchers around the world are working on a science, the better it is for that science. If China is investing a lot in AI that's fine; at the end of the day, we're all going to take advantage of the progress that's going to come of that research.

However, I think the part about the Chinese government potentially using this technology either for military purposes or for internal policing is scary. If you take the current state of the science and build systems that will recognize people, recognize faces, and track them, then essentially you can build a Big Brother society in just a few years. It's quite technically feasible and it is creating even more danger for democracy around the world. That is really something to be concerned about. It's not just states like China where this could happen, either; it could also happen in liberal democracies if they slip towards autocratic rule, as we have seen in some countries.

Regarding the military race to use AI, we shouldn't confuse killer robots with the use of AI in the military. I'm not saying that we should completely ban the use of AI in the military. For example, if the military uses AI to build weapons that will destroy killer robots, then that's a good thing. What is immoral is to have these robots kill humans. It's not like we all have to use AI immorally. We can build defensive weapons, and that could be useful to stop the race.

MARTIN FORD: It sounds like you feel there's definitely a role for regulation in terms of autonomous weapons?

YOSHUA BENGIO: There's a role for regulation everywhere. In the areas where AI is going to have a social impact, then we at least have to think about regulation. We have to consider what the right social mechanism is that will make sure that AI is used for good.

MARTIN FORD: And you think governments are equipped to take on that question?

YOSHUA BENGIO: I don't trust companies to do it by themselves because their main focus is on maximizing profits. Of course, they're also trying to remain popular among their users or customers, but they're not completely transparent about what they do. It's not always clear that those objectives that they're implementing correspond to the well-being of the population in general.

I think governments have a really important role to play, and it's not just individual governments, it's the international community because many of these questions are not just local questions, they're international questions.

MARTIN FORD: Do you believe that the benefits to all of this are going to clearly outweigh the risks?

YOSHUA BENGIO: They'll only outweigh the risks if we act wisely. That's why it's so important to have those discussions. That's why we don't want to move straight ahead with blinkers on; we have to keep our eyes open to all of the potential dangers that are lurking.

MARTIN FORD: Where do you think this discussion should be taking place now? Is it something primarily think tanks and universities should do, or do you think this should be part of the political discussion both nationally and internationally?

YOSHUA BENGIO: It should totally be part of the political discussion. I was invited to speak at a meeting of G7 ministers, and one of the questions discussed was, "How do we develop AI in a way that's both economically positive and keeps the trust of the people?", because people today do have concerns. The answer is to not do things in secret or in ivory towers, but instead to have an open discussion where everybody around the table, including every citizen, should be part of the discussion. We're going to have to make collective choices about what kind of future we want, and because AI is so powerful, every citizen should understand at some level what the issues are.

ARCHITECTS OF INTELLIGENCE

YOSHUA BENGIO *is Full Professor of the Department of Computer Science and Operations Research, scientific director of the Montreal Institute for Learning Algorithms (Mila), CIFAR Program co-director of the CIFAR program on Learning in Machines and Brains, Canada Research Chair in* Statistical Learning Algorithms. *Together with Ian Goodfellow and Aaron Courville, he wrote* Deep Learning, *one of the defining textbooks on the subject. The book is available for free from https://www.deeplearningbook.org.*

YOSHUA BENGIO

> **❝** *Once an AGI gets past kindergarten reading level, it will shoot beyond anything that any human being has ever done, and it will have a much bigger knowledge base than any human ever has.*

STUART J. RUSSELL

PROFESSOR OF COMPUTER SCIENCE,
UNIVERSITY OF CALIFORNIA, BERKELEY

Stuart J. Russell is widely recognized as one of the world's leading contributors in the field of artificial intelligence. He is a Professor of Computer Science and Director of the Center for Human-Compatible Artificial Intelligence at The University of California, Berkeley. Stuart is the co-author of the leading AI textbook, Artificial Intelligence: A Modern Approach, *which is in use at over 1,300 colleges and universities throughout the world.*

MARTIN FORD: Given that you co-wrote the standard textbook on AI in use today, I thought it might be interesting if you could define some key AI terms. What is your definition of artificial intelligence? What does it encompass? What types of computer science problems would be included in that arena? Could you compare it or contrast it with machine learning?

STUART J. RUSSELL: Let me give you, shall we say, the standard definition of artificial intelligence, which is similar to the one in the book and is now quite widely accepted: An entity is intelligent to the extent that it does the right thing, meaning that its actions are expected to achieve its objectives. The definition applies to both humans and machines. This notion of doing the right thing is the key unifying principle of AI. When we break this principle down and look deeply at what is required to do the right thing in the real world, we realize that a successful AI system needs some key abilities, including perception, vision, speech recognition, and action.

These abilities help us to define artificial intelligence. We're talking about the ability to control robot manipulators, and everything that happens in robotics. We're talking about the ability to make decisions, to plan, and to problem-solve. We're talking about the ability to communicate, and so natural language understanding also becomes extremely important to AI.

We're also talking about an ability to internally know things. It's very hard to function successfully in the real world if you don't actually know anything. To understand how we know things, we enter the scientific field that we call knowledge representation. This is where we study how knowledge can be stored internally and then processed by reasoning algorithms, such as automated logical deduction and probabilistic inference algorithms.

Then there is learning. Learning is a key ability for modern artificial intelligence. Machine learning has always been a subfield of AI, and it simply means improving your ability to do the right thing as a result of experience. That could be learning how to perceive better by seeing labeled examples of objects. That could also mean learning how to reason better by experience—such as discovering which reasoning steps turn out to be useful for solving a problem, and which reasoning steps turn out to be less useful.

AlphaGo, for example, is a modern AI Go program that recently beat the best human world-champion players, and it really does learn. It learns how to reason better from experience. As well as learning to evaluate positions, AlphaGo learns how to control its own deliberations so that it more effectively reaches high decision-quality moves more quickly, with less computation.

MARTIN FORD: Can you also define neural networks and deep learning?

STUART J. RUSSELL: Yes, in machine learning one of the standard techniques is called "supervised learning," where we give the AI system a set of examples of a concept, along with a description and a label for each example in the set. For example, we might have a photograph, where we've got all the pixels in the image, and then we have a label saying that this is a photograph of a boat, or of a Dalmatian dog, or of a bowl of cherries. In supervised learning for this task, the goal is to find a predictor, or a hypothesis, for how to classify images in general.

From these supervised training examples, we try to give an AI the ability to recognize pictures of, say, Dalmatian dogs, and the ability to predict how other pictures of Dalmatian dogs might look.

One way of representing the hypothesis, or the predictor, is a neural net. A neural net is essentially a complicated circuit with many layers. The input into this circuit could be the values of pixels from pictures of Dalmatian dogs. Then, as those input values propagate through the circuit, new values are calculated at each layer of the circuit. At the end, we have the outputs of the neural network, which are the predictions about what kind of object is being recognized.

So hopefully, if there's a Dalmatian dog in our input image, then by the time all those numbers and pixel values propagate through the neural network and all of its layers and connections, the output indicator for a Dalmatian dog will light up with a high value, and the output indicator for a bowl of cherries will have a low value. We then say that the neural network has correctly recognized a Dalmatian dog.

MARTIN FORD: How do you get a neural network to recognize images?

STUART J. RUSSELL: This is where the learning process comes in. The circuit has adjustable connection strengths between all its connections, and what the learning algorithms do is adjust those connection strengths so that the network tends to give the correct predictions on the training examples. Then if you're lucky, the neural network will also give correct predictions on new images that it hasn't seen before. And that's a neural network!

Going one step further, deep learning is where we have neural networks that have many layers. There is no required minimum for a neural network to be deep, but we would usually say that two or three layers is not a deep learning network, while four or more layers is deep learning.

Some deep learning networks get up to one thousand layers or more. By having many layers in deep learning, we can represent a very complex transformation between the input and output, by a composition of much simpler transformations, each represented by one of those layers in the network.

The deep learning hypothesis suggests that many layers make it easier for the learning algorithm to find a predictor, to set all the connection strengths in the network so that it does a good job.

We are just beginning now to get some theoretical understanding of when and why the deep learning hypothesis is correct, but to a large extent, it's still a kind of magic, because it really didn't have to happen that way. There seems to be a property of images in the real world, and there is some property of sound and speech signals in the real world, such that when you connect that kind of data to a deep network it will—for some reason—be relatively easy to learn a good predictor. But why this happens is still anyone's guess.

MARTIN FORD: Deep learning is receiving enormous amounts of attention right now, and it would be easy to come away with the impression that artificial intelligence is synonymous with deep learning. But deep learning is really just one relatively small part of the field, isn't it?

STUART J. RUSSELL: Yes, it would be a huge mistake for someone to think that deep learning is the same thing as artificial intelligence, because the ability to distinguish Dalmatian dogs from bowls of cherries is useful but it is still only a very small part of what we need to give an artificial intelligence in order for it to be successful. Perception and image recognition are both important aspects of operating successfully in the real world, but deep learning is only one part of the picture.

AlphaGo, and its successor AlphaZero, created a lot of media attention around deep learning with stunning advances in Go and Chess, but they're really a hybrid of classical search-based AI and a deep learning algorithm that evaluates each game position that the classical AI system searches through. While the ability to distinguish between good and bad positions is central to AlphaGo, it cannot play world-champion-level Go just by deep learning.

Self-driving car systems also use a hybrid of classical search-based AI and deep learning. Self-driving cars are not just pure deep learning systems, because that does not work very well. Many driving situations need classical rules for an AI to be successful. For example, if you're in the middle lane and you want to change lanes to the right, and there's someone trying to pass you on the inside, then you should wait for them to go by first before you pull over. For road situations that require lookahead, because no satisfactory rule is available, it may be necessary to imagine various actions that the car could take as well as the various actions that other cars might take, and then decide if those outcomes are good or bad.

While perception is very important, and deep learning lends itself well to perception, there are many different types of ability that we need to give an AI system. This is particularly true when we're talking about activities that span over long timescales, like going on a vacation. Or very complex actions like building a factory. There's no possibility that those kinds of activities can be orchestrated by purely deep learning black-box systems.

Let me take the factory example to close my point about the limitations of deep learning here. Let's imagine we try to use deep learning to build a factory. (After all, we humans know how to build a factory, don't we?) So, we'll take billions of previous examples of building factories to train a deep learning algorithm; we'll show it all the ways that people have built factories. We take all that data and we put it into a deep learning system and then it knows how to build factories. Could we do that? No, it's just a complete pipe dream. There is no such data, and it wouldn't make any sense, even if we had it, to try to build factories that way.

We need knowledge to build factories. We need to be able to construct plans. We need to be able to reason about physical obstructions and the structural properties of the buildings. We can build AI systems to work out these real-world problems, but it isn't achieved by deep learning. Building a factory requires a different type of AI altogether.

MARTIN FORD: Are there recent advances in AI that have struck you as being more than just incremental? What would you point to that is at the absolute forefront of the field right now?

STUART J. RUSSELL: It's a good question, because a lot of the things that are in the news at the moment are not really conceptual breakthroughs, they are just demos. The chess victory of Deep Blue over Kasparov is a perfect example. Deep Blue was basically a demo of algorithms that were designed 30 years earlier and had been gradually enhanced and then deployed on increasingly powerful hardware, until they could beat a world chess champion. But the actual conceptual breakthroughs behind Deep Blue were in how to design a chess program: how the lookahead works; the alpha-beta algorithm for reducing the amount of searching that had to be done; and some of the techniques for designing the evaluation functions. So, as is often the case, the media described the victory of Deep Blue over Kasparov as a breakthrough when in fact, the breakthrough had occurred decades earlier.

The same thing is still happening today as well. For instance, a lot of the recent AI reports about perception and speech recognition, and headlines about dictation accuracy being close to or exceeding human dictation accuracy, are all very impressive practical engineering results, but they are again demos of conceptual breakthroughs that happened much earlier—from the early deep learning systems and convolutional networks that date right back to the late '80s and early '90s.

It's been something of a surprise that we already had the tools decades ago to do perception successfully; we just weren't using them properly. By applying modern engineering to older breakthroughs, by collecting large datasets and processing them across very large networks on the latest hardware, we've managed to create a lot of interest recently in AI, but these have not necessarily been at the real forefront of AI.

MARTIN FORD: Do you think DeepMind's AlphaZero is a good example of a technology that's right on the frontier of AI research?

STUART J. RUSSELL: I think AlphaZero was interesting. To me, it was not particularly a surprise that you could use the same basic software that played Go to also play chess and Shogi at world-champion level. So, it was not at the forefront of AI in that sense.

I mean, it certainly gives you pause when you think that AlphaZero, in the space of less than twenty-four hours, learned to play at superhuman levels in three different games using the same software. But that's more a vindication of an approach to AI that says that if you have a clear understanding of the problem class, especially deterministic, two-player, turn-taking, fully-observable games with known rules, then those kinds of problems are amenable to a well-designed class of AI algorithms. And these algorithms have been around for some time—algorithms that can learn good evaluation functions and use classical methods for controlling search.

It's also clear that if you want to extend those techniques to other classes of problems, you're going to have to come up with different algorithmic structures. For example, partial observability—meaning that you can't see the board, so to speak—requires a different class of algorithm. There's nothing AlphaZero can do to play poker, for example, or to drive a car. Those tasks require an AI system that can estimate things that it can't see. AlphaZero assumes that the pieces on the board are the pieces on the board, and that's that.

MARTIN FORD: There was also a poker playing AI system developed at Carnegie Mellon University, called Libratus? Did they achieve a genuine AI breakthrough there?

STUART J. RUSSELL: Carnegie Mellon's Libratus poker AI was another very impressive hybrid AI example: it was a combination of several different algorithmic contributions that were pieced together from research that's happened over the last 10 or 15 years. There has been a lot of progress in dealing with games like poker, which are games of partial information. One of the things that happens with partial-information games, like poker, is that you must have a randomized playing strategy because if, say, you always bluff, then people figure out that you're bluffing and then they call your bluff. But if you never bluff, then you can never steal a game from your opponent when you have a weak hand. It's long been known, therefore, that for these kinds of card games, you should randomize your playing behavior, and bluff with a certain probability.

The key to playing poker extremely well is adjusting those probabilities for how to bet; that is, how often to bet more than your hand really justifies, and how often to bet less. The calculations for these probabilities are feasible for an AI, and they can be done very exactly, but only for small versions of poker, for example where there are only a few cards in a pack. It's very hard for an AI to do these calculations accurately for the full game of poker. As a result, over the decade or so that people have been working on scaling up poker, we've gradually seen improvements in the accuracy and efficiency of how to calculate these probabilities for larger and larger versions of poker.

So yes, Libratus is another impressive modern AI application. But whether the techniques are at all scalable, given that it has taken a decade to go from one version of poker to another slightly larger version of poker, I'm not convinced. I think there's also a reasonable question about how much those game-theoretic ideas in poker extend into the real world. We're not aware of doing much randomization in our normal day-to-day lives, even though—for sure—the world is full of agents; so it ought to be game-theoretic, and yet we're not aware of randomizing very much in our day-to-day lives.

MARTIN FORD: Self-driving cars are one of the highest-profile applications of AI. What is your estimate for when fully autonomous vehicles will become a truly practical technology? Imagine you're in a random place in Manhattan, and you call up an Uber, and it's going to arrive with no one in it, and then it will take you to another random place that you specify. How far off is that realistically, do you think?

STUART J. RUSSELL: Yes, the timeline for self-driving cars is a concrete question, and it's also an economically important question because companies are investing a great deal in these projects.

It is worth noting that the first actual self-driving car, operating on a public road, was 30 years ago! That was Ernst Dickmanns' demo in Germany of a car driving on the freeway, changing lanes, and overtaking other vehicles. The difficulty of course is trust: while you can run a successful demonstration for a short time, you need an AI system to run for decades with no significant failures in order to qualify as a safe vehicle.

The challenge, then, is to build an AI system that people are willing to trust themselves and their kids to, and I don't think we're quite there.

Results from vehicles that are being tested in California at the moment indicate that humans still feel they must intervene as frequently as once every mile of road testing. There are more successful AI driving projects, such as Waymo, which is the Google subsidiary working on this, that have some respectable records; but they are still, I think, several years away from being able to do this in a wide range of conditions.

Most of these tests have been conducted in good conditions on well-marked roads. And as you know, when you're driving at night and it's pouring with rain, and there are lights reflecting off the road, and there may also be roadworks, and they might have moved the lane markers, and so on … if you had followed the old lane markers, you'd have driven straight into a wall by now. I think in those kinds of circumstances, it's really hard for AI systems. That's why I think that we'll be lucky if the self-driving car problem is solved sufficiently in the next five years.

Of course, I don't know how much patience the major car companies have. I do think everyone is committed to the idea that AI-driven cars are going to come, and of course the major car companies feel they must be there early or miss a major opportunity.

MARTIN FORD: I usually tell people a 10-15-year time frame when they ask me about self-driving cars. Your estimate of five years seems quite optimistic.

STUART J. RUSSELL: Yes, five years is optimistic. As I said, I think we'll be lucky if we see driverless cars in five years, and it could well be longer. One thing that is clear, though, is that many of the early ideas of fairly simple architectures for driverless cars are now being abandoned, as we gain more experience.

In the early versions of Google's car, they had chip-based vision systems that were pretty good at detecting other vehicles, lane markers, obstacles, and pedestrians. Those vision systems passed that kind of information effectively in a sort of logical form and then the controller applied logical rules telling the car what to do. The problem was that every day, Google found themselves adding new rules. Perhaps they would go into a traffic circle—or a roundabout, as we call them in England—and there would be a little girl riding her bicycle the wrong way around the traffic circle. They didn't have a rule for that circumstance. So, then they have to add a new one, and so on, and so on. I think that there is probably no possibility that this type of architecture is ever going to work in the long run, because there are always more rules that should be encoded, and it can be a matter of life and death on the road if a particular rule is missing.

By contrast, we don't play chess or Go by having a bunch of rules specific to one exact position or another—for instance, saying if the person's king is here and their rook is there, and their queen is there, then make this move. That's not how we write chess programs. We write chess programs by knowing the rules of chess and then examining the consequences of various possible actions.

A self-driving car AI must deal with unexpected circumstances on the road in the same way, not through special rules. It should use this form of lookahead-based decision-making when it doesn't have a ready-made policy for how to operate in the current circumstance. If an AI doesn't have this approach as a fallback, then it's going to fall through the cracks in some situations and fail to drive safely. That's not good enough in the real world, of course.

MARTIN FORD: You've noted the limitations in current narrow or specialized AI technology. Let's talk about the prospects for AGI, which promises to someday solve these problems. Can you explain exactly what Artificial General Intelligence is? What does AGI really mean, and what are the main hurdles we need to overcome before we can achieve AGI?

STUART J. RUSSELL: Artificial General Intelligence is a recently coined term, and it really is just a reminder of our real goals in AI—a general-purpose intelligence much like our own. In that sense, AGI is actually what we've always called artificial intelligence. We're just not finished yet, and we have not created AGI yet.

The goal of AI has always been to create general-purpose intelligent machines. AGI is also a reminder that the "general-purpose" part of our AI goals has often been neglected in favor of more specific subtasks and application tasks. This is because it's been easier so far to solve subtasks in the real world, such as playing chess. If we look again at AlphaZero for a moment, it generally works within the class of two-player deterministic fully-observable board games. However, it is not a general algorithm that can work across all classes of problems. AlphaZero can't handle partial observability; it can't handle unpredictability; and it assumes that the rules are known. AlphaZero can't handle unknown physics, as it were.

Now if we could gradually remove those limitations around AlphaZero, we'd eventually have an AI system that could learn to operate successfully in pretty much any circumstance. We could ask it to design a new high-speed watercraft, or to lay the table for dinner. We could ask it to figure out what's wrong with our dog and it should be able to do that—perhaps even by reading everything about canine medicine that's ever been known and using that information to figure out what's wrong with our dog.

This kind of capability is thought to reflect the generality of intelligence that humans exhibit. And in principle a human being, given enough time, could also do all of those things, and so very much more. That is the notion of generality that we have in mind when we talk about AGI: a truly general-purpose artificial intelligence.

Of course, there may be other things that humans can't do that an AGI will be able to do. We can't multiply million-digit numbers in our heads, and computers can do that relatively easily. So, we assume that in fact, machines may be able to exhibit greater generality than humans do.

However, it's also worth pointing out that it's very unlikely that there will ever be a point where machines are comparable to human beings in the following sense. As soon as machines can read, then a machine can basically read all the books ever written; and no human can read even a tiny fraction of all the books that have ever been written. Therefore, once an AGI gets past kindergarten reading level, it will shoot beyond anything that any human being has ever done, and it will have a much bigger knowledge base than any human ever has.

And so, in that sense and many other senses, what's likely to happen is that machines will far exceed human capabilities along various important dimensions. There may be other dimensions along which they're fairly stunted and so they're not going to look like humans in that sense. This doesn't mean that a comparison between humans and AGI machines is meaningless though: what will matter in the long run is our relationship with machines, and the ability of the AGI machine to operate in our world.

There are dimensions of intelligence (for example, short-term memory) where humans are actually exceeded by apes; but nonetheless, there's no doubt which of the species is dominant. And if you are a gorilla or a chimpanzee, your future is entirely in the hands of humans. Now that is because, despite our fairly pathetic short-term memories compared to gorillas and apes, we are able to dominate them because of our decision-making capabilities in the real world.

We will undoubtedly face this same issue when we create AGI: how to avoid the fate of the gorilla and the chimpanzee, and not cede control of our own future to that AGI.

MARTIN FORD: That's a scary question. Earlier, you talked about how conceptual breakthroughs in AI often run decades ahead of reality. Do you see any indications that the conceptual breakthroughs for creating AGI have already been made, or is AGI still far in the future?

STUART J. RUSSELL: I do feel that many of the conceptual building blocks towards AGI pieces are already here, yes. We can start to explore this question by asking ourselves: "Why can't deep learning systems be the basis for AGI, what's wrong with them?"

A lot of people might answer our question by saying: "Deep learning systems are fine, but we don't know how to store knowledge, or how to do reasoning, or how to build more expressive kinds of models, because deep learning systems are just circuits, and circuits are not very expressive after all."

And for sure, it's because circuits are not very expressive that no one thinks about writing payroll software using circuits. We instead use programming languages to create payroll software. Payroll software written using circuits would be billions of pages long and completely useless and inflexible. By comparison, programming languages are very expressive and very powerful. In fact, they are the most powerful things that can exist for expressing algorithmic processes.

In fact, we already know how to represent knowledge and how to do reasoning: we have developed computational logic over quite a long time now. Even predating computers, people were thinking about algorithmic procedures for doing logical reasoning.

And so, arguably, some of the conceptual building blocks for AGI have already been here for decades. We just haven't figured out yet how to combine those with the very impressive learning capacities of deep learning.

The human race has also already built a technology called probabilistic programming, which I will say does combine learning capabilities with the expressive power of logical languages and programming languages. Mathematically speaking, such a probabilistic programming system is a way of writing down probability models which can then be combined with evidence, using probabilistic inference to produce predictions.

STUART J. RUSSELL

In my group we have a language called BLOG, which stands for Bayesian Logic. BLOG is a probabilistic modeling language, so you can write down what you know in the form of a BLOG model. You then combine that knowledge with data, and you run inference, which in turn makes predictions.

A real-world example of such a system is the monitoring system for the nuclear test-ban treaty. The way it works is that we write down what we know about the geophysics of the earth, including the propagation of seismic signals through the earth, the detection of seismic signals, the presence of noise, the locations of detection stations, and so on. That's the model—which is expressed in a formal language, along with all the uncertainties: for example, uncertainty in our ability to predict the speed of propagation of a signal through the earth. The data is the raw seismic information coming from the detection stations that are scattered around the world. Then there is the prediction: What seismic events took place today? Where did they take place? How deep were they? How big were they? And perhaps: Which ones are likely to be nuclear explosions? This system is an active monitoring system today for the test-ban treaty, and it seems to be working pretty well.

So, to summarize, I think that many of the conceptual building blocks needed for AGI or human-level intelligence are already here. But there are some missing pieces. One of them is a clear approach to how natural language can be understood to produce knowledge structures upon which reasoning processes can operate. The canonical example might be: How can an AGI read a chemistry textbook and then solve a bunch of chemistry exam problems—not multiple choice but real chemistry exam problems—and solve them for the right reasons, demonstrating the derivations and the arguments that produced the answers? And then, presumably if that's done in a way that's elegant and principled, the AGI should then be able to read a physics textbook and a biology textbook and a materials textbook, and so on.

MARTIN FORD: Or we might imagine an AGI system acquiring knowledge from, say, a history book and then applying what it's learned to a simulation of contemporary geopolitics, or something like that, where it's really moving knowledge and applying it in an entirely different domain?

STUART J. RUSSELL: Yes, I think that's a good example because it relates to the ability of an AI system to then be able to manipulate the real world in a geopolitical sense or a financial sense.

If, for example, the AI is advising a CEO on corporate strategy, it might be able to effectively outplay all the other companies by devising some amazing product marketing acquisition strategies, and so on.

So, I'd say that the ability to understand language, and then to operate with the results of that understanding, is one important breakthrough for AGI that still needs to happen.

Another AGI breakthrough still to happen is the ability to operate over long timescales. While AlphaZero is an amazingly good problem-solving system which can think 20, sometimes 30 steps into the future, that is still nothing compared to what the human brain does every moment. Humans, in our primitive steps, use motor control signals that we send to our muscles; and just typing a paragraph of text is several tens of millions of motor control commands. So those 20 or 30 steps by AlphaZero would only get an AGI only a few milliseconds into the future. As we talked about earlier, AlphaZero would be totally useless for planning the activity of a robot.

MARTIN FORD: How do humans even solve this problem with so many calculations and decisions to be made as they navigate the world?

STUART J. RUSSELL: The only way that humans and robots can operate in the real world is to operate at multiple scales of abstraction. We don't plan our lives in terms of exactly which thing are we going to actuate in exactly which order. We instead plan our lives in terms of "OK, this afternoon I'm going try to write another chapter of my book" and then: "It's going to be about such and such." Or things like, "Tomorrow I'm going to get on the plane and fly back to Paris."

Those are our abstract actions. And then as we start to plan them in more detail, we break them down into finer steps. That's common sense for humans. We do this all the time, but we actually don't understand very well how to have AI systems do this. In particular, we don't understand yet how to have AI systems construct those high-level actions in the first place. Behavior is surely organized hierarchically into these layers of abstraction, but where does the hierarchy come from? How do we create it and then use it?

If we can solve this problem for AI, if machines can start to construct their own behavioral hierarchies that allow them to operate successfully in complex environments over long timescales, that will be a huge breakthrough for AGI that takes us a long way towards a human-level functionality in the real world.

MARTIN FORD: What is your prediction for when we might achieve AGI?

STUART J. RUSSELL: These kinds of breakthroughs have nothing to do with bigger datasets or faster machines, and so we can't make any kind of quantitative prediction about when they're going to occur.

I always tell the story of what happened in nuclear physics. The consensus view as expressed by Ernest Rutherford on September 11th, 1933, was that it would never be possible to extract atomic energy from atoms. So, his prediction was "never", but what turned out to be the case was that the next morning Leo Szilard read Rutherford's speech, became annoyed by it, and invented a nuclear chain reaction mediated by neutrons! Rutherford's prediction was "never" and the truth was about 16 hours later. In a similar way, it feels quite futile for me to make a quantitative prediction about when these breakthroughs in AGI will arrive, but Rutherford's story is a good one.

MARTIN FORD: Do you expect AGI to happen in your lifetime?

STUART J. RUSSELL: When pressed, I will sometimes say yes, I expect AGI to happen in my children's lifetime. Of course, that's me hedging a bit because we may have some life extension technologies in place by then, so that could stretch it out quite a bit.

But given that we kind of understand enough about these breakthroughs to at least describe them, and that people certainly have inklings of what their solutions might be, suggests to me that we're just waiting for a bit of inspiration.

Furthermore, a lot of very smart people are working on these problems, probably more than ever in the history of the field, mainly because of Google, Facebook, Baidu, and so on. Enormous resources are being put into AI now. There's also enormous student interest in AI because it's so exciting right now.

So, all those things lead one to believe that the rate of breakthroughs occurring is probably likely to be quite high. These breakthroughs are certainly comparable in magnitude to a dozen of the conceptual breakthroughs that happened over the last 60 years of AI.

So that is why most AI researchers have a feeling that AGI is something in the not-too-distant future. It's not thousands of years in the future, and it's probably not even hundreds of years in the future.

MARTIN FORD: What do you think will happen when the first AGI is created?

STUART J. RUSSELL: When it happens, it's not going to be a single finishing line that we cross. It's going to be along several dimensions. We'll see machines exceeding human capacities, just as they have in arithmetic, and now chess, Go, and in video games. We'll see various other dimensions of intelligence and classes of problems that fall, one after the other; and those will then have implications for what AI systems can do in the real world. AGI systems may, for example, have strategic reasoning tools that are superhuman, and we use those for military and corporate strategy, and so on. But those tools may precede the ability to read and understand complex text.

An early AGI system, by itself, still won't be able to learn everything about how the world works or be able to control that world.

We'll still need to provide a lot of the knowledge to those early AGI systems. These AGIs are not going to look like humans though, and they won't have even roughly the same abilities across even roughly the same spectrum as humans. These AGI systems are going to be very spiky in different directions.

MARTIN FORD: I want to talk more about the risks associated with AI and AGI. I know that's an important focus of your recent work.

Let's start with the economic risks of AI, which is the thing that, of course, I've written about in my previous book, *Rise of the Robots*. A lot of people believe that we are on the leading edge of something on the scale of a new industrial revolution. Something that's going to be totally transformative in terms of the job market, the economy and so forth. Where do you fall on that? Is that overhyped, or would you line up with that assertion?

STUART J. RUSSELL: We've discussed how the timeline for breakthroughs in AI and AGI is hard to predict. Those are the breakthroughs that will enable an AI to do a lot of the jobs that humans do right now. It's also quite hard to forecast which sequence of employment categories are going to be at risk from machine replacement and a timeline around that.

However, what I see in a lot of the discussions and presentations from people talking about this, is that there's probably an over-estimate of what current AI technologies are able to do and also, the difficulty of integrating what we know how to do into the existing extremely complex functionality of corporations and governments, and so on.

I do agree that a lot of jobs that have existed for the last few hundred years are repetitive, and the humans who are doing them are basically exchangeable. If it's a job where you hire people by the hundred or by the thousand to do it, and you can identify what that person does as a particular task that is then repeated over and over again, those kinds of jobs are going to be susceptible. That's because you could say that, in those jobs, we are using humans as robots. So, it's not surprising that when we have real robots, they're going to be able to do those jobs.

I also think that the current mindset among governments is: "Oh, well then. I guess we really need to start training people to be data scientists, because that's the job of the future—or robot engineers." This clearly isn't the solution because we don't need a billion data scientists and robot engineers: we just need a few million. This might be a strategy for a small country like Singapore; or where I am currently, in Dubai, it might also be a viable strategy. But it's not a viable strategy for any major country because there is simply not going to be enough jobs in those areas. That's not to say that there are no jobs now: there certainly are, and training more people to do them makes sense; but this simply is not a solution to the long-term problem.

There are really only two futures for the human economy that I see in the long run.

The first is that effectively, most people are not doing anything that's considered economically productive. They're not involved in economic exchange of work for pay in any form, and this is the vision of the universal basic income: that there is a sector of the economy that is largely automated and incredibly productive, and that productivity generates wealth, in the form of goods and services, that in one way or another ends up subsidizing the economic viability of everyone else. That to me does not seem like a very interesting world to live in, at least not by itself, without a lot of other things needed to go on to make life worth living and provide sufficient incentive for people to do all of the things that we do now. For example, going to school, learning and training, and becoming experts in various areas. It's hard to see the motivation for acquiring a good education when it doesn't have any economic function.

The second of the two futures I can see in the long run is that even though machines will be doing a lot of goods and basic services like transportation, there are still things that people can do which improve the quality of life for themselves and for others. There are people who are able to teach, to inspire people to live richer, more interesting, more varied and more fulfilling lives, whether that's teaching people to appreciate literature or music, how to build, or even how to survive in the wilderness.

MARTIN FORD: Do you think we can navigate as individuals and as a species towards a positive future, once AI has changed our economy?

STUART J. RUSSELL: Yes, I really do, but I think that a positive future will require human intervention to help people live positive lives. We need to start actively navigating, right now, towards a future that can present the most constructive challenges and the most interesting experiences in life for people. A world that can build emotional resilience and nurture a generally constructive and positive attitude to one's own life—and to the lives of others. At the moment, we are pretty terrible at doing that. So, we have to start changing that now.

I think that we'll also need to fundamentally change our attitude about what science is for and what it can do for us. I have a cell phone in my pocket, and the human race probably spent on the order of a trillion dollars on the science and engineering that went into ultimately creating things like my cell phone. And yet we spend almost nothing on understanding how people can live interesting and fulfilling lives, and how we can help people around us do that. I think as a race that we will need to start acknowledging that if we help another person in the right way, it creates enormous value for them for the rest of their lives. Right now, we have almost no science base for how to do this, we have no degree programs in how to do it, we have very few journals about it, and those that are trying are not taken very seriously.

The future can have a perfectly functioning economy where people who are expert in living life well, and helping other people, can provide those kinds of services.

Those services may be coaching, they may be teaching, they may be consoling, or maybe collaborating, so that we can all really have a fantastic future.

It's not a grim future at all: it's a far better future than what we have at present; but it requires rethinking our education system, our science base, our economic structures.

We need now to understand how this will function from an economic point of view in terms of the future distribution of income. We want to avoid a situation where there are the super-rich who own the means of production—the robots and the AI systems—and then there are their servants, and then there is the rest of the world doing nothing. That's sort of the worst possible outcome from an economic point of view.

So, I do think that there is a positive future that makes sense once AI has changed the human economy, but we need to get a better handle on what that's going to look like now, so that we can construct a plan for getting there.

MARTIN FORD: You've worked on applying machine learning to medical data at both Berkeley and nearby UCSF. Do you think artificial intelligence will create a more positive future for humans through advances in healthcare and medicine?

STUART J. RUSSELL: I think so, yes, but I also think that medicine is an area where we know a great deal about human physiology—and so to me, knowledge-based or model-based approaches are more likely to succeed than data-driven machine learning systems.

I don't think that deep learning is going to work for a lot of important medical applications. The idea that today we can just collect terabytes of data from millions of patients and then throw that data into a black-box learning algorithm, doesn't make sense to me. There may be some areas of medicine where data-driven machine learning works very well of course. Genomic data is one area; and predicting human susceptibility to various kinds of genetically-related diseases. Also, I think, deep learning AI will be strong at predicting the potential efficacy of particular drugs.

But these examples are a long way from an AI being able to act like a doctor and being able to decide, perhaps, that a patient has a blocked ventricle in the brain that's interfering with the circulation of cerebral spinal fluid. To really do that, is more like diagnosing which part of a car is not working. If you have no idea how cars work, then figuring out that it's the fan belt that's broken is going to be very, very difficult.

Of course, if you're an expert car mechanic and you know how it all works, and you've got some symptoms to work with, maybe there's a kind of a flapping noise and that the car's overheating, then you generally can figure it out quickly. And it's going to be the same with human physiology, except that there is a significant effort that must be put in into building these models of human physiology.

A lot effort was already put in to these models in the '60s and '70s, and they have helped AI systems in medicine progress to some degree. But today we have technology that can in particular represent the uncertainty in those models. Mechanical systems models are deterministic and have specific parameter values: they represent exactly one completely predictable, fictitious human.

Today's probabilistic models, on the other hand, can represent an entire population, and they can accurately reflect the degree of uncertainty we might have about being able to predict, for example, exactly when someone is going to have a heart attack. It's very hard to predict things like heart attacks on an individual level, but we can predict that there's a certain probability per person, which might be increased during extreme exercise or stress, and that this probability would depend on various characteristics of the individual.

This more modern and probabilistic approach behaves much more reasonably than previous systems. Probabilistic systems enable us to combine the classical models of human physiology with observation and real-time data, to make strong diagnosis and plan treatments.

MARTIN FORD: I know you've focused a lot on the potential risks of weaponized AI. Could you talk more about that?

STUART J. RUSSELL: Yes, I think autonomous weapons are now creating the prospect of a new arms race. This arms race may already be leading towards the development of lethal autonomous weapons. These autonomous weapons can be given some mission description that the weapon has the ability to achieve by itself, such as identifying, selecting, and attacking human targets.

There are moral arguments that this will cross a fundamental line for artificial intelligence: that we're handing over the power over life and death to a machine to decide, and that is a fundamental reduction in the way we value human life and the dignity of human life.

But I think a more practical argument is that a logical consequence of autonomy is scalability. Since no supervision is required by an individual human for each individual autonomous weapon, someone could launch as many weapons as they want. Someone can launch an attack, where five guys in a control room could launch 10,000,000 weapons and wipe out all males between the age of 12 and 60 in some country. So, these can be weapons of mass destruction, and they have this property of scalability: someone could launch an attack with 10, or 1,000, or 1,000,000 or 10,000,000 weapons.

With nuclear weapons, if they were used at all, someone would be crossing a major threshold which we've managed to avoid so far as a race, by the skin of our teeth. We have managed to avoid crossing that threshold since 1945. But autonomous weapons don't have such a threshold, and so things can more smoothly escalate. They are also easily proliferated, so once they are manufactured in very large numbers it's quite likely they'll be on the international arms market and they'll be accessible to people who have less scruples than, you know, the Western powers.

MARTIN FORD: There's a lot of technology transfer between commercial applications and potential military applications. You can buy a drone on Amazon that could potentially be weaponized...

STUART J. RUSSELL: So, at the moment, you can buy a drone that's remotely piloted, maybe with first-person vision. You could certainly attach a little bomb to it and deliver it and kill someone, but that's a remotely piloted vehicle, which is different. It's not scalable because you can't launch 10,000,000 of those unless you've got 10,000,000 pilots. So, someone would need a whole country trained to do that, of course, or they could also give those 10,000,000 people machine guns and then go and kill people. Thankfully we have an international system of control of sanctions, and military preparedness, and so on—to try to prevent these things from happening. But we don't have an international system of control that would work against autonomous weapons.

MARTIN FORD: Still, couldn't a few people in a basement somewhere develop their own autonomous control system and then deploy it on commercially available drones? How would we be able control those kinds of homemade AI weapons?

STUART J. RUSSELL: Yes, something resembling the software that controls a self-driving car could conceivably be deployed to control a quadcopter that delivers a bomb. Then you might have something like a homemade autonomous weapon. It could be that under a treaty, there would be a verification mechanism that would require the cooperation of drone manufacturers and the people who make chips for self-driving cars and so on, so that anyone ordering large quantities would be noticed—in the same way that anyone ordering large quantities of precursor chemicals for chemical weapons is not going to get away with it because the corporation is required, by the chemical weapons treaty, to know its customer and to report any unusual attempts that are made to purchase large quantities of certain dangerous products.

I think it will be possible to have a fairly effective regime that could prevent very large diversions of civilian technology to create autonomous weapons. Bad things would still happen, and I think this may be inevitable, because in small numbers it will likely always be feasible for homemade autonomous weapons to be built. In small numbers, though, autonomous weapons don't have a huge advantage over a piloted weapon. If you're going to launch an attack with ten or twenty weapons, you might as well pilot them because you can probably find ten or twenty people to do that.

There are other risks of course with AI and warfare, such as where an AI system may accidentally escalate warfare when machines misinterpret some signal and start attacking each other. And the future risk of a cyber-infiltration means that you may think you have a robust defense based on autonomous weapons when in fact, all your weapons have been compromised and are going to turn on you instead when a conflict begins. So that all contributes to strategic uncertainty, which is not great at all.

MARTIN FORD: These are scary scenarios. You've also produced a short film called *Slaughterbots*, which is quite a terrifying video.

STUART J. RUSSELL: We made the video really just to illustrate these concepts because I felt that, despite our best efforts to write about them and give presentations about them, that somehow the message wasn't getting through. People were still saying, "oh, autonomous weapons are science fiction." They were still imagining it as Skynet and Terminators, as a technology that doesn't exist. So, we were simply trying to point out that we're not talking about spontaneously evil weapons, and we're not talking about taking over the world—but we also not talking about science fiction any more.

These AI warfare technologies are feasible today, and they bring some new kinds of extreme risks. We're talking about scalable weapons of mass destruction falling into the wrong hands. These weapons could inflict enormous damage on human populations. So, that's autonomous weapons.

MARTIN FORD: In 2014, you published a letter, along with the late Stephen Hawking and the physicists Max Tegmark and Frank Wilczek, warning that we aren't taking the risks associated with advanced AI seriously enough. It's notable that you were the only computer scientist among the authors. Could you tell the story behind that letter and what led you to write it?[1]

STUART J. RUSSELL: So, it's an interesting story. It started when I got a call from National Public Radio, who wanted to interview me about this movie called *Transcendence*. I was living in Paris at the time and the movie wasn't out in Paris, so I hadn't seen it yet.

I happened to have a stopover in Boston on the way back from a conference in Iceland, so I got off the plane in Boston and I went to the movie theatre to watch the movie. I'm sitting there towards the front of the theatre, and I don't really know what's going to happen in the movie at all and then, "Oh, look! It's showing Berkeley computer science department. That's kind of funny." Johnny Depp is playing the AI professor, "Oh, that's kind of interesting." He's giving a talk about AI, and then someone, some anti-AI terrorist decides to shoot him. So, I'm sort of involuntarily shrinking down in my seat seeing this happening, because that could really be me at that time. Then the basic plot of the movie is that before he dies they manage to upload his brain into a big quantum computer and the combination of those two things creates a super-intelligent entity that threatens to take over the world because it very rapidly develops all kinds of amazing new technologies.

---

1 The letter is available at: https://www.independent.co.uk/news/science/stephen-hawking-transcend-ence-looks-at-the-implications-of-artificial-intelligence-but-are-we-taking-9313474.html.

So anyway, we wrote an article that was, at least superficially, a review of the movie, but it was really saying, "You know, although this is just a movie, the underlying message is real: which is that if—or when—we create machines that can have a dominant effect on the real world, then that can present a very serious problem for us: that we could, in fact, cede control over our futures to other entities besides humans."

The problem is very straightforward: our intelligence is what gives us our ability to control the world; and so, intelligence represents power over the world. If something has a greater degree of intelligence, then it has more power.

We are already on the way to creating things that are much more powerful than us; but somehow, we have to make sure that they never, ever, have any power. So, when we describe the AI situation like that, people say, "Oh, I see. OK, there's a problem."

MARTIN FORD: And yet, a lot of prominent AI researchers are quite dismissive of these concerns...

STUART J. RUSSELL: Let me talk about these AI denialists. There are various arguments that people put forward as to why we shouldn't pay any attention to the AI problem, and that there are just too many of these arguments to count. I've collected somewhere between 25 and 30 distinct arguments, but they all share a single property, which is that they simply do not make any sense. They don't really stand up to scrutiny. Just to give you one example, something you'll often hear is, "well, you know, it's absolutely not a problem because we'll just be able to switch them off." That is like saying that beating AlphaZero at Go is absolutely not a problem. You just put the white pieces in the right place, you know? It just doesn't stand up to five seconds of scrutiny.

A lot of these AI denialist arguments, I think, reflect a kind of a knee-jerk defensive reaction. Perhaps some people think, "I'm an AI researcher. I feel threatened by this thought, and therefore I'm going to keep this thought out of my head and find some reason to keep it out of my head." That's one of my theories about why some otherwise very informed people will try to deny that AI is going to become a problem for humans.

This even extends to some mainstream people in the AI community who deny that AI will ever be successful, which is ironic because we've spent 60 years fending off philosophers, who have denied that the AI field will ever be successful. We've also spent those 60 years demonstrating and proving, one time after another, how things that the philosophers said would be impossible, can indeed happen—such as beating the world champion in chess.

Now, suddenly some people in the AI field are saying that AI is never going to succeed, and so there isn't anything to worry about.

This is a completely pathological reaction if you ask me. It seems prudent, just as with nuclear energy and atomic weapons, to assume that human ingenuity will, in fact, overcome the obstacles and achieve intelligence of a kind that's sufficient to present at least, potentially the threat of ceding control. It seems prudent to prepare for that and try to figure out how to design systems in such a way that that can't happen. So that's my goal: to help us prepare for the artificial intelligence threat.

MARTIN FORD: How should we address that threat?

STUART J. RUSSELL: The key to the problem is that we have made a slight mistake in the way that we define AI, and so I have a reconstructed a new definition for AI that goes as follows.

First of all, if we want to build artificial intelligence, we'd better figure out what it means to be intelligent. This means that we must draw from thousands of years of tradition, philosophy, economics and other disciplines. The idea of intelligence is that a human being is intelligent to the extent that their actions can be expected to achieve their objectives. This is the idea sometimes called rational behavior; and it contains within it various sub-kinds of intelligence, like the ability to reason; the ability to plan; the ability to perceive; and so on. Those are all kind of required capabilities for acting intelligently in the real world.

The problem with that is that if we succeed in creating artificial intelligence and machines with those abilities, then unless their objectives happen to be perfectly aligned with those of humans, then we've created something that's extremely intelligent, but with objectives that are different from ours. And then, if that AI is more intelligent than us, then it's going to attain its objectives—and we, probably, are not!

The negative consequences for humans are without limit. The mistake is in the way we have transferred the notion of intelligence, a concept that makes sense for humans, over to machines.

We don't want machines with our type of intelligence. We actually want machines whose actions can be expected to achieve our objectives, not their objectives.

The original idea we had for AI was that to make an intelligent machine, we should construct optimizers: things that choose actions really well when we give them an objective. Then off it goes and achieves our objective. That's probably a mistake. It's worked up to now—but only because we haven't made very intelligent machines, and the ones we have made we've only put in mini-worlds, like the simulated chessboard, the simulated Go board, and so on.

When the AI that humans have so far made, get out into the real-world, that's when things can go wrong, and we saw an example of this with the flash crash. With the flash crash, there was a bunch of trading algorithms, some of them fairly simple, but some of them fairly complicated AI-based decision-making and learning systems. Out there in the real world, during the flash crash things went catastrophically wrong and those machines crashed the stock market. They eliminated more than a trillion dollars of value in equities in the space of a few minutes. The flash crash was a warning signal about our AI.

The right way to think about AI is that we should be making machines which act in ways to help us achieve our objectives through them, but where we absolutely do not put our objectives directly into the machine!

My vision is that AI must always be designed to try to help us achieve our objectives, but that AI systems should not be assumed to know what those objectives are.

If we make AI this way, then there is always an explicit uncertainty about the nature of the objectives that an AI is obliged to pursue. It turns out that this uncertainty actually is the margin of safety that we require.

I'll give you an example to demonstrate this margin of safety that we really do need. Let's go back to an old idea that we can—if we ever need to—just switch the machine off if we get into trouble. Well, of course, you know, if the machine has an objective like, "fetch the coffee," then obviously a sufficiently intelligent machine realizes that if someone switches it off, then it's not going to be able to fetch the coffee. If its life's mission, if its objective, is to fetch the coffee, then logically it will take steps to prevent itself from being switched off. It will disable the Off switch. It will possibly neutralize anyone who might attempt to switch it off. So, you can imagine all these unanticipated consequences of a simple objective like "fetch the coffee," when you have a sufficiently intelligent machine.

Now in my vision for AI, we instead design the machine so that although it still wants to "fetch the coffee" it understands that there are a lot of other things that human beings might care about, but it doesn't really know what those are! In that situation, the AI understands that it might do something that the human doesn't like—and if the human switches it off, that's to prevent something that would make the human unhappy. Since in this vision the goal of the machine is to avoid making the human unhappy, even though the AI doesn't know what that means, it actually has an incentive to allow itself to be switched off.

We can take this particular vision for AI and put it into mathematics, and show that the margin of safety (meaning, in this case, the incentive that the machine has to allow itself to be switched off) is directly related to the uncertainty it has about the human objective. As we eliminate that uncertainty, and the machine starts to believe that it knows, for sure, what the true objective really is, then that margin of safety begins to disappear again, and the machine will ultimately stop us from switching it off.

In this way, we can show that, at least in a simplified mathematical framework, that when you design machines this way—with explicit uncertainty about the objective that they are to pursue—then they can be provably beneficial, meaning that you are provably better off with this machine than without.

What I've shared here is an indication that there may be a way of conceiving of AI which is a little bit different from how we've been thinking about AI so far, that there are ways to build an AI system that has much better properties, in terms of safety and control.

MARTIN FORD: Related to these issues of AI safety and control, a lot of people worry about an arms race with other countries, especially China. Is that something we should take seriously, something we should be very concerned about?

STUART J. RUSSELL: Nick Bostrom and others have raised a concern that, if a party feels that strategic dominance in AI is a critical part of their national security and economic leadership, then that party will be driven to develop the capabilities of AI systems—as fast as possible, and yes, without worrying too much about the controllability issues.

At a high level, that sounds like a plausible argument. On the other hand, as we produce AI products that can operate out there in the real world, there will be a clear economic incentive to make sure that they remain under control.

To explore this kind of scenario, let's think about a product that might come along fairly soon: a reasonably intelligent personal assistant that keeps track of your activities, conversations, relationships and so on, and kind of runs your life in the way that a good professional human assistant might help you. Now, if such a system does not have a good understanding of human preferences, and acts in ways that that are unsafe in ways that we've already talked about, then people are simply not going to buy it. If it misunderstands these things, then it might book you into a $20,000-a-night hotel room, or it might cancel a meeting with the vice president because you're supposed to go to the dentist.

In those kinds of situations, the AI is misunderstanding your preferences and, rather than being humble about its understanding of your preferences, it thinks that it knows what you want, and it is just being plain wrong about it. I've cited in other forums the example of a domestic robot that doesn't understand that the nutritional value of a cat is a lot less than the sentimental value of a cat, and so it just decides to cook the cat for dinner. If that happened, that would be the end of the domestic robot industry. No one is going to want a robot in its house that could make that kind of mistake.

Today, AI companies that are producing increasingly intelligent products have to solve at least a version of this problem in order for their products to be good AI systems.

We need to get the AI community to understand that AI that is not controllable and safe, is just not good AI.

In the same way that a bridge that falls down is simply not a good bridge, we need to recognize that AI that is not controllable and safe, is just not good AI. Civil engineers don't go around saying, "Oh yeah, I design bridges that don't fall down, you know, unlike the other guy, he designs bridges that fall down." It's just built into the meaning of the word "bridge" that it's not supposed to fall down.

This should be built into the meaning of what we mean when we define AI. We need to define AI in such a way that it remains under the control of the humans that it's supposed to be working for, in any country. And we need to define AI so that it has, now and in the future, properties that we call corrigibility: that it is able to be switched off, and that it is able to be corrected if it's doing something that we don't like.

If we can get everyone in AI, around the world, to understand that these are just necessary characteristics of good AI, then I think we move a long way forward in making the future prospects of the field of AI much, much brighter.

There's also no better way to kill the field of AI than to have a major control failure, just as the nuclear industry killed itself through Chernobyl and Fukushima. AI will kill itself if we fail to address the control issue.

MARTIN FORD: So, on balance, are you an optimist? Do you think that things are going to work out?

STUART J. RUSSELL: Yes, I do think that I'm an optimist. I think there's a long way to go. We are just scratching the surface of this control problem, but the first scratching seems to be productive, and so I'm reasonably optimistic that there is a path of AI development that leads us to what we might describe as "provably beneficial AI systems."

Of course, there is the risk that even if we do solve the control problem and even if we do build provably beneficial AI systems, that there will be some parties who choose not to use them. The risk here is that one party or another chooses only to magnify the capabilities of AI without regarding the safety aspects.

This could be the Dr. Evil character type, the Austin Powers villain who wants to take over the world and accidentally releases an AI system that ends up being catastrophic for everyone. Or it could be a much more sociological risk, where it starts off as very nice for society to have capable, controllable AI but we then

67

overuse it. In those risk scenarios, we head towards an enfeebled human society where we've moved too much of our knowledge and too much of our decision-making into machines, and we can never recover it. We could eventually lose our entire agency as humans along this societal path.

This societal picture is how the future is depicted in the WALL-E movie, where humanity is off on spaceships and being looked after by machines. Humanity gradually becomes fatter and lazier and stupider. That's an old theme in science fiction and it's very clearly illustrated in the WALL-E movie. That is a future that we need to be concerned about, assuming we successfully navigate all the other risks that we've been discussing.

As an optimist, I can also see a future where AI systems are well enough designed that they're saying to humans, "Don't use us. Get on and learn stuff yourself. Keep your own capabilities, propagate civilization through humans, not through machines."

Of course, we might still ignore a helpful and well-design AI, if we prove to be too lazy and greedy as a race; and then we'll pay the price. In that sense, this really might become more of a sociocultural problem, and I do think that we need to do work as a human race to prepare and make sure this doesn't happen.

STUART J. RUSSELL

STUART J. RUSSELL *is a professor of electrical engineering and computer science at the University of California Berkeley and is widely recognized as one of the world's leading contributors in the field of artificial intelligence. He is the co-author, along with Peter Norvig, of* Artificial Intelligence: A Modern Approach, *which is the leading AI textbook currently in use at over 1300 colleges and universities in 118 countries.*

Stuart received his undergraduate degree in Physics from Wadham College, Oxford in 1982 and his PhD in Computer Science from Stanford in 1986. His research has covered many topics related to AI, such as machine learning, knowledge representation, and computer vision, and he has received numerous awards and distinctions, including the IJCAI Computers and Thought Award and election as a fellow to the American Association for the Advancement of Science, the Association for the Advancement of Artificial Intelligence and the Association of Computing Machinery.

“ *In the past when AI has been overhyped—including backpropagation in the 1980s—people were expecting it to do great things, and it didn't actually do things as great as they hoped. Today, it's already done great things, so it can't possibly all be just hype.*

GEOFFREY HINTON

EMERITUS DISTINGUISHED PROFESSOR OF COMPUTER SCIENCE,
UNIVERSITY OF TORONTO
VICE PRESIDENT & ENGINEERING FELLOW, GOOGLE

Geoffrey Hinton is sometimes known as the Godfather of Deep Learning, and he has been the driving force behind some of its key technologies, such as backpropagation, Boltzmann machines, and the Capsules neural network. In addition to his roles at Google and the University of Toronto, he is also Chief Scientific Advisor of the Vector Institute for Artificial Intelligence.

MARTIN FORD: You're most famous for working on the backpropagation algorithm. Could you explain what backpropagation is?

GEOFFREY HINTON: The best way to explain it is by explaining what it isn't. When most people think about neural networks, there's an obvious algorithm for training them: Imagine you have a network that has layers of neurons, and you have an input at the bottom layer, and an output at the top layer. Each neuron has a weight associated with each connection. What each neuron does is look at the neurons in the layer below and it multiplies the activity of a neuron in the layer below by the weight, then adds all that up and gives an output that's a function of that sum. By adjusting the weights on the connections, you can get networks that do anything you like, such as looking at a picture of a cat and labeling it as a cat.

The question is, how should you adjust the weights so that the network does what you want? There's a very simple algorithm that will actually work but is incredibly slow—it's a dumb mutation algorithm—where you start with random weights on all the connections, and you give your network a set of examples and see how well it works. You then take one of those weights, and you change it a little bit, and now you give it another set of examples to see if it works better or worse than it did before. If it works better than it did before, you keep the change you made. If it works worse than it did before, you don't keep that change, or perhaps you change the weight in the opposite direction. Then you take another weight, and you do the same thing.

You have to go around all of the weights, and for each weight, you have to measure how well the network does on a set of examples, with each weight having to be updated multiple times. It is an incredibly slow algorithm, but it works, and it'll do whatever you want.

Backpropagation is basically a way of achieving the same thing. It's a way of tinkering with the weights so that the network does what you want, but unlike the dumb algorithm, it's much, much faster. It's faster by a factor of how many weights there are in the network. If you've got a network with a billion weights, backpropagation is going to be a billion times faster than the dumb algorithm.

The dumb algorithm works by having you adjust one of the weights slightly, followed by you measuring to see how well the network does. For evolution, that's what you've got to do because the process that takes you from your genes to the finished product depends on the environment you're in. There's no way you can predict exactly what the phenotype will look like from the genotype, or how successful the phenotype will be because that depends on what's going on in the world.

In a neural net, however, the processor takes you from the input and the weights to how successful you are in producing the right output. You have control over that whole process because it's all going on inside the neural net; you know all the weights that are involved. Backpropagation makes use of all that by sending information backward through the net. Using the fact that it knows all the weights, it can compute in parallel for every single weight in the network, whether you should make it a little bit bigger or smaller to improve the output.

The difference is that in evolution, you *measure* the effect of a change, and in backpropagation, you *compute* what the effect would be of making a change, and you can do that for all the weights at once with no interference. With backpropagation you can adjust the weights rapidly because you can give it a few examples, then backpropagate the discrepancies between what it said and what it should have said, and now you can figure out how to change all of the weights simultaneously to make all of them a little bit better. You still need to do the process a number of times, but it's much faster than the evolutionary approach.

MARTIN FORD: The backpropagation algorithm was originally created by David Rumelhart, correct, and you took that work forward?

GEOFFREY HINTON: Lots of different people invented different versions of backpropagation before David Rumelhart. They were mainly independent inventions, and it's something I feel I've got too much credit for. I've seen things in the press that say I invented backpropagation, and that's completely wrong. It's one of these rare cases when an academic feels he's got too much credit for something! My main contribution was to show how you can use it for learning distributed representations, so I'd like to set the record straight on that.

In 1981, I was a postdoc in San Diego, California and David Rumelhart came up with the basic idea of backpropagation, so it's his invention. Myself and Ronald Williams worked with him on formulating it properly. We got it working, but we didn't do anything particularly impressive with it, and we didn't publish anything.

After that, I went off to Carnegie Mellon and worked on the Boltzmann machine, which I think of as a much more interesting idea, even though it doesn't work as well. Then in 1984, I went back and tried backpropagation again so I could compare it with the Boltzmann machine, and discovered it actually worked much better, so I started communicating with David Rumelhart again.

What got me really excited about backpropagation was what I called the family trees task, where you could show that backpropagation can learn distributed representations. I had been interested in the brain having distributed representations since high school, and finally, we had an efficient way to learn them! If you gave it a problem, such as if I was to input two words and it has to output the third word that goes with that, it would learn distributed representations for the words, and those distributed representations would capture the meanings of the words.

Back in the mid-1980s, when computers were very slow, I used a simple example where you would have a family tree, and I would tell you about relationships within that family tree. I would tell you things like Charlotte's mother is Victoria, so I would say Charlotte and mother, and the correct answer is Victoria. I would also say Charlotte and father, and the correct answer is James. Once I've said those two things, because it's a very regular family tree with no divorces, you could use conventional AI to infer using your knowledge of family relations that Victoria must be the spouse of James because Victoria is Charlotte's mother and James is Charlotte's father. The neural net could infer that too, but it didn't do it by using rules of inference, it did it by learning a bunch of features for each person. Victoria and Charlotte would both be a bunch of separate features, and then by using interactions between those vectors of features, that would cause the output to be the features for the correct person. From the features for Charlotte and from the features for mother, it could derive the features for Victoria, and when you trained it, it would learn to do that. The most exciting thing was that for these different words, it would learn these feature vectors, and it was learning distributed representations of words.

We submitted a paper to *Nature* in 1986 that had this example of backpropagation learning distributed features of words, and I talked to one of the referees of the paper, and that was what got him really excited about it, that this system was learning these distributed representations. He was a psychologist, and he understood that having a learning algorithm that could learn representations of things was a big breakthrough. My contribution was not discovering the backpropagation algorithm, that was something Rumelhart had pretty much figured out, it was showing that backpropagation would learn these distributed representations, and that was what was interesting to psychologists, and eventually, to AI people.

Quite a few years later, in the early 1990s, Yoshua Bengio rediscovered the same kind of network but at a time where computers were faster. Yoshua was applying it to language, so he would take real text, taking a few words as context, and then try and predict the next word. He showed that the neural network was pretty good at that and that it would discover these distributed representations of words. It made a big impact because the backpropagation algorithm could learn representations and you didn't have to put them in by hand. People like Yann LeCun had been doing that in computer vision for a while. He was showing that backpropagation would learn good filters for processing visual input in order to make good decisions, and that was a bit more obvious because we knew the brain did things like that. The fact that backpropagation would learn distributed representations that captured the meanings and the syntax of words was a big breakthrough.

MARTIN FORD: Is it correct to say that at that time using neural networks was still not a primary thrust of AI research? It's only quite recently this has come to the forefront.

GEOFFREY HINTON: There's some truth to that, but you also need to make a distinction between AI and machine learning on the one hand, and psychology on the other hand. Once backpropagation became popular in 1986, a lot of psychologists got interested in it, and they didn't really lose their interest in it, they kept believing that it was an interesting algorithm, maybe not what the brain did, but an interesting way of developing representations. Occasionally, you see the idea that there were only a few people working on it, but that's not true. In psychology, lots of people stayed interested in it. What happened in AI was that in the late 1980s, Yann LeCun got something impressive working for recognizing handwritten digits, and there were various other moderately impressive applications of backpropagation from things like speech recognition to predicting credit card fraud. However, the proponents of backpropagation thought it was going to do amazing things, and they probably did oversell it. It didn't really live up to the expectations we had for it. We thought it was going to be amazing, but actually, it was just pretty good.

In the early 1990s, other machine learning methods on small datasets turned out to work better than backpropagation and required fewer things to be fiddled with to get them to work well. In particular, something called the support vector machine did better at recognizing handwritten digits than backpropagation, and handwritten digits had been a classic example of backpropagation doing something really well. Because of that, the machine learning community really lost interest in backpropagation. They decided that there was too much fiddling involved, it didn't work well enough to be worth all that fiddling, and it was hopeless to think that just from the inputs and outputs you could learn multiple layers of hidden representations. Each layer would be a whole bunch of feature detectors that represent in a particular way.

The idea of backpropagation was that you'd learn lots of layers, and then you'd be able to do amazing things, but we had great difficulty learning more than a few layers, and we couldn't do amazing things. The general consensus among statisticians and people in AI was that we were wishful thinkers. We thought that just from the inputs and outputs, you should be able to learn all these weights; and that was just unrealistic. You were going to have to wire in lots of knowledge to make anything work.

That was the view of people in computer vision until 2012. Most people in computer vision thought this stuff was crazy, even though Yann LeCun sometimes got systems working better than the best computer vision systems, they still thought this stuff was crazy, it wasn't the right way to do vision. They even rejected papers by Yann, even though they worked better than the best computer vision systems on particular problems, because the referees thought it was the wrong way to do things. That's a lovely example of scientists saying, "We've already decided what the answer has to look like, and anything that doesn't look like the answer we believe in is of no interest."

In the end, science won out, and two of my students won a big public competition, and they won it dramatically. They got almost half the error rate of the best computer vision systems, and they were using mainly techniques developed in Yann LeCun's lab but mixed in with a few of our own techniques as well.

MARTIN FORD: This was the ImageNet competition?

GEOFFREY HINTON: Yes, and what happened then was what should happen in science. One method that people used to think of as complete nonsense had now worked much better than the method they believed in, and within two years, they all switched. So, for things like object classification, nobody would dream of trying to do it without using a neural network now.

MARTIN FORD: This was back in 2012, I believe. Was that the inflection point for deep learning?

GEOFFREY HINTON: For computer vision, that was the inflection point. For speech, the inflection point was a few years earlier. Two different graduate students at Toronto showed in 2009 that you could make a better speech recognizer using deep learning. They went as interns to IBM and Microsoft, and a third student took their system to Google. The basic system that they had built was developed further, and over the next few years, all these companies' labs converted to doing speech recognition using neural nets. Initially, it was just using neural networks for the frontend of their system, but eventually, it was using neural nets for the whole system. Many of the best people in speech recognition had switched to believing in neural networks before 2012, but the big public impact was in 2012, when the vision community, almost overnight, got turned on its head and this crazy approach turned out to win.

MARTIN FORD: If you read the press now, you get the impression that neural networks and deep learning are equivalent to artificial intelligence—that it's the whole field.

GEOFFREY HINTON: For most of my career, there was artificial intelligence, which meant the logic-based idea of making intelligent systems by putting in rules that allowed them to process symbol strings. People believed that's what intelligence was, and that's how they were going to make artificial intelligence. They thought intelligence consists of processing symbol strings according to rules, they just had to figure out what the symbol strings were and what the rules were, and that was AI. Then there was this other thing that wasn't AI at all, and that was neural networks. It was an attempt to make intelligence by mimicking how the brain learns.

Notice that standard AI wasn't particularly interested in learning. In the 1970s, they would always say that learning's not the point. You have to figure out what the rules are and what the symbolic expressions they're manipulating are, and we can worry about learning later. Why? Because the main point is reasoning. Until you've figured out how it does reasoning, there's no point thinking about learning. The logic-based people were interested in symbolic reasoning, whereas the neural network-based people were interested in learning, perception, and motor control. They're trying to solve different problems, and we believe that reasoning is something that evolutionarily comes very late in people, and it's not the way to understand the basics of how the brain works. It's built on top of something that's designed for something else.

What's happened now is that industry and government use "AI" to mean deep learning, and so you get some really paradoxical things. In Toronto, we've received a lot of money from the industry and government for setting up the Vector Institute, which does basic research into deep learning, but also helps the industry do deep learning better and educates people in deep learning. Of course, other people would like some of this money, and another university claimed they had more people doing AI than in Toronto and produced citation figures as evidence. That's because they used classical AI. They used citations of conventional AI to say they should get some of this money for deep learning, and so this confusion in the meaning of AI is quite serious. It would be much better if we just didn't use the term "AI."

MARTIN FORD: Do you really think that AI should just be focused on neural networks and that everything else is irrelevant?

GEOFFREY HINTON: I think we should say that the general idea of AI is making intelligent systems that aren't biological, they are artificial, and they can do clever things. Then there's what AI came to mean over a long period, which is what's sometimes called good old-fashioned AI: representing things using symbolic expressions. For most academics—at least, the older academics—that's what AI means: that commitment to manipulating symbolic expressions as a way to achieve intelligence.

I think that old-fashioned notion of AI is just wrong. I think they're making a very naive mistake. They believe that if you have symbols coming in and you have symbols coming out, then it must be symbols in-between all the way. What's in-between is nothing like strings of symbols, it's big vectors of neural activity. I think the basic premise of conventional AI is just wrong.

MARTIN FORD: You gave an interview toward the end of 2017 where you said that you were suspicious of the backpropagation algorithm and that it needed to be thrown out and we needed to start from scratch.[1] That created a lot of disturbance, so I wanted to ask what you meant by that.

GEOFFREY HINTON: The problem was that the context of the conversation wasn't properly reported. I was talking about trying to understand the brain, and I was raising the issue that backpropagation may not be the right way to understand the brain. We don't know for sure, but there are some reasons now for believing that the brain might not use backpropagation. I said that if the brain doesn't use backpropagation, then whatever the brain is using would be an interesting candidate for artificial systems. I didn't at all mean that we should throw out backpropagation. Backpropagation is the mainstay of all the deep learning that works, and I don't think we should get rid of it.

MARTIN FORD: Presumably, it could be refined going forward?

GEOFFREY HINTON: There's going to be all sorts of ways of improving it, and there may well be other algorithms that are not backpropagation that also work, but I don't think we should stop doing backpropagation. That would be crazy.

MARTIN FORD: How did you become interested in artificial intelligence? What was the path that took you to your focus on neural networks?

GEOFFREY HINTON: My story begins at high school, where I had a friend called Inman Harvey who was a very good mathematician who got interested in the idea that the brain might work like a hologram.

MARTIN FORD: A hologram being a three-dimensional representation?

GEOFFREY HINTON: Well, the important thing about a proper hologram is that if you take a hologram and you cut it in half, you do not get half the picture, but instead you get a fuzzy picture of the whole scene. In a hologram, information about the scene is distributed across the whole hologram, which is very different from what we're used to. It's very different from a photograph, where if you cut out a piece of a photograph you lose the information about what was in that piece of the photograph, it doesn't just make the whole photograph go fuzzier.

---

1 See: https://www.axios.com/artificial-intelligence-pioneer-says-we-need-to-start-over-1513305524-f619efbd-9db0-4947-a9b2-7a4c310a28fe.html

Inman was interested in the idea that human memory might work like that, where an individual neuron is not responsible for storing an individual memory. He suggested that what's happening in the brain is that you adjust the connection strengths between neurons across the whole brain to store each memory, and that it's basically a distributed representation. At that time, holograms were an obvious example of distributed representation.

People misunderstand what's meant by distributed representation, but what I think it means is you're trying to represent some things—maybe concepts—and each concept is represented by activity in a whole bunch of neurons, and each neuron is involved in the representations of many different concepts. It's very different from a one-to-one mapping between neurons and concepts. That was the first thing that got me interested in the brain. We were also interested in how brains might learn things by adjusting connection strengths, and so I've been interested in that basically the whole time.

MARTIN FORD: When you were at high school? Wow. So how did your thinking develop when you went to university?

GEOFFREY HINTON: One of the things I studied at university was physiology. I was excited by physiology because I wanted to learn how the brain worked. Toward the end of the course they told us how neurons send action potentials. There were experiments done on the giant squid axon, figuring out how an action potential propagated along an axon, and it turned out that was how the brain worked. It was rather disappointing to discover, however, that they didn't have any kind of computational model of how things were represented or learned.

After that, I switched to psychology, thinking they would tell me how the brain worked, but this was at Cambridge, and at that time it was still recovering from behaviorism, so psychology was largely about rats in boxes. There was some cognitive psychology then but they were fairly non-computational, and I didn't really get much sense that they were ever going to figure out how the brain worked.

During the psychology course, I did a project on child development. I was looking at children between the ages of two and five, and how the way that they attend to different perceptual properties changes as they develop. The idea is that when they're very young, they're mainly interested in color and texture, but as they get older, they become more interested in shape. I conducted an experiment where I would show the children three objects, of which one was the odd one out, for example, two yellow circles and a red circle. I trained the children to point at the odd one out, something that even very young children can learn to do.

I'd also train them on two yellow triangles and one yellow circle, and then they'd have to point at the circle because that was the odd one out on shape. Once they'd been trained on simple examples where there was a clear odd one out, I would then give them a test example like a yellow triangle, a yellow circle, and a red circle. The idea was that if they were more interested in color than shape, then the odd one out would be the red circle, but if they were more interested in shape than color, then the odd one out would be the yellow triangle. That was all well and good, and for a couple of children, they pointed out either the yellow triangle that was a different shape or the red circle that was a different color. I remember, though, that when I first did the test with one bright five-year-old, he pointed at the red circle, and he said, "You've painted that one the wrong color."

The model that I was trying to corroborate was a very dumb, vague model that said, "when they're little, children attend more to color and as they get bigger, they attend more to shape." It's an incredibly primitive model that doesn't say how anything works, it's just a slight change in emphasis from color to shape. Then, I was confronted by this kid who looks at them and says, "You've painted that one the wrong color." Here's an information processing system that has learned what the task is from the training examples, and because he thinks there should be an odd one out, he realizes there isn't a single odd one out, and that I must have made a mistake, and the mistake was probably that I painted that one the wrong color.

Nothing in the model of children that I was testing allowed for that level of complexity at all. This was hugely more complex than any of the models in psychology. It was an information processing system that was smart and could figure out what was going on, and for me, that was the end of psychology. The models they had were hopelessly inadequate compared with the complexity of what they were dealing with.

MARTIN FORD: After leaving the field of psychology, how did you end up going into artificial intelligence?

GEOFFREY HINTON: Well, before I moved into the world of AI, I became a carpenter, and whilst I enjoyed it, I wasn't an expert at it. During that time, I met a really good carpenter, and it was highly depressing, so because of that I went back to academia.

MARTIN FORD: Well, given the other path that opened up for you, it's probably a good thing that you weren't a great carpenter!

GEOFFREY HINTON: Following my attempt at carpentry, I worked as a research assistant on a psychology project trying to understand how language develops in very young children, and how it is influenced by social class. I was responsible for creating a questionnaire that would assess the attitude of the mother toward their child's language development. I cycled out to a very poor suburb of Bristol, and I knocked on the door of the first mother I was due to talk to. She invited me in and gave me a cup of tea, and then I asked her my first question, which was: "What's your attitude towards your child's use of language?" She replied, "If he uses language, we hit him." So that was pretty much it for my career as a social psychologist.

After that I went into AI and became a graduate student in artificial intelligence at The University of Edinburgh. My adviser was a very distinguished scientist called Christopher Longuet-Higgins who'd initially been a professor of chemistry at Cambridge and had then switched fields to artificial intelligence. He was very interested in how the brain might work—and in particular, studying things like holograms. He had realized that computer modeling was the way to understand the brain, and he was working on that, and that's why I originally signed up with him. Unfortunately for me, about the same time that I signed up with him, he changed his mind. He decided that these neural models were not the way to understand intelligence, and the actual way to understand intelligence was to try and understand language.

It's worth remembering that at the time, there were some impressive models—using symbol processing—of systems that could talk about arrangements of blocks. An American professor of computer science called Terry Winograd wrote a very nice thesis that showed how you could get a computer to understand some language and to answer questions, and it would actually follow commands. You could say to it, "put the block that's in the blue box on top of the red cube," and it would understand and do that. It was only in a simulation, but it would understand the sentence. That impressed Christopher Longuet-Higgins a lot, and he wanted me to work on that, but I wanted to keep working on neural networks.

Now, Christopher was a very honorable guy, but we completely disagreed on what I should do. I kept refusing to do what he said, but he kept me on anyway. I continued my work on neural networks, and eventually, I did a thesis on neural networks, though at the time, neural networks didn't work very well and there was a consensus that they were just nonsense.

MARTIN FORD: When was this in relation to Marvin Minsky and Seymour Papert's *Perceptrons* book?

GEOFFREY HINTON: This was in the early '70s, and Minsky and Papert's book came out in the late '60s. Almost everybody in artificial intelligence thought that was the end of neural networks. They thought that trying to understand intelligence by studying neural networks was like trying to understand intelligence by studying transistors; it just wasn't the way to do it. They thought intelligence was all about programs, and you had to understand what programs the brain was using.

These two paradigms were completely different, they aimed to try and solve different problems, and they used completely different methods and different kinds of mathematics. Back then, it wasn't at all clear which was going to be the winning paradigm. It's still not clear to some people today.

What was interesting, was that some of the people most associated with logic actually believed in the neural net paradigm. The biggest examples are John von Neumann and Alan Turing, who both thought that big networks of simulated neurons were a good way to study intelligence and figure out how those things work. However, the dominant approach in AI was symbol processing inspired by logic. In logic, you take symbol strings and alter them to arrive at new symbol strings, and people thought that must be how reasoning works.

They thought neural nets were far too low-level, and that they were all about implementation, just like how transistors are the implementation layer in a computer. They didn't think you could understand intelligence by looking at how the brain is implemented, they thought you could only understand it by looking at intelligence in itself, and that's what the conventional AI approach was.

I think it was disastrously wrong, something that we're now seeing. The success of deep learning is showing that the neural net paradigm is actually far more successful than the logic-based paradigm, but back then in the 1970s, that was not what people thought.

MARTIN FORD: I've seen a lot of articles in the press suggesting deep learning is being overhyped, and this hype could lead to disappointment and then less investment, and so forth. I've even seen the phrase "AI Winter" being used. Is that a real fear? Is this potentially a dead end, or do you think that neural networks are the future of AI?

GEOFFREY HINTON: In the past when AI has been overhyped—including backpropagation in the 1980s—people were expecting it to do great things, and it didn't actually do things as great as they hoped. Today, it's already done great things, so it can't possibly all be just hype. It's how your cell phone recognizes speech, it's how a computer can recognize things in photos, and it's how Google does machine translation. Hype means you're making big promises, and you're not going to live up to them, but if you've already achieved them, that's clearly not hype.

I occasionally see an advertisement on the web that says it's going to be a 19.9 trillion-dollar industry. That seems like rather a big number, and that might be hype, but the idea that it's a multi-billion-dollar industry clearly isn't hype, because multiple people have put billions of dollars into it and it's worked for them.

MARTIN FORD: Do you believe the best strategy going forward is to continue to invest exclusively in neural networks? Some people still believe in symbolic AI, and they think there's potentially a need for a hybrid approach that incorporates both deep learning and more traditional approaches. Would you be open to that, or do you think the field should focus only on neural networks?

GEOFFREY HINTON: I think big vectors of neural activities interacting with each other is how the brain works, and it's how AI is going to work. We should definitely try and figure out how the brain does reasoning, but I think that's going to come fairly late compared with other things.

I don't believe hybrid systems are the answer. Let's use the car industry as an analogy. There are some good things about a petrol engine, like you can carry a lot of energy in a small tank, but there are also some really bad things about petrol engines. Then there are electric motors, which have a lot to be said in their favor compared with petrol engines. Some people in the car industry agreed that electrical engines were achieving progress and then said they'd make a hybrid system and use the electric motor to inject the petrol into the engine. That's how people in conventional AI are thinking. They have to admit that deep learning is doing amazing things, and they want to use deep learning as a kind of low-level servant to provide them with what they need to make their symbolic reasoning work. It's just an attempt to hang on to the view they already have, without really comprehending that they're being swept away.

MARTIN FORD: Thinking more in terms of the future of the field, I know your latest project is something you're calling *Capsules*, which I believe is inspired by the columns in the brain. Do you feel that it's important to study the brain and be informed by that, and to incorporate those insights into what you're doing with neural networks?

GEOFFREY HINTON: Capsules is a combination of half a dozen different ideas, and it's complicated and speculative. So far, it's had some small successes, but it's not guaranteed to work. It's probably too early to talk about that in detail, but yes, it is inspired by the brain.

When people talk about using neuroscience in neural networks, most people have a very naive idea of science. If you're trying to understand the brain, there's going to be some basic principles, and there's going to be a whole lot of details. What we're after is the basic principles, and we expect the details all to be very different if we use different kinds of hardware. The hardware we have in graphics processor units (GPUs) is very different from the hardware in the brain, and one might expect lots of differences, but we can still look for principles. An example of a principle is that most of the knowledge in your brain comes from learning, it doesn't come from people telling you facts that you then store as facts.

With conventional AI, people thought that you have this big database of facts. You also have some rules of inference. If I want to give you some knowledge, what I do is simply express one of these facts in some language and then transplant it into your head, and now you have the knowledge. That's completely different from what happens in neural networks: You have a whole lot of parameters in your head, that is weights of connections between neurons, and I have a whole lot of weights of connections between the neurons in my head, and there's no way that you can give me your connection strengths. Anyway, they wouldn't be any use to me because my neural network's not exactly the same as yours. What you have to do is somehow convey information about how you are working so that I can work the same way, and you do that by giving me examples of inputs and outputs.

For example, if you look at a tweet from Donald Trump, it's a big mistake to think that what Trump is doing is conveying facts. That's not what he's doing. What Trump is doing is saying that given a particular situation, here's a way you might choose to respond. A Trump follower can then see the situation, they can see how Trump thinks they ought to respond, and they can learn to respond the same way as Trump. It's not that some proposition is being conveyed from Trump to the follower, it's that a way of reacting to things has been conveyed by example. That's very different from a system that has a big store of facts, and you can copy facts from one system to another.

MARTIN FORD: Is it true that the vast majority of applications of deep learning rely heavily on labeled data, or what's called supervised learning, and that we still need to solve unsupervised learning?

GEOFFREY HINTON: That's not entirely true. There's a lot of reliance on labeled data, but there are some subtleties in what counts as labeled data. For example, if I give you a big string of text and I ask you to try and predict the next word, then I'm using the next word as a label of what the right answer is, given the previous words. In that sense, it's labeled, but I didn't need an extra label over and above the data. If I give you an image and you want to recognize cats, then I need to give you a label "cat," and the label "cat" is not part of the image. I'm having to create these extra labels, and that's hard work.

If I'm just trying to predict what happens next, that's supervised learning because what happens next acts as the label, but I don't need to add extra labels. There's this thing in between unlabeled data and labeled data, which is predicting what comes next.

MARTIN FORD: If you look at the way a child learns, though, it's mostly wandering around the environment and learning in a very unsupervised way.

GEOFFREY HINTON: Going back to what I just said, the child is wandering around the environment trying to predict what happens next. Then when what happens next comes along, that event is labeled to tell it whether it got it right or not. The point is, with both those terms, "supervised" and "unsupervised," it's not clear how you apply them to predicting what happens next.

There's a nice clear case of supervised learning, which is that I give you an image and I give you the label "cat," then you have to say it's a cat, then there's a nice clear case of unsupervised learning, which is if I give you a bunch of images, and you have to build representations of what's going on in the images. Finally, there's something that doesn't fall simply into either camp, which is if I give you a sequence of images and you have to predict the next image. It's not clear in that case whether you should call that supervised learning or unsupervised learning, and that causes a lot of confusion.

MARTIN FORD: Would you view solving a general form of unsupervised learning as being one of the primary obstacles that needs to be overcome?

GEOFFREY HINTON: Yes. But in that sense, one form of unsupervised learning is predicting what happens next, and my point is that you can apply supervised learning algorithms to do that.

MARTIN FORD: What do you think about AGI, and how would you define that? I would take it to mean human-level artificial intelligence, namely an AI that can reason in a general way, like a human. Is that your definition, or would you say it's something else?

GEOFFREY HINTON: I'm happy with that definition, but I think people have various assumptions of what the future's going to look like. People think that we're going to get individual AIs that get smarter and smarter, but I think there are two things wrong with that picture. One is that deep learning, or neural networks are going to get much better than us at some things, while they're still quite a lot worse than us at other things. It's not like they're going to get uniformly better at everything. They're going to be much better, for example, at interpreting medical images, while they're still a whole lot worse at reasoning about them. In that sense, it's not going to be uniform.

The second thing that's wrong is that people always think about it as individual AIs, and they ignore the social aspect of it. Just for pure computational reasons, making very advanced intelligence is going to involve making communities of intelligent systems because a community can see much more data than an individual system. If it's all a question of seeing a lot of data, then we're going to have to distribute that data across lots of different intelligent systems and have them communicate with one another so that between them, as a community, they can learn from a huge amount of data meaning that in the future, the community aspect of it is going to be essential.

MARTIN FORD: Do you envision it as being an emergent property of connected intelligences on the internet?

GEOFFREY HINTON: No, it's the same with people. The reason that you know most of what you know is not because you yourself extracted that information from data, it's because other people, over many years, have extracted information from data. They then gave you training experiences that allowed you to get to the same understanding without having to do the raw extraction from data. I think it'll be like that with artificial intelligence too.

MARTIN FORD: Do you think AGI, whether it's an individual system or a group of systems that interact, is feasible?

GEOFFREY HINTON: Oh, yes. I mean OpenAI already has something that plays quite sophisticated computer games as a team.

MARTIN FORD: When do you think it might be feasible for an artificial intelligence, or a group of AIs that come together, to have the same reasoning, intelligence, and capability as a human being?

GEOFFREY HINTON: If you go for reasoning, I think that's going to be one of the things we get really good at later on, but it's going to be quite a long time before big neural networks are really as good as people at reasoning. That being said, they'll be better at all sorts of other things before we get to that point.

MARTIN FORD: What about for a holistic AGI, though, where a computer system's intelligence is as good as a person?

GEOFFREY HINTON: I think there's a presupposition that the way AIs can develop is by making individuals that are general-purpose robots like you see on *Star Trek*.

If your question is, "When are we going to get a Commander Data?", then I don't think that's how things are going to develop. I don't think we're going to get single, general-purpose things like that. I also think, in terms of general reasoning capacity, it's not going to happen for quite a long time.

MARTIN FORD: Think of it in terms of passing the Turing test, and not for five minutes but for two hours, so that you can have a wide-ranging conversation that's as good as a human being. Is that feasible, whether it's one system or some community of systems?

GEOFFREY HINTON: I think there's a reasonable amount of probability that it will happen in somewhere between 10 and 100 years. I think there's a very small probability, it'll happen before the end of the next decade, and I think there's also a big probability that humanity gets wiped out by other things before the next 100 years occurs.

MARTIN FORD: Do you mean through other existential threats like a nuclear war or a plague?

GEOFFREY HINTON: Yes, I think so. In other words, I think there are two existential threats that are much bigger than AI. One is global nuclear war, and the other is a disgruntled graduate student in a molecular biology lab making a virus that's extremely contagious, extremely lethal, and has a very long incubation time. I think that's what people should be worried about, not ultra-intelligent systems.

MARTIN FORD: Some people, such as Demis Hassabis at DeepMind, do believe that they can build the kind of system that you're saying you don't think is going to come into existence. How do you view that? Do you think that it is a futile task?

GEOFFREY HINTON: No, I view that as Demis and me having different predictions about the future.

MARTIN FORD: Let's talk about the potential risks of AI. One particular challenge that I've written about is the potential impact on the job market and the economy. Do you think that all of this could cause a new Industrial Revolution and completely transform the job market? If so, is that something we need to worry about, or is that another thing that's perhaps overhyped?

GEOFFREY HINTON: If you can dramatically increase productivity and make more goodies to go around, that should be a good thing. Whether or not it turns out to be a good thing depends entirely on the social system, and doesn't depend at all on the technology. People are looking at the technology as if the technological advances are a problem. The problem is in the social systems, and whether we're going to have a social system that shares fairly, or one that focuses all the improvement on the 1% and treats the rest of the people like dirt. That's nothing to do with technology.

MARTIN FORD: That problem comes about, though, because a lot of jobs could be eliminated—in particular, jobs that are predictable and easily automated. One social response to that is a basic income, is that something that you agree with?

GEOFFREY HINTON: Yes, I think a basic income is a very sensible idea.

MARTIN FORD: Do you think, then, that policy responses are required to address this? Some people take a view that we should just let it play out, but that's perhaps irresponsible.

GEOFFREY HINTON: I moved to Canada because it has a higher taxation rate and because I think taxes done right are good things. What governments ought to be is mechanisms put in place so that when people act in their own self-interest, it helps everybody. High taxation is one such mechanism: when people get rich, everybody else gets helped by the taxes. I certainly agree that there's a lot of work to be done in making sure that AI benefits everybody.

MARTIN FORD: What about some of the other risks that you would associate with AI, such as weaponization?

GEOFFREY HINTON: Yes, I am concerned by some of the things that President Putin has said recently. I think people should be very active now in trying to get the international community to treat weapons that can kill people without a person in the loop the same way as they treat chemical warfare and weapons of mass destruction.

MARTIN FORD: Would you favor some kind of a moratorium on that type of research and development?

GEOFFREY HINTON: You're not going to get a moratorium on that type of research, just as you haven't had a moratorium on the development of nerve agents, but you do have international mechanisms in place that have stopped them being widely used.

MARTIN FORD: What about other risks, beyond the military weapon use? Are there other issues, like privacy and transparency?

GEOFFREY HINTON: I think using it to manipulate elections and to manipulate voters is worrying. Cambridge Analytica was set up by Bob Mercer who was a machine learning person, and you've seen that Cambridge Analytica did a lot of damage. We have to take that seriously.

MARTIN FORD: Do you think that there's a place for regulation?

GEOFFREY HINTON: Yes, lots of regulation. It's a very interesting issue, but I'm not an expert on it, so don't have much to offer.

MARTIN FORD: What about the global arms race in general AI, do you think it's important that one country doesn't get too far ahead of the others?

GEOFFREY HINTON: What you're talking about is global politics. For a long time, Britain was a dominant nation, and they didn't behave very well, and then it was America, and they didn't behave very well, and if it becomes the Chinese, I don't expect them to behave very well.

MARTIN FORD: Should we have some form of industrial policy? Should the United States and other Western governments focus on AI and make it a national priority?

GEOFFREY HINTON: There are going to be huge technological developments, and countries would be crazy not to try and keep up with that, so obviously, I think there should be a lot of investment in it. That seems common sense to me.

MARTIN FORD: Overall, are you optimistic about all of this? Do you think that the rewards from AI are going to outweigh the downsides?

GEOFFREY HINTON: I hope the rewards will outweigh the downsides, but I don't know whether they will, and that's an issue of social systems, not with the technology.

MARTIN FORD: There's an enormous talent shortage in AI and everyone's hiring. Is there any advice you would give to a young person that wants to get into this field, anything that might help attract more people and enable them to become expert in AI and in deep learning, that you can offer?

GEOFFREY HINTON: I'm worried that there may not be enough people who are critical of the basics. The idea of Capsules is to say, maybe some of the basic ways we're doing things aren't the best way of doing things, and we should throw a wider net. We should think about alternatives to some of the very basic assumptions we're making. The one piece of advice I give people is that if you have intuitions that what people are doing is wrong and that there could be something better, you should follow your intuitions.

You're quite likely to be wrong, but unless people follow the intuitions when they have them about how to change things radically, we're going to get stuck. One worry is that I think the most fertile source of genuinely new ideas is graduate students being well advised in a university. They have the freedom to come up with genuinely new ideas, and they learn enough so that they're not just repeating history, and we need to preserve that. People doing a master's degree and then going straight into the industry aren't going to come up with radically new ideas. I think you need to sit and think for a few years.

MARTIN FORD: There seems to be a hub of deep learning coalescing in Canada. Is that just random, or is there something special about Canada that helped with that?

GEOFFREY HINTON: The Canadian Institute for Advanced Research (CIFAR) provided funding for basic research in high-risk areas, and that was very important. There's also a lot of good luck in that both Yann LeCun, who was briefly my postdoc, and Yoshua Bengio were also in Canada. The three of us could form a collaboration that was very fruitful, and the Canadian Institute for Advanced Research funded that collaboration. This was at a time when all of us would have been a bit isolated in a fairly hostile environment—the environment for deep learning was fairly hostile until quite recently—it was very helpful to have this funding that allowed us to spend quite a lot of time with each other in small meetings, where we could really share unpublished ideas.

MARTIN FORD: So, it was a strategic investment on the part of the Canadian government to keep deep learning alive?

GEOFFREY HINTON: Yes. Basically, the Canadian government is significantly investing in advanced deep learning by spending half a million dollars a year, which is pretty efficient for something that's going to turn into a multi-billion-dollar industry.

MARTIN FORD: Speaking of Canadians, do you have any interaction with your fellow faculty member, Jordan Peterson? It seems like there's all kinds of disruption coming out of the University of Toronto...

GEOFFREY HINTON: Ha! Well, all I'll say about that is that he's someone who doesn't know when to keep his mouth shut.

ARCHITECTS OF INTELLIGENCE

GEOFFREY HINTON *received his undergraduate degree from Kings College, Cambridge and his PhD in Artificial Intelligence from the University of Edinburgh in 1978. After five years as a faculty member at Carnegie-Mellon University, he became a fellow of the Canadian Institute for Advanced Research and moved to the Department of Computer Science at the University of Toronto where he is now an Emeritus Distinguished Professor. He is also a Vice President & Engineering Fellow at Google and Chief Scientific Adviser of the Vector Institute for Artificial Intelligence.*

Geoff was one of the researchers who introduced the backpropagation algorithm and the first to use backpropagation for learning word embeddings. His other contributions to neural network research include Boltzmann machines, distributed representations, time-delay neural nets, mixtures of experts, variational learning and deep learning. His research group in Toronto made seminal breakthroughs in deep learning that revolutionized speech recognition and object classification.

Geoff is a fellow of the UK Royal Society, a foreign member of the US National Academy of Engineering and a foreign member of the American Academy of Arts and Sciences. His awards include the David E. Rumelhart prize, the IJCAI award for research excellence, the Killam prize for Engineering, the IEEE Frank Rosenblatt medal, the IEEE James Clerk Maxwell Gold medal, the NEC C&C award, the BBVA award, and the NSERC Herzberg Gold Medal, which is Canada's top award in science and engineering.

GEOFFREY HINTON

> **❝** *The concern is not that [an AGI] would hate or resent us for enslaving it, or that suddenly a spark of consciousness would arise and it would rebel, but rather that it would be very competently pursuing an objective that differs from what we really want. Then you get a future shaped in accordance with alien criteria.*

NICK BOSTROM

PROFESSOR, UNIVERSITY OF OXFORD AND DIRECTOR OF THE FUTURE OF HUMANITY INSTITUTE

Nick Bostrom is widely recognized as one of the world's top experts on superintelligence and the existential risks that AI and machine learning could potentially pose for humanity. He is the Founding Director of the Future of Humanity Institute at the University of Oxford, a multidisciplinary research institute studying big-picture questions about humanity and its prospects. He is a prolific author of over 200 publications, including the 2014 New York Times *bestseller* Superintelligence: Paths, Dangers, Strategies.

MARTIN FORD: You've written about the risks of creating a superintelligence—an entity that could emerge when an AGI system turns its energies toward improving itself, creating a recursive improvement loop that results in an intelligence that is vastly superior to humans.

NICK BOSTROM: Yes, that's one scenario and one problem, but there are other scenarios and other ways this transition to a machine intelligence era could unfold, and there are certainly, other problems one could be worried about.

MARTIN FORD: One idea you've focused on especially is the control or alignment problem where a machine intelligence's goals or values might result in outcomes that are harmful to humanity. Can you go into more detail on what that alignment problem, or control problem, is in layman's terms?

NICK BOSTROM: Well, one distinctive problem with very advanced AI systems that's different from other technologies is that it presents not only the possibility of humans misusing the technology—that's something we see with other technologies, of course—but also the possibility that the technology could misuse itself, as it were. In other words, you create an artificial agent or a process that has its own goals and objectives, and it is very capable of achieving those objectives because, in this scenario, it is superintelligent. The concern is that the objectives that this powerful system is trying to optimize for are different from our human values, and maybe even at cross-purposes with what we want to achieve in the world. Then if you have humans trying to achieve one thing and a superintelligent system trying to achieve something different, it might well be that the superintelligence wins and gets its way.

The concern is not that it would hate or resent us for enslaving it, or that suddenly a spark of consciousness would arise and it would rebel, but rather that it would be very competently pursuing an objective that differs from what we really want. Then you get a future shaped in accordance with alien criteria. The control problem, or the alignment problem, then is how do you engineer AI systems so that they are an extension of human will? In the sense that we have our intentions shape their behavior as opposed to a random, unforeseen and unwanted objective cropping up there?

MARTIN FORD: You have a famous example of a system that manufactures paperclips. The idea is that when a system is conceived and given an objective, it pursues that goal with a superintelligent competence, but it does it in a way that doesn't consider common sense, so it ends up harming us. The example you give is a system that turns the whole universe into paperclips because it's a paperclip optimizer. Is that a good articulation of the alignment problem?

NICK BOSTROM: The paperclip example is a stand-in for a wider category of possible failures where you ask a system to do one thing and, perhaps, initially things turn out pretty well but then it races to a conclusion that is beyond our control. It's a cartoon example, where you design an AI to operate a paperclip factory. It's dumb initially, but the smarter it gets, the better it operates the paperclip factory, and the owner of this factory is very pleased and wants to make more progress. However, when the AI becomes sufficiently smart, it realizes that there are other ways of achieving an even greater number of paperclips in the world, which might then involve taking control away from humans and indeed turning the whole planet into paperclips or into space probes that can go out and transform the universe into more paperclips.

The point here is that you could substitute almost any other goal you want for paperclips and if you think through what it would mean for that goal to be truly maximized in this world, that unless you're really, really careful about how you specify your goals, you will find that as a side effect of maximizing for that goal human beings and the things we care about would be stamped out.

MARTIN FORD: When I hear this problem described, it's always given as a situation where we give the system a goal, and then it pursues that goal in a way that we're not happy with. However, I never hear of a system that simply changes its goal, and I don't quite understand why that is not a concern. Why couldn't a superintelligent system at some point just decide to have different goals or objectives? Humans do it all of the time!

NICK BOSTROM: The reason why this seems less of a concern is that although a superintelligence would have the ability to change its goals, you have to consider the criteria it uses to choose its goals. It would make that choice based on the goals it has at that moment. In most situations, it would be a very poor strategic move for an agent to change its goals because it can predict that in the future, there will then not be an agent pursuing its current goal but instead an agent pursuing some different goal. This would tend to produce outcomes that would rank lower by its current goals, which by definition here are what it is using as the criteria by which to select actions. So, once you have a sufficiently sophisticated reasoning system, you expect it to figure this out and therefore be able to achieve internal goal stability to

Humans are a mess. We don't have a particular goal from which all the other objectives we pursue are sub-goals. We have different parts of our minds that are pulling in different directions, and if you increase our hormone levels, we suddenly change those values. Humans are not stable in the same way as machines, and maybe don't have a very clean, compact description as goal-maximizing agents. That's why it can seem that we humans sometimes decide to change our goals. It's not so much us deciding to change our goals; it's our goals just changing. Alternatively, by "goals," we don't mean our fundamental criteria for judging things, but just some particular objective, which of course can change as circumstances change or we discover new plans.

MARTIN FORD: A lot of the research going into this is informed by neural science, though, so there are ideas coming from the human brain being injected into machine intelligence. Imagine a superintelligence that has at its disposal all of human knowledge. It would be able to read all of human history. It would read about powerful individuals, and how they had different objectives and goals. The machine could also conceivably be subject to pathologies. The human brain has all kinds of problems, and there are drugs that can change the way the brain works. How do we know there's not something comparable in the machine space?

NICK BOSTROM: I think there well could be, particularly in the earlier stages of development, before the machine achieves sufficient understanding of how AI works to be able to modify itself without messing itself up. Ultimately, there are convergent instrumental reasons for developing technology to prevent your goals from being corrupted. I would expect a sufficiently capable system to develop those technologies for goal stability, and indeed it might place some priority on developing them. However, if it's in a rush or if it's not yet very capable—if it's roughly at the human level—the possibility certainly exists that things could get scrambled. A change might be implemented with the hope that it would maybe make it a more effective thinker, but it turns out to have some side effect in changing its objective function.

MARTIN FORD: The other thing that I worry about is that it's always a concern about how the machine is not going to do what we want, where "we" applies to collective humanity as though there's some sort of universal set of human desires or values. Yet, if you look at the world today, that's really not the case. The world has different cultures with different value sets. It seems to me that it might matter quite a lot where the first machine intelligence is developed. Is it naive to talk about the machine and all of humanity as being one entity? To me, it just seems like things are a lot messier than that

NICK BOSTROM: You try to break up the big problem into smaller problems in order then to make progress on them. You try to break out one component of the overall challenge, in this case that is the technical problem of how to achieve AI alignment with any human values to get the machine to do what its developers want it to do. Unless you have a solution to that, you don't have the privilege even to try for a solution to the wider, political problems of ensuring that we humans will then use this powerful technology for some beneficial purpose.

You need to solve the technical problem to get the opportunity to squabble over whose values, or in what degrees different values should guide the use of this technology. It is true, of course, that even if you have a solution to the technical control problem, you've really only solved part of the overall challenge. You also then need to figure out a way that we can use this peacefully and in a way that benefits all of humanity.

MARTIN FORD: Is solving that technical control problem, in terms of how to build a machine that remains aligned with the objective, what you're working on at the Future of Humanity Institute, and what other think tanks like OpenAI and the Machine Intelligence Research Institute are focusing on?

NICK BOSTROM: Yes, that's right. We do have a group working on that, but we're also working on other things. We also have a governance of AI group, that is focused on the governance problems related to advances in machine intelligence.

MARTIN FORD: Do you think that think tanks like yours are an appropriate level of resource allocation for AI governance, or do you think that governments should jump into this at a larger scale?

NICK BOSTROM: I think there could be more resources on AI safety. It's not actually just us: DeepMind also has an AI safety group that we work with, but I do think more resources would be beneficial. There is already a lot more talent and money now than there was even four years ago. In percentage terms, there has been a rapid growth trajectory, even though in absolute terms it's still a very small field.

MARTIN FORD: Do you think that superintelligence concerns should be more in the public sphere? Do you want to see presidential candidates in the United States talking about superintelligence?

NICK BOSTROM: Not really. It's still a bit too early to seek involvement from states and governments because right now it's not exactly clear what one would want them to do that would be helpful at this point in time. The nature of the problem first needs to be clarified and understood better, and there's a lot of work that can be done without having governments come in. I don't see any need right now for any particular regulations with respect to machine superintelligence. There are all kinds of things related to near-term AI applications where there might be various roles for governments to play.

If you're going to have flying drones everywhere in the cities, or self-driving cars on the streets, then there presumably needs to be a framework that regulates them. The extent that AI will have an impact on the economy and the labor market is also something that should be of interest to people running education systems or setting economic policy. I still think superintelligence is a little bit outside the purview of politicians, who mainly think about what might happen during their tenure.

MARTIN FORD: So, when Elon Musk says superintelligence is a bigger threat than North Korea, could that rhetoric potentially make things worse?

NICK BOSTROM: If you are getting into this prematurely, with a view to there being a big arms race, which could lead to a more competitive situation where voices for caution and global cooperation get sidelined, then yes, that could actually make things worse rather than better. I think one can wait until there is a clear concrete thing that one actually would need and want governments to do in relation to superintelligence, and then one can try to get them activated. Until that time, there's still a huge amount of work that we can do, for example, in collaboration with the AI development community and with companies and academic institutions that are working with AI, so let's get on with that groundwork for the time being.

MARTIN FORD: How did you come to your role in the AI community? How did you first become interested in AI, and how did your career develop to the point it's at right now?

NICK BOSTROM: I've been interested in artificial intelligence for as long as I can remember. I studied artificial intelligence, and later computational neuroscience, at university, as well as other topics, like theoretical physics. I did this because I thought that firstly, AI technology could eventually be transformative in the world, and secondly because it's very interesting intellectually to try to figure out how thinking is produced by the brain or in a computer.

I published some work about superintelligence in the mid-1990s, and I had the opportunity in 2006 to create the Future of Humanity Institute (FHI) at Oxford University. Together with my colleagues, I work full-time on the implications of future technologies for the future of humanity, with a particular focus—some might say an obsession—on the future of machine intelligence. That then resulted in 2014 in my book *Superintelligence: Paths, Dangers, Strategies*. Currently, we have two groups within the FHI. One group focuses on technical computer science work on the alignment problem, so trying to craft algorithms for scalable control methods. The other group focuses on governance, policy, ethics and the social implications of advances in machine intelligence.

MARTIN FORD: In your work at the Future of Humanity Institute you've focused on a variety of existential risks, not just AI-related dangers, right?

NICK BOSTROM: That's right, but we're also looking at the existential opportunities, we are not blind to the upside of technology.

MARTIN FORD: Tell me about some of the other risks you've looked at, and why you've chosen to focus so much on machine intelligence above all.

NICK BOSTROM: At the FHI, we're interested in really big-picture questions, the things that could fundamentally change the human condition in some way. We're not trying to study what next year's iPhone might be like, but instead things that could change some fundamental parameter of what it means to be human—questions that shape the future destiny of Earth-originating intelligent life. From that perspective, we are interested in existential risk—things that could permanently destroy human civilization—and also things that could permanently shape our trajectory into the future. I think technology is maybe the most plausible source for such fundamental reshapers of humanity, and within technology there are just a few that plausibly present either existential risks or existential opportunities; AI might be the foremost amongst those. FHI also has a group working on the biosecurity risks coming out of biotechnology, and we're interested more generally in how you put these different considerations together—a macro strategy, as we call it.

Why AI in particular? I think that if AI were to be successful at its original goal, which all along has been not just to automate specific tasks but to replicate in machine substrates the general-purpose learning ability and planning ability that makes us humans smart, then that would quite literally be the last invention that humans ever needed to make. If achieved, it would have enormous implications not just in AI, but across all technological fields, and indeed all areas where human intelligence currently is useful.

MARTIN FORD: What about climate change, for example? Is that on your list of existential threats?

NICK BOSTROM: Not so much, partly because we prefer to focus where we think our efforts might make a big difference, which tends to be areas where the questions have been relatively neglected. There are tons of people currently working on climate change across the world. Also, it's hard to see how the planet getting a few degrees warmer would cause the extinction of the human species, or permanently destroy the future. So, for those and some other reasons, that's not been at the center of our own efforts, although we might cast a sideways glance at it on occasion by trying to sum up the overall picture of the challenges that humanity confronts.

MARTIN FORD: So, you would argue that the risk from advanced AI is actually more significant than from climate change, and that we're allocating our resources and investment in these questions incorrectly? That sounds like a very controversial view.

NICK BOSTROM: I do think that there is some misallocation, and it's not just between those two fields in particular. In general, I don't think that we as a human civilization allocate our attention that wisely. If we imagine humans as having an amount of concern capital, chips of concern or fear that we can spread around on different things that threaten human civilization, I don't think we are that sophisticated in how we choose to allocate those concern chips.

If you look back over the last century, there has been at any given point in time maybe one big global concern that all intellectually educated people are supposed to be fixated on, and it's changed over time. So maybe 100 years ago, it was dysgenics, where intellectuals were worrying about the deterioration of the human stock. Then during the Cold War, obviously nuclear Armageddon was a big concern, and then for a while, it was overpopulation. Currently, I would say it's global warming, although AI has, over the last couple of years, been creeping up there.

MARTIN FORD: That's perhaps largely due to the influence of people like Elon Musk talking about it. Do you think that's a positive thing that he's been so vocal, or is there a danger that it becomes overhyped or it draws uninformed people into the discussion?

NICK BOSTROM: I think so far it has been met positively. When I was writing my book, it was striking how neglected the whole topic of AI was. There were a lot of people working on AI, but very few people thinking about what would happen if AI were to succeed. It also wasn't the kind of topic you could have a serious conversation with people about because they would dismiss it as just science fiction, but that's now changed.

I think that's valuable, and maybe as a consequence of this having become a more mainstream topic, it's now possible to do research and publish technical papers on things like the alignment problem. There are a number of research groups doing just that, including here at the FHI, where we have joint technical research seminars with DeepMind, also OpenAI has a number of AI safety researchers, and there are other groups like the Machine Intelligence Research Institute at Berkeley. I'm not sure whether there would have been as much talent flowing into this field unless the profile of the whole challenge had first been raised. What is most needed today is not further alarm or further hand-wringing with people screaming for attention, the challenge now is more to channel this existing concern and interest in constructive directions and to get on with the work.

MARTIN FORD: Is it true to say that the risks you worry about in terms of machine intelligence are really all dependent on achieving AGI and beyond that, superintelligence? The risks associated with narrow AI are probably significant, but not what you would characterize as existential.

NICK BOSTROM: That's correct. We do also have some interest in these more near-term applications of machine intelligence, which are interesting in their own right and also worth having a conversation about. I think the trouble arises when these two different contexts, the near term, and the long term get thrown into the same pot and confused.

MARTIN FORD: What are some of the near-term risks that we need to worry about over the next five years or so?

NICK BOSTROM: In the near term, I think primarily there are things that I would be very excited about and look forward to having roll out. In the near-term context, the upside far outweighs the downside. Just look across to the economy and at all the areas where having smarter algorithms could make a positive difference. Even a low-key, boring algorithm running in the background in a big logistic center predicting demand curves more accurately would enable you to reduce the amount of stock, and therefore cut prices for consumers.

In healthcare, the same neural networks that can recognize cats, dogs, and faces could recognize tumors in x-ray images and assist radiologists in making more accurate diagnoses. Those neural networks might run in the background and help optimize patient flows and track outcomes. You could name almost any area, and there would probably be creative ways to use these new techniques that are emerging from machine learning to good effect.

I think that's a very exciting field, with a lot of opportunity for entrepreneurs. From a scientific point of view as well, it's really exciting to begin to understand a little bit about how intelligence works and how perception is performed by the brain and in these neural systems.

MARTIN FORD: A lot of people worry about the near-term risks of things like autonomous weapons that can make their own decisions about who to kill. Do you support a ban on weapons of those types?

NICK BOSTROM: It would be positive if the world could avoid immediately jumping into another arms race, where huge amounts of money are spent perfecting killer robots. Broadly speaking, I'd prefer that machine intelligence is used for peaceful purposes, and not to develop new ways of destroying us. I think if one zooms in, it becomes a little bit less clear exactly what it is that one would want to see banned by a treaty.

There's a move to say that humans must be in the loop and that we should not have autonomous drones make targeting decisions on their own, and maybe that is possible. However, the alternative is that you have exactly the same system in place, but instead of the drone deciding to fire a missile, a19-year-old sits in Arlington, Virginia in front of a computer screen and has the job that whenever a window pops up on the screen saying "Fire," they need to press a red button. If that's what human oversight amounts to, then it's not clear that it really makes that much of a difference from having the whole system be completely autonomous. I think maybe more important is that there is some accountability, and there's somebody whose butt you can kick if things go wrong.

MARTIN FORD: There are certain situations you can imagine where an autonomous machine might be preferable. Thinking of policing rather than military applications, we've had incidents in the United States of what appears to be police racism, for example. A properly designed AI-driven robotic system in a situation like that would not be biased. It would also be prepared to take a bullet first, and shoot second, which is really not an option for a human being.

NICK BOSTROM: Preferably we shouldn't be fighting any wars between ourselves at all, but if there are going to be wars, maybe it's better if it's machines killing machines rather than young men shooting holes in other young men. If there are going to be strikes against specific combatants, maybe you can make precision strikes that only kill the people you're trying to kill, and don't create collateral damage with civilians. That's why I'm saying that the overall calculation becomes a little bit more complex when one considers the specifics, and what exactly the rule or agreement is that one would want to be implemented with regard to lethal autonomous weapons.

There are other areas of application that also raise interesting ethical questions such as in surveillance, or the management of data flows, marketing, and advertising, which might matter as much for the long-term outcome of human civilization as these more direct applications of drones to kill or injure people.

MARTIN FORD: Do you feel there is a role for regulation of these technologies?

NICK BOSTROM: Some regulation, for sure. If you're going to have killer drones, you don't want any old criminal to be able to easily assassinate public officials from five kilometers away using a drone with facial recognition software. Likewise, you don't want to have amateurs flying drones across airports and causing big delays. I'm sure a form of military framework will be required as we get more of these drones traversing spaces where humans are traveling for other purposes.

MARTIN FORD: It's been about four years since your book *Superintelligence: Paths, Dangers, Strategies* was published. Are things progressing at the rate that you expected?

NICK BOSTROM: Progress has been faster than expected over the last few years, with big advances in deep learning in particular.

MARTIN FORD: You had a table in your book where you said that having a computer beat the best Go player in the world was a decade out, so that would have been roughly 2024. As things turned out, it actually occurred just two years after you published the book.

NICK BOSTROM: I think the statement I made was that if progress continued at the same rate as it had been going over the last several years, then one would expect a Go Grand Champion machine to occur about a decade after the book was written. However, the progress was faster than that, partly because there was a specific effort toward solving Go. DeepMind took on the challenge and assigned some good people to the task, and put a lot of computing power onto it. It was certainly a milestone, though, and a demonstration of the impressive capabilities of these deep learning systems.

MARTIN FORD: What are the major milestones or hurdles that you would point to that stand between us and AGI?

NICK BOSTROM: There are several big challenges remaining in machine learning, such as needing better techniques for unsupervised learning. If you think about how adult humans come to know all the things we do, only a small fraction of that is done through explicit instruction. Most of it is by us just observing what's going on and using that sensory feed to improve our world models. We also do a lot of trial and error as toddlers, banging different things into one another and seeing what happens.

In order to get really highly effective machine intelligent systems, we also need algorithms that can make more use of unsupervised and unlabeled data. As humans, we tend to organize a lot of our world knowledge in causal terms, and that's something that is not really done much by current neural networks. It's more about finding statistical regularities in complex patterns, but not really organizing that as objects that can have various kinds of causal impacts on other objects. So, that would be one aspect.

I also think that there are advances needed in planning and a number of other areas as well, and it is not as if there are no ideas out there on how to achieve these things. There are limited techniques available that can do various aspects of these things relatively poorly, and I think that there just needs to be a great deal of improvement in those areas in order for us to get all the way to full human general intelligence.

MARTIN FORD: DeepMind seems to be one of the very few companies that's focused specifically on AGI. Are there other players that you would point to that are doing important work, that you think may be competitive with what DeepMind is doing?

NICK BOSTROM: DeepMind is certainly among the leaders, but there are many places where there is exciting work being done on machine learning or work that might eventually contribute to achieving artificial general intelligence. Google itself has another world-class AI research group in the form of Google Brain. Other big tech companies now have their own AI labs: Facebook, Baidu, and Microsoft have quite a lot of research in AI going on.

In academia, there are a number of excellent places. Canada has Montreal and Toronto, both of which are world-leading deep learning universities, and the likes of Berkeley, Oxford, Stanford, and Carnegie Mellon also have a lot of researchers in the field. It's not just a Western thing, countries like China are investing greatly in building up their domestic capacity.

MARTIN FORD: Those are not focused specifically on AGI, though.

NICK BOSTROM: Yes, but it's a fuzzy boundary. Among those groups currently overtly working towards AGI, aside from DeepMind, I guess OpenAI would be another group that one could point to.

MARTIN FORD: Do you think the Turing test is a good way to determine if we've reached AGI, or do we need another test for intelligence?

NICK BOSTROM: It's not so bad if what you want is a rough-and-ready criterion for when you have fully succeeded. I'm talking about a full-blown, difficult version of the Turing test. Something where you can have experts interrogate the system for an hour, or something like that. I think that's an AI-complete problem. It can't be solved other than by developing general artificial intelligence. If what you're interested in is gauging the rate of progress, say, or establishing benchmarks to know what to shoot for next with your AI research team, then the Turing test is maybe not such a good objective.

MARTIN FORD: Because it turns into a gimmick if it's at a smaller scale?

NICK BOSTROM: Yes. There's a way of doing it right, but that's too difficult, and we don't know at all how to do that right now. If you wanted incremental progress on the Turing test, what you would get would be these systems that have a lot of canned answers plugged in, and clever tricks and gimmicks, but that actually don't move you any closer to real AGI. If you want to make progress in the lab, or if you want to measure the rate of progress in the world, then you need other benchmarks that plug more into what is actually getting us further down the road, and that will eventually lead to fully general AI.

MARTIN FORD: What about consciousness? Is that something that might automatically emerge from an intelligent system, or is that an entirely independent phenomenon?

NICK BOSTROM: It depends on what you mean by consciousness. One sense of the word is the ability to have a functional form of self-awareness, that is, you're able to model yourself as an actor in the world and reflect on how different things might change you as an agent. You can think of yourself as persisting through time. These things come more or less as a side effect of creating more intelligent systems that can build better models of all kinds of aspects of reality, and that includes themselves.

Another sense of the word "consciousness" is this phenomenal experiential field that we have that we think has moral significance. For example, if somebody is actually consciously suffering, then it's a morally bad thing. It means something more than just that they tend to run away from noxious stimuli because they actually experience it inside of themselves as a subjective feeling. It's harder to know whether that phenomenal experience will automatically arise just as a side effect of making machine systems smarter. It might even be possible to design machine systems that don't have qualia but could still be very capable. Given that we don't really have a very clear grasp of what the necessary and sufficient conditions are for morally relevant forms of consciousness, we must accept the possibility that machine intelligences could attain consciousness, maybe even long before they become human-level or superintelligent.

We think many non-human animals have more of the relevant forms of experience. Even with something as simple as a mouse, if you want to conduct medical research on mice, there is a set of protocols and guidelines that you have to follow. You have to anesthetize a mouse before you perform surgery on it, for example, because we think it would suffer if you just carved it up without anesthesia. If we have machine-intelligent systems, say, with the same behavioral repertoire and cognitive complexity as a mouse, then it seems to be a live question whether at that point it might not also start to reach levels of consciousness that would give it some degree of moral status and limit what we can do to it. At least it seems we shouldn't be dismissing that possibility out of hand. The mere possibility that it could be conscious might already be sufficient grounds for some obligations on our part to do, at least if they're easy to do, things that will make the machine have a better-quality life.

MARTIN FORD: So, in a sense, the risks here run both ways? We worry about the risk of AI harming us, but there's also the risk that perhaps we're going to enslave a conscious entity or cause it to suffer. It sounds to me that there is no definitive way that we're ever going to know if a machine is truly conscious. There's nothing like the Turing test for consciousness. I believe you're conscious because you're the same species I am, and I believe I'm conscious, but you don't have that kind of connection with a machine. It's a very difficult question to answer.

NICK BOSTROM: Yes, I think it is difficult. I wouldn't say species membership is the main criterion here that we use to posit consciousness, there are a lot of human beings that are not conscious. Maybe they are in a coma, or they are fetuses, or they could be brain dead, or under deep anesthesia. Most people also think you can be a non-human being, for instance, certain animals, let us say, have various degrees and forms of conscious experience. So, we are able to project it outside our own species, but I think it is true that it will be a challenge for human empathy to extend the requisite level of moral consideration to digital minds, should such come to exist.

We have a hard enough time with animals. Our treatment of animals, particularly in meat production, leaves much to be desired, and animals have faces and can squeak! If you have an invisible process inside a microprocessor, it's going to be much harder for humans to recognize that there could be a sentient mind in there that deserves consideration. Even today, it seems like one of those crazy topics that you can't really take seriously. It's like a discussion for a philosophical seminar rather than a real issue, like algorithmic discrimination is, or killer drones.

Ultimately, it needs to be moved out of this sphere of crazy topics that only professional philosophers talk about, and into a topic that you could have a reasonable public debate about. It needs to happen gradually, but I think maybe it's time to start affecting that shift, just as the topic of what AI might do for the human condition has moved from science-fiction into a more mainstream conversation over the last few years.

MARTIN FORD: What do you think about the impact on the job market and the economy that artificial intelligence might have? How big a disruption do you think that could be and do you think that's something we need to be giving a lot of attention to?

NICK BOSTROM: In the very short term, I think that there might be a tendency to exaggerate the impacts on the labor market. It is going to take time to really roll out systems on a large enough scale to have a big impact. Over time, though, I do think that advances in machine learning will have an increasingly large impact on human labor markets and if you fully succeed with artificial intelligence, then yes, artificial intelligence could basically do everything. In some respects, the ultimate goal is full unemployment. The reason why we do technology, and why we do automation is so that we don't have to put in so much effort to achieve a given outcome. You can do more with less, and that's the gestalt of technology.

MARTIN FORD: That's the utopian vision. So, would you support, for example, a basic income as a mechanism to make sure that everyone can enjoy the fruits of all this progress?

NICK BOSTROM: Some functional analog of that could start to look increasingly desirable over time. If AI truly succeeds, and we resolve the technical control problem and have some reasonable governance, then an enormous bonanza of explosive economic growth takes place. Even a small slice of that would be ample enough to give everybody a really great life, so it seems one should at the minimum do that. If we develop superintelligence, we will all carry a slice of the risk of this development, whether we like it or not. It seems only fair, then, that everybody should also get some slice of the upside if things go well.

I think that should be part of the vision of how machine superintelligence should be used in the world; at least a big chunk of it should be for the common good of all of humanity. That's also consistent with having private incentives for developers, but the pie, if we really hit the jackpot, would be so large that we should make sure that everybody has a fantastic quality of life. That could take the form of some kind of universal basic income or there could be other schemes, but the net result of that should be that everybody sees a great gain in terms of their economic resources. There will also be other benefits—like better technologies, better healthcare, and so forth—that superintelligence could enable.

MARTIN FORD: What are your thoughts on the concern that China could reach AGI first, or at the same time as us? It seems to me that the values of whatever culture develops this technology do matter.

NICK BOSTROM: I think it might matter less which particular culture happens to develop it first. It matters more how competent the particular people or group that are developing it are, and whether they have the opportunity to be careful. This is one of the concerns with a racing dynamic, where you have a lot of different competitors racing to get to some kind of finish line first—in a tight race you are forced to throw caution to the wind. The race would go to whoever squanders the least effort on safety, and that would be a very undesirable situation.

We would rather have whoever it is that develops the first superintelligence to have the option at the end of the development process to pause for six months, or maybe a couple of years to double-check their systems and install whatever extra safeguards they can think of. Only then would they slowly and cautiously amplify the system's capabilities up to the superhuman level. You don't want them to be rushed by the fact that some competitor is nipping at their heels. When thinking about what the most desirable strategic situation for humanity is when superintelligence arises in the future, it seems that one important desideratum is that the competitive dynamics should be allayed as much as possible.

MARTIN FORD: If we do have a "fast takeoff" scenario where the intelligence can recursively improve itself, though, then there is an enormous first-mover advantage. Whoever gets there first could essentially be uncatchable, so there's a huge incentive for exactly the kind of competition that you're saying isn't a good thing.

NICK BOSTROM: In certain scenarios, yes, you could have dynamics like that, but I think the earlier point I made about pursuing this with a credible commitment to using it for the global good is important here, not only from an ethical point of view but also from the point of view of reducing the intensity of the racing dynamic. It would be good if all the competitors feel that even if they don't win the race, they're still going to benefit tremendously. That will then make it more feasible to have some arrangement in the end where the leader can get a clean shot at this without being rushed.

MARTIN FORD: That calls for some sort of international coordination, and humanity's track record isn't that great. Compared to the chemical weapons ban and the nuclear non-proliferation act, it sounds like AI would be an even greater challenge in terms of verifying that people aren't cheating, even if you did have some sort of agreement.

NICK BOSTROM: In some respects it would be more challenging, and in other respects maybe less challenging. The human game has often been played around scarcity—there is a very limited set of resources, and if one person or country has those resources, then somebody else does not have them. With AI there is the opportunity for abundance in many respects, and that can make it easier to form cooperative arrangements.

MARTIN FORD: Do you think that we will solve these problems and that AI will be a positive force overall?

NICK BOSTROM: I'm full of both hopes and fears. I would like to emphasize the upsides here, both in the short term and longer term. Because of my job and my book, people always ask me about the risks and downsides, but a big part of me is also hugely excited and eager to see all the beneficial uses that this technology could be put to and I hope that this could be a great blessing for the world.

ARCHITECTS OF INTELLIGENCE

NICK BOSTROM *is a Professor at Oxford University, where he is the founding Director of the Future of Humanity Institute. He also directs the Governance of Artificial Intelligence Program. Nick studied at the University of Gothenburg, Stockholm University and Kings College London prior to receiving his PhD in philosophy from the London School of Economics in 2000. He is the author of some 200 publications, including* Anthropic Bias *(2002),* Global Catastrophic Risks *(2008),* Human Enhancement *(2009), and* Superintelligence: Paths, Dangers, Strategies *(2014), a* New York Times *bestseller.*

Nick has a background in physics, artificial intelligence, and mathematical logic as well as philosophy. He is recipient of a Eugene R. Gannon Award (one person selected annually worldwide from the fields of philosophy, mathematics, the arts and other humanities, and the natural sciences). He has been listed on Foreign Policy's *Top 100 Global Thinkers list twice; and he was included on* Prospect *magazine's* World Thinkers *list, the youngest person in the top 15 from all fields and the highest-ranked analytic philosopher. His writings have been translated into 24 languages. There have been more than 100 translations and reprints of his works.*

NICK BOSTROM

> ❝ *A human can learn to drive a car in 15 hours of training without crashing into anything. If you want to use the current reinforcement learning methods to train a car to drive itself, the machine will have to drive off cliffs 10,000 times before it figures out how not to do that.*

YANN LECUN

VP & CHIEF AI SCIENTIST, FACEBOOK
PROFESSOR OF COMPUTER SCIENCE, NYU

Yann LeCun has been involved in the academic and industry side of AI and Machine Learning for over 30 years. Prior to joining Facebook, Yann worked at AT&T's Bell Labs, where he is credited with developing convolutional neural networks—a machine learning architecture inspired by the brain's visual cortex. Along with Geoff Hinton and Yoshua Bengio, Yann is part of a small group of researchers whose effort and persistence led directly to the current revolution in deep learning neural networks.

MARTIN FORD: Let's jump right in and talk about the deep learning revolution that's been unfolding over the past decade or so. How did that get started? Am I right that it was the confluence of some refinements to neural network technology, together with much faster computers and an explosion in the amount of training data available?

YANN LECUN: Yes, but it was more deliberate than that. With the emergence of the backpropagation algorithm in 1986-87, people were able to train neural nets with multiple layers, which was something that the old models didn't do. This resulted in a wave of interest that lasted right through to around 1995 before petering out.

Then in 2003, Geoffrey Hinton, Yoshua Bengio, and I got together and said, we know these techniques are eventually going to win out, and we need to get together and hash out a plan to renew the community interest in these methods. That's what became deep learning. It was a deliberate conspiracy, if you will.

MARTIN FORD: Looking back, did you imagine the extent to which you would be successful? Today, people think artificial intelligence and deep learning are synonymous.

YANN LECUN: Yes and no. Yes, in the sense that we knew eventually those techniques would come to the fore for computer vision, speech recognition, and maybe a couple of other things—but no, we didn't realize it would become synonymous with deep learning.

We didn't realize that there would be so much of an interest from the wider industry that it would create a new industry altogether. We didn't realize that there would be so much interest from the public, and that it would not just revolutionize computer vision and speech recognition, but also natural language understanding, robotics, medical imaging analysis, and that it would enable self-driving cars that actually work. That took us by surprise, that's for sure.

Back in the early '90s, I would have thought that that this kind of progress would have happened slightly earlier but more progressively, rather than the big revolution that occurred around 2013.

MARTIN FORD: How did you first become interested in AI and machine learning?

YANN LECUN: As a kid, I was interested in science and engineering and the big scientific questions—life, intelligence, the origin of humanity. Artificial intelligence was something that fascinated me, even though it didn't really exist as a field in France during the 1960s and 1970s. Even with a fascination for those questions, when I finished high school I believed that I would eventually become an engineer rather than a scientist, so I began my studies in the field of engineering.

Early on in my studies, around 1980, I stumbled on a philosophy book which was a transcription of a debate between Jean Piaget, the developmental psychologist, and Noam Chomsky, the linguist, called, *Language and Learning: The Debate Between Jean Piaget and Noam Chomsky*. The book contained a really interesting debate between the concepts of nature and nurture and the emergence of language and intelligence.

On the side of Piaget in the debate was Seymour Papert, who was a professor at MIT in computer science and who was involved with early machine learning and arguably actually killed the field off in the first wave of neural nets in the late 1960s. Here he was, 10 years later, singing the praise of a very simple machine learning model called the perceptron that had been invented in the 1950s, and that he had been working on in the 1960s. That was the first time I read about the concept of a learning machine, and I was absolutely fascinated by the idea that a machine could learn. I thought learning was an integral part of intelligence.

As an undergrad, I dug up all the literature I could find about machine learning and did a couple of projects on it. I discovered that nobody in the West was working on neural nets. A few Japanese researchers were working on what became known as neural networks, but no one in the West was, because the field had been killed in the late '60s in part by Seymour Papert and Marvin Minsky, the famous American AI researcher.

I carried on working on neural nets on my own, and I did a PhD in 1987 titled, *Modeles connexionnistes de l'apprentissage (Connectionist learning models)*. My advisor, Maurice Milgram, was not actually working on this topic, and he told me outright, "I can be your official advisor, but I can't help you technically."

I discovered through my work that in the early 1980s, there was a community of people around the world who were working on neural nets, and I connected with them and ended up discovering things like backpropagation in parallel with people like David Rumelhart and Geoffrey Hinton.

MARTIN FORD: So, in the early 1980s there was a lot of research in this area going on in Canada?

YANN LECUN: No, this was the United States. Canada was not on the map for this type of research yet. In the early 1980s, Geoffrey Hinton was a postdoc at the University of California, San Diego where he was working with cognitive scientists like David Rumelhart and Jay McClelland. Eventually they published a book explaining psychology by simple neural nets and models of computation. Geoffrey then became Associate Professor at Carnegie Mellon University, and only moved to Toronto in 1987. That's when I also moved to Toronto, where I was a postdoc in his lab for one year.

MARTIN FORD: I was an undergraduate studying computer engineering in the early 1980s, and I don't recall much exposure to neural networks at all. It was a concept that was out there, but it was definitely very much marginalized. Now, in 2018, that has changed dramatically.

YANN LECUN: It was worse than marginalized. In the '70s and early '80s it was anathema within the community. You couldn't publish a paper that even mentioned the phrase neural networks because it would immediately be rejected by your peers.

In fact, Geoffrey Hinton and Terry Sejnowski published a very famous paper in 1983 called, *Optimal Perceptual Inference*, which described an early deep learning or neural network model. Hinton and Sejnowski had to use code words to avoid mentioning that it was a neural network. Even the title of their paper was cryptic; it was all very strange!

MARTIN FORD: One of the main innovations you're known for is the convolutional neural network. Could you explain what that is and how it's different from other approaches in deep learning?

YANN LECUN: The motivation for convolutional neural networks was building a neural network that was appropriate for recognizing images. It turned out to be useful for a wide-range of tasks, such as speech recognition and language translation. It's somewhat inspired by the architecture of the visual cortex in animals or humans.

David Hubel and Torsten Wiesel did some Nobel prize-winning work in neuroscience in the 1950s and 1960s about the type of functions that the neurons in the visual cortex perform and how they're connected with each other.

A convolutional network is a particular way of connecting the neurons with each other in such a way that the processing that takes place is appropriate for things like images. I should add that we don't normally call them neurons because they're not really an accurate reflection of biological neurons.

The basic principle of how the neurons are connected is that they're organized in multiple layers and each neuron in the first layer is connected with a small patch of pixels in the input image. Each neuron computes a weighted sum of its inputs. The weights are the quantities that are modified by learning. The neurons only see a tiny window of pixels of the input, and there's a whole bunch of neurons that look at the same little window. Then, there's a whole bunch of neurons that look at another slightly shifted window, but this bunch performs the same operation as the other bunch. If you have a neuron that detects a particular motif in one window, you're going to have another neuron that detects exactly the same motif in the next window and other neurons for all windows across the image.

Once you put all those neurons together and you realize what kind of mathematical operation they do, that operation is called a discrete convolution, which is why this is called a convolutional net.

That's the first layer, and then there's a second layer, which is a non-linearity layer—basically a threshold where each neuron turns on or turns off if the weighted sum computed by the convolution layer is above or below the threshold.

Finally, there's a third layer that performs what's called a pooling operation. I'm not going to cover it in detail, but it basically plays a role in making sure that when the input image is slightly shifted or deformed, the output responses don't change that much. That's a way of building a bit of invariance to distortion shifts or deformation of the object in the input image.

The convolutional net is basically a stack of layers of this type—convolution, non-linearity, pooling. You stack multiple layers of those, and by the time you get to the top, you have neurons that are supposed to detect individual objects.

You might have a neuron that turns on if you put an image of a horse in the image, and then you have one for cars, people, chairs, and all other categories you might want to recognize.

The trick is that the function that this neural network is doing is determined by the strength of the connections between the neurons, the weights, and those are not programmed; they're trained.

This is what is learned when you train the neural net. You show it the image of a horse, and if it doesn't say "horse," you tell it that it's wrong and here is the answer that it should have said. Then by using the backpropagation algorithm, it adjusts all the weights of all the connections in the network so that next time you show the same image of a horse, the output would be closer to the one you want, and you keep doing this for thousands of images.

MARTIN FORD: That process of training a network by giving it images of cats or horses, and so on, is what's called supervised learning, correct? Is it true to say that supervised learning is the dominant approach today, and that it takes huge amounts of data?

YANN LECUN: Exactly. Almost all of the applications of deep learning today use supervised learning.

Supervised learning is when you give the correct answer to the machine when you're training it, and then it corrects itself to give the correct answer. The magic of it is that after it's been trained, it produces a correct answer most of the time in categories that it's been trained on, even for images it's never seen before. You're correct, that does typically require a lot of samples, at least the first time you train the network.

MARTIN FORD: How do you see the field moving forward in the future? Supervised learning is very different from the way a human child learns. You could point at a cat once and say, "there's a cat," and that one sample might be enough for a child to learn. That's dramatically different from where AI is today.

YANN LECUN: Well, yes and no. As I said, the first time you train a convolutional network you train it with thousands, possibly even millions of images of various categories. If you then want to add a new category, for example if the machine has never seen a cat and you want to train it to recognize cats, then it only requires a few samples of cats. That is because it has already been trained to recognize images of any type and it knows how to represent images; it knows what an object is, and it knows a lot of things about various objects. So, to train it to recognize a new object, you just show it a few samples, and you just need to train a couple of the top layers.

MARTIN FORD: So, if you trained a network to recognize other kinds of animals like dogs and bears, then would it only take a small amount of data to get to a cat? That seems not so different from what a child is probably doing.

YANN LECUN: But it is different, and that's the unfortunate thing. The way a child learns (and animals, for that matter) is that most of the learning they do is before you can tell them, "this is a cat." In the first few months of life, babies learn a huge amount by observation without having any notion of language. They learn an enormous amount of knowledge about how the world works just by observation and with a little interaction with the world.

This sort of accumulation of enormous amounts of background knowledge about the world is what we don't know how to do with machines. We don't know what to call this, some people call this unsupervised learning, but it's a loaded term. It's sometimes called predictive learning, or imputative learning. I call it self-supervised learning. It's the kind of learning where you don't train for a task, you just observe the world and figure out how it works, essentially.

MARTIN FORD: Would reinforcement learning, or learning by practice with a reward for succeeding, be in the category of unsupervised learning?

YANN LECUN: No, that's a different category altogether. There are three categories essentially; it's more of a continuum, but there is reinforcement learning, supervised learning, and self-supervised learning.

Reinforcement learning is learning by trial and error, getting rewards when you succeed and not getting rewards when you don't succeed. That form of learning in its purest form is incredibly inefficient in terms of samples, and as a consequence works well for games, where you can try things as many times as you want, but doesn't work in many real-world scenarios.

You can use reinforcement learning to train a machine to play Go or chess. That works really well, as we've seen with AlphaGo, for example, but it requires a ridiculous number of samples or trials. A machine has to basically play more games than all of humanity in the last 3,000 years to reach good performance, and it works really well if you can do that, but it is often impractical in the real world.

If you want to use reinforcement learning to train a robot to grab objects, it will take a ridiculous amount of time to achieve that. A human can learn to drive a car in 15 hours of training without crashing into anything. If you want to use the current reinforcement learning methods to train a car to drive itself, the machine will have to drive off cliffs 10,000 times before it figures out how not to do that.

MARTIN FORD: I guess that's the argument for simulation.

YANN LECUN: I don't agree. It might be an argument for simulation, but it's also an argument for the fact that the kind of learning that we can do as humans is very, very different from pure reinforcement learning.

It's more akin to what people call model-based reinforcement learning. This is where you have your internal model of the world that allows you to predict that when you turn the wheel in a particular direction then the car is going to go in a particular direction, and if another car comes in front you're going to hit it, or if there is a cliff you are going to fall off that cliff. You have this predictive model that allows you to predict in advance the consequence of your actions. As a result, you can plan ahead and not take the actions that result in bad outcomes.

Learning to drive in this context is called model-based reinforcement learning, and that's one of the things we don't really know how to do. There is a name for it, but there's no real way to make it work reliably! Most of the learning is not in the reinforcement, it's in learning the predictive models in a self-supervised manner, and that's the main problem we don't know how to solve today.

MARTIN FORD: Is this an area that you're focused on with your work at Facebook?

YANN LECUN: Yes, it is one of the things that we're working on at Facebook. We're working on a lot of different things, including getting machines to learn by observation from different data sources—learning how the world works. We're building a model of the world so that perhaps some form of common sense will emerge and perhaps that model could be used as kind of a predictive model that would allow a machine to learn the way people do without having to try and fail 10,000 times before they've succeeded.

MARTIN FORD: Some people argue that deep learning alone is not going to be enough, or that there needs to be more structure in the networks, some kind of intelligent design from the onset. You seem to be a strong believer in the idea that intelligence will emerge organically from relatively generic neural networks.

YANN LECUN: I think that would be an exaggeration. Everybody agrees that there is a need for some structure, the question is how much, and what kind of structure is needed. I guess when you say that some people believe that there should be structures such as logic and reasoning, you're probably referring to Gary Marcus and maybe Oren Etzioni.

I actually had a debate with Gary Marcus on this earlier today. Gary's view isn't particularly well accepted in the community because he's been writing critically about deep learning, but he's not been contributing to it. That's not the case for Oren Etzioni because he's been in the field for a while, but his view is considerably milder than Gary's. The one thing all of us agree on, though, is that there is a need for some structure.

In fact, the very idea of convolutional networks is to put a structure in neural networks. Convolutional networks are not a blank slate, they do have a little bit of structure. The question is, if we want AI to emerge, and we're talking general intelligence or human-level AI, how much structure do we need? That's where people's views may differ, like whether we need explicit structures that will allow a machine to manipulate symbols, or if we need explicit structures for representing hierarchical structures in language.

A lot of my colleagues, like Geoffrey Hinton and Yoshua Bengio, agree that in the long run we won't need precise specific structures for this. It might be useful in the short term because we may not have figured out a general learning method for self-supervised learning. So, one way to cut corners is to hardwire the architecture; that is a perfectly fine thing to do. In the long run, though, it's not clear how much of that we need. The microstructure of the cortex seems to be very, very uniform all over, whether you're looking at the visual or prefrontal cortex.

MARTIN FORD: Does the brain use something like backpropagation?

YANN LECUN: We don't really know. There are more fundamental questions than that, though. Most of the learning algorithms that people have come up with essentially consist of minimizing some objective function.

We don't even know if the brain minimizes an objective function. If the brain does minimize an objective function, does it do it through a gradient-based method? Does the brain have some way of estimating in which direction to modify all of its synaptic connections in such a way as to improve this objective function? We don't know that. If it estimates that gradient, does it do it by some form of backpropagation?

It's probably not backpropagation as we know it, but it could be a form of approximation of gradient estimation that is very similar to backpropagation. Yoshua Bengio has been working on biologically plausible forms of gradient estimation, so it's not entirely impossible that the brain does some sort of gradient estimation of some objective function, we just simply don't know.

MARTIN FORD: What other important topics are you working on at Facebook?

YANN LECUN: We're working on a lot of fundamental research and questions on machine learning, so things that have more to do with applied mathematics and optimization. We are working on reinforcement learning, and we are also working on something called generative models, which are a form of self-supervised or predictive learning.

MARTIN FORD: Is Facebook working on building systems that can actually carry out a conversation?

YANN LECUN: What I've mentioned so far are the fundamental topics of research, but there are a whole bunch of application areas.

Facebook is very active in computer vision, and I think we can claim to have the best computer vision research group in the world. It's a mature group and there are a lot of really cool activities there. We're putting quite a lot of work into natural language processing, and that includes translation, summarization, text categorization—figuring out what topic a text talks about, as well as dialog systems. Actually, dialog systems are a very important area of research for virtual assistants, question and answering systems, and so on.

MARTIN FORD: Do you anticipate the creation of an AI that someday could pass the Turing test?

YANN LECUN: It's going to happen at some point, but the Turing test is not actually an interesting test. In fact, I don't think a lot of people in the AI field at the moment consider the Turing test to be a good test. It's too easy to trick it, and to some extent, the Turing test has already been and gone.

We give a lot of importance to language as humans because we are used to discussing intelligent topics with other humans through language. However, language is sort of an epiphenomenon of intelligence, and when I say this, my colleagues who work on natural language processing disagree vehemently!

Look at orangutans, who are essentially almost as smart as we are. They have a huge amount of common sense and very good models of the world, and they can build tools, just like humans. However, they don't have language, they're not social animals, and they barely interact with other members of the species outside the non-linguistic mother-and-child interaction. There is a whole component of intelligence that has nothing to do with language, and we are ignoring this if we reduce AI to just satisfying the Turing test.

MARTIN FORD: What is the path to artificial general intelligence and what do we need to overcome to get there?

YANN LECUN: There are probably other problems that we do not see at the moment that we're going to eventually encounter, but one thing I think we'll need to figure out is the ability that babies and animals have to learn how the world works by observation in the first few days, weeks, and months of life.

In that time, you learn that the world is three-dimensional. You learn that there are objects that move in front of others in different ways when you move your head. You learn object permanence, so you learn that when an object is hidden behind another one, it's still there. As time goes on, you learn about gravity, inertia, and rigidity—very basic concepts that are learnt essentially by observation.

Babies don't have a huge amount of means to act on the world, but they observe a lot, and they learn a huge amount by observing. Baby animals also do this. They probably have more hardwired stuff, but it's very similar.

Until we figure out how to do this unsupervised/self-supervised/predictive learning, we're not going to make significant progress because I think that's the key to learning enough background knowledge about the world so that common sense will emerge. That's the main hurdle. There are more technical subproblems of this that I can't get into, like prediction under uncertainty, but that's the main thing.

How long is it going to take before we figure out a way to train machines so that they learn how the world works by watching YouTube videos? That's not entirely clear. We could have a breakthrough in two years that might take another 10 years to actually make it work, or it might take 10 or 20 years. I have no idea when it will happen, but I do know it has to happen.

That's just the first mountain we have to climb, and we don't know how many mountains are behind it. There might be other huge issues and major questions that we do not see yet because we haven't been there yet and it's unexplored territory.

It will probably take 10 years before we find this kind of breakthrough and before it has some consequence in the real world, and that has to happen way before we reach human-level artificial general intelligence. The question is, once we clear this hurdle, what other problems are going to pop up?

How much prior structure do we need to build into those systems for them to actually work appropriately and be stable, and for them to have intrinsic motivations so that they behave properly around humans? There's a whole lot of problems that will absolutely pop up, so AGI might take 50 years, it might take 100 years, I'm not too sure.

MARTIN FORD: But you think it's achievable?

YANN LECUN: Oh, definitely.

MARTIN FORD: Do you think it's inevitable?

YANN LECUN: Yes, there's no question about that.

MARTIN FORD: When you think of an AGI, would it be conscious, or could it be a zombie with no conscious experience at all?

YANN LECUN: We don't know what that means. We have no idea what consciousness is. I think it's a non-problem. It's one of those questions that in the end, when you realize how things actually work, you realize that question was immaterial.

Back in the 17th century when people figured out that the image in the back of the eye on the retina forms upside down, they were puzzled by the fact that we see right-side up. When you understand what kind of processing is required after this, and that it doesn't really matter in which order the pixels come, you realize it's kind of a funny question because it doesn't make any sense. It's the same thing here. I think consciousness is a subjective experience and it could be a very simple epiphenomenon of being smart.

There are several hypotheses for what causes this illusion of consciousness—because I think it is an illusion. One possibility is that we have essentially a single engine in our prefrontal cortex that allows us to model the world, and a conscious decision to pay attention to a particular situation configures that model of the world for the situation at hand.

The conscious state is sort of an important form of attention, if you will. We may not have the same conscious experience if our brain were ten times the size and we didn't have a single engine to model the world, but a whole bunch of them.

MARTIN FORD: Let's talk about some of the risks associated with AI. Do you believe that we're on the cusp of a big economic disruption with the potential for wide spread job losses?

YANN LECUN: I'm not an economist, but I'm obviously interested in those questions, too. I've talked to a bunch of economists, and I've attended a number of conferences with a whole bunch of very famous economists who were discussing those very questions. First of all, what they say is that AI is what they call a general-purpose technology or GPT for short. What that means is that it's a piece of technology that will diffuse into all corners of the economy and transform pretty much how we do everything. I'm not saying this; they are saying this. If

I was saying this, I would sound self-serving or arrogant, and I would not repeat it unless I had heard it from other people who know what they're talking about. So, they're saying this, and I didn't really realize that this was the case before I heard them say it. They say this is something on the scale of electricity, the steam engine, or the electric motor.

One thing I'm worried about, and this was before talking to the economists, is the problem of technological unemployment. The idea that technology progresses rapidly and the skills that are required by the new economy are not matched by the skills of the population. A whole proportion of the population suddenly doesn't have the right skills, and it's left behind.

You would think that as technological progress accelerates, there'd be more and more people left behind, but what the economists say is that the speed at which a piece of technology disseminates in the economy is actually limited by the proportion of people who are not trained to use it. In other words, the more people are left behind, the less quickly the technology can diffuse in the economy. It's interesting because it means that the evil has kind of a self-regulating mechanism in it. We're not going to have widely disseminated AI technology unless a significant proportion of the population is trained to actually take advantage of it, and the example they use to demonstrate this is computer technology.

Computer technology popped up in the 1960s and 1970s but did not have an impact on productivity on the economy until the 1990s because it took that long for people to get familiar with keyboards, mice, etc., and for software and computers to become cheap enough for them to have mass appeal.

MARTIN FORD: I think there is a question of whether this time is different relative to those historical cases, because machines are taking on cognitive capability now.

You now have machines that can learn to do a lot of routine, predictable things, and a significant percentage of our workforce is engaged in things that are predictable. So, I think the disruption could turn out to be bigger this time than what we've seen in the past.

YANN LECUN: I don't actually think that's the case. I don't think that we're going to face mass unemployment because of the appearance of this technology. I think certainly the economic landscape is going to be vastly different in the same way that 100 years ago most of the population were working in the fields, and now it's 2% of the population.

Certainly, over the next several decades, you're going to see this kind of shift and people are going to have to retrain for it. We'll need some form of continuous learning, and it's not going to be easy for everyone. I don't believe, though, that we're going to run out of jobs. I heard an economist say, "We're not going to run out of jobs because we're not going to run out of problems."

The upcoming AI systems are going to be an amplification of human intelligence in the way that mechanical machines have been an amplification of physical strength. They're not going to be a replacement. It's not like just because AI systems that analyze MRI images would be better at detecting tumors, then radiologists are out of a job. It's going to be a very different job, and it's going to be a much more interesting job. They're going to spend their time doing more interesting things like talking to patients instead of staring at screens for 8 hours a day.

MARTIN FORD: Not everyone's a doctor, though. A lot of people are taxi drivers or truck drivers or fast food workers and they may have a harder time transitioning.

YANN LECUN: What's going to happen is the value of things and services is going to change. Everything that's by done by machine is going to get a lot cheaper, and anything that's done by humans is going to get more expensive. We're going to pay more for authentic human experience, and the stuff that can be done by machine is going to get cheap.

As an example, you can buy a Blu-ray player for $46. If you think about how much incredibly sophisticated technology goes into a Blu-ray player, it's insane that it costs $46. It's got technology in the form of blue lasers that didn't exist 20 years ago. It's got an incredibly precise servo mechanism to drive the laser to microns of precision. It's also got, H.264 video compression and superfast processors. It has a ridiculous amount of technology that goes in there, and it's $46 because it's essentially mass-produced by machines. Now, go on the web and search for a handmade ceramic salad bowl, and the first couple of hits you're going to get are going to propose handmade ceramic bowl, a 10,000-year-old technology, for something in the region of $500. Why $500?

Because it's handmade and you're paying for the human experience and the human connection. You can download a piece of music for a buck, but then if you want to go to a show where that music is being played live, it's going to be $200. That's for human experience.

The value of things is going to change, with more value placed on human experience and less to things that are automated. A taxi ride is going to be cheap because it can be driven by the AI system, but a restaurant where an actual person serves you or an actual human cook creates something, is going to be more expensive.

MARTIN FORD: That does presume that everyone's got a skill or talent that's marketable, which I'm not sure is true. What do you think of the idea of a universal basic income as a way to adapt to these changes?

YANN LECUN: I'm not an economist, so I don't have an informed opinion on this, but every economist I talked to seemed against the idea of a universal basic income. They all agree with the fact that as a result of increased inequality brought about by technological progress, some measures have to be taken by governments to compensate. All of them believe this has to do with fiscal policy in the form of taxing, and wealth and income redistribution.

This income inequality is something that is particularly apparent in the US, but also to a smaller scale in Western Europe. The Gini index—a measure of income inequality—of France or Scandinavia is around 25 or 30. In the US, it's 45, and that's the same level as third-world countries. In the US, Erik Brynjolfsson, an economist at MIT, wrote a couple of books with his colleague from MIT, Andrew McAfee, studying the impact of technology on the economy. They say that the median income of a household in America has been flat since the 1980s where we had Reaganomics and the lowering of taxes for higher incomes, whereas productivity has gone up more or less continuously. None of that occurred in Western Europe. So, it's purely down to fiscal policy. It's maybe fueled by technological progress, but there are easy things that governments can do to compensate for the disruption, and they're just not doing it in the US.

MARTIN FORD: What other risks are there, beyond the impact on the job market and economy, that come coupled with AI?

YANN LECUN: Let me start with one thing we should not worry about, the Terminator scenario. This idea that somehow we'll come up with the secret to artificial general intelligence, and that we'll create a human-level intelligence that will escape our control and all of a sudden robots will want to take over the world. The desire to take over the world is not correlated with intelligence, it's correlated with testosterone.

We have a lot of examples today in American politics, clearly illustrating that the desire for power is not correlated with intelligence.

MARTIN FORD: There is a pretty reasoned argument, though, that Nick Bostrom, in particular, has raised. The problem is not an innate need to take over the world, but rather that an AI could be given a goal and then it might decide to pursue that goal in a way that turns out to be harmful to us.

YANN LECUN: So, somehow we're smart enough to build artificial general intelligence machines, then the first thing we do is tell them to build as many paper clips as they can and they turn the entire universe into paper clips? That sounds unrealistic to me.

MARTIN FORD: I think Nick intends that as kind of a cartoonish example. Those kinds of scenarios all seem far-fetched, but if you are truly talking about superintelligence, then you would have a machine that might act in ways that would be incomprehensible to us.

YANN LECUN: Well, there is the issue of objective function design. All of those scenarios assume that somehow, you're going to design the objective function— the intrinsic motivations—of those machines in advance, and that if you get it wrong, they're going to do crazy things. That's not the way humans are built. Our intrinsic objective functions are not hardwired. A piece of it is hardwired in a sense that we have the instinct to eat, breathe, and reproduce, but a lot of our behavior and value system is learned.

We can very much do the same with machines, where their value system is going to be trained and we're going to train them to essentially behave in society and be beneficial to humanity. It's not just a problem of designing those functions but also training them, and it's much easier to train an entity to behave. We do it with our kids to educate them in what's right and wrong, and if we know how to do it with kids why wouldn't we be able to do this with robots or AI systems?

Clearly, there are issues there, but it's a bit like we haven't invented the internal combustion engine yet and we are already worrying that we're not going to be able to invent the brake and the safety belt. The problem of inventing the internal combustion engine is considerably more complicated than inventing brakes and safety belts.

MARTIN FORD: What do you think of the fast takeoff scenario, where you have recursive improvement that happens at an extraordinary rate, and before you know it, we've got something that makes us look like a mouse or an insect in comparison?

YANN LECUN: I absolutely do not believe in that. Clearly there's going to be continuous improvement, and certainly, the more intelligent machines become, the more they're going to help us design the next generation. It's already the case, and it's going to accelerate.

There is some sort of differential equation that governs the progress of technology, the economy, consumption of resources, communication, the sophistication of technology, and all that stuff. There's a whole bunch of friction terms in this equation that is completely ignored by the proponent of singularity or fast takeoff. Every physical process at some point has to saturate, by exhausting resources if nothing else. So, I don't believe in a fast takeoff. It's a fallacy that someone will figure out the secret to AGI, then all of a sudden, we're going to go from machines that are as intelligent as a rat to some that are as intelligent as an orangutan, and then a week later they are more intelligent than us, and then a month later, way more intelligent.

There's also no reason necessarily to believe that being way more intelligent than a single human will allow a machine to be completely superior to a single human. Humans can get killed by viruses that are extremely stupid, but they are specialized to kill us.

If we can build an artificial intelligence system that has general intelligence in that sense, then we can probably also build a more specialized intelligence designed to destroy the first one. It would be much more efficient at killing the AGI because more specialized machines are more efficient than general ones. I just think that every issue has its own solution built in.

MARTIN FORD: So, what should we legitimately be worried about in the next decade or two?

YANN LECUN: Economic disruption is clearly an issue. It's not an issue without a solution, but it's an issue with considerable political obstacles, particularly in cultures like the US where income and wealth redistribution are not something that's culturally accepted. There is an issue of disseminating the technology so that it doesn't only profit the developed world, but it's shared across the world.

There is a concentration of power. Currently, AI research is very public and open, but it's widely deployed by a relatively small number of companies at the moment. It's going to take a while before it's used by a wider swath of the economy and that's a redistribution of the cards of power. That will affect the world in some ways, it may be positive but it may also be negative, and we need to ensure that it's positive.

I think the acceleration of technological progress and the emergence of AI is going to prompt governments to invest more massively into education, particularly continuous education because people are going to have to learn new jobs. That's a real aspect of the disruption that needs to be dealt with. It's not something that doesn't have a solution, it's just a problem that people have to realize exists in order for them to solve it.

If you have a government that doesn't even believe in established scientific facts like global warming, how can they believe in this kind of stuff? There are a lot of issues of this type, including ones in the area of bias and equity. If we use supervised learning to train our systems, they're going to reflect the biases that are in the data, so how can you make sure they don't prolong the status quo in terms of biases?

MARTIN FORD: The problem there is that the biases are encapsulated in the data so that a machine learning algorithm would naturally acquire them. One would hope that it might be much easier to fix bias in an algorithm than in a human.

YANN LECUN: Absolutely. I'm actually quite optimistic in that dimension because I think it would indeed be a lot easier to reduce bias in a machine than it currently is with people. People are biased in ways that are extremely difficult to fix.

MARTIN FORD: Do you worry about military applications, like autonomous weapons?

YANN LECUN: Yes and no. Yes, because of course AI technology can be used for building weapons, but some people, like Stuart Russell, have characterized a potential new generation of AI-powered weapons as weapons of mass destruction and I completely disagree with that.

I think the way that militaries are going to use AI technology is exactly the opposite. It's for what the military calls, surgical actions. You don't drop a bomb that destroys an entire building, you send in your drone that just puts the person you are interested in capturing to sleep; it could be non-lethal.

When it gets to that point, it makes the military look more like police. Is that good in the long term? I don't think anyone can guess. It's less destructive than nukes—it can't be more destructive than nukes!

MARTIN FORD: Do you worry about a race with China in terms of advancing artificial intelligence? They have over a billion people, so they have got more data and along with that, fewer constraints on privacy. Is that going to give them an advantage in moving forward?

YANN LECUN: I don't think so. I think currently progress in the science is not conditioned on the wide availability of data. There may be more than 1 billion people in China, but the proportion of people who are actually involved in technology and research is actually relatively small.

There's no question that it will grow, China is really progressing in that direction. I think the style of government and the type of education they have may be stifling for creativity after a while. There is good work coming out of China, though, with some very smart people there, and they're going to make contributions to this field.

There was the same kind of fear of the West being overrun by Japanese technology in the 1980s, and it happened for a while and then it kind of saturated. Then it was the Koreans, and now it's the Chinese. There are going to be big mutations in Chinese society that will have to happen over the next few decades that will probably change the situation completely.

MARTIN FORD: Do you think that AI needs to be regulated at some level? Is there a place for government regulation for the kind of research you're doing and the systems that you're building?

YANN LECUN: While I don't think there is any point in regulating AI research at the moment, I do think there is certainly a need for regulating applications. Not because they use AI, but because of the domain of applications that they are.

Take the use of AI in the context of drug design; you always want to regulate how drugs are being tested, how they are deployed, and how they are used. It's already the case. Take self-driving cars: cars are regulated, and there are strict road safety regulations. Certainly, those are application areas where existing regulations might need to be tweaked because AI is going to become preponderant.

However, I don't see any need for the regulation of AI at the moment.

MARTIN FORD: So, I assume you disagree quite strongly with the kind of rhetoric Elon Musk has been using?

YANN LECUN: Oh, I completely and absolutely disagree with him. I've talked to him several times, but I don't know where his views are coming from. He's a very smart guy and I'm in awe of some of his projects, but I'm not sure what his motivation is. He wants to save humanity, so maybe he needs another existential threat for it. I think he is genuinely worried, but none of us have been able to convince him that Bostrom-style, hard take-off scenarios are not going to happen.

MARTIN FORD: Are you an optimist overall? Do you believe that the benefits of AI are going to outweigh the downsides?

YANN LECUN: Yes, I would agree with that.

MARTIN FORD: In what areas do you think it will bring the most benefits?

YANN LECUN: Well, I really hope that we figure out the way to get machines to learn like baby humans and animals. That's my scientific program for the next few years. I also hope we're going to make some convincing breakthrough before the people funding all this research get tired, because that's what happened in previous decades.

MARTIN FORD: You've warned that AI is being overhyped and that this might even lead to another "AI Winter." Do you really think there's a risk of that? Deep learning has become so central to the business models of Google, Facebook, Amazon, Tencent, and all these other incredibly wealthy corporations. So, it seems hard to imagine that investment in the technology would fall off dramatically.

YANN LECUN: I don't think we're going to see an AI winter in the way we saw before because there is a big industry around it and there are real applications that are bringing real revenue to these companies.

There's still a huge amount of investment, with the hope that, for example, self-driving cars are going to be working in the next five years and that medical imaging is going to be radically revolutionized. Those are probably going to be the most visible effects over the next few years, medicine and health care, transportation, and information access.

Virtual assistants are another case. They are only mildly useful today because they're kind of scripted by hand. They don't have any common sense, and they don't really understand what you tell them at a deep level. The question is whether we need to solve the AGI problem before we get virtual assistants that are not frustrating, or whether we can make more continuous progress before that. Right now, I don't know.

When that becomes available, though, that's going to change a lot of how people interact with each other and how people interact with the digital world. If everyone has a personal assistant that has human-level intelligence, that's going to make a huge difference.

I don't know if you've seen the movie *Her*? It's not a bad depiction in some ways of what might happen. Among all the sci-fi movies on AI, it's probably one of the least ridiculous.

I think a lot of AI-related technology is going to be widely available in the hands of people because of hardware progress. There's a lot of effort now to develop low-power and cheap hardware that can fit in your smartphone or your vacuum cleaner that can run a convolutional network on 100 milliwatts of power, and the chip can be bought for 3 bucks. That's going to change a lot of how the world around us works.

Instead of going randomly around your room, your vacuum cleaner is now going to be able to see where it needs to go, and your lawnmower is going to be able to mow your lawn without running over your flowerbeds. It's not just your car that will drive itself.

It might also have interesting environmental consequences, like wildlife monitoring. AI is going to be in the hands of everyone because of progress in hardware technology that is specialized for deep learning, and that's coming in the next 2 or 3 years.

YANN LECUN *is a Vice President and Chief AI Scientist at Facebook, as well as a professor of computer science at New York University. Along with Geoff Hinton and Yoshua Bengio, Yann is part of the so-called "Canadian Mafia"—the trio of researchers whose effort and persistence led directly to the current revolution in deep learning neural networks.*

Prior to joining Facebook, Yann worked at AT&T's Bell Labs, where he is credited with developing convolutional neural networks—a machine learning architecture inspired by the brain's visual cortex. Yann used convolutional neural nets to develop a handwriting recognition system that became widely used in ATMs and at banks to read the information on checks. In recent years, deep convolutional nets, powered by ever faster computer hardware, have revolutionized computer image recognition and analysis.

Yann received an Electrical Engineer Diploma from Ecole Superieure d'Ingenieurs en Electrotechnique et Electronique (ESIEE) in Paris, and a PhD in Computer Science from Universite Pierre et Marie Curie in 1987. He later worked as a post-doctoral researcher in Geoff Hinton's lab at the University of Toronto. He joined Facebook in 2013 to establish and run the Facebook AI Research (FAIR) organization, headquartered in New York City.

YANN LECUN

> **❝** *If we look around, whether you're looking at AI groups in companies, AI professors in academia, AI PhD students or AI presenters at top AI conferences, no matter where you cut it: we lack diversity. We lack women, and we lack under-represented minorities.*

FEI-FEI LI

PROFESSOR OF COMPUTER SCIENCE, STANFORD
CHIEF SCIENTIST, GOOGLE CLOUD

Fei-Fei Li is Professor of Computer Science at Stanford University, and Director of the Stanford Artificial Intelligence Lab (SAIL). Working in areas of computer vision and cognitive neuroscience, Fei-Fei builds smart algorithms that enable computers and robots to see and think, inspired by the way the human brain works in the real world. Fei-Fei is Chief Scientist, AI and Machine Learning at Google Cloud, where she works to advance and democratize AI. Fei-Fei is a strong proponent of diversity and inclusion in artificial intelligence and co-founded AI4ALL, an organization to attract more women and people from underrepresented groups into the field.

MARTIN FORD: Let's talk about your career trajectory. How did you first become interested in AI, and how did that lead to your current position at Stanford?

FEI-FEI LI: I've always been something of a STEM student, so the sciences have always appealed to me, and in particular I love physics. I went to Princeton University where I majored in Physics, and a by-product of studying physics is that I became fascinated by the fundamentals of the universe. Questions like, where does the universe come from? What does it mean to exist? Where is the universe going? The fundamental quest of human curiosity.

In my research I noticed something really interesting: since the beginning of the 20th century, we've seen a great awakening of modern physics, due to the likes of Einstein and Schoenberg, who towards the end of their lives became fascinated not only by the physical matter of the universe but by life, and biology, and by the fundamental questions of being. I became very fascinated by these questions as well. When I started to study, I realized that my real interest in life is not to discover physical matters but to understand intelligence—which defines human life.

MARTIN FORD: Was this when you were in China?

FEI-FEI LI: I was in the US, at Princeton Physics, when my intellectual interest in AI and neuroscience began. When I applied for a PhD there I was very lucky, and to this day, it's still a bit of a rare combination to do what I did—which was both neuroscience and AI.

MARTIN FORD: Do you think then that it's an important advantage to study both of those fields rather than to focus exclusively on a computer-science-driven approach?

FEI-FEI LI: I think it gives me a unique angle because I consider myself a scientist, and so when I approach AI, what drives me is scientific hypotheses and the scientific quest. The field of AI is about thinking machines, making machines intelligent, and I like to work on problems at the core of conquering machine intelligence.

Coming from a cognitive neuroscience background, I take an algorithmic point of view, and a detailed modeling point of view. So, I find the connection between the brain and machine learning fascinating. I also think a lot about human-inspired tasks that drive AI advances: the real-world tasks that our natural intelligence had to solve through evolution. My background has in this way given me a unique angle and approach to working with AI.

MARTIN FORD: Your focus has really been on computer vision, and you've made the point that, in evolutionary terms, the development of the eye likely led to the development of the brain itself. The brain was providing the compute power to interpret images, and so maybe understanding vision is the gateway to intelligence. Am I correct in that line of thinking?

FEI-FEI LI: Yes, you're right. Language is a huge part of human intelligence, of course: along with speech, tactile awareness, decision-making, and reasoning. But visual intelligence is embedded in all of these things.

If you look at the way nature designed our brain, half of the human brain is involved in human intelligence, and that human intelligence is intimately related to a motor system, to decision-making, to emotion, to intention, and to language. The human brain does not just happen to recognize isolated objects; these functions are an integral part of what deeply defines human intelligence.

MARTIN FORD: Could you sketch out some of the work you've done in computer or machine vision?

FEI-FEI LI: During the first decade of the 21st century, object recognition was the holy grail that the field of computer vision was working on. Object recognition is a building block for all vision. As humans, if we open our eyes and look around our environment, we recognize almost every object we look at. Recognition is critically important for us to be able to navigate the world, understand the world, communicate about the world, and do things in the world. Object recognition was a very lofty holy grail in computer vision, and we were using tools such as machine learning at that time.

Then in the mid-2000s, as I transitioned from a PhD student to become a professor, it became obvious that computer vision as a field was stuck, and that the machine learning models were not making huge progress. Back then, the whole international community was benchmarking autorecognition tasks with around 20 different objects.

So, along with my students and collaborators, we started thinking deeply about how we might make a quantum leap forward. We began to see that it was just not going to be sufficient for us to work with such a small-scale problem involving 20 objects to reach the lofty goal of object recognition. I was very much inspired by human cognition at this point, and the developmental story of any child, where the first few years of development involves a huge amount of data. Children engage in a huge amount of experimenting with their world, seeing the world, and just taking it in. Coincidentally, at was just at this time that the internet had boomed into a global phenomenon that provided a lot of big data.

I wanted to do a pretty crazy project that would take all the pictures we could find on the internet, organize them into concepts that mattered to humans, and label those images. As it turned out, this crazy idea turned into the project called ImageNet, with 15 million images organized into 22,000 labels.

We immediately open-sourced ImageNet for the world, because to this day I believe in the democratization of technology. We released the entire 15 million images to the world and started to run international competitions for researchers to work on the ImageNet problems: not on the tiny small-scale problems but on the problems that mattered to humans and applications.

Fast-forward to 2012, and I think we see the turning point in object recognition for a lot of people. The winner of the 2012 ImageNet competition created a convergence of ImageNet, GPU computing power, and convolutional neural networks as an algorithm. Geoffrey Hinton wrote a seminal paper that, for me, was Phase One in achieving the holy grail of object recognition.

MARTIN FORD: Did you continue this project?

FEI-FEI LI: For the next two years, I worked on taking object recognition a step further. If we again look at human development, babies start by babbling, a few words, and then they start making sentences. I have a two-year-old daughter and a six-year-old son. The two-year-old is making a lot of sentences, which is huge developmental progress, something that humans do as intelligent agents and animals. Inspired by this human development, I started working on the problem of how to enable computers to speak sentences when they see pictures, rather than just labeling a chair or a cat.

We were working on this problem using deep learning models for a few years. In 2015, I talked about the project at the TED2015 conference. The title of my talk was *How we're teaching computers to understand pictures*, and I discussed enabling computers to be able to understand the content of an image and summarize it in a human, natural-language sentence which could then be communicated.

MARTIN FORD: The way algorithms are trained is quite different from what happens with a human baby or young child. Children for the most part are not getting labeled data—they just figure things out. And even when you point to a cat and say, "look there's a cat," you certainly don't have to do that a hundred thousand times. Once or twice is probably enough. There's a pretty remarkable difference in terms of how a human being can learn from the unstructured, real-time data we meet in the world, versus the supervised learning that's done with AI now.

FEI-FEI LI: You totally nailed it, and this is why as an AI scientist I wake up so excited every day because there's so much to work with. Some part of the work has inspiration from humans, but a large part of the work does not resemble humans at all. As you say, the success today of neural networks and deep learning mostly involve supervised pattern recognition, which means that it's a very narrow sliver of capabilities compared to general human intelligence.

I gave a talk at Google's I/O conference this year, where I was again using the example of my two-year-old daughter. A couple of months ago, I watched her on a baby monitor escape from her crib by learning the cracks in the system, a potential path to escape from the crib. I saw her open her sleeping bag, which I had particularly modified in order to prevent her from opening and get herself out. That kind of coordinated intelligence to a visual motor, planning, reasoning, emotion, intention, and persistence, is really nowhere to be seen in our current AI. We've got a lot of work to do, and it's really important to recognize that.

MARTIN FORD: Do you think there will likely be breakthroughs that allow computers to learn more like children? Are people actively working on how to solve this problem?

FEI-FEI LI: There are absolutely people working on that, especially within the research community. A lot of us are working on the next horizon problem. In my own lab at Stanford, we are working on robotic learning problems where the AI is learning by imitation, which is much more natural than learning by supervised labels.

As kids, we watch how other humans do things and then we do it; so, the field is now starting to get into inverse reinforcement learning algorithms, and neuro-programming algorithms. There is a lot of new exploration, and DeepMind is doing that. Google Brain is doing that; Stanford is doing that; and MIT is doing that. I'm very hopeful that in our lifetime we'll be seeing a lot more AI breakthroughs, given the incredible amount of global investment in this area. We also see a lot of effort in the research community to look at algorithms beyond supervised learning.

Dating when a breakthrough will come, is much harder to predict. I learned, as a scientist, not to predict scientific breakthroughs, because they come serendipitously, and they come when a lot of ingredients in history converge. But I'm very hopeful that in our lifetime we'll be seeing a lot more AI breakthroughs given the incredible amount of global investment in this area.

MARTIN FORD: I know you're the chief scientist for Google Cloud. A point that I always make when I give presentations is that AI and machine learning are going to be like a utility—almost like electricity—something that can be deployed almost anywhere. It seems to me that integrating AI into the cloud is one of the first steps toward making the technology universally available. Is that in line with your vision?

FEI-FEI LI: As a professor, every seven or eight years there is a built-in encouragement for sabbaticals where we leave the university for a couple of years to explore a different line of work or to refresh yourself. Two years ago, I was very sure that I wanted to join an industry to really democratize AI technologies, because AI has advanced to a point where some of the technology that is now working, like supervised learning and pattern recognition, is doing good things for society. And like you say, if you think about disseminating technology like AI, the best and biggest platform is a cloud because there's no other computing on any platform which humanity has invented that reaches as many people. Google Cloud alone, at any moment, is empowering, helping, or serving billions of people.

I was therefore very happy to be invited as chief scientist of Google Cloud, where the mission is to democratize AI. This is about creating products that empower businesses and partners, and then taking the feedback from customers and working with them closely to improve the technology itself. This way we can close that loop between the democratization of AI and the advancement AI. I'm overseeing both the research part of cloud AI as well as the product of cloud AI, and we've been here since January 2017.

An example of what we're doing is a product we created that's called AutoML. This is a unique product on the market to really lower the entry barrier of AI as much as much as possible—so that AI can be delivered to people who don't do AI. The customer pain point is that so many businesses need customized models to help them to tackle their own problems. So, in the context of computer vision, if say I were a retailer, I might need a model to recognize my logo. If I were *National Geographic* magazine, I might need a model to recognize wild animals. If I worked in the agricultural industry, I might need a model to recognize apples. People have all kinds of use cases, but not everybody has the machinery expertise to create the AI.

Seeing this problem, we built the AutoML product so that as long as someone knows what they need, such as, "I need it for apples versus oranges," and you bring the training data, we will do everything for you. So, from your perspective, it's all automatic and delivers a customized machine learning model for your problem. We rolled AutoML out in January, and tens of thousands of customers have signed up to this service. It's been very rewarding to see this democratization of cutting-edge AI.

MARTIN FORD: It sounds like AutoML, if it makes machine learning accessible to less technical people, could easily result in a sort of explosion of all kinds of AI applications created by different people with different objectives.

FEI-FEI LI: Yes, exactly! In fact, I used a Cambrian explosion analogy in one of my presentations.

MARTIN FORD: Today there is an enormous focus on neural networks and deep learning. Do you think that's the way forward? You obviously believe that deep learning will be refined over time, but you do think that it is really the foundational technology that's going to lead AI into the future? Or is there another thing out there that's completely different, where we're going to end up throwing away deep learning and back propagation and all of that, and have something entirely new?

FEI-FEI LI: If you look at human civilization, the path of scientific progress is always built upon undoing yourself. There isn't a moment in history where scientists would have said that there's nothing more to come, that there's no refinement left. This is especially true for AI, which is such a nascent field that's only been around for 16 years. Compared to fields like physics, biology, and chemistry, which have hundreds if not thousands of years of history, AI still has a lot to progress.

As an AI scientist, I do not philosophically believe we've finished our task, that convolutional neural networks and deep learning are the answers to everything—not by a huge margin. As you said earlier, a lot of problems are not labeled data or involve lots of training examples. Looking at the history of civilization and the things it's taught us, we cannot possibly think we've reached a destination yet. As my two-year-old kid escaping the crib story tells us, we don't have any AI that is close to that level of intelligence sophistication.

MARTIN FORD: What particular projects would you point to that you think are at the forefront of research in AI?

FEI-FEI LI: In my own lab, we have been doing a project that goes way beyond ImageNet, called the Visual Genome Project. In this project, we've thought deeply about the visual world, and we have recognized that ImageNet is very impoverished. ImageNet just gives some discreet labels of objects on the picture or visual scene, whereas in real visual scenes, objects are connected, humans and objects are doing a lot of things. There's also the connection between vision and language, so Visual Genome Project is really what one would call the next step beyond ImageNet. It's designed to really focus on the relationships between the visual world and our language, so we've been doing a lot of work in pushing that forwards.

Another direction I'm super excited about involves AI and healthcare. We're currently working on a project in my lab that's inspired by a focus on one particular element of healthcare—care itself. The topic of care touches a lot of people. Care is the process of taking care of patients, but if you look at our hospital system, for example, there are a lot of inefficiencies: low quality care, lack of monitoring, errors, and high costs associated with the whole healthcare delivery process. Just look at the mistakes of the surgery world, and the lack of hygiene that can result in hospitals acquiring infections. There's also the lack of help and of awareness in senior home care. There are a lot of problems in care.

We recognized, about five years ago, that the technology that could help healthcare delivery is very similar to the top technology of self-driving cars and

AI. We need smart sensors to sense the environment and the mood, and we need algorithms to make sense of the data collected and give feedback to clinicians, nurses, the patient and family members. So, we started pioneering this AI for healthcare delivery area of research. We're working with Stanford children's hospital, Utah's Intermountain Hospital, and San Francisco's unlocked senior homes. We recently published an opinion piece in the New England Journal of Medicine. I think it's very exciting because it's using cutting-edge AI technology, like the ones self-driving cars use, but it's applied to an area that is so deeply critical for human needs and wellbeing.

MARTIN FORD: I want to talk about the path to artificial general intelligence (AGI). What you think the major hurdles that we would need to surmount are?

FEI-FEI LI: I want to answer your question in two parts. The first part I'll answer more narrowly on the question about the path to AGI, and in the second part, I want to talk about what I think the framework and frame of mind should be for the future development of AI.

So, let's first define AGI, because this isn't about AI versus AGI: it's all on one continuum. We all recognize today's AI is very narrow and task specific, focusing on pattern recognition with labeled data, but as we make AI more advanced, that is going to be relaxed, and so in a way, the future of AI and AGI is one blurred definition. I guess the general definition of AGI would be the kind of intelligence that is contextualized, situationally aware, nuanced, multifaceted and multidimensional— and one that has the kind of learning capability that humans do, which is not only through big data but also through unsupervised learning, reinforcement learning, virtual learning, and various kinds of learning.

If we use that as a definition of AGI, then I think the path to AGI is a continued exploration of algorithms that are beyond just supervised. I also believe that it's important to recognize the interdisciplinary need for collaborations in brain science, cognitive science, and behavior science. A lot of AI's technology, whether it's the hypothesis of the task or the evaluation or the conjecture of algorithms, can touch on related areas like brain science and cognitive science. It's also really critical that we invest and advocate for this collaboration and interdisciplinary approach. I've actually written about this in my New York Times editorial opinion piece in March 2018 titled, *How to Make A.I. That's Good for People.*

MARTIN FORD: Right, I read that, and I know you've been advocating a comprehensive framework for the next phase of AI development.

FEI-FEI LI: Yes, I did that because AI has graduated from an academic and niche subject area into a much bigger field that impacts human lives in very profound ways. So how do we divide AI, and how do we create AI in the next phase, for the future?

There are three core components or elements of human-centered AI. The first component is advancing AI itself, which has a lot to do with what I was just talking about: interdisciplinary research and work, on AI, across neuroscience and cognitive science.

The second component of human-centered AI is really the technology and application; the human-centered technology. We talk a lot about AI replacing humans in terms of a job scenario, but there are way more opportunities for AI to enhance humans and augment humans. The opportunities are much, much wider and I think we should advocate and invest in technology that is about collaboration and interaction between humans and machines. That's robotics, natural language processing, human-centric design, and all that.

The third component of human-centered AI recognizes that computer science alone cannot address all the AI opportunities and issues. It's a deeply impactful technology to humanity, so we should be bringing in economists to talk about jobs, to talk about bigger organizations, to talk about finance. We should bring in policymakers and law scholars and ethicists to talk about regulations, to talk about bias, to talk about security and privacy. We should work with historians, with artists, with anthropologists, and with philosophers—to look at the different implications and new areas of AI research. These are really the three elements that are about human-centered AI for the next phase.

MARTIN FORD: When you talk about human-centered AI, you're trying to address some concerns that have been raised, and I wanted to touch on some of those. There's this idea that there is a true existential threat, something that's been raised by Nick Bostrom, Elon Musk, and Stephen Hawking, where super intelligence could happen very rapidly, a recursive self-improvement loop. I've heard people say that your AutoML might be one step toward that because you're using technology to design other machine learning systems. What do you think about that?

FEI-FEI LI: I think that it's healthy that we have thought leaders like Nick Bostrom to conjecture a fairly troubling future of AI, or at least send warning signs of things that could impact us in ways that we didn't expect. But I think it's important to contextualize that, because in the long history of human civilization, every time a new social order or technology has been invented, it's had that same potential to disrupt the human world in unexpected and deeply profound ways.

I also think that it's healthy to have different ways of exploring these important questions through a diversity of voices. And from voices coming from different development paths. It's good to have Nick, who is a philosopher, to philosophize the potentials. Nick's is one type of voice in the social discourse of AI. I think we need many voices to contribute.

MARTIN FORD: That particular concern really has been given a lot of weight by people like Elon Musk who attracts a lot of attention by saying, for example, that AI is a bigger threat than North Korea. Do you think that's over the top, or should we really be that concerned as a society, at this point in time?

FEI-FEI LI: By definition, we tend to remember over-the-top statements. As a scientist and as a scholar I tend to focus on arguments that are built on deeper and well substantiated evidence and logical deduction. It's really not important whether I judge a particular sentence or not.

The important thing is what we do with the opportunities we have now, and what each one of us is doing. For example, I'm more vocal to discuss the bias and lack of diversity in AI, and so that's what I speak about, because it's much more important to look at what I do.

MARTIN FORD: So, the existential threat is pretty far in the future?

FEI-FEI LI: Well like I said, it's healthy that some people are thinking about that existential threat.

MARTIN FORD: You mentioned briefly the impact on jobs, and this is something that I've written about a lot, in fact, it's what my previous book was about. You said that there are definitely opportunities to enhance people—but at the same time, there is this intersection of technology and capitalism, and businesses always have a very strong motive to eliminate labor if they can. That's happened throughout history. It seems as though we're at an inflection point today, where there are soon going to be tools that are able to automate a much broader range of tasks than anything in the past. These tools will replace cognitive and intellectual tasks, and not just manual work. Is there potential for lots of job losses, deskilling of jobs, depressed wages, and so forth?

FEI-FEI LI: I don't pretend to be an economist, but capitalism is one form of human societal order and it is what, 100 years old? What I'm saying is that no one can predict that capitalism is the only form of human society going forward; nor can anyone predict how technology is going to morph in that future society.

My argument is that AI, as a technology with a lot of potentials, has an opportunity to make life a lot better, to make work more productive. I've been working with doctors for five years, and I get that there are parts of doctors' work that can be potentially replaced by a machine. But I really want that part to be replaced, because I see our doctors overworked, overwhelmed, and their brilliance is sometimes not used in the ways that it should be used. I want to see our doctors having time to talk to patients, having time to talking to each other, and having time to understand and optimize for the best treatment of diseases. I want to see our doctors having time to do the detective work that some rare or harder illnesses need.

AI as a technology has so much potential to enhance and augment labor, in addition to just replace it, and I hope that we see more and more of that. This is something that we've got evidence of in history. Computers automated a lot of jobs away from office typists some 40 years ago. But what we see is new jobs, we now have software engineers as a new job, we have people doing way more interesting work around the office. The same went with ATM machines: when they started to automate some of these transactions in the bank, the number of tellers actually increased because there were more financial services that could be done by humans—and the mundane cash deposit or withdrawal can now be done by ATM machines. It's not a black and white story at all, and it's our work together that defines how things go.

MARTIN FORD: Let's talk about some of the other topics you've focused on, like diversity and bias. It seems to me that these are two separate things, really. The bias comes about because it's encapsulated in the human-generated data that machine learning algorithms are trained on, whereas diversity is more of an issue of who's working in AI.

FEI-FEI LI: First of all, I don't think they're as separate as you think because at the end of the day, it's the values that humans bring to machines. If we have a machine learning pipeline, starting with the data itself, then when that data is biased our machine learning outcome will be biased. And some forms of bias might have even fatal implications. But that itself is potentially linked to the development process of the pipeline. I just want to make a philosophical point that they are actually potentially linked.

That now said, I agree with you that bias and diversity can be treated a little more separately. For example, in terms of data bias resulting in machine learning outcome bias, a lot of academia researchers are recognizing this now, and working on ways to expose that kind of bias. They're also modifying algorithms to respond to bias in a way to try to correct it that way. This exposure to the bias of products and technology, from academia to industry, is really healthy, and it keeps the industry on their toes.

MARTIN FORD: You must have to deal with machine learning bias at Google. How do you address it?

FEI-FEI LI: Google now has a whole group of researchers working on machine learning bias and "explainability" because the pressure is there to tackle bias, to deliver a better product, and we want to be helping others. It's still early days, but it's so critical that this area of research gets invested and that there's more development in that.

On the topic of diversity and the bias of people, I think it's a huge crisis. We've not solved the issue of diversity in our workforces, especially in STEM. Then with tech and AI being so nascent and yet so impactful as a technology, this problem is exacerbated. If we look around, whether you're looking at AI groups in companies, AI professors in academia, AI PhD students or AI presenters at top AI conferences, no matter where you cut it: we lack diversity. We lack women, and we lack under-represented minorities.

MARTIN FORD: I know you started the AI4ALL project, which is focused on attracting women and underrepresented minorities into the field of AI. Could you talk about that?

FEI-FEI LI: Yes, that lack of representation we've been discussing led to me start the Stanford AI4ALL project four years ago. One important effort we can make is to inspire high school students, before they go to college and decide on their major and future career, and to invite them into AI research and AI study. We especially think that, for underrepresented minorities who are inspired by human missions in AI, they respond to the kind of bigger-than-themselves motivations and inspiration. As a result, we've crafted this summer curriculum every year at Stanford, for the past four years, and invited high school girls to participate in AI. This was so successful that in 2017 we formed a national nonprofit organization called AI4ALL and started to replicate this model and invite other universities to participate.

A year later, we have six universities targeting different areas where AI has really struggled to get people involved. In addition to Stanford and Simon Fraser University, we've also got Berkeley targeting AI for low-income students, Princeton focusing on AI for racial minorities, Christopher Newport University doing AI for off-the-rails students, and Boston University doing AI for girls. These have only been running for a small amount of time, but we're hoping to mushroom the program and continue to invite future leaders of AI from a much more diverse background.

MARTIN FORD: I wanted to ask if you think there's a place for the regulation of artificial intelligence. Is that something you'd like to see? Would you advocate for the government taking more of an interest, in terms of making rules, or do you think that the AI community can solve these problems internally?

FEI-FEI LI: I actually don't think AI, if you mean the AI technologists, can solve all the AI problems by themselves: our world is interconnected, human lives are intertwined, and we all depend on each other.

No matter how much AI that I make happen, I still drive on the same highway, breathe the same air, and send my kids to community schools. I think that we need to have a very humanistic view of this and recognize that for any technology to have this profound impact, we need to invite all sectors of life and society to participate.

I also think the government has a huge role, which is to invest in basic science, research, and education of AI. Because if we want to have the transparent technology, and if we want to have the fair technology, and if we want to have more people who can understand and impact this technology in positive ways, then the government needs to invest in our universities, research institutes and schools to educate people about AI and support basic science research. I'm not trained as a policymaker, but I talk to some policymakers, and I talk to my friends. Whether it's about privacy, fairness, dissemination, or collaboration, I see a role the government can play.

MARTIN FORD: The final thing I want to ask you about is this perceived AI arms race, especially with China. How seriously do you take that, and is it something we should worry about?

China does have a different system, a more authoritarian system, and a much bigger population which means more data to train algorithms on and less restrictions regarding privacy and so forth. Are we at risk of falling behind in AI leadership?

FEI-FEI LI: Right now, we're living in a major hype-cycle of modern physics and how that can transform technology, whether it's nuclear technology, or electrical technology.

One hundred years later, will we ask ourselves the question: which person owned modern physics? Will we try to name the company or country that owned modern physics and everything after the industrial revolution? I think it will be difficult for any of us to answer those questions. My point is, as a scientist and as an educator, that the human quest for knowledge and truth has no borders. If there is a fundamental principle of science, it is that these are the universal truths and quests for these truths, which we all seek as a species together. And AI is a science in my opinion.

From that point of view, as a basic scientist and as an educator, I work with people from all backgrounds. My Stanford lab literally consists of students from every continent. With the technology we create, whether it's automation or it's healthcare, we hope to benefit everyone.

Of course, there is going to be competition between companies and between regions, and I hope that's healthy. Healthy competition means that we respect each other, we respect the market, we respect the users and consumers, and we respect the laws, even if it's cross-border laws or international laws. As a scientist, that's what I advocate for, and I continue to publish in the open source domain to educate students of all colors and nations, and I want to collaborate with people of all backgrounds.

More Information about AI4ALL can be found at http://ai-4-all.org/.

FEI-FEI LI is *Chief Scientist, AI and Machine Learning at Google Cloud, Professor of Computer Science at Stanford University, and Director of both the Stanford Artificial Intelligence Lab and the Stanford Vision Lab. Fei-Fei received her undergraduate degree in physics from Princeton University and her PhD in electrical engineering from the California Institute of Technology. Her work has focused on computer vision and cognitive neural science and she is widely published in top academic journals. She is the co-founder of AI4ALL, an organization focused on attracting women and people from underrepresented groups into the field of AI, which began at Stanford and has now scaled up to universities across the United States.*

FEI-FEI LI

> **❝** *Games are just our training domain. We're not doing all this work just to solve games; we want to build these general algorithms that we can apply to real-world problems.*

DEMIS HASSABIS

CO-FOUNDER & CEO OF DEEPMIND
AI RESEARCHER AND NEUROSCIENTIST

Demis Hassabis is a former child chess prodigy, who started coding and designing video games professionally at age 16. After graduating from Cambridge University, Demis spent a decade leading and founding successful startups focused on video games and simulation. He returned to academia to complete a PhD in cognitive neuroscience at University College London, followed by postdoctoral research at MIT and Harvard. He co-founded DeepMind in 2010. DeepMind was acquired by Google in 2014 and is now part of Alphabet's portfolio of companies.

MARTIN FORD: I know you had a very strong interest in chess and video games when you were younger. How has that influenced your career in AI research and your decision to found DeepMind?

DEMIS HASSABIS: I was a professional chess player in my childhood with aspirations of becoming the world chess champion. I was an introspective kid and I wanted to improve my game, so I used to think a lot about how my brain was coming up with these ideas for moves. What are the processes that are going on there when you make a great move or a blunder? So, very early on I started to think a lot about thinking, and that led me to my interest in things like neuroscience later on in my life.

Chess, of course, has a deeper role in AI. The game itself has been one of the main problem areas for AI research since the dawn of AI. Some of the early pioneers in AI like Alan Turing and Claude Shannon were very interested in computer chess. When I was 8 years old, I purchased my first computer using the winnings from the chess tournaments that I entered. One of the first programs that I remember writing was for a game called *Othello*—also known as *Reversi*—and while it's a simpler game than chess, I used the same ideas that those early AI pioneers had been using in their chess programs, like alpha-beta search, and so on. That was my first exposure to writing an AI program.

My love of chess and games got me into programming, and specifically into writing AI for games. The next stage for me was to combine my love of games and programming into writing commercial videogames. One key theme that you'll see in a lot of my games, from *Theme Park* (1994) to *Republic: The Revolution* (2003), was that they had simulation at the heart of their gameplay. The games presented players with sandboxes with characters in them that reacted to the way that you played. It was AI underpinning those characters, and that was always the part that I worked on specifically.

The other thing that I was doing with games was training my mind on certain capabilities. For example, with chess, I think it's a great thing for kids to learn at school because it teaches problem-solving, planning, and all sorts of other meta-skills that I think are then useful and translatable to other domains. Looking back, perhaps all of that information was in my subconscious when I started DeepMind and started using games as a training environment for our AI systems.

The final step for me, before starting DeepMind, was taking undergraduate computer science course at Cambridge University. At the time, which was the early 2000s, I felt that as a field we didn't have quite enough ideas to try and attempt to climb the Everest of AGI. This led me to my PhD in Neuroscience because I felt we needed a better understanding of how the brain solved some of these complex capabilities, so that we could be inspired by that to come up with new algorithmic ideas. I learned a lot about memory and imagination—topics that we didn't at the time, and in some cases still don't, know how to get machines to do. All those different strands then came together into DeepMind.

MARTIN FORD: Your focus then, right from the beginning, has been on machine intelligence and especially AGI?

DEMIS HASSABIS: Exactly. I've known I wanted to do this as a career since my early teens. That journey started with my first computer. I realized straight away that a computer was a magical tool because most machines extend your physical capability, but here was a machine that could extend your mental capabilities.

I still get excited by the fact that you can write a program to crunch a scientific problem, set it running, go off to sleep, and then when you wake up in the morning it's solved it. It's almost like outsourcing your problems to the machine. This led me to think of AI as the natural next step, or even the end step, where we get machines to be smarter in themselves so they're not just executing what you're giving them, but they're actually able to come up with their own solutions.

I've always wanted to work on learning systems that learn for themselves, and I've always been interested in the philosophical idea of what is intelligence and how can we recreate that phenomena artificially, which is what led me to create DeepMind.

MARTIN FORD: There aren't many examples of pure AGI companies around. One reason is that there's not really a business model for doing that; it's hard to generate revenue in the short term. How did DeepMind overcome that?

DEMIS HASSABIS: From the beginning, we were an AGI company, and we were very clear about that. Our mission statement of solving intelligence was there from the beginning. As you can imagine, trying to pitch that to standard venture capitalists was quite hard.

Our thesis was that because what we were building was a general-purpose technology, if you could build it powerfully enough, general enough, and capable enough, then there should be hundreds of amazing applications for it. You'd be inundated with incoming possibilities and opportunities, but you would require a large amount of upfront research first from a group of very talented people that we'd need to get together. We thought that was defensible because of the small number of people in the world that could actually work on this, especially if you think back to 2009 and 2010 when we first started out. You could probably count less than 100 people that could contribute to that type of work. Then there was the question of can we demonstrate clear and measurable progress?

The problem with having a large and long-term research goal is how do your funders get confidence that you actually know what you're talking about? With a typical company, your metric is your product and the number of users, something that's easily measurable. The reason why a company like DeepMind is so rare is that's very hard for an external non-specialist, like a venture capitalist, to judge whether you're making sense and your plan really is sensible, or whether you're just crazy.

The line is very thin, especially when you're going very far out, and in 2009 and 2010 no one was talking about AI. AI was not the hot topic that it is today. It was really difficult for me to get my initial seed funding because of the previous 30 years of failed promises in AI. We had some very strong hypotheses as to why that was, and those were the pillars that we were basing DeepMind on. Things like taking inspiration from neuroscience, which had massively improved our understanding of the brain in the last 10 years; doing learning systems not traditional expert systems; using benchmarking and simulations for the rapid development and testing of AI. There was a set of things that we committed to that turned out to be correct and were our explanations for why AI hadn't improved in the previous years. Another very powerful thing was that these new techniques required a lot of computing power, which was now becoming available in the form of GPUs.

Our thesis made sense to us, and in the end, we managed to convince enough people, but it was hard because we were operating at that point within a very skeptical, non-fashionable domain. Even in academia, AI was frowned upon. It had been rebranded "machine learning," and people who worked on AI were considered to be fringe elements. It's amazing to see how quickly all of that has changed.

MARTIN FORD: Eventually you were able to secure the funding to be viable as an independent company. But then you decided to let Google acquire DeepMind. Can you tell me about the rationale behind the acquisition and how that happened?

DEMIS HASSABIS: It's worth noting that we had no plans to sell, partly because we figured no big corporate would understand our value until DeepMind started producing products. It's also not fair to say that we didn't have a business model. We did, we just hadn't gone very far down the line of executing it. We did already have some cool technology, DQN (deep Q-network—our first general-purpose learning model) and our Atari work had already been done by 2013. But then Larry Page, the Co-Founder of Google, heard about us through some of our investors and out of the blue in 2013 I received an email from Alan Eustace, who was running search and research at Google, saying that Larry's heard of DeepMind and he'd like to have a chat.

That was the start, but the process took a long time because there were a lot of things I wanted to be sure of before we joined forces with Google. But at the end of the day, I became convinced that by combining with Google's strengths and resources— their computing power and their ability to construct a much bigger team, we would be able to execute on our mission much more quickly. It wasn't to do with money, our investors were willing to increase funding to keep us going independently, but DeepMind has always been about delivering AGI and using it for the benefit of the world, and there was an opportunity with Google to accelerate that.

Larry and the people at Google were just as passionate about AI as I was, and they understood how important the work we would do would be. They agreed to give us autonomy as to our research roadmap and our culture, and also to staying in London, which was very important to me. Finally, they also agreed to have an ethics board concerning our technology, which was very unusual but very prescient of them.

MARTIN FORD: Why did you choose to be in London, and not Silicon Valley? Is that a Demis Hassabis or a DeepMind thing?

DEMIS HASSABIS: Both really. I'm a born-and-bred Londoner, and I love London, but at the same time, I thought it was a competitive advantage because the UK and Europe have amazing universities in the field of AI like Cambridge and Oxford. But also, at the time there was no real ambitious research company in the UK, or really in Europe, so our hiring prospects were high, especially with all these universities outputting great postgraduate and graduate students.

In 2018 there are now a number of companies in Europe, but we were the first in AI who were doing deep research. But more culturally, I think it's important that we have more stakeholders and cultures involved in making AI, not just Silicon Valley in the United States, but also European sensibilities and Canadian, and so on. Ultimately, this is going to be of global significance and having different voices about how to use it, what to use it for, and how to distribute the proceeds, is important.

MARTIN FORD: I believe you're also opening up labs in other European cities?

DEMIS HASSABIS: We've opened a small research lab in Paris, which is our first continental European office. We've also opened two labs in Canada in Alberta and Montreal. More recently, since joining Google, we now have an applied team office in Mountain View, California who are right next to the Google teams that we work with.

MARTIN FORD: How closely do you work with the other AI teams at Google?

DEMIS HASSABIS: Google's a huge place, and there are thousands of people working on every aspect of machine learning and AI, from both a very applied perspective to a pure research point of view. As a result of that, there are a number of team leads who all know each other, and there's a lot of cross-collaboration, both with product teams and research teams. It tends to be ad hoc, so it depends on individual researchers or individual topics, but we keep each other informed at a high level of our overall research directions.

At DeepMind, we're quite different from other teams in that we're pretty focused around this one moonshot goal of AGI. We're organized around a long-term roadmap, which is our neuroscience-based thesis, which talks about what intelligence is and what's required to get there.

MARTIN FORD: DeepMind's accomplishments with AlphaGo are well documented. There's even a documentary film about it[1], so I wanted to focus more on your latest innovation, AlphaZero, and on your plans for the future. It seems to me that you've

1 https://www.alphagomovie.com/

demonstrated something very close to a general solution for information-complete two-player games; in other words, games where everything that can be known is available there on the board or in terms of pixels on the screen. Going forward, are you finished with that type of game? Are you planning to move on to more complex games with hidden information, and so forth?

DEMIS HASSABIS: There's a new version of AlphaZero that we're going to publish soon that's even more improved, and as you've said, you can think of that as a solution to two-player perfect-information games like chess, Go, shogi, and so on. Of course, the real world is not made up of perfect information, so as you've said, the next step is to create systems that can deal with that. We're already working on that, and one example of this is our work with the PC strategy game, StarCraft, which has a very complicated action space. It's very complex because you build units, so it's not static in terms of what pieces you have, like in chess. It's also real time, and the game has hidden information, for example, the "fog of war" that obscures onscreen information until you explore that area.

Beyond that, games are just our training domain. We're not doing all this work just to solve games; we want to build these general algorithms that we can apply to real-world problems.

MARTIN FORD: So far, your focus has primarily been on combining deep learning with reinforcement learning. That's basically learning by practice, where the system repeatedly attempts something, and there's a reward function that drives it toward success. I've heard you say that you believe that reinforcement learning offers a viable path to general intelligence, that it might be sufficient to get there. Is that your primary focus going forward?

DEMIS HASSABIS: Going forward, yes, it is. I think that technique is extremely powerful, but you need to combine it with other things to scale it. Reinforcement learning has been around for a long time, but it was only used in very small toy problems because it was very difficult for anyone to scale up that learning in any way. In our Atari work, we combined that with deep learning, which did the processing of the screen, and the model of the environment you're in. Deep learning is amazing at scaling, so combining that with reinforcement learning allowed it to scale to these large problems that we've now tackled in AlphaGo and DQN—all of these things that people would have told you was impossible 10 years ago.

I think we proved that first part. The reason we were so confident about it and why we backed it when we did was because in my opinion reinforcement learning will become as big as deep learning in the next few years. DeepMind is one of the few companies that take that seriously because, from the neuroscience perspective, we know that the brain uses a form of reinforcement learning as one of its learning mechanisms, it's called temporal difference learning, and we know the dopamine system implements that. Your dopamine neurons track the prediction errors your brain is making, and then you strengthen your synapses according to those reward signals. The brain works along these principles, and the brain is our only example of general intelligence, which is why we take neuroscience very seriously here. To us, that must be a viable solution to the problem of general intelligence. It may not be the only one, but from a biologically inspired standpoint, it seems reinforcement learning is sufficient once you scale it up enough. Of course, there are many technical challenges with doing that, and many of them are unsolved.

MARTIN FORD: Still, when a child learns things like language or an understanding of the world, it doesn't really seem like reinforcement learning for the most part. It's unsupervised learning, as no one's giving the child labeled data the way we would do with ImageNet. Yet somehow, a young child can learn organically directly from the environment. But it seems to be more driven by observation or random interaction with the environment rather than learning by practice with a specific goal in mind.

DEMIS HASSABIS: A child learns with many mechanisms, it's not like the brain only uses one. The child gets supervised learning from their parents, teachers, or their peers and they do unsupervised learning when they're just experimenting with stuff, with no goal in mind. They also do reward learning and reinforcement learning when they do something, and they get a reward for it.

We work on all three of those, and they're all going to be needed for intelligence. Unsupervised learning is hugely important, and we're working on that. The question here is, are there intrinsic motivations that evolution has designed in us that end up being proxies for reward, which then guide the unsupervised learning? Just look at information gain. There is strong evidence showing that gaining information is intrinsically rewarding to your brain.

Another thing would be novelty seeking. We know that seeing novel things releases dopamine in the brain, so that means novelty is intrinsically rewarding. In a sense, it could be that these intrinsic motivations that we have chemically in our brains are guiding what seems to us to be unstructured play or unsupervised learning. If the brain finds finding information and structure rewarding in itself, then that's a hugely useful motivation for unsupervised learning; you're just going to try and find structure, no matter what, and it seems like the brain is doing that.

Depending on what you determine as the reward, some of these things could be intrinsic rewards that could be guiding the unsupervised learning. I find that it is useful to think about intelligence in the framework of reinforcement learning.

MARTIN FORD: One thing that's obvious from listening to you is that you combine a deep interest in both neuroscience and computer science. Is that combined approach true for DeepMind as a whole? How does the company integrate knowledge and talent from those two areas?

DEMIS HASSABIS: I'm definitely right in the middle for both those fields, as I'm equally trained in both. I would say DeepMind is clearly more skewed towards machine learning; however, our biggest single group here at DeepMind is made up of neuroscientists led by Matt Botvinick, an amazing neuroscientist and professor from Princeton. We take it very seriously.

The problem with neuroscience is that it's a massive field in itself, way bigger than machine learning. If you as a machine-learning person wanted to quickly find out which parts of neuroscience would be useful to you, then you'd be stuck. There's no book that's going to tell you that, there's just a mass of research work, and you'll have to figure out for yourself how to parse that information and find the nuggets that could be useful from an AI perspective. Most of that neuroscience research is being undertaken for medical research, psychology, or for neuroscience itself. Neuroscientists aren't designing those experiments thinking they would be useful for AI. 99% of that literature is not useful to you as an AI researcher and so you have to get really good at training yourself to navigate and pick out what are the right influences and what is the right level of influence for each of those.

Quite a lot of people talk about neuroscience inspiring AI work, but I don't think a lot of them really have concrete ideas on how to do that. Let's explore two extremes. One is you could try and reverse-engineer the brain, which is what quite a lot of people are attempting to do in their approach to AI, and I mean literally reverse-engineer the brain on a cortical level, a prime example being the Blue Brain Project.

MARTIN FORD: That's being directed by Henry Markram, right?

DEMIS HASSABIS: Right, and he's literally trying to reverse-engineer cortical columns. It may be interesting neuroscience but, in my view, that is not the most efficient path towards building AI because it's too low-level. What we're interested in at DeepMind is a systems-level understanding of the brain and the algorithms the brain implements, the capabilities it has, the functions it has, and the representations it uses.

DeepMind is not looking at the exact specifics of the wetware or how the biology actually instantiates it, we can abstract all of that away. That makes sense, because why would you imagine an in-silico system would have to mimic an in-carbo system because there are completely different strengths and weaknesses about those two systems. In silicon, there's no reason why you would want to copy the exact permutation details of, say a hippocampus. On the other hand, I am very interested in the computations and the functions that the hippocampus has, like episodic memory, navigating in space, and the grid cells it uses. These are all systems-level influences from neuroscience and showcase our interest in the functions, representations and the algorithms that the brain uses, not the exact details of implementation.

MARTIN FORD: You often hear the analogy that airplanes don't flap their wings. Airplanes achieve flight, but don't precisely mimic what birds do.

DEMIS HASSABIS: That's a great example. At DeepMind, we're trying to understand aerodynamics by looking at birds, and then abstracting the principles of aerodynamics and building a fixed-wing plane.

Of course, people who built planes were inspired by birds. The Wright Brothers knew that heavier-than-air flight was possible because they'd seen birds. Before the airfoil was invented, they tried without success to use deformable wings, but they were more like birds gliding. What you've got to do is look at nature, and then try and abstract away the things that are not important for the phenomenon you're after in that case, flying and in our case, intelligence. But that doesn't mean that that didn't help your search process.

My point is that you don't know yet what the outcome looks like. If you're trying to build something artificial like intelligence and it doesn't work straight away, how do you know that you're looking in the right place? Is your 20-person team wasting their time, or should you push a bit harder, and maybe you'll crack it next year? Because of that, having neuroscience as a guide can allow me to make much bigger, much stronger bets on things like that.

A great example of this is reinforcement learning. I know reinforcement learning has to be scalable because the brain does scale it. If you didn't know that the brain implemented reinforcement learning and it wasn't scaling, how would you know on a practical level if you should spend another two years on this? It's very important to narrow down the search space that you're exploring as a team or a company, and I think that's a meta-point that is often missed by people that ignore neuroscience.

MARTIN FORD: I think you've made the point that the work in AI could also inform research being done in neuroscience. DeepMind just came out with a result on grid cells used in navigation, and it sounds like you've got them to emerge organically in a neural network. In other words, the same basic structure naturally arises in both the biological brain and in artificial neural networks, which seems pretty remarkable.

DEMIS HASSABIS: I'm very excited about that because it's one of our biggest breakthroughs in the last year. Edvard Moser and May-Britt Moser, who discovered grid cells and won the Nobel Prize for their work both wrote to us very excited about this finding because it means that, possibly, these grid cells are not just a function of the wiring of the brain, but actually may be the most optimal way of representing space from a computational sense. That's a huge and important finding for the neuroscientists because what they're speculating now is that maybe the brain isn't necessarily hardwired to create grid cells. Perhaps if you have that structure of neurons and you just expose them to space, that is the most efficient coding any system would come up with.

We've also recently created a whole new theory around how the prefrontal cortex might work, based on looking at our AI algorithms and what they were doing, and then having our neuroscientists translate that into how the brain might work.

I think that this is the beginning of seeing many more examples of AI ideas and algorithms inspiring us to look at things in a different way in the brain or looking for new things in the brain, or as an analysis tool to experiment with our ideas about how we think the brain might work.

As a neuroscientist, I think that the journey we're on of building neuroscience-inspired AI is one of the best ways to address some of the complex questions we have about the brain. If we build an AI system that's based on neuroscience, we can then compare it to the human brain and maybe start gleaning some information about its unique characteristics. We could start shedding light on some of the profound mysteries of the mind like the nature of consciousness, creativity, and dreaming. I think that comparing the brain to an algorithmic construct could be a way to understand that.

MARTIN FORD: It sounds like you think there could be some discoverable general principles of intelligence that are substrate-independent. To return to the flight analogy, you might call it "the aerodynamics of intelligence."

DEMIS HASSABIS: That's right, and if you extract that general principle, then it must be useful for understanding the particular instance of the human brain.

MARTIN FORD: Can you talk about some of the practical applications that you imagine happening within the next 10 years? How are your breakthroughs going to be applied in the real world in the relatively near future?

DEMIS HASSABIS: We're already seeing lots of things in practice. All over the world people are interacting with AI today through machine translation, image analysis, and computer vision.

DeepMind has started working on quite a few things, like optimizing the energy being used in Google's data centers. We've worked on WaveNet, the very human-like text-to-speech system that's now in the Google Assistant in all Android-powered phones. We use AI in recommendation systems, in Google Play, and even on behind-the-scenes elements like saving battery life on your Android phone. Things that everyone uses every single day. We're finding that because they're general algorithms, they're coming up all over the place, so I think that's just the beginning.

What I'm hoping will come through next are the collaborations we have in healthcare. An example of this is our work with the famous UK eye hospital,

Moorfields, where we're looking at diagnosing macular degeneration from your retina scans. We published the results from the first phase of our joint research partnership in Nature Medicine, and they show that our AI system can quickly interpret eye scans from routine clinical practice with unprecedented accuracy. It can also correctly recommend how patients should be referred for treatment for over 50 sight-threatening eye diseases as accurately as world-leading expert doctors.

There are other teams doing similar work for diseases like skin cancer. Over the next five years, I think healthcare will be one of the biggest areas to see a benefit from the work we're all doing in the field.

What I'm really personally excited about, and this is something I think we're on the cusp of, is using AI to actually help with scientific problems. We're working on things like protein folding, but you can imagine its use in material design, drug discovery and chemistry. People are using AI to analyze data from the Large Hadron Collider to searching for exoplanets. There's a lot of really cool areas of masses of data that we as human experts find hard to identify the structure in that I think this kind of AI is going to become increasingly used for. I'm hoping that over the next 10 years this will result in an advancement in the speed of scientific breakthroughs in some really fundamental areas.

MARTIN FORD: What does the path to AGI look like? What would you say are the main hurdles that will have to be surmounted before we have human-level AI?

DEMIS HASSABIS: From the beginning of DeepMind we identified some big milestones, such as the learning of abstract, conceptual knowledge, and then using that for transfer learning. Transfer learning is where you usefully transfer your knowledge from one domain to a new domain that you've never seen before, it's something humans are amazing at. If you give me a new task, I won't be terrible at it out of the box because I'll bring some knowledge from similar things or structural things, and I can start dealing with it straight away. That's something that computer systems are pretty terrible at because they require lots of data and they're very inefficient. We need to improve that.

Another milestone is that we need to get better at language understanding, and another is replicating things that old AI systems were able to do, like symbolic manipulation, but using our new techniques. We're a long way from all of those, but they would be really big milestones if they were to happen. If you look at where we were in 2010, just eight years ago, we've already achieved some big things that were milestones to us, like AlphaGo, but there are more to come. So those would be the big ones for me, concepts and transfer learning.

MARTIN FORD: When we do achieve AGI, do you imagine intelligence being coupled with consciousness? Is it something that would automatically emerge, or is consciousness a completely separate thing?

DEMIS HASSABIS: That's one of the interesting questions that this journey will address. I don't know the answer to it at the moment, but that's one of the very exciting things about the work that both we and others are doing in this field.

My hunch currently would be that consciousness and intelligence are double-dissociable. You can have intelligence without consciousness, and you can have consciousness without human-level intelligence. I'm pretty sure smart animals have some level of consciousness and self-awareness, but they're obviously not that intelligent at least compared to humans, and I can imagine building machines that are phenomenally intelligent by some measures but would not feel conscious to us in any way at all.

MARTIN FORD: Like an intelligent zombie, something that has no inner experience.

DEMIS HASSABIS: Something that wouldn't feel sentient in the way we feel about other humans. Now that's a philosophical question, because the problem is, as we see with the Turing test, how would we know if it was behaving in the same way as we were? The Occam's razor explanation is to say that if you're exhibiting the same behavior as I exhibit, and you're made from the same stuff as I'm made from, and I know what I feel, then I can assume you're feeling the same thing as me. Why would you not?

What's interesting with a machine is that they could exhibit the same behavior as a human, if we designed them like that, but they're on a different substrate. If you're not on the same substrate then that Occam's razor idea doesn't hold as strongly. It may be that they are conscious in some sense, but we don't feel it in the same way because we don't have that additional assumption to rely on. If you break down why we think each of us is conscious, I think that's a very important assumption, if you're operating on the same substrate as me, why would it feel different to your substrate?

MARTIN FORD: Do you believe machine consciousness is possible? There are some people that argue consciousness is fundamentally a biological phenomenon.

DEMIS HASSABIS: I am actually open-minded about that, in the sense that I don't think we know. It could well turn out that there's something very special about biological systems. There are people like Sir Roger Penrose that think it's to do with quantum consciousness, in which case a classical computer wouldn't have it, but it's an open question. That's why I think the path we're on will shed some light on it because I actually think we don't know whether that's a limit or not. Either way, it will be fascinating because it would be pretty amazing if it turned out that you couldn't build consciousness at all on a machine. That would tell us a lot about what consciousness is and where it resides.

MARTIN FORD: What about the risks and the downsides associated with AGI? Elon Musk has talked about "raising the demon" and an existential threat. There's also Nick Bostrom, who I know is on DeepMind's advisory board and has written a lot on this idea. What do you think about these fears? Should we be worried?

DEMIS HASSABIS: I've talked to them a lot about these things. As always, the soundbites seem extreme but it's a lot more nuanced when you talk to any of these people in person.

My view on it is that I'm in the middle. The reason I work on AI is because I think it's going to be the most beneficial thing to humanity ever. I think it's going to unlock our potential within science and medicine in all sorts of ways. As with any powerful technology, and AI could be especially powerful because it's so general, the technology itself is neutral. It depends on how we as humans decide to design and deploy it, what we decide to use it for, and how we decide to distribute the gains.

There are a lot of complications there, but those are more like geopolitical issues that we need to solve as a society. A lot of what Nick Bostrom worries about are the technical questions we have to get right, such as the control problem and the value alignment problem. My view is that on those issues we do need a lot more research because we've only just got to the point now where there are systems that can even do anything interesting at all.

We're still at a very nascent stage. Five years ago, you might as well have been talking about philosophy because no one had anything that was interesting. We've now got AlphaGo and a few other interesting technologies that are still very nascent, but we're now at the point where we should start reverse-engineering those things and experimenting on them by building visualization and analysis tools. We've got teams doing this to better understand what these black-box systems are doing and how we interpret their behavior.

MARTIN FORD: Are you confident that we'll be able to manage the risks that come along with advanced AI?

DEMIS HASSABIS: Yes, I'm very confident, and the reason is that we're at the inflection point where we've just got these things working, and not that much effort has yet gone into reverse engineering them and understanding them, and that's happening now. Over the next decade, most of these systems won't be black-box in the sense that we mean now. We'll have a good handle on what's going on with these systems, and that will lead to a better understanding of how to control the systems and what their limits are mathematically, and then that could lead into best practices and protocols.

I'm pretty confident that path will address a lot of the technical issues that people like Nick Bostrom are worried about, like the collateral consequences of goals not being set correctly. To make advances in that, my view has always been that the best science occurs when theory and practice—empirical work—go hand in hand, and for this subject and field, empirical work experiments are engineering.

A lot of the fears that some of the people not working at the coalface of this technology have won't hold once we actually have a much better understanding of these systems. That's not to say that I think that there's nothing to worry about, because I think we should worry about these things. There are plenty of near-term questions to resolve as well—like how do we test these systems as we deploy them in products? Some of the long-term problems are so hard that we want to be thinking about them in the time we have right now, well ahead of when we're going to need the answers.

We also need to be able to inform the research that has to be done to come up with the solutions to some of those questions that are posed by people like Nick Bostrom. We are actively thinking about these problems and we're taking them seriously, but I'm a big believer in human ingenuity to overcome those problems if you put enough brainpower on it collectively around the world.

MARTIN FORD: What about the risks that will arise long before AGI is achieved? For example, autonomous weapons. I know you've been very outspoken about AI being used in military applications.

DEMIS HASSABIS: These are very important questions. At DeepMind, we start from the premise that AI applications should remain under meaningful human control, and be used for socially beneficial purposes. This means banning the development and deployment of fully autonomous weapons, since it requires a meaningful level of human judgment and control to ensure that weapons are used in ways that are necessary and proportionate. We've expressed this view in a number of ways, including signing an open letter and supporting the Future of Life Institute's pledge on the subject.

MARTIN FORD: It's worth pointing out even though chemical weapons are in fact banned, they have still been used. All of this requires global coordination and it seems that rivalries between countries could push things in the other direction. For example, there is a perceived AI race with China. They do have a much more authoritarian system of government. Should we worry that they will gain an advantage in AI?

DEMIS HASSABIS: I don't think it's a race in that sense because we know all the researchers and there's a lot of collaboration. We publish papers openly and I know that for example Tencent has created an AlphaGo clone, so I know many of the researchers there. I do think that if there's going to be coordination and perhaps even regulation and best practices down the road, it's important that it's international and the whole world adopts that. It doesn't work if some countries don't adopt those principles. However, that's not an issue that's unique to AI. There are many other problems that we're already grappling with that are a question of global coordination and organization—the obvious one being climate change.

MARTIN FORD: What about the economic impact of all of this? Is there going to be a big disruption of the job market and perhaps rising unemployment and inequality?

DEMIS HASSABIS: I think there's been very minimal disruption so far from AI, it's just been part of the technology disruption in general. AI is going to be hugely transformative, though. Some people believe that it's going to be on the scale of the Industrial Revolution or electricity, while other people believe it's going to be a class of its own above that, and that's something I think that remains to be seen. Maybe it will mean we're in a world of abundance, where there are huge productivity gains everywhere? Nobody knows for sure. The key thing is to make sure those benefits are shared with everyone.

I think that's the key thing, whether that's universal basic income, or it's done in some other form. There are lots of economists debating these things, and we need to think very carefully about how everyone in society will benefit from those presumably huge productivity gains, which must be coming in, otherwise it wouldn't be so disruptive.

MARTIN FORD: Yes, that's basically the argument that I've been making, that it's fundamentally a distributional problem and that a large part of our population is in danger of being left behind. But it is a staggering political challenge to come up with a new paradigm that will create an economy that works for everyone.

DEMIS HASSABIS: Right.

Whenever I meet an economist, I think they should be working quite hard on this problem, but it's difficult to because they can't really envisage how it could be so productive because people have been talking about massive productivity gains for 100 years.

My dad studied economics at university, and he was saying that in the late 1960s a lot of people were seriously talking about that: "What is everyone going to do in the 1980s when we have so much abundance, and we don't have to work?" That, of course, never happened, in the 1980s or since then, and we're working harder than ever. I think a lot of people are not sure if it's ever going to be like that, but if it does end up that we have a lot of extra resources and productivity, then we've got to distribute it widely and equitably, and I think if we do that, then I don't see a problem with it.

MARTIN FORD: Is it safe to say that you're an optimist? I'd guess that you see AI as transformative and that it's arguably going to be one of the best things that's ever happened to humanity. Assuming, of course, that we manage it wisely?

DEMIS HASSABIS: Definitely, and that's why I've worked towards it my whole life. All of the things I've been doing that we covered in the first part of our discussion have been building towards achieving that. I would be quite pessimistic about the way the world's going, if AI was not going to come along. I actually think there's a lot of problems in the world that require better solutions, like climate change, Alzheimer's research or water purification. I can give you a list of things that are going to get worse over time. What is a worry is that I don't see how we're going to get the global coordination and the excess resources or activity to solve them. But ultimately, I'm actually optimistic about the world because a transformative technology like AI is coming.

DEMIS HASSABIS *is a former child chess prodigy who finished his high school exams two years early before coding the multi-million selling simulation game* Theme Park *at age 17. Following graduation from Cambridge University with a Double First in Computer Science he founded the pioneering videogames company Elixir Studios producing award winning games for global publishers such as Vivendi Universal. After a decade of experience leading successful technology startups, Demis returned to academia to complete a PhD in cognitive neuroscience at University College London, followed by postdoctoral research at MIT and Harvard. His research into the neural mechanisms underlying imagination and planning was listed in the top ten scientific breakthroughs of 2007 by the journal* Science.

Demis is a five-time World Games Champion, and a Fellow of the Royal Society of Arts and the Royal Academy of Engineering, winning the Academy's Silver Medal. In 2017 he was named in the Time 100 list of the world's most influential people, and in 2018 was awarded a CBE for services to science and technology. He was elected as a Fellow of the Royal Society, has been a recipient of the Society's Mullard Award, and was also awarded an Honorary Doctorate by Imperial College London.

Demis co-founded DeepMind along with Shane Legg and Mustafa Suleyman in 2010. DeepMind was acquired by Google in 2014 and is now part of Alphabet. In 2016 DeepMind's AlphaGo system defeated Lee Sedol, arguably the world's best player of the ancient game of Go. That match is chronicled in the documentary film AlphaGo *(https://www.alphagomovie.com/).*

> *The rise of supervised learning has created a lot of opportunities in probably every major industry. Supervised learning is incredibly valuable and will transform multiple industries, but I think there is a lot of room for something even better to be invented.*

ANDREW NG

CEO, LANDING AI & GENERAL PARTNER, AI FUND
ADJUNCT PROFESSOR COMPUTER SCIENCE, STANFORD

Andrew Ng is widely recognized for his contributions to artificial intelligence and deep learning, as both an academic researcher and an entrepreneur. He co-founded both the Google Brain project and the online education company, Coursera. He then became the chief scientist at Baidu, where he built an industry-leading AI research group. Andrew played a major role in the transformation of both Google and Baidu into AI-driven organizations. In 2018 he established AI Fund, a venture capital firm focused on building startup companies in the AI space from scratch.

MARTIN FORD: Let's start by talking about the future of AI. There's been remarkable success, but also enormous hype, associated with deep learning. Do you feel that deep learning is the way forward and—the primary idea that will continue to underlie progress in AI? Or is it possible that an entirely new approach will replace it in the long run?

ANDREW NG: I really hope there's something else out there better than deep learning. All of the economic value driven by this recent rise of AI is down to supervised learning—basically learning input and output mappings. For example, with self-driving cars the input is a video picture of what's in front of your car, and the output is the actual position of the other cars. There are other examples, speech recognition has an input of an audio clip and an output of a text transcript, machine translation has an input of English text and an output of Chinese text, say.

Deep learning is incredibly effective for learning these input/output mappings and this is called supervised learning, but I think that artificial intelligence is much bigger than supervised learning.

The rise of supervised learning has created a lot of opportunities in probably every major industry. Supervised learning is incredibly valuable and will transform multiple industries, but I think that there is a lot of room for something even better to be invented. It's hard to say right now exactly what that would be, though.

MARTIN FORD: What about the path to artificial general intelligence? What would you say are the primary breakthroughs that have to occur for us to get to AGI?

ANDREW NG: I think the path is very unclear. One of the things we will probably need is unsupervised learning. For example, today in order to teach a computer what a coffee mug is we show it thousands of coffee mugs, but no child's parents, no matter how patient and loving, ever pointed out thousands of coffee mugs to that child. The way that children learn is by wandering around the world and soaking in images and audio. The experience of being a child allows them to learn what a coffee mug is. The ability to learn from unlabeled data, without parents or labelers pointing out thousands of coffee mugs, will be crucial to making our systems more intelligent.

I think one of the problems in AI is that we've made a lot of progress in building specialized intelligence or narrow intelligence, and very little progress towards AGI. The problem is, both of these things are called AI. AI turns out to be incredibly valuable for online advertising, speech recognition and self-driving cars, but it's specialized intelligence, not general. Much of what the public sees is progress in building specialized intelligence and they think that we are therefore making rapid progress toward artificial general intelligence. It's just not true.

I would love to get to AGI, but the path is very unclear. I think that individuals that are less knowledgeable about AI have used very simplistic extrapolations, and that has led to unnecessary amounts of hype about AI.

MARTIN FORD: Do you expect AGI to be achieved in your lifetime?

ANDREW NG: The honest answer is that I really don't know. I would love to see AGI in my lifetime, but I think there's a good chance it'll be further out than that.

MARTIN FORD: How did you become interested in AI? And how did that lead to such a varied career trajectory?

ANDREW NG: My first encounter with neural networks was when I was in high school where I did an office assistant internship. There may not seem like an obvious link between an internship and neural networks, but during the course of my internship I thought about how we could automate some of the work that I was doing, and that was the earliest time I was thinking about neural networks. I wound up doing my bachelor's at Carnegie Mellon, my master's from MIT and a PhD, with a thesis titled, *Shaping and Policy Search in Reinforcement Learning*, from the University of California, Berkeley.

For about the next twelve years I taught at the Stanford University Department of Computer Science and the Department of Electrical Engineering as a professor. Then between 2011 and 2012, I was a founding member of the Google Brain team, which helped transform Google into the AI company that we now perceive it to be.

MARTIN FORD: And Google Brain was the first attempt to really use deep learning at Google, correct?

ANDREW NG: To an extent. There had been some small-scale projects based around neural networks, but the Google Brain team really was the force that took deep learning into many parts of Google. The first thing I did when I was leading the Brain team was to teach a class within Google for around 100 engineers. This helped teach a lot of Google engineers about deep learning, and it created a lot of allies and partners for the Google Brain team and opened up deep learning to a lot more people.

The first two projects we did were partnering with the speech team, which I think helped transform speech recognition at Google, and working on unsupervised learning, which led to the somewhat infamous Google cat. This is where we set an unsupervised neural network free on YouTube data and it learned to recognize cats. Unsupervised learning isn't what actually creates the most value today, but that was a nice technology demonstration of the type of scale we could achieve using Google's compute cluster at the time. We were able to do very large-scale deep learning algorithms.

MARTIN FORD: You stayed at Google until 2012. What came next for you?

ANDREW NG: Towards the end of my time at Google, I felt that deep learning should move toward GPUs. As a result, I wound up doing that work at Stanford University rather than at Google. In fact, I remember a conversation that I had with Geoff Hinton at NIPS, the annual conference on Neural Information Processing Systems, where I was trying to use GPUs, and I think that later influenced his work with Alex Krizhevsky and influenced, quite a lot of people to then adopt GPUs for deep learning.

I was lucky to be teaching at Stanford at the time because being here in Silicon Valley, we saw the signals that GPGPU (general-purpose GPU) computing was coming. We were in the right place at the right time and we had friends at Stanford working on GPGPUs, so we saw the ability of GPUs to help scale up deep learning algorithms earlier than almost everyone else.

My former student at Stanford, Adam Coates was actually the reason I decided to pitch the Google Brain team to Larry Page in a bid to get Larry to approve me using a lot of their computers to build a very large neural network. It was really one figure that was generated by Adam Coates, where the x-axis was the amount of data, and the y-axis was the performance of an algorithm. Adam generated this figure showing that the more data we could train these deep learning algorithms on, the better they'd perform.

MARTIN FORD: After that you went on to start Coursera with Daphne Koller, who is also interviewed in this book. Then you moved on to Baidu. Can you describe your path through those roles?

ANDREW NG: Yes, I helped to start Coursera with Daphne because I wanted to scale online teaching both around AI and other things to millions of people around the world. I felt that the Google Brain team already had tremendous momentum at that point, so I was very happy to hand the reins over to Jeff Dean and move on to Coursera. I worked at building Coursera from the ground up for a couple of years until 2014 when I stepped away from my day-to-day work there to go and work at Baidu's AI Group. Just as Google Brain helped transform Google into the AI company you perceive it to be today, the Baidu AI group did a lot of work to transform Baidu into the AI company that a lot of people now perceive Baidu to be. At Baidu, I built a team that built technology, supported existing business units, and then systematically initiated new businesses using AI.

After three years there the team was running very well, so I decided to move on again this time becoming the CEO of Landing AI and a general partner at AI Fund.

MARTIN FORD: You've been instrumental in transforming both Google and Baidu into AI-driven companies, and it sounds like now you want to scale that out and transform everything else. Is that your vision for AI Fund and Landing AI?

ANDREW NG: Yes, I'm done transforming large web search engines, and now I'd rather go and transform some other industries. At Landing AI, I help to transform companies using AI. There are a lot of opportunities in AI for incumbent companies, so Landing AI is focused on helping those companies that already exist to transform and embrace those AI opportunities. AI Fund takes this a step further, looking at the opportunities for new startups and new businesses to be created from scratch built around AI technologies.

These are very different models with different opportunities. For example, if you look at the recent major technological transformation of the internet, incumbent companies like Apple and Microsoft did a great job transforming themselves to be internet companies. However, you only have to look at how big the "startups," like Google, Amazon, Baidu, and Facebook are now and how they did such a great job building incredibly valuable businesses based on the rise of the internet.

With the rise of AI there will also be some incumbent companies, ironically many of them were startups in the previous age, like Google, Amazon, Facebook, and Baidu, that'll do very well with the rise of AI. AI Fund is trying to create the new startup companies that leverage these new AI capabilities we have. We want to find or create the next Google or Facebook.

MARTIN FORD: There are a lot of people who say that the incumbents like Google and Baidu are essentially unshakable because they have access to so much data, and that creates a barrier to entry for smaller companies. Do you think startups and smaller companies are going to struggle to get traction in the AI space?

ANDREW NG: That data asset that the large search engines have definitely creates a highly defensible barrier to the web search business, but at the same time, it's not obvious how web search clickstream data is useful for medical diagnosis or for manufacturing or for personalized educational tutors, for example.

I think data is actually verticalized, so building a defensible business in one vertical can be done with a lot of data from that vertical. Just as electricity transformed multiple industries 100 years ago, AI will transform multiple industries, and I think that there is plenty of room for multiple companies to be very successful.

MARTIN FORD: You mentioned AI Fund, which you founded recently and which I think operates differently from other venture capital funds. What is your vision for AI Fund, and how is it unique?

ANDREW NG: Yes. AI Fund is extremely different from most venture capital funds, and I think most venture capital funds are in the business of trying to identify winners, while we're in the business of creating winners. We build startups from scratch, and we tell entrepreneurs that if you already have a pitch deck, you're probably at too late a stage for us.

ANDREW NG

We bring in teams as employees and work with them, mentor them, and support them, whatever is needed to try and build a successful startup from scratch. We actually tell people that if you're interested in working with us, don't send us a pitch deck, send us a resume and then we'll work together to flesh out the startup idea.

MARTIN FORD: Do most people that come to you already have an idea, or do you help them come up with something?

ANDREW NG: If they have an idea we're happy to talk about it, but my team has a long list of ideas that we think are promising but we don't have the bandwidth to invest in. When people join us, we're very happy to share this long list of ideas with them to see which ones fit.

MARTIN FORD: It sounds like your strategy is to attract AI talent in part by offering the opportunity and infrastructure to found a startup venture.

ANDREW NG: Yes, building a successful AI company takes more than AI talent. We focus so much on the technology because it's advancing so quickly, but building a strong AI team often needs a portfolio of different skills ranging from the tech, to the business strategy, to product, to marketing, to business development. Our role is building full stack teams that are able to build concrete business verticals. The technology is super important, but a startup is much more than technology.

MARTIN FORD: So far, it seems that any AI startup that demonstrates real potential gets acquired by one of the huge tech firms. Do you think that eventually there'll be AI startups that will go on to have IPOs and become public companies?

ANDREW NG: I really hope there'll be plenty of great AI startups that are not just acquired by much larger startups. Initial public offering as a tactic is not the goal, but I certainly hope that there'll be many very successful AI startups that will end up thriving as standalone entities for a long time. We don't really have a financial goal; the goal is to do something good in the world. I'd be really sad if every AI startup ends up being acquired by a bigger company, and I don't think we're headed there.

MARTIN FORD: Lately, I've heard a number of people express the view that deep learning is over-hyped and might soon "hit a wall" in terms of continued progress.

191

There have even been suggestions that a new AI Winter could be on the horizon. Do you think that's a real risk? Could disillusionment lead to a big drop off in investment?

ANDREW NG: No, I don't think there'll be another AI winter, but I do think there needs to be a reset of expectations about AGI. In the earlier AI winters, there was a lot of hype about technologies that ultimately did not really deliver. The technologies that were hyped were really not that useful, and the amount of value created by those earlier generations of technology was vastly less than expected. I think that's what caused the AI winters.

In the current era, if you look at the number of people actually working on deep learning projects to date, it's much greater than six months ago, and six months ago, it was much greater than six months before that. The number of concrete projects in deep learning, the number of people researching it, the number of people learning it, and the number of companies being built on it means the amount of revenue being generated is actually growing very strongly.

The fundamentals of the economics support continued investment in deep learning. Large companies are continuing to back deep learning strongly, and it's not based on just hopes and dreams, it's based on the results we're already seeing. That will see confidence continue to grow. Now, I do think we need to reset the expectations about AI as a whole, and AGI in particular. I think the rise of deep learning was unfortunately coupled with false hopes and dreams of a sure path to achieving AGI, and I think that resetting everyone's expectations about that would be very helpful.

MARTIN FORD: So, aside from unrealistic expectations about AGI, do you think we will continue to see consistent progress with the use of deep learning in more narrow applications?

ANDREW NG: I think there are a lot of limitations to the current generation of AI. AI is a broad category, though, and I think when people discuss AI, what they really mean is the specific toolset of backpropagation, supervised learning, and neural networks. That is the most common piece of deep learning that people are working on right now.

Of course, deep learning is limited, just like the internet is limited, and electricity is limited. Just because we invented electricity as a utility, it didn't suddenly solve all of the problems of humanity. In the same way, backpropagation will not solve all the problems of humanity, but it is turning out to be incredibly valuable, and we're nowhere near done building out all the things we could do with neural networks trained by backpropagation. We're just in the early phases of figuring out the implications of even the current generation of technology.

Sometimes, when I'm giving a talk about AI, the first thing I say is "AI is not magic, it can't do everything." I think it's very strange that we live in a world where anyone even has to say sentences like that—that there's a technology that cannot do everything.

The huge problem that AI has had is what I call the communications problem. There's been tremendous progress in narrow artificial intelligence and also real progress in artificial general intelligence, but both of these things are called AI. So, tremendous progress in economics and value through narrow artificial intelligence is rightly causing people to see that there's tremendous progress in AI, but it's also causing people to falsely reason that there's tremendous progress in AGI as well. Frankly, I do not see much progress. Other than having faster computers and data, and progress at a very general level, I do not see specific progress toward AGI.

MARTIN FORD: There seem to be two general camps with regard to the future of AI. Some people believe it will be neural networks all the way, while others think a hybrid approach that incorporates ideas from other areas, for example symbolic logic, will be required to achieve continued progress. What's your view?

ANDREW NG: I think it depends on whether you're talking short term or long term. At Landing AI we use hybrids all the time to build solutions for industrial partners. There's often a hybrid of deep learning tools together with, say, traditional computer vision tools because when your datasets are small, deep learning by itself isn't always the best tool. Part of the skill of being an AI person is knowing when to use a hybrid and how to put everything together. That's how we deliver tons of short-term useful applications.

On balance, there's been a shift from traditional tools toward deep learning, especially when you have a lot of data, but there are still plenty of problems in the world where you have only small datasets, and then the skill is in designing the hybrid and getting the right mix of techniques.

I think in the long term, if we ever move toward more human-level intelligence, maybe not for AGI but more flexible learning algorithms, I think that we'll continue to see a shift toward neural networks, but one of the most exciting things yet to be invented will be other algorithms that are much better than backpropagation. Just like alternating current power is incredibly limited, but also incredibly useful, I think backpropagation is also incredibly limited, but incredibly useful, and I don't see any contradiction in those circumstances.

MARTIN FORD: So, as far as you're concerned, neural networks are clearly the best technology to take AI forward?

ANDREW NG: I think that for the foreseeable future, neural networks will have a very central place in the AI world. I don't see any candidates on the horizon for replacing neural networks, that's not to say that there won't be something on the horizon in the future.

MARTIN FORD: I recently spoke with Judea Pearl, and he believes very strongly that AI needs a causal model in order to progress and that current AI research isn't giving enough attention to that. How would you respond to that view?

ANDREW NG: There are hundreds of different things that deep learning doesn't do, and causality is one of them. There are other things, such as not doing explainability well enough; we need to sort out how to defend against adversarial attacks; we need to get a lot better at learning from small datasets rather than big datasets; we need to get much better at transfer or multitask learning; we need to figure out how to use unlabeled data better. So yes, there are a lot of things that backpropagation doesn't do well, and again causality is one of them. When I look at the amount of high value projects being created, I don't see causality as a hindering factor in them, but of course we'd love to make progress there. We'd love to make progress in all of those things I mentioned.

MARTIN FORD: You mentioned adversarial attacks. I've seen research indicating that it is fairly easy to trick deep learning networks using manufactured data. Is that going to be a big problem as this technology becomes more prevalent?

ANDREW NG: I think it is already a problem, especially in anti-fraud. When I was head of the Baidu AI team we were constantly fighting against fraudsters both attacking AI systems and using AI tools to commit fraud. This is not a futuristic thing. I'm not fighting that war right now, because I'm not leading an anti-fraud team, but I have led teams and you feel very adversarial and very zero-sum when you're fighting against fraud. The fraudsters are very smart and very sophisticated, and just as we think multiple steps ahead, they think multiple steps ahead. As the technology evolves, the attacks and the defenses will both have to evolve. This is something that those of us shipping products in the AI community have been dealing with for a few years already.

MARTIN FORD: What about privacy issues? In China especially, facial recognition technology is becoming ubiquitous. Do you think we run the risk that AI is going to be deployed to create an Orwellian surveillance state?

ANDREW NG: I'm not an expert on that, so I'll defer to others. One thing that I would say, is that one trend we see with many rises in technology is the potential for greater concentration of power. I think this is true of the internet, and this is true again with the rise of AI. It becomes possible for smaller and smaller groups to be more and more powerful. The concentration of power can happen at the level of corporations, where corporations with relatively few employees can have a bigger influence, or at the level of governments.

The technology available to small groups is more powerful than ever before. For example, one of the risks of AI that we have already seen is the ability of a small group to influence the way very large numbers of people vote, and the implications of that on democracy is something that we need to pay close attention to, to make sure that democracy is able to defend itself so that votes are truly fair and representative of the interests of the population. What we saw in the recent US election was based more on internet technologies rather than AI technologies, but the opportunity is there. Before that, television had a huge effect on democracy and how people voted. As technology evolves, the nature and texture of governance and democracy changes, which is why we have to constantly refresh our commitment to protecting society from its abuse.

MARTIN FORD: Let's talk about one of the highest-profile applications of AI: self-driving cars. How far off are they really? Imagine you're in a city and you're going to call for a fully autonomous car that will take you from one random location to another. What's the time frame for when you think that becomes a widely available service?

ANDREW NG: I think that self-driving cars in geofenced regions will come relatively soon, possibly by the end of this year, but that self-driving cars in more general circumstances will be a long way off, possibly multiple decades.

MARTIN FORD: By geofenced, you mean autonomous cars that are running essentially on virtual trolley tracks, or in other words only on routes that have been intensively mapped?

ANDREW NG: Exactly! A while back I co-authored a Wired article talking about Train Terrain[1] about how I think self-driving cars might roll out. We'll need infrastructure changes, and societal and legal changes, before we'll see mass adoption of self-driving cars.

I have been fortunate to have seen the self-driving industry evolve for over 20 years now. As an undergraduate at Carnegie Mellon in the late '90s, I did a class with Dean Pomerleau working on their autonomous car project that steered the vehicle based an input video image. The technology was great, but it wasn't ready for its time. Then at Stanford, I was a peripheral part of the DARPA Urban Challenge in 2007.

We flew down to Victorville, and it was the first time I saw so many self-driving cars in the same place. The whole Stanford team were all fascinated for the first five minutes, watching all these cars zip around without drivers, and the surprising thing was that after five minutes, we acclimatized to it, and we turned our backs to it. We just chatted with each other while self-driving cars zipped passed us 10 meters away, and we weren't paying attention. One thing that's remarkable about humanity is how quickly we acclimatize to new technologies, and I feel that it's not going to be too long before self-driving cars are no longer called self-driving cars, they're just called cars.

MARTIN FORD: I know you're on the board of directors of the self-driving car company Drive.ai. Do you have an estimate for when their technology will be in general use?

ANDREW NG: They're driving round in Texas right now. Let's see, what time is it? Someone's just taken one and gone for lunch. The important thing is how

---

1 https://www.wired.com/2016/03/self-driving-cars-wont-work-change-roads-attitudes/

mundane that is. Someone's just gone out for lunch, like any normal day, and they've done it by getting in a self-driving car.

MARTIN FORD: How do you feel about the progress you've seen in self-driving cars so far? How has it compared with your expectations?

ANDREW NG: I don't like hype, and I feel like a few companies have spoken publicly and described what I think of as unrealistic timelines about the adoption of self-driving cars. I think that self-driving cars will change transportation, and will make human life much better. However, I think that everyone having a realistic roadmap to self-driving cars is much better than having CEOs stand on stage and proclaim unrealistic timelines. I think the self-driving world is working toward more realistic programs for bringing the tech to market, and I think that's a very good thing.

MARTIN FORD: How do you feel about the role of government regulation, both for self-driving cars and AI more generally?

ANDREW NG: The automotive industry has always been heavily regulated because of safety, and I think that the regulation of transportation needs to be rethought in light of AI and self-driving cars. Countries with more thoughtful regulation will advance faster to embrace the possibilities enabled by, for example, AI-driven healthcare systems, self-driving cars, or AI-driven educational systems, and I think countries that are less thoughtful about regulation will risk falling behind.

Regulation should be in these specific industry verticals because we can have a good debate about the outcomes. We can more easily define what we do and do not want to happen. I find it less useful to regulate AI broadly. I think that the act of thinking through the impact of AI in specific verticals for regulation will not only help the verticals grow but will also help AI develop the right solutions and be adopted faster across verticals.

I think self-driving cars are only a microcosm of a broader theme here, which is the government. Every time there is a technological breakthrough, regulators must act. Regulators have to act to make sure that democracy is defended, even in the era of the internet and the era of artificial intelligence. In addition to defending democracy, governments must act to make sure that their countries are well positioned for the rise of AI.

Assuming that one of governments' primary responsibilities is the well-being of their citizens, I think that governments that act wisely can help their nations ride the rise of AI, to much better outcomes for their people. In fact, even today, some governments use the internet much better than other governments. This is about external websites and services to citizens, as well as internal ones, in terms of, how are your government IT services organized?

Singapore has an integrated healthcare system, where every patient has a unique patient ID, and this allows for the integration of healthcare records in a way that is the envy of many other nations. Now, Singapore's a small country, so maybe it's easier for Singapore than a larger country, but the way the Singapore government has shifted the healthcare system to use the internet better, has a huge impact on the healthcare system, and on the health of the Singaporean citizens.

MARTIN FORD: It sounds like you think the relationship between government and AI should extend beyond just regulating the technology.

ANDREW NG: I think governments have a huge role to play in the rise of AI and in making sure that first, governance is done well with AI. For instance, should we better allocate government personnel using AI? How about the forestry resources, can we allocate that better using AI? Can AI help us set better economic policies? Can the government weed out fraud—maybe tax fraud—better and more efficiently using AI? I think AI will have hundreds of applications in governance, just as AI has hundreds of applications in the big AI companies. Governments should use AI well for themselves.

For the ecosystem as well, I think public-private partnerships will accelerate the growth of domestic industry, and governments that make thoughtful regulation about self-driving cars will see self-driving accelerate in their communities. I'm very committed to my home state of California, but California regulations do not allow self-driving car companies to do certain things, which is why many self-driving car companies can't have their home bases in California and are now almost forced to operate outside of California.

I think that both at the state level as well as at the nation level, countries that have thoughtful policies about self-driving cars, about drones, and about the adoption of AI in payment systems and in healthcare systems, for example—those countries with thoughtful policies in all of these verticals will see much faster progress in how these amazing new tools can be brought to bear on some of the most important problems for their citizens. Beyond regulation and public-private partnership, to accelerate the adoption of these amazing tools, I think governments also need to come up with solutions in education and on the jobs issue.

MARTIN FORD: The impact on jobs and the economy is an area that I've written about a lot. Do you think we may be on the brink of a massive disruption that could result in widespread job losses?

ANDREW NG: Yes, and I think it's the biggest ethical problem facing AI. Whilst the technology is very good at creating wealth in some segments of society, we have frankly left large parts of the United States and also large parts of the world behind. If we want to create not just a wealthy society but a fair one, then we still have a lot of important work to do. Frankly, that's one of the reasons why I remain very engaged in online education.

I think our world is pretty good at rewarding people who have the required skills at a particular time. If we can educate people to reskill even as their jobs are displaced by technology, then we have a much better chance of making sure that this next wave of wealth creation ends up being distributed in a more equitable way. A lot of the hype about evil AI killer robots distracts leaders from the much harder, but much more important conversation about what we do about jobs.

MARTIN FORD: What do you think of a universal basic income as part of a solution to that problem?

ANDREW NG: I don't support a universal basic income, but I do think a conditional basic income is a much better idea. There's a lot about the dignity of work and I actually favor a conditional basic income in which unemployed individuals can be paid to study. This would increase the odds that someone that's unemployed will gain the skills they need to re-enter the workforce and contribute back to the tax base that is paying for the conditional basic income.

I think in today's world, there are a lot of jobs in the gig economy, where you can earn enough of a wage to get by, but there isn't much room for lifting up yourself or your family. I am very concerned about an unconditional basic income causing a greater proportion of the human population to become trapped doing this low-wage, low-skilled work.

A conditional basic income that encourages people to keep learning and keep studying will make many individuals and families better off because we're helping people get the training they need to then do higher-value and better-paying jobs. We see economists write reports with statistics like "in 20 years, 50% of jobs are at risk of automation," and that's really scary, but the flip side is that the other 50% of jobs are not at risk of automation.

In fact, we can't find enough people to do some of these jobs. We can't find enough healthcare workers, we can't find enough teachers in the United States, and surprisingly we can't seem to find enough wind turbine technicians.

The question is, how do people whose jobs are displaced take on these other great-paying, very valuable jobs that we just can't find enough people to do? The answer is not for everyone to learn to program. Yes, I think a lot of people should learn to program, but we also need to skill up more people in those areas of healthcare, education, and wind turbine technicians, and other in-demand rising categories of jobs.

I think we're moving away from a world where you have one career in your lifetime. Technology changes so fast that there will be people that thought they were doing one thing when they went to college that will realize that the career they set out toward when they were 17-years-old is no longer viable, and that they should branch into a different career.

We've seen how millennials are more likely to hop among jobs, where you go from being a product manager in one company to the product manager of a different company. I think that in the future, increasingly we'll see people going from being a material scientist in one company to being a biologist in a different company, to being a security researcher in a third company. This won't happen overnight, it will take a long time to change. Interestingly, though, in my world of deep learning, I already see many people doing deep learning that did not major in computer science, they did subjects like physics, astronomy, or pure mathematics.

MARTIN FORD: Is there any particular advice you'd give to a young person who is interested in a career in AI, or in deep learning specifically? Should they focus entirely on computer science or is brain science, or the study of cognition in humans also important?

ANDREW NG: I would say to study computer science, machine learning, and deep learning. Knowledge of brain science or physics is all useful, but the most time-efficient route to a career in AI is computer science, machine learning and deep learning. Because of YouTube videos, talks, and books, I think it's easier than ever for someone to find materials and study by themselves, just step by step. Things don't happen overnight, but step by step, I think it's possible for almost anyone to become great at AI.

There are a couple of pieces of advice that I tend to give to people. Firstly, people don't like to hear that it takes hard work to master a new field, but it does take hard work, and the people who are willing to work hard at it will learn faster. I know that it's not possible for everyone to learn a certain number of hours every week, but people that are able to find more time to study will just learn faster.

The other piece of advice I tend to give people is that let's say you're currently a doctor and you want to break into AI—as a doctor you'd be uniquely positioned to do very valuable work in healthcare that very few others can do. If you are currently a physicist, see if there are some ideas on AI applied to physics. If you're a book publisher, see if there's some work you can do with AI in book publishing, because that's one way to leverage your unique strengths and to complement that with AI, rather than competing on a more even playing field with the fresh college grad stepping into AI.

MARTIN FORD: Beyond the possible impact on jobs, what are the other risks associated with AI that you think we should be concerned about now or in the relatively near future?

ANDREW NG: I like to relate AI to electricity. Electricity is incredibly powerful and on average has been used for tremendous good, but it can also be used to harm people. AI is the same. In the end, it's up to individuals, as well as companies and governments, to try to make sure we use this new superpower in positive and ethical ways.

I think that bias in AI is another major issue. AI that learns from human-generated text data can pick up on health, gender, and racial stereotypes. AI teams are aware of this and are actively working on this, and I am very encouraged that today we have better ideas for reducing bias in AI than we do for reducing bias in humans.

MARTIN FORD: Addressing bias in people is very difficult, so it does seem like it might be an easier problem to solve in software.

ANDREW NG: Yes, you can zero a number in an AI piece of software and it will exhibit much less gender bias, we don't have similarly effective ways of reducing gender bias in people. I think that soon we might see that AI systems will be less biased than many humans. That is not to say that we should be satisfied with just having less bias, there's still a lot of work to do and we should keep on working to reduce that bias.

MARTIN FORD: What about the concern that a superintelligent system might someday break free of our control and pose a genuine threat to humanity?

ANDREW NG: I've said before that worrying about AGI evil killer robots today is like worrying about overpopulation on the planet Mars. A century from now I hope that we will have colonized the planet Mars. By that time, it may well be overpopulated and polluted, and we might even have children dying on Mars from pollution. It's not that I'm heartless and don't care about those dying children—I would love to find a solution to that, but we haven't even landed on the planet yet, so I find it difficult to productively work on that problem.

MARTIN FORD: You don't think then that there's any realistic fear of what people call the "fast takeoff" scenario, where an AGI system goes through a recursive self-improvement cycle and rapidly becomes superintelligent?

ANDREW NG: A lot of the hype about superintelligence and exponential growth were based on very naive and very simplistic extrapolations. It's easy to hype almost anything. I don't think that there is a significant risk of superintelligence coming out of nowhere and it happening in a blink of an eye, in the same way that I don't see Mars becoming overpopulated overnight.

MARTIN FORD: What about the question of competition with China? It's often pointed out that China has certain advantages, like access to more data due to a larger population and fewer concerns about privacy. Are they going to outrun us in AI research?

ANDREW NG: How did the competition for electricity play out? Some countries like the United States have a much more robust electrical grid than some developing economies, so that's great for the United States. However, I think the global AI race is much less of a race than the popular press sometimes presents it to be. AI is an amazing capability, and I think every country should figure out what to do with this new capability, but I think that it is much less of a race than the popular press suggests.

MARTIN FORD: AI clearly does have military applications, though, and potentially could be used to create automated weapons. There's currently a debate in the United Nations about banning fully autonomous weapons, so it's clearly something people are concerned about. That's not futuristic AGI-related stuff, but rather something we could see quite soon. Should we be worried?

ANDREW NG: The internal combustion engine, electricity, and integrated circuits all created tremendous good, but they were all useful for the military. It's the same with any new technology, including AI.

MARTIN FORD: You're clearly an optimist where AI is concerned. I assume you believe that the benefits are going to outweigh the risks as artificial intelligence advances?

ANDREW NG: Yes, I do. I've been fortunate to be on the front lines, shipping AI products for the last several years and I've seen firsthand the way that better speech recognition, better web search, and better optimized logistics networks help people.

This is the way that I think about the world, which may be a very naïve way. The world's gotten really complicated, and the world's not the way I want it to be. Frankly, I miss the times when I could listen to political leaders and business leaders, and take much more of what they said at face value.

I miss the times when I had greater confidence in many companies and leaders to behave in an ethical way and to mean what they say and say what they mean. If you think about your as-yet-unborn grandchildren or your unborn great-great-grandchildren, I don't think the world is yet the way that you want it to be for them to grow up in. I want democracy to work better, and I want the world to be fairer. I want more people to behave ethically and to think about the actual impact on other people, and I want the world to be fairer, for everyone to have access to and gain an education. I want people to work hard, but to work hard and to keep studying, and to do work that they find meaningful, and I think many parts of the world are not yet the way I think we would all like it to be.

Every time there's a technological disruption, it gives us the opportunity to make a change. I would like my teams, as well as other people around the world to take a shot at making the world a better place in the ways that we want it to be. I know that sounds like I'm a dreamer, but that's what I actually want to do.

MARTIN FORD: I think that's a great vision. I guess the problem is that it's a decision for society as a whole to set us on the path to that kind of optimistic future. Are you confident that we'll make the right choices?

ANDREW NG: I don't think it will be in a straight line, but I think there are enough honest, ethical, and well-meaning people in the world to have a very good shot at it.

ANDREW NG

ANDREW NG *is one of the most recognizable names in AI and machine learning. He co-founded the Google Brain deep learning project as well as the online education company Coursera. Between 2014 and 2017, he was a vice president and chief scientist at Baidu, where he built the company's AI group into an organization with several thousand people. He is generally credited with playing a major role in the transformation of both Google and Baidu into AI-driven companies.*

Since leaving Baidu, Andrew has undertaken a number of projects including launching deeplearning.ai, an online education platform geared toward educating deep learning experts, as well as Landing AI, which seeks to transform enterprises with AI. He's currently the chairman of Woebot, a startup focused on mental health applications for AI and is on the board of directors of self-driving car company Drive.ai. He is also the founder and General Partner at AI Fund, a venture capital firm that builds new AI startups from the ground up.

Andrew is currently an adjunct professor, and formerly the associate professor and Director of the AI Lab at Stanford University. He received his undergraduate degree in computer science from Carnegie Mellon University, his master's degree from MIT, and his PhD from The University of California, Berkeley.

> **❝** *I feel that this view, about the existential threat that robots are going to take over humanity, takes away our agency as humans. At the end of the day, we're designing these systems, and we get to say how they are deployed, we can turn the switch off.*

RANA EL KALIOUBY

CEO & CO-FOUNDER OF AFFECTIVA

Rana el Kaliouby is the co-founder and CEO of Affectiva, a startup company that specializes in AI systems that sense and understand human emotions. Affectiva is developing cutting-edge AI technologies that apply machine learning, deep learning, and data science to bring new levels of emotional intelligence to AI. Rana is an active participant in international forums that focus on ethical issues and the regulation of AI to help ensure the technology has a positive impact on society. She was selected as a Young Global Leader by the World Economic Forum in 2017.

MARTIN FORD: I want to begin by exploring your background; I'm especially interested in how you became involved with AI and how your trajectory went from an academic background to where you are today with your company, Affectiva.

RANA EL KALIOUBY: I grew up around the Middle East, being born in Cairo, Egypt and spending much of my childhood in Kuwait. During this time, I found myself experimenting with early computers, as a result of both my parents being in technology, and my dad would bring home the old Atari machines where we would pick them apart. Fast-forward and that grew into my undergraduate course where I majored in Computer Science at the American University in Cairo. I guess you could say this is where the thinking behind Affectiva first came into play. During this time, I became fascinated by how technology changes how humans connect with one another. Nowadays a lot of our communication is mediated via technology, and so the special way that we connect with technology, but also with one another, fascinates me.

The next step was to do a PhD. I received a scholarship to work with the Computer Science department at Cambridge University, which, on a side note, was something that was quite unusual for a young Egyptian and Muslim woman to do. This was in the year 2000, so it was before we all had smartphones, but at the time I was quite interested in this idea of human-computer interaction and how our interface is going to evolve over the next few years.

Through my own experience, I realized that I was spending a lot of time in front of my machine, where I was coding and writing all these research papers, which opened me to two realizations. The first realization was that the laptop I was using (remember no smartphones yet) was supposedly quite intimate with me. I mean, I was spending a lot of hours with it, and while it knew a lot of things about me—like if I was writing a Word document or coding—it had no idea how I was feeling. It knew my location, it knew my identity, but it was just completely oblivious to my emotional and cognitive state.

In that sense my laptop reminded me of Microsoft Clippy, where you would be writing a paper, and then this paper-clip would show up, do a little twirl, and it would say, "Oh, it looks like you're writing a letter! Do you need any help?" Clippy would often show up at the weirdest times, for example when I was super-stressed and my deadline was in 15 minutes... and the paperclip would do its funny little cheesy thing. Clippy helped me realize that we have an opportunity here, because there's an emotional intelligence gap with our technology.

The other thing that was kind of very clear is that this machine mediated a lot of my communication with my family back home. During my PhD, there were times when I was that homesick, and I would be chatting with my family in tears, and yet they'd have no idea because I was hiding behind my screen. It made me feel very lonely and I realized how all of the rich non-verbal communications that we have when we're face to face, in a phone conversation or a video conference, are all lost in cyberspace when we are interacting digitally.

MARTIN FORD: So, your own life experiences led you to become interested in the idea of technology that could understand human emotions. Did your PhD focus much on exploring this idea?

RANA EL KALIOUBY: Yes, I became intrigued by the idea that we're building a lot of smartness into our technologies but not a lot of emotional intelligence, and this was an idea that I started to explore during my PhD. It all began during one of my very early presentations at Cambridge, where I was talking to an audience about how curious I was about how we might build computers that could read emotions. I explained during the presentation how I am, myself, a very expressive person—that I'm very attuned to people's facial expressions, and how intriguing I found it to think about how we could get a computer to do the same. A fellow PhD student popped up and said, "Have you looked into autism because people on the autism spectrum also find it very challenging to read facial expressions and non-verbal behaviors?" As a result of that question, I ended up collaborating very closely with the Cambridge Autism Research Center during my PhD. They had an amazing dataset that they'd compiled to help kids on the autism spectrum to learn about different facial expressions.

Machine learning needs a lot of data, and so I borrowed their dataset to train the algorithms I was creating, on how to read different emotions, something that showed some really promising results. This data opened up an opportunity to focus not just on the happy/sad emotions, but also on the many nuanced emotions that we see in everyday life, such as confusion, interest, anxiety or boredom.

I could soon see that we had this tool that we could package up and provide as a training tool for individuals on the autism spectrum. This is where I realized that my work wasn't just about improving human-computer machine interfaces, but also about improving human communication and human connection.

When I completed my PhD at Cambridge, I met with the MIT professor, Rosalind Picard, who authored the book *Affective Computing*, and would later co-found Affectiva with me. But back in 1998, Rosalind posited that technology needs to be able to identify human emotions and respond to those emotions.

Long story short, we ended up chatting, and Rosalind invited me to join her lab at the MIT Media Lab. The project that brought me over to the US was a National Science Foundation project that would take my technology of reading emotions and, by integrating it with a camera, we could apply it for kids on the autism spectrum.

MARTIN FORD: In one of the articles I read about you, I think you described an "emotional hearing aid" for autistic kids. Is this what you are referring to? Did that invention stay at the conceptual level or did it become a practical product?

RANA EL KALIOUBY: I joined MIT in 2006, and between then and 2009 we partnered with a school in Providence, Rhode Island, and they were focused on kids on the autism spectrum. We deployed our technology there, and we would take prototypes to the kids and have them try it, and they would say "this doesn't feel quite right," so we iterated the system until it began to succeed. Eventually, we were able to demonstrate that the kids who were using the technology were having a lot more eye contact, and they were doing a lot more than just looking at people's faces.

Imagine how these kids, somewhere on the spectrum of autism, would wear these pairs of glasses with a camera facing outwards. When we first started doing this research, a lot of the camera data we got was just of the floor or the ceiling: the kids weren't even looking at the face. But the input that we got, from working with these kids, allowed us to build real-time feedback that helped encourage them to make face contact. Once those kids started to do that, we gave them feedback on what kind of emotions people are displaying. It all looked very promising.

You've got to remember that Media Lab is a unique academic department at MIT, in the sense that it has very strong ties to industry, to the point where about 80% of the lab's funding comes from Fortune 500 companies. So twice a year, we would host these companies for what we called Sponsor Week, where it was very demo-or-die because you had to actually show what you were working on. A PowerPoint wouldn't cut it!

So, twice a year between 2006 and 2008 we'd invite all these folks over to MIT, and we would demo the autism prototype. During these kinds of events, companies like Pepsi would ask if we'd thought about applying this work to test whether advertising was effective. And Procter & Gamble wanted to use it to test its latest shower gels, because it wanted to know if people liked the smells or not. Toyota wanted to use it for driver state monitoring, and The Bank of America wanted to optimize the banking experience. We explored getting some more research assistants to help develop the ideas that our funders wanted, but we soon realized that this was not research anymore, that it was in fact a commercial opportunity.

I was apprehensive about leaving academia, but I was starting to get a little frustrated that in academia you do all these prototypes, but they never get deployed at scale. With a company, I felt we had an opportunity to scale and bring products to market, and to change how people communicate and do things on a day-to-day basis.

MARTIN FORD: It sounds like Affectiva has been very customer-driven. Many startups try to create a product in anticipation of a market being there; but in your case, the customers told you exactly what they wanted, and you responded directly to that.

RANA EL KALIOUBY: You're absolutely right, and it quickly became apparent that we were sitting on a potentially huge commercial opportunity. Collectively, Rosalind and I felt that between us we had started this field, we were thought leaders, and that we wanted to do it in a very ethical way as well—which was core to us.

MARTIN FORD: What are you working on at Affectiva now, and what's your overall vision for where it's going to go in the future?

RANA EL KALIOUBY: Our overall vision is that we're on a mission to humanize technology. We're starting to see technology permeate every aspect of our life. We're also starting to see how interfaces are becoming conversational, and that our devices are becoming more perceptual—and a lot more potentially relational. We're forming these tight relationships with our cars, our phones, and our smart-enabled devices like Amazon's Alexa or Apple's Siri.

If you think about a lot of people who are building these devices, right now, they're focused on the cognitive intelligence aspect of these devices, and they're not paying much attention to the emotional intelligence. But if you look at humans, it's not just your IQ that matters in how successful you are in your professional and personal life; it's often really about your emotional and social intelligence. Are you able to understand the mental states of people around you? Are you able to adapt your behavior to take that into consideration and then motivate them to change their behavior, or persuade them to take action?

All of these situations, where we are asking people to take action, we all need to be emotionally intelligent to get to that point. I think that this is equally true for technology that is going to be interfacing with you on a day-to-day basis and potentially asking you to do things.

Whether that is helping you sleep better, eat better, exercise more, work more productively, or be more social, whatever that technology is, it needs to consider your mental state when it tries to persuade you to take part in them.

My thesis is that this kind of interface between humans and machines is going to become ubiquitous, that it will just be ingrained in the future human-machine interfaces, whether it's our car, our phone or smart devices at our home or in the office. We will just be coexisting and collaborating with these new devices, and new kinds of interfaces.

MARTIN FORD: Could you sketch out some of the specific things you're working on? I know you're doing something with monitoring drivers in cars to make sure they are attentive.

RANA EL KALIOUBY: Yes, the issue today around monitoring drivers in cars is that there are so many situations to cater for, that Affectiva as a company has focused specifically on situations that are ethical, and where there's a good product-market fit. And of course, for where the markets are ready.

When Affectiva started in 2009, the first kind of low-hanging market opportunities were in advertising testing, as I mentioned, and today Affectiva works with a quarter of the Fortune Global 500 companies to help them understand the emotional connection their advertising creates with their consumers.

Often, companies will spend millions of dollars to create an advertisement that's funny or one that tugs at your heart. But they have no idea if they struck the right emotional chord with you. The only way that they could find that sort of thing out, before our technology existed, was to ask people. So, if you, Martin Ford, were the person watching the ad, then you'd get a survey, and it would say, "Hey, did you like this ad? Did you think it was funny? Are you going to buy the product?" And the problem with that is that it's very unreliable and very biased data.

So now, with our technology, as you're watching the ad, with your consent it will analyze on a moment-by-moment basis all your facial expressions and aggregate that over the thousands of people who watched that same ad. The result is an unbiased, objective set of data around how people respond emotionally to the advertising. We can then correlate that data with things like customer purchase intent, or even actual sales data and virality.

Today we have all these KPIs that can be tracked, and we're able to tie the emotional response to actual consumer behavior. That's a product of ours that's in 87 countries, from the US and China to India, but also smaller countries like Iraq and Vietnam. It's a pretty robust product at this point, and it's been amazing because it allows us to collect data from all over the world, and it's all very spontaneous data. It's data that, I would argue, even Facebook and Google don't have because it's not just your profile picture, it's you sitting in your bedroom one night, watching a shampoo ad. That's the data we have, and that's what drives our algorithm.

MARTIN FORD: What are you analyzing? Is it mostly based on facial expressions or also on other things like voice?

RANA EL KALIOUBY: Well, when we first started, we worked with just the face, but about eighteen months ago we went back to the drawing board and asked: how do we as humans monitor the responses of other humans?

People are pretty good at monitoring the mental states of the people around them, and we know that about 55% of the signals we use are in facial expression and your gestures, while about 38% of the signal we respond to is from tone of voice. So how fast someone is speaking, the pitch, and how much energy is in the voice. Only 7% of the signal is in the text and the actual choice of words that someone uses!

Now when you think of the entire industry of sentiment analysis, the multi-billion-dollar industry of people listening to tweets and analyzing text messages and all that, it only accounts for 7% of how humans communicate. What I like to think about what we're doing here, is trying to capture the other 93% of non-verbal communication.

So, back to your questions: about eighteen months ago I started a speech team that looks at these prosodic paralinguistic features. They would look at the tone of voice and the occurrence of speech events, such as how many times you say "um" or how many times you laughed. All of these speech events are independent of the actual words that we're saying. Affectiva technology now combines these things and takes what we call a multimodal approach, where different modalities are combined, to truly understand a person's cognitive, social or emotional state.

MARTIN FORD: Are the emotional indicators you look for consistent across languages and cultures, or are there significant differences between populations?

RANA EL KALIOUBY: If you take facial expressions or even the tone of a person's voice, the underlying expressions are universal. A smile is a smile everywhere in the world. However, we are seeing this additional layer of cultural display norms, or rules, that depict when people portray their emotions, or how often, or how intensely they show their emotion. We see examples of people amplifying their emotions, dampening their emotions, or even masking their emotions altogether. We particularly see signs of masking in Asian markets, where Asian populations are less likely to show negative emotions, for instance. So, in Asia we see an increased incidence of what we call a social smile, or a politeness smile. Those are not expressions of joy, but are more themed around saying, "I acknowledge you," and in that sense they are a very social signal.

By and large, everything is universal. There are cultural nuances, of course, and because we have all this data, we've been able to build region-specific and sometimes even country-specific norms. We have so much data in China, for instance, that China is its own norm. Instead of comparing a Chinese individual's response to say, a chocolate ad, we compare a Chinese individual to the subpopulation that's most like them. And this particular approach has been critical to our success in monitoring emotional states in different cultures around the world.

MARTIN FORD: I guess then that other applications you're working on are oriented toward safety, for example monitoring drivers or the operators of dangerous equipment to make sure they stay attentive?

RANA EL KALIOUBY: Absolutely. In fact in the last year we've started to get a ton of inbound interest from the automotive industry. It's really exciting because it's a major market opportunity for Affectiva and we're solving two interesting problems for the car industry.

In the cars of today, where there is an active driver, safety is a huge issue. And safety will continue to be an issue, even when we have semi-autonomous vehicles like Tesla that can drive themselves for a while but do still need a co-pilot to be paying attention.

Using Affectiva software, we're able to monitor the driver or the co-pilot for things like drowsiness, distraction, fatigue and even intoxication. In the case of intoxication, we would alert the driver or also even potentially have the car intervene. Intervention could be anything from changing the music to blasting a little bit of cold air, or tightening the seat belt, all the way to potentially saying, "You know what? I'm the car, and I feel I could be a safer driver than you are right now. I'm taking control over." There's a lot of actions the car can take once it understands the level of attention and how impaired a driver is. So, that's one class of use cases.

The other problem we're solving for the automotive industry is around the occupant experience. Let's look into the future where we have fully autonomous vehicles and robot-taxis, where there's no driver in the car at all. In those situations, the car needs to understand the state of the occupants such as, how many people are in the car, what's their relationship, are they in a conversation, or even do we have a baby in the car that's potentially getting left behind? Once you understand the mood of the occupants in the car, you can personalize the experience.

The robot-taxi could make product recommendations or route recommendations. This would also introduce new business models for auto companies, especially premium brands like a BMW or a Porsche, because right now they're all about the driving experience. But in the future, it's not going to be about driving anymore: it's going to be about transforming and redefining that transport, that mobility experience. Modern transport is a very exciting market, and we're spending a lot of our mindshare building products for that industry, and also for those partnered with Tier 1 companies.

MARTIN FORD: Do you see potential applications in healthcare? Given that we do have a mental health crisis, I wonder if you think the kind of technology you're building at Affectiva might help in areas like counseling?

RANA EL KALIOUBY: Healthcare is probably what I'm most excited about, because we know that there are facial and vocal biomarkers of depression, and we know that there are signs that could be predictive of suicidal intent in a person. Think about how often we are in front of our devices and our phones, that's an opportunity to collect very objective data.

Right now, you can only ask a person, on a scale from 1 to 10, how depressed they are, or how suicidal they are. It's just not accurate. But we now have the opportunity to collect data at scale and build a baseline model of who someone is and what their baseline mental state or mental health state is. Once we have that data, if someone starts to deviate from their normal baseline, then a system can signal that to the person themselves, to their family members or even maybe a healthcare professional.

Then imagine how we could use these same metrics to analyze the efficacy of different treatments. The person could try cognitive behavioral therapy or certain drugs, and we would be able to quantify, very accurately and very objectively over time, if those treatments were effective or not. I feel that there's a real potential here to understand anxiety, stress, and depression, and be able to quantify it.

MARTIN FORD: I want to move into a discussion about the ethics of AI. It's easy to think of things that people might find disturbing about this kind of technology. For example, during a negotiation, if your system was secretly watching someone and giving the other side information about their responses, that would create an unfair advantage. Or it could be used for some form of wider workplace surveillance. Monitoring someone when they're driving to make sure they're attentive would probably be okay with most people, but they might feel very different about the idea of your system watching an office worker sitting in front of a computer. How do you address those concerns?

RANA EL KALIOUBY: There's a little history lesson here about when Rosalind, myself, and our first employee met around Rosalind's kitchen table and we were thinking: Affectiva is going to get tested, so what are our boundaries and what's non-negotiable? In the end, we landed on this core value of respecting that people's emotions are a very personal type of data. From then on, we agreed that we would only take on situations where people are explicitly consenting and opting in to share that data. And, ideally, where they're also getting some value in return for sharing that data.

These are things that Affectiva has been tested on. In 2011, we were running low on funds, but we had the opportunity for funding from a security agency that had a venture arm, and it was very interested in using the technology for surveillance and security. Even though most people know that when they go to an airport, they're being watched, we just felt that this was not in line with our core value of consent and opt-in, so we declined the offer even though the money was there. At Affectiva, we've stayed away from applications where we feel that people aren't necessarily opting in and the value equation is not balanced.

When you think about the applications around the workplace, this question does become very interesting because the same tool could be used in ways that might be very empowering—or of course, very like Big Brother. I do think it would be super-interesting if people wanted to opt-in, anonymously, and employers were able to then get a sentiment score, or just an overall view, of whether people are stressed in the office—or whether people are engaged and happy.

Another great example would be where a CEO is giving a presentation, to people dialed in from around the world, and the machine indicates whether or not the message is resonating as they CEO intends. Are the goals exciting? Are people motivated? These are core questions that if we're all co-located, it would be easy to collect; but now, with everybody distributed, it's just really hard to get a sense of these things. However, if you turn it around and use the same technology to say, "OK. I'm going to pick on a certain member of staff because they seemed really disengaged," then that's a total abuse of the data.

Another example would be where we have a version of the technology that tracks how meetings go, and at the end of every meeting, it can give people feedback. It would give you feedback like, "you rambled for 30 minutes, and you were pretty hostile towards so-and-so, you should be a little bit more thoughtful or more empathetic." You can easily imagine how this technology could be used as a coach to help staff negotiate better or be a more thoughtful team member; but at the same time, you could use it to hurt people's careers.

I would like to think of us as advocating for situations where people can get the data back, and they can learn something about it, and it could help them advance their social and emotional intelligence skills.

MARTIN FORD: Let's delve into the technology you're using. I know that you use deep learning quite heavily. How do you feel about that as a technology? There has been some recent pushback, with some people suggesting that progress in deep learning is going to slow or even hit a wall, and that another approach will be needed. How do you feel about the use of neural networks and how they're going to evolve in the future?

RANA EL KALIOUBY: Back when I did my PhD, I used dynamic Bayesian networks to quantify and build these classifiers. Then a couple of years ago we moved all our science infrastructure to be deep learning-based, and we have absolutely reaped the benefits of that.

I would say that we haven't even maxed out yet on deep learning. With more data combined with these deep neural nets, we see increases in the accuracy and robustness of our analysis across so many different situations.

Deep learning being awesome, I don't think that it's the be-all, end-all to all of our needs. It's still pretty much supervised, so you still need to have some labeled data to track these classifiers. I think of it as an awesome tool within this bigger bucket of machine learning, but deep learning is not going to be the only tool that we use.

MARTIN FORD: Thinking more generally now, let's talk about the march towards artificial general intelligence. What are the hurdles involved? Is AGI something that is feasible, realistic or even something you expect to see in your lifetime?

RANA EL KALIOUBY: We're many, many, many, many, many years away from an AGI and the reason I say that is because when you look at all the examples of AI that we have today, all of them are pretty narrow. Today's AI does one thing well, but they all had to be bootstrapped in one way or another, even if they learned how to play a game from scratch.

I think there are sub-assumptions, or some level of sub-curation, that happens with the dataset, which has allowed that algorithm to learn whatever it learns, and I don't think that we've yet figured out how to give it human-level intelligence.

Even if you look at the best natural language processing system that we have today, and you give it something like a third-grade test, it doesn't pass.

MARTIN FORD: What are your thoughts about the intersection between AGI and emotion? A lot of your work is primarily focused on getting machines to understand emotion, but flipping the coin, what about having a machine that exhibits emotion? Do you think that's an important part of what AGI would be, or do you imagine a zombie-like machine that has no emotional sense at all?

RANA EL KALIOUBY: I would say that we are already there, right now, in terms of machines exhibiting emotions. Affectiva has developed an emotion-sensing platform, and a lot of our partners use this sensing platform to actuate machine behavior. Whether that technology is a car, or a social robot, an emotion-sensing platform can take our human metrics as input, and that data can be used to decide how a robot is going to respond. Those responses could be the things that a robot says from our stimuli, just like Amazon Alexa responds today.

Of course, if you're asking Amazon Alexa to order something and it keeps getting it wrong, then you're now getting annoyed. But instead of Alexa just being completely oblivious to all of that, your Alexa device could say, "OK, I'm sorry. I realize I'm getting this wrong. Let me try again." Alexa could acknowledge our level of frustration and it could then incorporate that into its response, and into what it actually does next. A robot could move its head, it could move around, it could write, and it could exhibit actions that we would translate into, "Oh! It looks like it's sorry."

I would argue that machine systems are already incorporating emotional cues in their actions, and that they can portray emotions, in any way that someone designs them to do so. That is quite different, of course, from the device actually having emotions, but we don't need to go there.

MARTIN FORD: I want to talk about the potential impact on jobs. How do you feel about that? Do you think that there is the potential for a big economic and job-market disruption from AI and robotics, or do you think that's perhaps been overhyped, and we shouldn't worry quite so much about it?

RANA EL KALIOUBY: I'd like to think of this as more of a human-technology partnership. I acknowledge that some jobs are going to cease to exist, but that's nothing new in the history of humanity. We've seen that shift of jobs over and over again, and so I think there's going to be a whole new class of jobs and job opportunities. While we can envision some of those new jobs now, we can't envision all of them.

I don't subscribe to the vision of a world where robots are going to take over and be in control, whilst humanity will just sit around and chill by the beach. I grew up in the Middle East during the time of the first Gulf War, so I've realized that there are so many problems in the world that need to be solved. I don't think we're anywhere close to a machine that's just going to wake up someday and be able to solve all these problems. So, to answer your question, I'm not concerned.

MARTIN FORD: If you think about a relatively routine job, for example a customer service job in a call center, it does sound like the technology you're creating might enable machines to do that more human element of the work as well. When I'm asked about this, which is often, I say the jobs that are most likely to be safe are the more human-oriented jobs, the ones that involve emotional intelligence. But it sounds like you're pushing the technology into this area as well, so it does seem that there's a very broad range of occupations that could be eventually be impacted, including some areas currently perceived as quite safe from automation.

RANA EL KALIOUBY: I think you're right about this, and let me give an example with nurses. At Affectiva, we are collaborating with companies that are building nurse avatars for our phones, and even installing social robots in our homes, which are designed to be a companion to terminally-ill patients. I don't think this is going to take the place of real nurses, but I do think it's going to change how nurses do their jobs.

You can easily imagine how a human nurse could be assigned to twenty patients, and each of these patients has access to a nurse avatar or a nurse robot. The human nurse only gets brought into the loop if there is a problem that the nurse robot can't deal with. The technology allows the nurse robot to manage so many more patients, and manage them longitudinally, in a way that's not possible today.

There's a similar example with teachers. I don't think intelligent learning systems are going to replace teachers, but they are going to augment them in places where there isn't access to enough teachers. It's like we're delegating these jobs to those mini-robots that could do parts of the job on our behalf.

I think this is even true for truck drivers. Nobody will be driving a truck in the next ten years, but someone is sitting at home and tele-operating 100 fleets out there and making sure that they're all on track. There may instead be a job where someone needs to intervene, every so often, and take human control of one of them.

MARTIN FORD: What is your response to some of the fears expressed about AI or AGI, in particular by Elon Musk, who has been very vocal about existential risks?

RANA EL KALIOUBY: There's a documentary on the internet called *Do You Trust This Computer?* which was partially funded by Elon Musk, and I was featured in it being interviewed.

MARTIN FORD: Yes, in fact, a couple of the other people I've interviewed in this book were also featured in that documentary.

RANA EL KALIOUBY: Having grown up in the Middle East, I feel that humanity has bigger problems than AI, so I'm not concerned.

I feel that this view, about the existential threat that robots are going to take over humanity, takes away our agency as humans. At the end of the day, we're designing these systems, and we get to say how they are deployed, we can turn the switch off. So, I don't subscribe to those fears. I do think that we have more imminent concerns with AI, and these have to do with the AI systems themselves and whether we are, through them, just perpetuating bias?

MARTIN FORD: So, you would say that bias is one of the more pressing issues that we're currently facing?

RANA EL KALIOUBY: Yes. Because the technology is moving so fast, while we train these algorithms, we don't necessarily know exactly what the algorithm or the neural network is learning. I fear that we are just rebuilding all the biases that exist in society by implementing them in these algorithms.

MARTIN FORD: Because the data is coming from people, so inevitably it incorporates their biases. You're saying that it isn't the algorithms that are biased, it's the data.

RANA EL KALIOUBY: Exactly, it's the data. It's how we're applying this data. So Affectiva, as a company, is very transparent about the fact that we need to make sure that the training data is representative of all the different ethnic groups, and that it has gender balance and age balance.

We need to be very thoughtful about how we train and validate these algorithms. This an ongoing concern, it's always a work in progress. There is always more that we can do to guard against these kinds of biases.

MARTIN FORD: But the positive side would be that while fixing bias in people is very hard, fixing bias in an algorithm, once you understand it, might be a lot easier. You could easily make an argument that relying on algorithms more in the future might lead to a world with much less bias or discrimination.

RANA EL KALIOUBY: Exactly. One great example is in hiring. Affectiva has partnered a company called HireVue, who use our technology in the hiring process. Instead of sending a Word resume, candidates send a video interview, and by using a combination of our algorithms and natural language processing classifiers, the system ranks and sorts those candidates based on their non-verbal communication, in addition to how they answered the questions. This algorithm is gender-blind, and it's ethnically blind. So, the first filters for these interviews do not consider gender and ethnicity.

HireVue has published a case study, with Unilever, where it shows that not only did it reduce its time to hire by 90%, but the process resulted in a 16% increase in the diversity of its incoming hiring population. I found that to be pretty cool.

MARTIN FORD: Do you think AI will need to be regulated? You've talked about how you've got very high ethical standards at Affectiva, but looking into the future, there's a real chance that your competitors are going to develop similar technologies but perhaps not adhere to the same standards. They might accept the contract from an authoritarian state, or the corporation that wants to secretly spy on its employees or customers, even if you would not. Given this, do you think there's going to be a need to regulate this type of technology?

RANA EL KALIOUBY: I'm a big advocate of regulation. Affectiva is part of the Partnership on AI consortium, and a member of the FATE working group, which is the Fair, Accountable, Transparent and Equitable AI.

Through working with these groups, our mandate is to develop guidelines that advocate for the equivalent of an FDA (Food and Drug Administration) process for AI. Alongside this work, Affectiva publishes best practices and guidelines for the industry. Since we are thought leaders, it is our responsibility to be an advocate for regulation, and to move the ball forward, as opposed to just saying, "Oh, yeah. We're just going to wait until legislation comes about." I don't think that that's the right solution.

I'm also a part of the World Economic Forum, on which there's an international forum council on robotics and AI. Through working with this forum, I've become fascinated by the cultural differences in how different countries think about AI. A great example can be seen in China, which is part of this council. We know that the Chinese government doesn't really care about ethics, and so it begs the question, how do you navigate that? Different nations think about AI regulation differently, which makes this difficult to answer the question.

MARTIN FORD: To end on an upbeat note, I assume you're an optimist? That you believe these technologies are, on balance, going to be beneficial for humanity?

RANA EL KALIOUBY: Yes, I would say that I'm an optimist because I believe that technology is neutral. What matters is how we decide to use it, and I think there's a potential for good, and we should, as an industry, follow the footsteps of my team, where we've decided to focus our mindshare on the positive applications of AI.

RANA EL KALIOUBY *is the CEO and co-founder of Affectiva, a company focused on emotion AI. She received her undergraduate and master's degrees from American University in Cairo, Egypt and her PhD from the Computer Lab at the University of Cambridge. She worked as a research scientist at the MIT Media Lab, where she developed technology to assist autistic children. That work led directly to the launch of Affectiva.*

Rana has received a number of awards and distinctions, including selection as a Young Global Leader in 2017 by the World Economic Forum. She was also featured on Fortune Magazine's 40 under 40 *and TechCrunch's* 40 Female founders who crushed it in 2016 *lists.*

RANA EL KALIOUBY

> **❝** *The scenario that I have is that we will send medical nanorobots into our bloodstream. [...] These robots will also go into the brain and provide virtual and augmented reality from within the nervous system rather than from devices attached to the outside of our bodies.*

RAY KURZWEIL

DIRECTOR OF ENGINEERING AT GOOGLE

Ray Kurzweil is one of the world's leading inventors, thinkers, and futurists. He has received 21 honorary doctorates, and honors from three US presidents. He is the recipient of the MIT Lemelson Prize for innovation and in 1999, he received the National Medal of Technology, the nation's highest honor in technology, from President Clinton. Ray is also a prolific writer, authoring 5 national bestsellers. In 2012, Ray became a Director of Engineering at Google—heading up a team of engineers developing machine intelligence and natural language understanding. Ray's first novel, Danielle, Chronicles of a Superheroine, *is being published in early 2019. Another book by Ray,* The Singularity is Nearer, *is expected to be published in late 2019.*

MARTIN FORD: How did you come to start out in AI?

RAY KURZWEIL: I first got involved in AI in 1962, which was only 6 years after the term was coined by Marvin Minsky and John McCarthy at the 1956 Dartmouth Conference in Hanover, New Hampshire.

The field of AI had already bifurcated into two warring camps: the symbolic school and the connectionist school. The symbolic school was definitely in the ascendancy with Marvin Minsky regarded as its leader. The connectionists were the upstarts, and one such person was Frank Rosenblatt at Cornell University, who had the first popularized neural net called the perceptron. I wrote them both letters and they both invited me to come up, so I first went to visit Minsky, where he spent all day with me and we struck up a rapport that would last for 55 years. We talked about AI, which at the time was a very obscure field that nobody was really paying attention to. He asked who I was going to see next, and when I mentioned Dr. Rosenblatt, he said that I shouldn't bother.

I then went to go and see Dr. Rosenblatt, who had this single-layer neural net called the perceptron; it was a hardware device that had a camera. I brought some printed letters to my meeting with Dr. Rosenblatt where his device recognized them perfectly as long as they were in Courier 10.

Other type styles didn't work as well, and he said, "Don't worry, I can take the output of the perceptron and feed it as the input to a secondary perceptron, then we can take the output of that and feed it to a third layer, and as we add layers it'll get smarter and generalize and be able to do all these remarkable things." I responded saying, "Have you tried that?", and he said, "well, not yet, but it's high on our research agenda."

Things didn't move quite as quickly back in the 1960s as they do today, and sadly he died 9 years later in 1971 never having tried that idea. The idea was remarkably prescient, however. All of the excitement we see now in neural nets is due to these deep neural networks with many layers. It was a pretty remarkable insight, as it really was not obvious that it would work.

In 1969, Minsky wrote his book, *Perceptrons*, with his colleague, Seymour Papert. The book basically proved a theorem that a perceptron could not devise answers that required the use of the XOR logical function, nor could they solve the connectedness problem. There are two maze-like images on the cover of that book, and if you look carefully, you can see one is fully connected, and the other is not. Making that classification is called the connectedness problem. The theorem proved that a perceptron could not do that. The book was very successful in killing all funding for connectionism for the next 25 years, which is something Minsky regretted, as shortly before he died he told me that he now appreciated the power of deep neural nets.

MARTIN FORD: Marvin Minsky did work on early connectionist neural nets back in the '50s, though, right?

RAY KURZWEIL: That's right, but he became disillusioned with them by the 1960s, and really didn't appreciate the power of multi-layer neural nets. It was not apparent until decades later when 3-layer neural nets were tried and they worked somewhat better. There was a problem going with too many layers, because of the exploding gradient or vanishing gradient problem, which is basically where the dynamic range of the values of the coefficients would decline because the numbers got too big or too small.

Geoffrey Hinton and a group of mathematicians solved that problem and now we can go to any number of levels. Their solution was that you recalibrate the information after each level, so it doesn't outstrip the range of values that can be represented and these 100-layer neural nets have been very successful. There's still a problem though, which is summarized by the motto, "Life begins at a billion examples."

One of the reasons I'm here at Google is that we do have a billion examples of some things like pictures of dogs and cats and other image categories that are annotated, but there are also lots of things we don't have a billion examples of. We have lots of examples of language, but they're not annotated with what they mean, and how could we annotate them anyway using language that we can't understand in the first place? There's a certain category of problems where we can work around that, and playing Go is a good example. The DeepMind system was trained on all of the online moves, which is in the order of a million moves. That's not a billion. That created a fair amateur player, but they need another 999 million examples, so where are they going to get them from?

MARTIN FORD: What you're getting at is that deep learning right now is very dependent on labeled data and what's called supervised learning.

RAY KURZWEIL: Right. One way to work around it is if you can simulate the world you're working in, then you can create your own training data, and that's what DeepMind did by having it play itself. They could annotate the moves with traditional annotation methods. Subsequently AlphaZero actually trained a neural net to improve on the annotation, so it was able to defeat AlphaGo 100 games to 0 starting with no human training data.

The question is, in what situations can you do that in? For example, another situation where we can do that is math, because we can simulate math. The axioms of number theory are no more complicated than the rules of Go.

Another situation is self-driving cars, even though driving is much more complex than a board game or the axioms of a math system. The way that worked is that Waymo created a pretty good system with a combination of methods and then drove millions of miles with humans at the wheel ready to take over. That generated enough data to create an accurate simulator of the world of driving. They've now driven on the order of a billion miles with simulated vehicles in the simulator, which has generated training data for a deep neural net designed to improve the algorithms. This has worked even though the world of driving is much more complex than a board game.

The next exciting area to attempt to simulate is the world of biology and medicine. If we could simulate biology, and it's not impossible, then we could do clinical trials in hours rather than years, and we could generate our own data just like we're doing with self-driving cars or board games or math.

That's not the only approach to the problem of providing sufficient training data. Humans can learn from much less data because we engage in transfer learning, using learning from situations which may be fairly different from what we are trying to learn. I have a different model of learning based on a rough idea of how the human neocortex works. In 1962 I came up with a thesis on how I thought the human brain works, and I've been thinking about thinking for the last 50 years. My model is not one big neural net, but rather many small modules, each of which can recognize a pattern. In my book, *How to Create a Mind*, I describe the neocortex as basically 300 million of those modules, and each can recognize a sequential pattern and accept a certain amount of variability. The modules are organized in a hierarchy, which is created through their own thinking. The system creates its own hierarchy.

That hierarchical model of the neocortex can learn from much less data. It's the same with humans. We can learn from a small amount of data because we can generalize information from one domain to another.

Larry Page, one of the co-founders of Google, liked my thesis in *How to Create a Mind* and recruited me to Google to apply those ideas to understanding language.

MARTIN FORD: Do you have any real-world examples of you applying those concepts to a Google product?

RAY KURZWEIL: Smart Reply on Gmail (which provides three suggestions to reply to each email) is one application from my team that uses this hierarchical system. We just introduced Talk to Books[1], where you ask a question in natural language and the system then reads 100,000 books in a half-second—that's 600 million sentences—and then returns the best answers that it can find from those 600 million sentences. It's all based on semantic understanding, not keywords.

At Google we're making progress in natural language, and language was the first invention of the neocortex. Language is hierarchical; we can share the hierarchical ideas we have in our neocortex with each other using the hierarchy of language. I think Alan Turing was prescient in basing the Turing test on language because I think it does require the full range of human thinking and human intelligence to create and understand language at human levels.

MARTIN FORD: Is your ultimate objective to extend this idea to actually build a machine that can pass the Turing test?

RAY KURZWEIL: Not everybody agrees with this, but I think the Turing test, if organized correctly, is actually a very good test of human-level intelligence. The issue is that in the brief paper that Turing wrote in 1950, it's really just a couple of paragraphs that talked about the Turing test, and he left out vital elements. For example, he

---

1 https://books.google.com/talktobooks/

didn't describe how to actually go about administering the test. The rules of the test are very complicated when you actually administer it, but if a computer is to pass a valid Turing test, I believe it will need to have the full range of human intelligence. Understanding language at human levels is the ultimate goal. If an AI could do that, it could read all documents and books and learn everything else. We're getting there a little bit at a time. We can understand enough of the semantics, for example to enable our Talk to Books application to come up with reasonable answers to questions, but it's still not at human levels. Mitch Kapor and I have a long-range bet on this for $20,000, with the proceeds to go to the charity of the winner's choice. I'm saying that an AI will pass the Turing test by 2029, whereas he's saying no.

MARTIN FORD: Would you agree that for the Turing test to be an effective test of intelligence, there probably shouldn't be a time limit at all? Just tricking someone for 15 minutes seems like a gimmick.

RAY KURZWEIL: Absolutely, and if you look at the rules that Mitch Kapor and I came up with, we gave a number of hours, and maybe even that's not enough time. The bottom line is that if an AI is really convincing you that it's human, then it passes the test. We can debate how long that needs to be—probably several hours if you have a sophisticated judge—but I agree that if the time is too short, then you might get away with simple tricks.

MARTIN FORD: I think it's easy to imagine an intelligent computer that just isn't very good at pretending to be human because it would be an alien intelligence. So, it seems likely that you could have a test where everyone agreed that the machine was intelligent, even though it didn't actually seem to be human. And we would probably want to recognize that as an adequate test as well.

RAY KURZWEIL: Whales and octopi have large brains and they exhibit intelligent behavior, but they're obviously not in a position to pass the Turing test. A Chinese person who speaks mandarin and not English would not pass the English Turing test, so there are lots of ways to be intelligent without passing the test. The key statement is the converse: In order to pass the test, you have to be intelligent.

MARTIN FORD: Do you believe that deep learning, combined with your hierarchical approach, is really the way forward, or do you think there needs to be some other massive paradigm shift in order to get us to AGI/human-level intelligence?

RAY KURZWEIL: No, I think humans use this hierarchical approach. Each of these modules is capable of doing learning, and I actually make the case in my book that in the brain they're not doing deep learning in each module, they're doing something equivalent to a Markov process, but it actually is better to use deep learning.

In our systems at Google we use deep learning to create vectors that represent the patterns in each module and then we have a hierarchy that goes beyond the deep learning paradigm. I think that's sufficient for AGI, though. The hierarchical approach is how the human brain does it in my view, and there's a lot of evidence now for that from the brain reverse engineering projects.

There's an argument that human brains follow a rule-based system rather than a connectionist one. People point out that humans are capable of having sharp distinctions and we're capable of doing logic. A key point is that connectionism can emulate a rule-based approach. A connectionist system in a certain situation might be so certain of its judgment that it looks and acts like a rule-based system, but then it's also able to deal with rare exceptions and the nuances of its apparent rules.

A rule-based system really cannot emulate a connectionist system, so the converse statement is not the case. Doug Lenat's "Cyc" is an impressive project, but I believe that it proves the limitations of a rule-based system. You reach a complexity ceiling, where the rules get so complex that if you try to fix one thing, you break three other things.

MARTIN FORD: Cyc is the project where people are manually trying to enter logic rules for common sense?

RAY KURZWEIL: Right. I'm not sure of the count, but they have a vast number of rules. They had a mode where it could print out its reasoning for a behavior and the explanations would go on for a number of pages and are very hard to follow. It's impressive work, but it does show that this is really not the approach, at least not by itself, and it's not how humans achieve intelligence. We don't have cascades of rules that we go through, we have this hierarchical self-organizing approach.

I think another advantage of a hierarchical, but connectionist approach is that it's better at explaining itself because you can look at the modules in the hierarchy and see which module influences which decision. When you have these massive

100-layer neural nets, they act like a big black box. It's very hard to understand its reasoning, though there have been some attempts to do that. I do think that this hierarchical spin on a connectionist approach is an effective approach, and that's how humans think.

MARTIN FORD: There are some structures, though, in the human brain, even at birth. For example, babies can recognize faces.

RAY KURZWEIL: We do have some feature generators. For example, in our brains we have this module called the fusiform gyrus that contains specialized circuitry and computes certain ratios, like the ratio of the tip of the nose to the end of the nose, or the distance between the eyes. There is set of a dozen or so fairly simple features, and experiments have shown that if we generate those features from images and then generate new images that have the same features—the same ratios—then people will immediately recognize them as a picture of that same person, even though other details have changed quite a bit in the image. There are various feature generators like that, some with audio information that we compute certain ratios and recognize partial overtones, and these features then feed into the hierarchical connectionist system. So, it is important to understand these feature generators, and there are some very specific features in recognizing faces, and that's what babies rely on.

MARTIN FORD: I'd like to talk about the path and the timing for Artificial General Intelligence (AGI). I'm assuming AGI and human-level AI are equivalent terms.

RAY KURZWEIL: They're synonyms, and I don't like the term AGI because I think it's an implicit criticism of AI. The goal of AI has always been to achieve greater and greater intelligence and ultimately to reach human levels of intelligence. As we've progressed, though, we've spun off separate fields. For example, once we mastered recognizing characters, it became the separate field of OCR. The same happened with speech recognition and robotics, and it was felt that the overarching field of AI was no longer focusing on general intelligence. My view is always that we'll get to general intelligence step by step by solving one problem at a time.

Another bit of color on that is that human performance in any type of task is a very broad range. What is the human performance level in Go? It's a broad range from a child who's playing their first game to the world champion. One thing we've seen is that once a computer can achieve human levels, even at the low end of that range, it very quickly soars past human performance. A little over a year ago computers were playing at a low-level in Go and then they quickly soared past that. More recently, AlphaZero soared past AlphaGo and beat it 100 games to 0, after training for a few hours.

Computers are also improving in their language understanding, but not at the same rate, because they don't yet have sufficient real-world knowledge. Computers currently can't do multi-chain reasoning very well, basically taking inferences from multiple statements while at the same time considering real-world knowledge. For example, on a third-grade language understanding test, a computer didn't understand that if a boy had muddy shoes he probably got them muddy by walking in the mud outside and if he got the mud on the kitchen floor it would make his mother mad. That may all seem obvious to us humans because we may have experienced that, but it's not obvious to the AI.

I don't think the process will be as quick to go from the average adult comprehension performance that we have now for computers on some language tests to superhuman performance because I think there are more fundamental issues to solve to do that. Nonetheless, human performance is a broad range, as we've seen, and once computers get in that range they can ultimately soar past it to become superhuman. The fact that they're performing at any kind of adult level in language understanding is very impressive because I feel that language requires the full range of human intelligence, and has the full range of human ambiguity and hierarchical thinking. To sum up, yes, AI is making very rapid progress and yes, all of this is using connectionist approaches.

I just had a discussion with my team here about what we have to do to pass the Turing test beyond what we've already done. We already have some level of language understanding. One key requirement is multi-chain reasoning—being able to consider the inferences and implications of concepts—that's a high priority. That's one area where chatbots routinely fail.

If I say I'm worried about my daughter's performance in nursery school, you wouldn't want to then ask three turns later, do you have any children? Chatbots do that kind of thing because they're not considering all the inferences of everything that has been said. As I mentioned, there is also the issue of real-world knowledge, but if we could understand all the implications of language, then real-world knowledge could be gained by reading and understanding the many documents available online. I think we have very good ideas on how to do those things and we have plenty of time to do them.

MARTIN FORD: You've been very straightforward for a long time that the year when you think human-level AI is going to arrive is 2029. Is that still the case?

RAY KURZWEIL: Yes. In my book, *The Age of Intelligent Machines*, which came out in 1989, I put a range around 2029 plus or minus a decade or so. In 1999 I published *The Age of Spiritual Machines* and made the specific prediction of 2029. Stanford University held a conference of AI experts to deal with this apparently startling prediction. At that time, we didn't have instant polling machines, so we basically had a show of hands. The consensus view then was it would take hundreds of years, with about a quarter of the group saying it would never happen.

In 2006 there was a conference at Dartmouth College celebrating the 50th anniversary of the 1956 Dartmouth conference, which I mentioned earlier, and there we did have instant polling devices and the consensus was about 50 years. 12 years later, in 2018 the consensus view now is about 20 to 30 years, so anywhere from 2038 to 2048, so I'm still more optimistic than the consensus of AI experts, but only slightly. My view and the consensus view of AI experts is getting closer together, but not because I've changed my view. There's a growing group of people who think I'm too conservative.

MARTIN FORD: 2029 is only 11 years away, which is not that far away really. I have an 11-year-old daughter, which really brings it into focus.

RAY KURZWEIL: The progress is exponential; look at the startling progress just in the last year. We've made dramatic advances in self-driving cars, language understanding, playing Go and many other areas. The pace is very rapid, both in hardware and software. In hardware, the exponential progression is even faster than for computation generally. We have been doubling the available computation for deep learning every three months over the past few years, compared to a doubling time of one year for computation in general.

MARTIN FORD: Some very smart people with a deep knowledge of AI are still predicting that it will take over 100 years, though. Do you think that is because they are falling into that trap of thinking linearly?

RAY KURZWEIL: A) they are thinking linearly, and B) they are subject to what I call the engineer's pessimism—that is being so focused on one problem and feeling that it's really hard because they haven't solved it yet, and extrapolating that they alone are going to solve the problem at the pace they're working on. It's a whole different discipline to consider the pace of progress in a field and how ideas interact with each other and study that as a phenomenon. Some people are just not able to grasp the exponential nature of progress, particularly when it comes to information technology.

Halfway through the human genome project, 1% had been collected after 7 years, and mainstream critics said, "I told you this wasn't going to work. 1% in 7 years means it's going to take 700 years, just like we said." My reaction was, "We finished one percent—We're almost done. We're doubling every year. 1% is only 7 doublings from 100%." And indeed, it was finished 7 years later.

A key question is why do some people readily get this, and other people don't? It's definitely not a function of accomplishment or intelligence. Some people who are not in professional fields understand this very readily because they can experience this progress just in their smartphones, and other people who are very accomplished and at the top of their field just have this very stubborn linear thinking. So, I really don't actually have an answer for that.

MARTIN FORD: You would agree though that it's not just about exponential progress in terms of computing speed or memory capacity? There are clearly some fundamental conceptual breakthroughs that have to happen in terms of teaching computers to learn from real time, unstructured data the way that human beings do, or in reasoning and imagination?

RAY KURZWEIL: Well, progress in software is also exponential, even though it has that unpredictable aspect that you're alluding to. There's a cross-fertilization of ideas that is inherently exponential, and once we have established performance at one level, ideas emerge to get to the next level.

There was a study done by the Obama administration scientific advisory board on this question. They examined how hardware and software progress compares. They took a dozen classical engineering and technical problems and looked at the advance quantitatively to see how much was attributable to hardware. Generally, over the previous 10 years from that point, it was about 1,000 to 1 in hardware, which is consistent with the implication of doubling in price performance every year. The software, as you might expect, varied, but in every case, it was greater than the hardware. Advances tend to be exponential. If you make an advance in software, it doesn't progress linearly; it progresses exponentially. On the overall progress is the product of the progress in hardware and software.

MARTIN FORD: The other date that you've given as a projection is 2045 for what you referred to as the singularity. I think most people associate that with an intelligence explosion or the advent of a true superintelligence. Is that the right way to think about it?

RAY KURZWEIL: There are actually two schools of thought on the singularity: there's a hard take off school and a soft take off school. I'm actually in the soft take off school that says we will continue to progress exponentially, which is daunting enough. The idea of an intelligence explosion is that there is a magic moment where a computer can access its own design and modify it and create a smarter version of itself, and that it keeps doing that in a very fast iterative loop and just explodes in its intelligence.

I think we've actually been doing that for thousands of years, ever since we created technology. We are certainly smarter as a result of our technology. Your smartphone is a brain extender, and it does make us smarter. It's an exponential process. A thousand years ago paradigm shifts and advances took centuries, and it looked like nothing was happening. Your grandparents lived the same lives you did, and you expected your grandchildren to do the same. Now, we see changes on an annual basis if not faster. It is exponential and that results in an acceleration of progress, but it's not an explosion in that sense.

I think we will achieve a human level of intelligence by 2029 and it's immediately going to be superhuman. Take for example our Talk to Books, you ask it a question and it reads 600 million sentences, 100,000 books, in half a second. Personally, it takes me hours to read 100,000 books!

Your smartphone right now is able to do searching based on keywords and other methods and search all human knowledge very quickly. Google search already goes beyond keyword search and has some semantic capability. The semantic understanding is not yet at human levels, but it's a billion times faster than human thinking. And both the software and the hardware will continue to improve at an exponential pace.

MARTIN FORD: You're also well known for your thoughts on using technology to expand and extend human life. Could you let me know more about that?

RAY KURZWEIL: One thesis of mine is that we're going to merge with the intelligent technology that we are creating. The scenario that I have is that we will send medical nanorobots into our bloodstream. One application of these medical nanorobots will be to extend our immune systems. That's what I call the third bridge to radical life extension. The first bridge is what we can do now, and bridge two is the perfecting of biotechnology and reprogramming the software of life. Bridge three constitutes these medical nanorobots to perfect the immune system. These robots will also go into the brain and provide virtual and augmented reality from within the nervous system rather than from devices attached to the outside of our bodies. The most important application of the medical nanorobots is that we will connect the top layers of our neocortex to synthetic neocortex in the cloud.

MARTIN FORD: Is this something that you're working on at Google?

RAY KURZWEIL: The projects I have done with my team here at Google use what I would call crude simulations of the neocortex. We don't have a perfect understanding of the neocortex yet, but we're approximating it with the knowledge we have now. We are able to do interesting applications with language now, but by the early 2030s we'll have very good simulations of the neocortex.

Just as your phone makes itself a million times smarter by accessing the cloud, we will do that directly from our brain. It's something that we already do through our smartphones, even though they're not inside our bodies and brains, which I think is an arbitrary distinction. We use our fingers and our eyes and ears, but they are nonetheless brain extenders. In the future, we'll be able to do that directly from our brains, but not just to perform tasks like search and language translation directly from our brains, but to actually connect the top layers of our neocortex to synthetic neocortex in the cloud.

Two million years ago, we didn't have these large foreheads, but as we evolved we got a bigger enclosure to accommodate more neocortex. What did we do with that? We put it at the top of the neocortical hierarchy. We were already doing a very good job at being primates, and now we were able to think at an even more abstract level.

That was the enabling factor for us to invent technology, science, language, and music. Every human culture that we have discovered has music, but no primate culture has music. Now that was a one-shot deal, we couldn't keep growing the enclosure because birth would have become impossible. This neocortical expansion two million years ago actually made birth pretty difficult as it was.

This new extension in the 2030s to our neocortex will not be a one-shot deal. Even as we speak, the cloud is doubling in power every year. It's not limited by a fixed enclosure, so the non-biological portion of our thinking will continue to grow. If we do the math, we will multiply our intelligence a billion-fold by 2045, and that's such a profound transformation that it's hard to see beyond that event horizon. So, we've borrowed this metaphor from physics of the event horizon and the difficulty of seeing beyond it.

Technologies such as Google Search and Talk to Books are at least a billion times faster than humans. It's not at human levels of intelligence yet, but once we get to that point, AI will take advantage of the enormous speed advantage which already exists and an ongoing exponential increase in capacity and capability. So that's the meaning of the singularity, it's a soft take off, but exponentials nonetheless become quite daunting. If you double something 30 times, you're multiplying by a billion.

MARTIN FORD: One of the areas where you've talked a lot about the singularity having an impact is in medicine and especially in the longevity of human life, and this is maybe one area where you've been criticized. I heard a presentation you gave at MIT last year where you said that within 10 years, most people might be able to achieve what you call "longevity escape velocity," and you also said that you think you personally might have achieved that already? Do you really believe it could happen that soon?

RAY KURZWEIL: We are now at a tipping point in terms of biotechnology. People look at medicine, and they assume that it is just going to plod along at the same hit or miss pace that they have been used to in the past. Medical research has essentially been hit or miss. Drug companies will go through a list of several thousand compounds to find something that has some impact, as opposed to actually understanding and systematically reprogramming the software of life.

It's not just a metaphor to say that our genetic processes are software. It is a string of data, and it evolved in an era where it was not in the interest of the human species for each individual to live very long because there were limited resources such as food. We are transforming from an era of scarcity to an era of abundance

Every aspect of biology as an information process has doubled in power every year. For example, genetic sequencing has done that. The first genome cost US $1 billion, and now we're close to $1,000. But our ability to not only collect this raw object code of life but to understand it, to model it, to simulate it, and most importantly to reprogram it, is also doubling in power every year.

We're now getting clinical applications—it's a trickle today, but it'll be a flood over the next decade. There are hundreds of profound interventions in process that are working their way through the regulatory pipeline. We can now fix a broken heart from a heart attack, that is, rejuvenate a heart with a low ejection fraction after a heart attack using reprogrammed adult stem cells. We can grow organs and are installing them successfully in primates. Immunotherapy is basically reprogramming the immune system. On its own, the immune system does not go against cancer because it did not evolve to go after diseases that tend to get us later on in life. We can actually reprogram it and turn it on to recognize cancer and treat it as a pathogen. This is a huge bright spot in cancer treatment, and there are remarkable trials where virtually every person in the trial goes from stage 4 terminal cancer to being in remission.

Medicine is going to be profoundly different in a decade from now. If you're diligent, I believe you will be able to achieve longevity escape velocity, which means that we'll be adding more time than is going by, not just to infant life expectancy but to your remaining life expectancy. It's not a guarantee, because you can still be hit by the proverbial bus tomorrow, and life expectancy is actually a complicated statistical concept, but the sands of time will start running in rather than running out. In another decade further out, we'll be able to reverse aging processes as well.

MARTIN FORD: I want to talk about the downsides and the risks of AI. I would say that sometimes you are unfairly criticized as being overly optimistic, maybe even a bit Pollyannaish, about all of this. Is there anything we should worry about in terms of these developments?

RAY KURZWEIL: I've written more about the downsides than anyone, and this was decades before Stephen Hawking or Elon Musk were expressing their concerns. There was extensive discussion of the downsides of GNR—Genetics, Nanotechnology, and Robotics (which means AI)—in my book, *The Age of Spiritual Machines*, which came out in 1999 that led Bill Joy to write his famous Wired cover story in January 2000 titled, *Why the Future Doesn't Need Us*.

MARTIN FORD: That was based upon a quote from Ted Kaczynski, the Unabomber, wasn't it?

RAY KURZWEIL: I have a quote from him on one page that sounds like a very level-headed expression of concern, and then you turn the page, and you see that this is from the Unabomber Manifesto. I discussed in quite some detail in that book the existential risk of GNR. In my 2005 book, *The Singularity is Near*, I go into the topic of GNR risks in a lot of detail. Chapter 8 is titled, "The Deeply Intertwined Promise versus Peril of GNR."

I'm optimistic that we'll make it through as a species. We get far more profound benefit than harm from technology, but you don't have to look very far to see the profound harm that has manifested itself, for example, in all of the destruction in the 20th century—even though the 20th century was actually the most peaceful century up to that time, and we're in a far more peaceful time now. The world is getting profoundly better, for example, poverty has been cut 95% in the last 200 years and literacy rates have gone from under 10% to over 90% in the world.

People's algorithm for whether the world is getting better or worse is "how often do I hear good news versus bad news?", and that's not a very good method. There was a poll taken of 24,000 people in about 26 countries asking this question, "Is poverty worldwide getting better or worse over the last 20 years?" 87% said, incorrectly, that it's getting worse. Only 1% said correctly that it's fallen by half or more in the last 20 years. Humans have an evolutionary preference for bad news. 10,000 years ago, it was very important that you paid attention to bad news, for example that little rustling in the leaves that might be a predator. That was more important to pay attention to than studying that your crops are half a percent better than last year, and we continue to have this preference for bad news.

MARTIN FORD: There's a step-change, though, between real risks and existential risks.

RAY KURZWEIL: Well, we've also done reasonably well with existential risks from information technology. Forty years ago, a group of visionary scientists saw both the promise and the peril of biotechnology, neither of which was close at hand at the time, and they held the first Asilomar Conference on biotechnology ethics. These ethical standards and strategies have been updated on a regular basis. That has worked very well. The number of people who have been harmed by intentional or accidental abuse or problems with biotechnology has been close to zero. We're now beginning to get the profound benefit that I alluded to, and that's going to become a flood over the next decade.

That's a success for this approach of comprehensive ethical standards, and technical strategies on how to keep the technology safe, and much of that is now baked into law. That doesn't mean we can cross danger from biotechnology off our list of concerns; we keep coming up with more powerful technologies like CRISPR and we have to keep reinventing the standards.

We had our first AI ethics Asilomar conference about 18 months ago where we came up with a set of ethical standards. I think they need further development, but it's an overall approach that can work. We have to give it a high priority.

MARTIN FORD: The concern that's really getting a lot of attention right now is what's called the control problem or the alignment problem, where a superintelligence might not have goals that are aligned with what's best for humanity. Do you take that seriously, and should work be done on that?

RAY KURZWEIL: Humans don't all have aligned goals with each other, and that's really the key issue. It's a misconception to talk about AI as a civilization apart, as if it's an alien invasion from Mars. We create tools to extend our own reach. We couldn't reach food at that higher branch 10,000 years ago, so we made a tool that extended our reach. We can't build a skyscraper with our bare hands, so we have machines that leverage the range of our muscles. A kid in Africa with a smartphone is connected to all of the human knowledge with a few keystrokes.

That is the role of technology; it enables us to go beyond our limitations, and that's what we are doing and will continue to do with AI. It's not us versus the AIs, which has been the theme of many AI futurist dystopian movies. We are going to merge with it. We already have. The fact that your phone is not physically inside your body and brain is a distinction without a difference, because it may as well be. We don't leave home without it, we're incomplete without it, nobody could do their work, get their education, or keep their relationships without their devices today, and we're getting more intimate with them.

I went to MIT because it was so advanced in 1965 that it had a computer. I had to take my bicycle across the campus to get to it and show my ID to get into the building, and now half a century later we're carrying them in our pockets, and we're using them constantly. They are integrated into our lives and will ultimately become integrated into our bodies and brains.

If you look at the conflict and warfare we've had over the millennia, it's been from humans having disagreements. I do think technology tends to actually create greater harmony and peace and democratization. You can trace the rise of democratization to improvements in communication. Two centuries ago, there was only one democracy in the world. There were half a dozen democracies one century ago. Now there are 123 democracies out of 192 recognized countries, that's 64% of the world. The world's not a perfect democracy, but democracy has actually been accepted as the standard today. It is the most peaceful time in human history, and every aspect of life is getting better, and this is due to the effect of technology which is becoming increasingly intelligent, and it's deeply integrated into who we are.

We have conflict today between different groups of humans, each of whom are amplified by their technology. That will continue to be the case, although I think there's this other theme that better communication technology harnesses our short-range empathy. We have a biological empathy for small groups of people, but that's now amplified by our ability to actually experience what happens to people half a world away. I think that's the key issue; we still have to manage our human relations as we increase our personal powers through technology.

MARTIN FORD: Let's talk about the potential for economic and job market disruption. I personally do think there's a lot of potential for jobs to be lost or deskilled and for greatly increasing inequality. I actually think it could be something that will be disruptive on the scale of a new Industrial Revolution.

RAY KURZWEIL: Let me ask you this: how did that last Industrial Revolution work out? Two hundred years ago, the weavers had enjoyed a guild that was passed down from generation to generation for hundreds of years. Their business model was turned on its head and disrupted when all these thread-spinning and cloth-weaving machines came out that completely upended their livelihoods. They predicted that more machines would come out and that most people would lose their jobs, and that employment would be enjoyed just by an elite. Part of that prediction came true—more textile machines were introduced and many types of skills and jobs were eliminated. However, employment went up, not down as society became more prosperous.

If I were a prescient futurist in 1900 I would point out that 38% of you work on farms and 25% of you work in factories, but I predict that 115 years from now, in 2015, that'll be 2% on farms, and 9% in factories. Everybody's reaction would be, "Oh my god I'm going to be out of work!" I would then say "Don't worry, the jobs that are eliminated are at the bottom of the skill ladder, and we are going to create an even larger number of jobs at the top of the skill ladder."

People would say, "Oh really, what new jobs?", and I'd say, "Well I don't know, we haven't invented them yet." People say we've destroyed many more jobs than we've created but that's not true, we've gone from 24 million jobs in 1900 to 142 million jobs today, and as a percentage of the population that goes from 31% to 44%. How do these new jobs compare? Well, for one thing, the average job today pays 11 times as much in constant dollars per hour than in 1900. As a result, we've shortened the work year from about 3,000 hours to 1,800 hours. People still make 6 times as much per year in constant dollars, and the jobs have become much more interesting. I think that's going to continue to be the case even in the next Industrial Revolution.

MARTIN FORD: The real question is whether this time it's different. What you say about what happened previously is certainly true, but it is also true, according to most estimates, that maybe half or more of the people in the workforce are doing things that are fundamentally predictable and relatively routine, and all those jobs are going to be potentially threatened by machine learning. Automating most of those predictable jobs does not require human-level AI.

There may be new kinds of work created for robotics engineers and deep learning researchers and all of that, but you cannot take all the people that are now flipping hamburgers or driving taxis and realistically expect to transition them into those kinds of jobs, even assuming that there are going to be a sufficient number of these new jobs. We're talking about a technology that can displace people cognitively, displace their brainpower, and it's going to be extraordinarily broad-based.

RAY KURZWEIL: Your model that's implicit in your prediction is us-versus-them, and what are the humans going to do versus the machines. We've already made ourselves smarter in order to do these higher-level types of jobs. We've made ourselves smarter not with things connected directly into our brains yet, but with intelligent devices. Nobody can do their jobs without these brain extenders, and the brain extenders are going to extend our brains even further, and they're going to be more closely integrated into our lives.

One thing that we did to improve our skills is education. We had 68,000 college students in 1870 and today we have 15 million. If you take them and all the people that service them, such as faculty and staff, it is about 20 percent of the workforce that is just involved in higher education, and we are constantly creating new things to do. The whole app economy did not exist about six years ago, and that forms a major part of the economy today. We're going to make ourselves smarter.

A whole other thesis that needs to be looked at in considering this question is the radical abundance thesis that I mentioned earlier. I had an on-stage dialogue with Christine Lagarde, the managing director of the IMF, at the annual International Monetary Fund meeting and she said, "Where's the economic growth associated with this? The digital world has these fantastic things, but fundamentally you can't eat information technology, you can't wear it, you can't live in it," and my response was, "All that's going to change."

"All those types of nominally physical products are going to become an information technology. We're going to grow food with vertical agriculture in AI-controlled buildings with hydroponic fruits and vegetables, and in vitro cloning of muscle tissue for meat, providing very high-quality food without chemicals at very low cost, and without animal suffering. Information technology has a 50% deflation rate; you get the same computation, communication, genetic sequencing that you could purchase a year ago for half the price, and this massive deflation is going to attend to these traditionally physical products."

MARTIN FORD: So, you think that technologies like 3D printing or robotic factories and agriculture could drive costs down for nearly everything?

RAY KURZWEIL: Exactly, 3D printing will print out clothing in the 2020s. We're not quite there yet for various reasons, but all that's moving in the right direction. The other physical things that we need will be printed out on 3D printers, including modules which will snap together a building in a matter of days. All the physical things we need will ultimately become facilitated by these AI-controlled information technologies.

Solar energy is being facilitated by applying deep learning to come up with better materials, and as a result, the cost of both energy storage and energy collection is coming down rapidly. The total amount of solar energy is doubling every two years, and the same trend exists with wind energy. Renewable energy is now only about five doublings, at two years per doubling, away from meeting 100% of our energy needs, by which time it will use one part in thousands of the energy from the sun or from the wind.

Christine Lagarde said, "OK, there is one resource that will never be an information technology, and that's land. We are already crowded together." I responded "That's only because we decided to crowd ourselves together and create cities so we could work and play together." People are already spreading out as our virtual communication becomes more robust. Try taking a train trip anywhere in the world and you will see that 95% of the land is unused.

We're going be able to provide a very high quality of living that's beyond what we consider a high standard of living today for everyone, for all of the human population, as we get to the 2030s. I made a prediction at TED that we will have universal basic income, which won't actually need to be that much to provide a very high standard of living, as we get into the 2030s.

MARTIN FORD: So, you're a proponent of a basic income, eventually? You agree that there won't be a job for everyone, or maybe everyone won't need a job, and that there'll be some other source of income for people, like a universal basic income?

RAY KURZWEIL: We assume that a job is a road to happiness. I think the key issue will be purpose and meaning. People will still compete to be able to contribute and get gratification.

MARTIN FORD: But you don't necessarily have to get paid for the thing that you get meaning from?

RAY KURZWEIL: I think we will change the economic model and we are already in the process of doing that. I mean, being a student in college is considered a worthwhile thing to do. It's not a job, but it's considered a worthwhile activity. You won't need income from a job in order to have a very good standard of living for the physical requirements of life, and we will continue to move up Maslow's hierarchy. We have been doing that, just compare today to 1900.

MARTIN FORD: What do you think about the perceived competition with China to get to advanced AI? China does have advantages in terms of having less regulation on things like privacy. Plus, their population is so much larger, which generates more data and also means they potentially have a lot more young Turings or von Neumanns in the pipeline.

RAY KURZWEIL: I don't think it's a zero-sum game. An engineer in China who comes up with a breakthrough in solar energy or in deep learning benefits all of us. China is publishing a lot just as the United States is, and the information is actually shared pretty widely. Look at Google, which put its TensorFlow deep learning framework into the public domain, and we did that in our group with the technology underlying Talk to Books and Smart Reply being made open source so people can use that.

I personally welcome the fact that China is emphasizing economic development and entrepreneurship. When I was in China recently the tremendous explosion of entrepreneurship was apparent. I would encourage China to move in the direction of free exchange of information. I think that's fundamental for this type of progress. All around the world we see Silicon Valley as a motivating model. Silicon Valley really is just a metaphor for entrepreneurship, the celebrating of experimenting, and calling failure experience. I think that's a good thing, I really don't see it as an international competition.

MARTIN FORD: But do you worry about the fact that China is an authoritarian state, and that these technologies do have, for example, military applications? Companies like Google and certainly DeepMind in London have been very clear that they don't want their technology used in anything that is even remotely military. Companies like

Tencent and Baidu in China don't really have the option to make that choice. Is that something we should worry about, that there's a kind of asymmetry going forward?

RAY KURZWEIL: Military use is a different issue from authoritarian government structure. I am concerned about the authoritarian orientation of the Chinese government, and I would encourage them to move toward greater freedom of information and democratic ways of governing. I think that will help them and everyone economically.

I think these political and social and philosophical issues remain very important. My concern is not that AI is going to go off and do something on its own, because I think it's deeply integrated with us. I'm concerned about the future of the human population, which is already a human technological civilization. We're going to continue to enhance ourselves through technology, and so the best way to assure the safety of AI is to attend to how we govern ourselves as humans.

RAY KURZWEIL *is widely recognized as one of the world's foremost inventors and futurists. Ray received his engineering degree from MIT, where he was mentored by Marvin Minsky, one of the founding fathers of the field of artificial intelligence. He went on to make major contributions in a variety of areas. He was the principal inventor of the first CCD flat-bed scanner, the first omni-font optical character recognition, the first print-to-speech reading machine for the blind, the first text-to-speech synthesizer, the first music synthesizer capable of recreating the grand piano and other orchestral instruments, and the first commercially marketed large-vocabulary speech recognition.*

Among Ray's many honors, he received a Grammy Award for outstanding achievements in music technology; he is the recipient of the National Medal of Technology *(the nation's highest honor in technology), was inducted into the* National Inventors Hall of Fame, *holds twenty-one honorary doctorates, and honors from three US presidents.*

Ray has written five national best-selling books, including New York Times *bestsellers* The Singularity Is Near *(2005) and* How To Create A Mind *(2012). He is Co-Founder and Chancellor of Singularity University and a Director of Engineering at Google, heading up a team developing machine intelligence and natural language understanding.*

Ray is known for his work on exponential progress in technology, which he has formalized as "The Law of Accelerating Returns." Over the course of decades, he has made a number of important predictions that have proven to be accurate.

Ray's first novel, Danielle, Chronicles of a Superheroine, *is being published in early 2019. Another book by Ray,* The Singularity is Nearer, *is expected to be published in late 2019.*

RAY KURZWEIL

> **❝** *I like to think of a world where more mundane routine tasks are taken off your plate. Maybe garbage cans that take themselves out and smart infrastructure to ensure that they disappear, or robots that will fold your laundry.*

DANIELA RUS

DIRECTOR OF MIT CSAIL

Daniela Rus is the Director of the Computer Science and Artificial Intelligence Laboratory (CSAIL) at MIT, one of the world's largest research organizations focused on AI and robotics. Daniela is a fellow of ACM, AAAI and IEEE, and a member of the National Academy of Engineering, and the American Academy for Arts and Science. Daniela leads research in robotics, mobile computing, and data science.

MARTIN FORD: Let's start by talking about your background and looking at how you became interested in AI and robotics.

DANIELA RUS: I've always been interested in science and science fiction, and when I was a kid I read all the popular science fiction books at the time. I grew up in Romania where we didn't have the range of media that you had in the US, but there was one show that I really enjoyed, and that's the original *Lost in Space*.

MARTIN FORD: I remember that. You're not the first person I've spoken to who has drawn their career inspiration from science fiction.

DANIELA RUS: I never missed an episode of *Lost in Space*, and I loved the cool geeky kid Will and the robot. I didn't imagine that I would do anything remotely associated with that at that time. I was lucky enough to be quite good at math and science, and by the time I got to college age I knew that I wanted to do something with math, but not pure math because it seemed too abstract. I studied computer science with a major in computer science and mathematics, and a minor in astronomy—the astronomy continuing the connection to my fantasies of what could be in other worlds.

Toward the end of my undergraduate degree I went to a talk given by John Hopcroft, the Turing Award-winning theoretical computer scientist, and in that talk, John said that classical computer science was finished. What he meant by that was that many of the graph-theoretic algorithms that were posed by the founders of the field of computing had solutions and it was time for the grand applications, which in his opinion were robots.

I found that an exciting idea, so I worked on my PhD with John Hopcroft because I wanted to make contributions to the field of robotics. However, at that time the field of robotics was not at all developed. For example, the only robot that was available to us was a big PUMA arm (Programmable Universal Manipulation Arm), an industrial manipulator that had little in common with my childhood fantasies of what robots should be. It got me thinking a lot about what I could contribute, and I ended up studying dexterous manipulation, but very much from a theoretical, computational point of view. I remember finishing my thesis and trying to implement my algorithms to go beyond simulation and create real systems. Unfortunately, the systems that were available at the time were the Utah/MIT hand and the Salisbury hand, and neither one of those hands was able to exert the kind of forces and torques that my algorithms required.

MARTIN FORD: It sounds to me like there was a big gap between where the physical machines were and where the algorithms were.

DANIELA RUS: Exactly. At the time, I really realized that a machine is actually a closed connection between body and brain, and for any task you want that machine to execute, you really needed a body capable of those tasks, and then you needed a brain to control the body to deliver what it was meant to do.

As a result, I became very interested in the interaction between body and brain, and challenging the notion of what a robot is. So industrial manipulators are excellent examples of robots, but they are not all that we could do with robots; there are so many other ways to envision robots.

Today in my lab, we have all kinds of very non-traditional robots. There are modular cellular robots, soft robots, robots built out of food, and even robots built out of paper. We're looking at new types of materials, new types of shapes, new types of architectures and different ways of imagining what the machine body ought to be. We also do a lot of work on the mathematical foundations of how those bodies operate, and I'm very interested in understanding and advancing the engineering of both the science of autonomy and of intelligence.

I became very interested in the connection between the hardware of the device and the algorithms that control the hardware. When I think about algorithms, I think that while it's very important to consider the solutions, it's also important to consider the mathematical foundations for those solutions because that's in some sense where we create the nuggets of knowledge that other people can build on.

MARTIN FORD: You're the director of the MIT Computer Science and Artificial Intelligence Laboratory (CSAIL), which is one of the most important research endeavors in not just robotics, but in AI generally. Could you explain what exactly CSAIL is?

DANIELA RUS: Our objective at CSAIL is to invent the future of computing to make the world better through computing, and to educate some of the best students in the world in research.

CSAIL is an extraordinary organization. When I was a student, I looked up to it as the Mount Olympus of technology and never imagined that I'd become a part of it. I like to think of CSAIL as the prophet for the future of computing, and the place where people envision how computing can be used to make the world better.

CSAIL actually has two parts, Computer Science (CS) and AI, both having a really deep history. The AI side of our organization goes back to 1956 when the field was invented and founded. In 1956, Marvin Minsky gathered his friends in New Hampshire where they spent a month, no doubt hiking in the woods, drinking wine and having great conversations, uninterrupted by social media, email, and smartphones.

When they emerged from the woods, they told the world that they had coined a new field of study: artificial intelligence. AI refers to the science and engineering of creating machines that exhibit human-level skills in how they perceive the world; in how they move in the world; in how they play games; in how they reason; in how they communicate; and even, in how they learn. Our researchers at CSAIL have been thinking about these questions and making groundbreaking contributions ever since, and it's an extraordinary privilege to be part of this community.

The computer science side goes back to 1963, when Bob Fano, a computer scientist and MIT professor, had the crazy idea that two people might use the same computer at the same time. You have to understand this was a big dream back then when computers were the size of rooms and you had to book time on them. Originally, it was set up as Project MAC, which stood for Machine-Aided Cognition, but there was a joke that it was actually named MAC after Minsky and Corby (Fernando "Corby" Corbató), who were the two technical leads for the CS and the AI side. Ever since the founding of the laboratory in 1963, our researchers have put a lot of effort into imagining what computing looks like and what it can accomplish.

Many of the things that you take for granted today have their roots in the research developed at CSAIL, such as the password, RSA encryption, the computer time-sharing systems that inspired Unix, the optical mouse, object-oriented programming, speech systems, mobile robots with computer vision, the free software movement, the list goes on. More recently CSAIL has been a leader in defining the cloud and cloud computing, and in democratizing education through Massive Open Online Courses (MOOCs) and in thinking about security, privacy, and many other aspects of computing.

DANIELA RUS

MARTIN FORD: How big is CSAIL today?

DANIELA RUS: CSAIL is the largest research laboratory at MIT, with over 1,000 members, and it cuts across 5 schools and 11 departments. CSAIL today has 115 faculty members, and each of these faculty members has a big dream about computing, which is such an important part of our ethos here. Some of our faculty members want to make computing better through algorithms, systems or networks, while others want to make life better for humanity with computing. For example, Shafi Goldwasser wants to make sure that we can have private conversations over the internet; and Tim Berners-Lee wants to create a bill of rights, a Magna Carta of the World Wide Web. We have researchers who want to make sure that if we get sick, the treatments that are available to us are personalized and customized to be as effective as they can be. We have researchers who want to advance what machines can do: Leslie Kaelbling wants to make Lieutenant-Commander Data, and Russ Tedrake wants to make robots that can fly. I want to make shape-shifting robots because I want to see a world with pervasive robots that support us in our cognitive and physical tasks.

This aspiration is really inspired by looking back at history and observing that only 20 years ago, computation was a task reserved for the expert few because computers were large, expensive, and difficult to handle, and it took knowledge to know what to do with them. All of that changed a decade ago when smartphones, cloud computing, and social media came along.

Today, so many people compute. You don't have to be an expert in order to use computing, and you use computing so much that you don't even know how much you depend on it. Try to imagine a day in your life without the world wide web and everything that enables. No social media; no communication through email; no GPS; no diagnosis in hospitals; no digital media; no digital music; no online shopping. It's just incredible to see how computation has permeated into the fabric of life. To me, this raises a very exciting and important question, which is: In this world that has been so changed by computation, what might it look like with robots and cognitive assistants helping us with physical and cognitive tasks?

MARTIN FORD: As a university-based organization, what's the balance between what you would classify as pure research and things that are more commercial and that end up actually developing into products? Do you spin off startups or work with commercial companies?

DANIELA RUS: We don't house companies; instead, we focus on training our students and giving them various options for what they could do when they graduate, whether that be joining the academic life, going into high-tech industry, or becoming entrepreneurs. We fully support all of those paths. For example, say a student creates a new type of system after several years of research, and all of a sudden there is an immediate application for the system. This is the kind of technological entrepreneurship that we embrace, and hundreds of companies have been spun out of CSAIL research, but the actual companies do not get housed by CSAIL.

We also don't create products, but that's not to say we ignore them. We're very excited about how our work could be turned into products, but generally, our mission is really to focus on the future. We think about problems that are 5 to 10 years out, and that's where most of our work is, but we also embrace the ideas that matter today.

MARTIN FORD: Let's talk about the future of robotics, which sounds like something you spend a great deal of your time thinking about. What's coming down the line in terms of future innovations?

DANIELA RUS: Our world has already been transformed by robotics. Today, doctors can connect with patients, and teachers can connect with students that are thousands of miles away. We have robots that help with packing on factory floors, we've got networked sensors that we deploy to monitor facilities, and we have 3D printing that creates customized goods. Our world has already been transformed by advances in artificial intelligence and robotics, and when we consider adding even more extensive capabilities from our AI and robot systems, extraordinary things will be possible.

At the high level, we have to picture a world where routine tasks will be taken off our plate because this is the sweet spot for where technology is today. These routine tasks could be physical tasks or could be computational or cognitive tasks.

You already see some of that in the rise of machine learning applications for various industries, but I like to think of a world where more mundane routine tasks are taken off your plate. Maybe garbage cans that take themselves out and smart infrastructure to ensure that they disappear, or robots that will fold your laundry. We will have transportation available in the same way that water

258

or electricity are available, and you will be able to go anywhere at any time. We will have intelligent assistants who will enable us to maximize our time at work and optimize our lives to live better and more healthily, and to work more efficiently. It will be extraordinary.

MARTIN FORD: What about self-driving cars? When will I be able to call a robot taxi in Manhattan and have it take me anywhere?

DANIELA RUS: I'm going to qualify my answer and say that certain autonomous driving technologies are available right now. Today's solutions are good for certain level 4 autonomy situations (the penultimate level before full autonomy, as defined by the Society of Automotive Engineers). We already have robot cars that can deliver people and packages, and that operate at low speeds in low-complexity environments where you have low interaction. Manhattan is a challenging case because traffic in Manhattan is super chaotic, but we do already have robot cars that could operate in retirement communities or business campuses, or in general places where there is not too much traffic. Nevertheless, those are still real-world places where you can expect other traffic, other people, and other vehicles.

Next, we have to think about how we extend this capability to make it applicable to bigger and more complex environments where you'll face more complex interactions at higher speeds. That technology is slowly coming, but there are still some serious challenges ahead. For instance, the sensors that we use in autonomous driving today are not very reliable in bad weather. We've still got a long way to go to reach level 5 autonomy where the car is fully autonomous in all weather conditions. These systems also have to be able to handle the kind of congestion that you find in New York City, and we have to become much better at integrating robot cars with human-driven cars. This is why thinking about mixed human/machine environments is very exciting and very important. Every year we see gradual improvements in the technology but getting to a complete solution, if I was to estimate, could take another decade.

There are, though, specific applications where we will see autonomy used commercially sooner than other applications. I believe that a retirement community could use autonomous shuttles today. I believe that long-distance driving with autonomous trucks is coming soon. It's a little bit simpler than driving in New York, but it's harder than what driving in a retirement community would look like because you have to drive at high speed, and there are a lot of corner cases and situations where maybe a human driver would have to step in. Let's say it's raining torrentially and you are on a treacherous mountain pass in the Rockies. To face that, you need to have a collaboration between a really great sensor and control system, and the human's reasoning and control capabilities. With autonomous driving on highways, we will see patches of autonomy interleaved with human assistance, or vice versa, and that will be sooner than 10 years, for sure, maybe 5.

MARTIN FORD: So in the next decade a lot of these problems would be solved, but not all of them. Maybe the service would be confined to specified routes or areas that are really well mapped?

DANIELA RUS: Well, not necessarily. Progress is happening. In our group we just released a paper that demonstrates one of the first systems capable of driving on country roads. So, on the one hand, the challenges are daunting, but on the other hand, 10 years is a long time. 20 years ago, Mark Weiser, who was the chief scientist at Xerox PARC, talked about pervasive computing and he was seen as a dreamer. Today, we have solutions for all of the situations he envisioned where computing would be used, and how computing would support us.

I want to be a technology optimist. I want to say that I see technology as something that has the huge potential to unite people rather than divide people, and to empower people rather than estrange people. In order to get there, though, we have to advance science and engineering to make technology more capable and more deployable.

We also have to embrace programs that enable broad education and allow people to become familiar with technology to the point where they can take advantage of it and where anyone could dream about how their lives could be better by the use of technology. That's something that's not possible with AI and robotics today because the solutions require expertise that most people don't have. We need to revisit how we educate people to ensure that everyone has the tools and the skills to take advantage of technology. The other thing that we can do is to continue to develop the technology side so that machines begin to adapt to people, rather than the other way around.

MARTIN FORD: In terms of ubiquitous personal robots that can actually do useful things, it seems to me that the limiting factor is really dexterity. The cliché is being able to ask a robot to go to the refrigerator and get you a beer. That's a real challenge in terms of the technology that we have today.

DANIELA RUS: Yes, I think you're right. We do currently see significantly greater successes in navigation than in manipulation, and these are two major types of capabilities for robots. The advances in navigation were enabled by hardware advances. When the LIDAR sensor—the laser scanner—was introduced, all of a sudden, the algorithms that didn't work with sonar started working, and that was transformational. We now had a reliable sensor that control algorithms could use in a robust way. As a result of that, mapping, planning, and localization took off, and that fueled the great enthusiasm in autonomous driving.

Coming back to dexterity, on the hardware side, most of our robot hands still look like they did 50 years ago. Most of our robot hands are still very rigid, industrial manipulators with a two-pronged pincer, and we need something different. I personally believe that we are getting closer because we are beginning to look at reimagining what a robot is. In particular, we have been working on soft robots and soft robot hands. We've shown that with soft robot hands—the kind that we can design and build in my lab—we are able to pick up objects and handle objects much more reliably and much more intuitively than what is possible with traditional two-finger grasps.

It works as follows: if you have a traditional robot hand where the fingers are all made out of metal, then they are capable of what is technically called "hard finger contact"—you put your finger on the object you're trying to grasp at one point, and that's the point at which you can exert forces and torques. If you have that kind of a setup, then you really need to know the precise geometry of the object that you're trying to pick up. You then need to calculate very precisely where to put your fingers on the surface of the object so that all their forces and torques balance out, and they can resist external forces and torques. This is called in technical literature, "the force closure and form closure problem." This problem requires very heavy computation, very precise execution, and very accurate knowledge of the object that you're trying to grasp.

That's not something that humans do when they grasp an object. As an experiment, try to grasp a cup with your fingernails—it is such a difficult task. As a human, you have a perfect knowledge of the object and where it is located, but you will

261

have a difficult time with that. With soft fingers, you actually don't need to know the exact geometry of the object you're trying to grasp because the fingers will comply to whatever the object surface is. Contact along a wider surface area means that you don't have to think precisely about where to place the fingers in order to reliably envelop and lift the object.

That translates into much more capable robots and much simpler algorithms. As a result, I'm very bullish about the future progress in grasping and manipulation. I think that soft hands, and in general, soft robots are going to be a very critical aspect of advancement in dexterity, just like the laser scanner was a critical aspect of advancing the navigation capabilities of robots.

That goes back to my observation that machines are made up of bodies and brains. If you change the body of the machine and you make it more capable, then you will be able to use different types of algorithms to control that robot. I'm very excited about soft robotics, and I'm very excited about the potential for soft robotics to impact an area of robotics that has been stagnant for many years. A lot of progress has been made in grasping and manipulation, but we do not have the kinds of capabilities that compare with those of natural systems, people or animals.

MARTIN FORD: Let's talk about progress in AI toward human-level artificial intelligence or AGI. What does that path look like, and how close are we?

DANIELA RUS: We have been working on AI problems for over 60 years, and if the founders of the field were able to see what we tout as great advances today, they would be very disappointed because it appears we have not made much progress. I don't think that AGI is in the near future for us at all.

I think that there is a great misunderstanding in the popular press about what artificial intelligence is and what it isn't. I think that today, most people who say "AI," actually mean machine learning, and more than that, they mean deep learning within machine learning.

I think that most people who talk about AI today tend to anthropomorphize what these terms mean. Someone who is not an expert says the word "intelligence" and only has one association with intelligence, and that is the intelligence of people.

When people say "machine learning," they imagine that the machine learned just like a human has learned. Yet these terms mean such different things in the technical context. If you think about what machine learning can do today, it's absolutely extraordinary. Machine learning is a process that starts with millions of usually manually labeled data points, and the system aims to learn a pattern that is prevalent in the data, or to make a prediction based on that data.

These systems can do this much better than humans because these systems can assimilate and correlate many more data points then humans are able to. However, when a system learns, for example, that there is a coffee mug in a photograph, what it is actually doing is it's saying that the pixels that form this blob that represents the coffee mug in the current photo are the same as other blobs that humans have labeled in images as coffee mugs. The system has no real idea what that coffee mug represents.

The system has no idea what to do with it, it doesn't know if you drink it, eat it, or if you throw it. If I told you that there is a coffee mug on my desk, you don't need to see that coffee mug in order to know what it is because you have the kind of reasoning and experience that machines today simply do not have.

To me, the gap between this and human-level intelligence is extraordinary, and it will take us a long time to get there. We have no idea of the processes that define our own intelligence, and no idea how our brain works. We have no idea how children work. We know a little bit about the brain, but that amount is insignificant to how much there is to know. The understanding of intelligence is one of the most profound questions in science today. We see progress at the intersection between neuroscience, cognitive science, and computer science.

MARTIN FORD: Is it possible that there might be an extraordinary breakthrough that really moves things along?

DANIELA RUS: That's possible. In our lab, we're very interested in figuring out whether we can make robots that will adapt to people. We started looking at whether we can detect and classify brain activity, which is a challenging problem.

We are mostly able to classify whether a person detects that something is wrong because of the "you are wrong" signal—called the "error-related potential." This is a signal that everyone makes, independent of their native tongue and independent of their circumstances. With the external sensors we have today, which are called EEG caps, we are fairly reliably able to detect the "you are wrong" signal. That's interesting because if we can do that, then we can imagine applications where workers could work side by side with robots, and they could observe the robots from a distance and correct their mistakes when a mistake is detected. In fact, we have a project that addresses this question.

What's interesting, though, is that these EEG caps are made up of 48 electrodes placed on your head—it's a very sparse, mechanical setup that reminds you of when computers were made up of levers. On the other hand, we have the ability to do invasive procedures to tap into neurons at the level of the neural cell, so you could actually stick probes into the human brain, and you could detect neural-level activity very precisely. There's a big gap between what we can do externally and what we can do invasively, and I wonder whether at some point we will have some kind of Moore's law improvement on sensing brain activity and observing brainwave activity at a much higher resolution.

MARTIN FORD: What about the risks and the downsides of all of this technology? One aspect is the potential impact on jobs. Are we looking at a big disruption that could eliminate a lot of work, and is that something we have to think about adapting to?

DANIELA RUS: Absolutely! Jobs are changing: jobs are going away, and jobs are being created. The McKinsey Global Institute published a study that gives some really important views. They looked at a number of professions and observed that there are certain tasks that can be automated with the level of machine capability today, and others that cannot.

If you do an analysis of how people spend time in various professions, there are certain categories of work. People spend time applying expertise; interacting with others; managing; doing data processing; doing data entry; doing predictable physical work; doing unpredictable physical work. Ultimately, there are tasks that can be automated and tasks that can't. The predictable physical work and the data tasks are routine tasks that can be automated with today's technologies, but the other tasks can't.

I'm actually very inspired by this because what I see is that technology can relieve us of routine work in order to give us time to focus on the more interesting parts of our work. Let's go through an example in healthcare. We have an autonomous wheelchair, and we have been talking with physical therapists about using this wheelchair. They are very excited about it because, at the moment, the physical therapist works with patients in the hospital in the following way:

For every new patient, the physical therapist has to go to the patient's bed where they have to put the patient in a wheelchair, push the patient to the gym where they'll work together in the gym and at the end of the hour, the physical therapist has to take the patient back to the patient's hospital bed. A significant amount of time is spent moving the patient around and not on patient care.

Now imagine if the physical therapist didn't have to do this. Imagine if the physical therapist could stay in the gym, and the patient would show up delivered by an autonomous wheelchair. Then both the patient and the physical therapist would have a much better experience. The patient would get more help from the physical therapist, and the physical therapist would focus on applying their expertise. I'm very excited about the possibility of enhancing the quality of time that we spend in our jobs and increasing our efficiency in our jobs.

A second observation is that in general, it is much easier for us to analyze what might go away than to imagine what might come back. For instance, in the 20th century, agricultural employment dropped from 40% to 2% in the United States. Nobody in the 20th century guessed that this would happen. Just consider, then, that only 10 years ago, when the computer industry was booming, nobody predicted the level of employment in social media; in app stores; in cloud computing; and even in other things like college counseling. There are so many jobs that employ a lot of people today that did not exist 10 years ago, and that people did not anticipate would exist. I think that it's exciting to think about the possibilities for the future and the new kinds of jobs that will be created as a result of technology.

MARTIN FORD: So, you think the jobs destroyed by technology and the new jobs created will balance out?

DANIELA RUS: Well, I do also have concerns. One concern is in the quality of jobs. Sometimes, when you introduce technology, the technology levels the playing field. For instance, it used to be that taxi drivers had to have a lot of expertise—they had to have great spatial reasoning, and they had to memorize large maps. With the advent of GPS, that level of skill is no longer needed. What that does is open the field for many more people to join the driving market, and that tends to lower the wages.

Another concern is that I wonder if people are going to be trained well enough for the good jobs that will be created as a result of technology. I think that there are only two ways to approach this challenge. In the short term, we have to figure out how to help people retrain themselves, how to help people gain the skills that are needed in order to fulfill some of the jobs that exist. I can't tell you how many times a day I hear, "We want your AI students. Can you send us any AI students?" Everyone wants experts in artificial intelligence and machine learning, so there are a lot of jobs, and there are also a lot of people who are looking for jobs. However, the skills that are in demand are not necessarily the skills that people have, so we need retraining programs to help people acquire those skills.

I'm a big believer in the fact that actually anybody can learn technology. My favorite example is a company called BitSource. BitSource was launched a couple of years back in Kentucky, and this company is retraining coal miners into data miners and has been a huge success. This company has trained a lot of the miners who lost their jobs and who are now in a position to get much better, much safer and much more enjoyable jobs. It's an example that actually tells us that with the right programs and the right support, we can actually help people in this transition period.

MARTIN FORD: Is that just in terms of retraining workers, or do we need to fundamentally change our entire educational system?

DANIELA RUS: In the 20th century we had reading, writing, and arithmetic that defined literacy. In the 21st century, we should expand what literacy means, and we should add computational thinking. If we teach in schools how to make things and how to breathe life into them by programming, we will empower our students. We can get them to the point where they can imagine anything and make it happen, and they will have the tools to make it happen. More importantly, by the time they finish high school, these students will have the technical skills that will be required in the future, and they will be exposed to a different way of learning that will enable them to help themselves for the future.

The final thing I want to say about the future of work is that our attitude toward learning will also have to change. Today, we operate with a sequential model of learning and working. What I mean by this is that most people spend some chunk of their lives studying and at some point, they say, "OK, we're done studying, now we're going to start working." With technology accelerating and bringing in new types of capabilities, though, I think it's very important to reconsider the sequential approach to learning. We should consider a more parallel approach to learning and working, where we will be open to acquiring new skills and applying those skills as a lifelong learning process.

MARTIN FORD: Some countries are making AI a strategic focus or adopting an explicit industrial policy geared toward AI and robotics. China, in particular, is investing massively in this area. Do you think that there is a race toward advanced AI, and is the US at risk of falling behind?

DANIELA RUS: When I look at what is happening in AI around the world, I think it is amazing. You have China, Canada, France, and the UK, among dozens of others, hugely investing in AI. Many countries are betting their future on AI, and I think we in the US should do too. I think we should consider the potential for AI, and we should increase the support and the funding of AI.

DANIELA RUS *is the Andrew (1956) and Erna Viterbi Professor of Electrical Engineering and Computer Science and Director of the Computer Science and Artificial Intelligence Laboratory (CSAIL) at MIT. Daniela's research interests are in robotics, artificial intelligence, and data science.*

The focus of her work is developing the science and engineering of autonomy, toward the long-term objective of enabling a future with machines pervasively integrated into the fabric of life, supporting people with cognitive and physical tasks. Her research addresses some of the gaps between where robots are today and the promise of pervasive robots: increasing the ability of machines to reason, learn, and adapt to complex tasks in human-centered environments, developing intuitive interfaces between robots and people, and creating the tools for designing and fabricating new robots quickly and efficiently. The applications of this work are broad and include transportation, manufacturing, agriculture, construction, monitoring the environment, underwater exploration, smart cities, medicine, and in-home tasks such as cooking.

Daniela serves as the Associate Director of MIT's Quest for Intelligence Core, and as Director of the Toyota-CSAIL Joint Research Center, whose focus is the advancement of AI research and its applications to intelligent vehicles. She is a member of the Toyota Research Institute advisory board.

Daniela is a Class of 2002 MacArthur Fellow, a fellow of ACM, AAAI and IEEE, and a member of the National Academy of Engineering and the American Academy of Arts and Sciences. She is the recipient of the 2017 Engelberger Robotics Award from the Robotics Industries Association. She earned her PhD in Computer Science from Cornell University.

Daniela has also worked on two collaborative projects with the Pilobolus Dance company at the intersection of technology and art. Seraph, a pastoral story about human-machine friendship, was choreographed in 2010 and performed in 2010-2011 in Boston and New York City. The Umbrella Project, a participatory performance exploring group behavior, was choreographed in 2012 and performed at PopTech 2012, in Cambridge, Baltimore, and Singapore.

DANIELA RUS

> **❝** *Somebody should be thinking about what the regulation of AI should look like. But I think the regulation shouldn't start with the view that its goal is to stop AI and put back the lid on a Pandora's box, or hold back the deployment of these technologies and try and turn the clock back.*

JAMES MANYIKA

CHAIRMAN AND DIRECTOR OF MCKINSEY GLOBAL INSTITUTE

James is a senior partner at McKinsey and Chairman of the McKinsey Global Institute, researching global economic and technology trends. James consults with the chief executives and founders of many of the world's leading technology companies. He leads research on AI and digital technologies and their impact on organizations, work, and the global economy. James was appointed by President Obama as vice chair of the Global Development Council at the White House and by US Commerce Secretaries to the Digital Economy Board and National Innovation Board. He is on the boards of the Oxford Internet Institute, MIT's Initiative on the Digital Economy, the Stanford-based 100-Year Study on AI, and he is a fellow at DeepMind.

MARTIN FORD: I thought we could start by having you trace your academic and career trajectory. I know you came from Zimbabwe. How did you get interested in robotics and artificial intelligence and then end up in your current role at McKinsey?

JAMES MANYIKA: I grew up in a segregated black township in what was then Rhodesia, before it became Zimbabwe. I was always inspired by the idea of science, partly because my father had been the first black Fulbright scholar from Zimbabwe to come to the United States of America in the early 1960s. While there, my father visited NASA at Cape Canaveral, where he watched rockets soar up into the sky. And in my early childhood after he came back from America, my father filled my head with the idea of science, space, and technology. So, I grew up in this segregated township, thinking about science and space, building model planes and machines out of whatever I could find.

When I got to university after the country had become Zimbabwe, my undergraduate degree was in electrical engineering with heavy doses of mathematics and computer science. And while there a visiting researcher from the University of Toronto got me involved in a project on neural networks. That's when I learned about Rumelhart Backpropagation and the use of logisti sigmoid functions in neural network algorithms.

Fast forward, I did well enough to get a Rhodes scholarship to go to Oxford University, where I was in the Programming Research Group, working under Tony Hoare, who is best known for inventing Quicksort and for his obsession with formal methods and axiomatic specifications of programming languages. I studied for a master's degree in mathematics and computer science and worked a lot on mathematical proofs and the development and verification of algorithms. By this time, I'd given up on the idea that I would be an astronaut, but I thought that at least if I worked on robotics and AI, I might get close to science related to space exploration.

I wound up in the Robotics Research Group at Oxford, where they were actually working on AI, but not many people called it that in those days because AI had a negative connotation at the time, after what had recently been a kind of "AI Winter" or a series of winters, where AI had underdelivered on its hype and expectations. So, they called their work everything but AI—it was machine perception, machine learning, it was robotics or just plain neural networks; but no-one in those days was comfortable calling their work AI. Now we have the opposite problem, everyone wants to call everything AI.

JAMES MANYIKA

MARTIN FORD: When was this?

JAMES MANYIKA: This was in 1991, when I started my PhD at the Robotics Research Group at Oxford. This part of my career really opened me to working with a number of different people in the robotics and AI fields. So, I met people like Andrew Blake and Lionel Tarassenko, who were working on neural networks; Michael Brady, now Sir Michael, who was working on machine vision; and I met Hugh Durrant-Whyte, who was working on distributed intelligence and robotic systems. He became my PhD advisor. We built a few autonomous vehicles together and we also wrote a book together drawing on the research and intelligence systems we were developing.

Through the research I was doing, I wound up collaborating with a team at the NASA Jet Propulsion Laboratory that was working on the Mars rover vehicle. NASA was interested in applying the machine perception systems and algorithms that they were developing to the Mars rover vehicle project. I figured that this was as close as I'm ever going to get to go into space!

MARTIN FORD: So, there was actually some code that you wrote running on the rover, on Mars?

JAMES MANYIKA: Yes, I was working with the Man Machine Systems group at JPL in Pasadena, California. I was one of several visiting scientists there working on these machine perception and navigation algorithms, and some of them found their way onto the modular and autonomous vehicle systems and other places.

That period at Oxford in the Robotics Research Group is what really sparked my interest in AI. I found machine perception particularly fascinating: the challenges of how to build learning algorithms for distributed and multi-agent systems, how to use machine learning algorithms to make sense of environments, and how to develop algorithms that could autonomously build models of those environments, in particular, environments where you had no prior knowledge of them and had to learn as you go—like the surface of Mars.

A lot of what I was working on had applications not just in machine vision, but in distributed networks and sensing and sensor fusion. We were building these neural network-based algorithms that were using a combination of Bayesian networks of the kind Judea Pearl had pioneered, Kalman filters and other estimation and prediction algorithms to essentially build machine learning systems. The idea was that these systems could learn from the environment, learn from input data from a wide range of sources of varying quality, and make predictions. They could build maps and gather knowledge of the environments that they were in; and then they might be able to make predictions and decisions, much like intelligent systems would.

So, eventually I met Rodney Brooks, who I'm still friends with today, during my visiting faculty fellowship at MIT, where I was working with the Robotics Group at MIT and the Sea Grant project that was building underwater robots. During this time, I also got to know people like Stuart Russell, who's a professor in robotics and AI at Berkeley, because he had spent time at Oxford in my research group. In fact, many of my colleagues from those days have continued to do pioneering work, people like John Leonard, now a Robotics Professor at MIT and Andrew Zisserman, at DeepMind. Despite the fact that I've wandered off into other areas in business and economics, I've stayed close to the work going on in AI and machine learning and try to keep up as best as I can.

MARTIN FORD: So, you started out with a very technical orientation, given that you were teaching at Oxford?

JAMES MANYIKA: Yes, I was on the faculty and a fellow at Balliol College, Oxford, and I was teaching students courses in mathematics and computer science and as well as on some of the research we were doing in robotics.

MARTIN FORD: It sounds like a pretty unusual jump from there to business and management consulting at McKinsey.

JAMES MANYIKA: That was actually as much by accident as anything else. I'd recently become engaged, and I had also received an offer from McKinsey to join them in Silicon Valley; and I thought it would be a brief, interesting detour, to go to McKinsey.

At the time, like many of my friends and colleagues, such as Bobby Rao, who had also been in the Robotics Research Lab with me, I was interested in building systems that could compete in the DARPA driverless car challenge. This was because a lot of our algorithms were applicable to autonomous vehicles and driverless cars and back then, the DARPA challenge was one of the places where you could apply those algorithms. All of my friends were moving to Silicon Valley then. Bobby was at that time a post-doc at Berkeley working with Stuart Russell and others, and so I thought I should take this McKinsey offer in San Francisco. It was a way to be close to Silicon Valley and to be close to where some of the action, including the DARPA challenge, was taking place.

MARTIN FORD: What is your role now at McKinsey?

JAMES MANYIKA: I've ended up doing two kinds of things. One is working with many of the pioneering technology companies in Silicon Valley, where I have been fortunate to work with and advise many founders and CEOs. The other part, which has grown over time, is leading research at the intersection of technology and its impact on business and the economy. I'm the chairman of the McKinsey Global Institute, where we research not just technology but also macroeconomic and global trends to understand their impact on business and the economy. We are privileged to have amazing academic advisors that include economists who also think a lot about technology's impacts, people like Erik Brynjolffson, Hal Varian, and Mike Spence, the Nobel laureate, and even Bob Solow in the past.

To link this back to AI, we've been looking a lot at disruptive technologies, and tracking the progress of AI, and I've stayed in constant dialogues as well as collaborated with AI friends like Eric Horvitz, Jeff Dean, Demis Hassabis, and Fei-Fei Li, and also learning from legends like Barbara Grosz. While I've tried to stay close to the technology and the science, my MGI colleagues and I have spent more time thinking about and researching the economic and business impacts of these technologies.

MARTIN FORD: I definitely want to delve into the economic and job market impact, but let's begin by talking about AI technology.

You mentioned that you were working on neural networks way back in the 1990s. Over the past few years, there's been this explosion in deep learning. How do you feel about that? Do you see deep learning as the holy grail going forward, or has it been overhyped?

JAMES MANYIKA: We're only just discovering the power of techniques such as deep learning and neural networks in their many forms, as well as other techniques like reinforcement learning and transfer learning. These techniques all still have enormous headroom; we're only just scratching the surface of where they can take us.

Deep learning techniques are helping us solve a huge number of particular problems, whether it's in image and object classification, natural language processing or generative AI, where we predict and create sequences and outputs whether its speech, images, and so forth. We're going to make a lot of progress in what is sometimes called "narrow AI," that is, solving particular areas and problems using these deep learning techniques.

In comparison, we're making slower progress on what is sometimes called "artificial general intelligence" or AGI. While we've made more progress recently than we've done in a long time, I still think progress is going to be much, much slower towards AGI, just because it involves a much more complex and difficult set of questions to answer and will require many more breakthroughs.

We need to figure out how to think about problems like transfer learning, because one of the things that humans do extraordinarily well is being able to learn something, over here, and then to be able to apply that learning in totally new environments or on a previously unencountered problem, over there. There are definitely some exciting new techniques coming up, whether in reinforcement learning or even simulated learning—the kinds of things that AlphaZero has begun to do—where you self-learn and self-create structures, as well start to solve wider and different categories of challenges, in the case of AlphaZero different kinds of games. In another direction the work that Jeff Dean and others at Google Brain are doing using AutoML is really exciting. That's very interesting from the point of helping us start to make progress in machines and neural networks that design themselves. These are just a few examples. One could say all of this progress is nudging us towards AGI. But these are really just small steps; much, much more is needed, there are whole areas of high-level reasoning etc. that we barely know how to tackle. This is why I think AGI is still quite a long way away.

Deep learning is certainly going to help us with narrow AI applications. We're going to see lots and lots and lots and lots of applications that are already being turned into new products and new companies. At the same time, it's worth pointing out that there are still some practical limitations to the use and application of machine learning, and we have pointed this out in some of our MGI work.

MARTIN FORD: Do you have any examples?

JAMES MANYIKA: For example, we know that many of these techniques still largely rely on labelled data, and there's still lots of limitations in terms of the availability of labelled data. Often this means that humans must label underlying data, which can be a sizable and error-prone chore. In fact, some autonomous vehicle companies are hiring hundreds of people to manually annotate hours of video from prototype vehicles to help train the algorithms. There are some new techniques that are emerging to get around the issue of needing labeled data, for example, in-stream supervision pioneered by Eric Horvitz and others; the use of techniques like Generative Adversarial Networks or GANs, which is a semi-supervised technique through which usable data can be generated in a way that reduces the need for datasets that require labeling by humans.

But then we still have a second challenge of needing such large and rich data sets. It is quite interesting that you can more or less identify those areas that are making spectacular progress simply by observing which areas have access to a huge amount of available data. So, it is no surprise that we have made more progress in machine vision than in other applications, because of the huge volume of images and now video being put on the internet every day. Now, there are some good reasons—regulatory, privacy, security, and otherwise—that may limit data availability to some extent. And this can also, in part, explain why different societies are going to experience differential rates of progress on making data available. Countries with large populations, naturally, generate larger volumes of data, and different data use standards may make it easier to access large health data sets, for example, and use that to train algorithms. So, in China you might see more progress in using AI in genomics and "omics" given larger available data sets.

So, data availability is a big deal and may explain why some areas of AI applications take off much faster in some places than others. But we've also got other limitations to deal with, like we still don't have generalized tools in AI and we still don't know how to solve general problems in AI. In fact, one of the fun things, and you may have seen this, is that people are now starting to define new forms of what used to be the Turing test.

MARTIN FORD: A new Turing Test? How would that work?

JAMES MANYIKA: Steve Wozniak, the co-founder of Apple, has actually proposed what he calls the "coffee test" as opposed to Turing tests, which are very narrow in many respects. A coffee test is kind of fun: until you get a system that can enter an average and previously unknown American home and somehow figure out how to make a cup of coffee, we've not solved AGI. The reason why that sounds trivial but at the same time quite profound is because you're solving a large number of unknowable and general problems in order to make that cup of coffee in an unknown home, where you don't know where things are going to be, what type of coffee maker it is or other tools they have, etc. That's very complex generalized problem-solving across numerous categories of problems that the system would have to do. Therefore, it may be that we need Turing tests of that form if you want to test for AGI, and maybe that's where we need to go.

I should point out the other limitation, which is the question of potential issues not so much in the algorithm, but in the data. This is a big question which tends to divide the AI community. One view is the idea that these machines are probably going to be less biased than humans. You can look at multiple examples, such as human judges and bail decisions where using an algorithm could take out many of the inherent human biases, including human fallibility and even time of day biases. Hiring and advancement decisions could be another similar area like this, thinking about Marianne Bertrand and Sendhil Mullainathan's work looking at the difference in calls back received by different racial groups who submitted identical resumes for jobs.

MARTIN FORD: That's something that has come up in a number of the conversations I've had for this book. The hope should be that AI can rise above human biases, but the catch always seems to be that that the data you're using to train the AI system encapsulates human bias, so the algorithm picks it up.

JAMES MANYIKA: Exactly, that's the other view of the bias question that recognizes that the data itself could actually be quite biased, both in its collection, the sampling rates—either through oversampling or undersampling—and what that means systematically, either to different groups of people or different kinds of profiles.

The general bias problem has been shown in quite a spectacular fashion in lending, in policing and criminal justice cases, and so in any dataset that we have want to use, we could have large-scale biases already built it, many likely unintended. Julia

Angwin and her colleagues at ProPublica have highlighted such biases in their work, as has MacArthur Fellow Sendhil Mullainathan and his colleagues. One of the most interesting findings to come out of that work, by the way, is that algorithms may be mathematically unable to satisfy different definitions of fairness at the same time, so deciding how we will define fairness is becoming a very important issue.

I think both views are valid. On the one hand, machine systems can help us overcome human bias and fallibility, and yet on the other hand, they could also introduce potentially larger issues of their own. This is another important limitation we're going to need to work our way through. But here again we are starting to make progress. I am particularly excited about the pioneering work that Silvia Chiappa at DeepMind is doing using counterfactual fairness and causal model approaches to tackle fairness and bias.

MARTIN FORD: That's because the data directly reflects the biases of people, right? If it's collected from people as they're behaving normally, using an online service or something, then the data is going to end up reflecting whatever biases they have.

JAMES MANYIKA: Right, but it can actually be a problem even if individuals aren't necessarily biased. I'll give you an example where you can't actually fault the humans per se, or their own biases, but that instead shows us how our society works in ways that create these challenges. Take the case of policing. We know that, for example, some neighborhoods are more policed than others and by definition, whenever neighborhoods are more policed, there's a lot more data collected about those neighborhoods for algorithms to use.

So, if we take two neighborhoods, one that is highly policed and one that is not— whether deliberately or not—the fact is that the data sampling differences across those two communities will have an impact on the predictions about crime. The actual collection itself may not have shown any bias, but because of oversampling in one neighborhood and undersampling in another, the use of that data could lead to biased predictions.

Another example of undersampling and oversampling can be seen in lending. In this example, it works the other way, where if you have a population that has more available transactions because they're using credit cards and making electronic payments, we have more data about that population. The oversampling there actually helps those populations, because we can make better predictions about them, whereas if you then have an undersampled population, because they're paying in cash and there is little available data, the algorithm could be less accurate for those populations, and as a result, more conservative in choosing to lend, which essentially biases the ultimate decisions. We have this issue too in facial recognitions systems which has been demonstrated in the work of Timnit Gebru, Joy Buolamwini, and others.

It may not be the biases that any human being has in developing the algorithms, but the way in which we've collected the data that the algorithms are trained on that introduces bias.

MARTIN FORD: What about other kinds of risks associated with AI? One issue that's gotten a lot of attention lately is the possibility of existential risk from superintelligence. What do you think are the things we should legitimately worry about?

JAMES MANYIKA: Well, there are lots of things to worry about. I remember a couple of years ago, a group of us, that included many of the AI pioneers and other luminaries, including the likes of Elon Musk and Stuart Russell, met in Puerto Rico to discuss progress in AI as well concerns and areas that needed more attention. The group ended up writing about what some of the issues are, in a paper that was published by Stuart Russell, and what we should worry about, and pointing out where there was not enough attention and research going into analyzing these areas. Since that meeting, the areas to worry about have begun to change a little bit in the last couple of years, but those areas included everything—including things like safety questions.

Here is one example. How do you stop a runaway algorithm? How do you stop a runaway machine that gets out of control? I don't mean in a *Terminator* sense, but even just in the narrow sense of an algorithm that is making wrong interpretations, leading to safety questions, or even simply upsetting people. For this we may need what has been referred to as the Big Red Button, something several research teams are working on DeepMind's work with gridworlds, for example, has demonstrated that many algorithms could theoretically learn how to turn off their own "off-switches".

Another issue is explainability. Here, explainability is a term used to discuss the problem that with neural networks: we don't always know which feature or which dataset influenced the AI decision or prediction, one way or the other. This can make it very hard to explain an AI's decision, to understand why it might be reaching a wrong decision. This can matter a great deal when predictions and decisions have consequential implications that may affect lives for example when AI is used in criminal justice situations or lending applications, as we've discussed. Recently, we've seen new techniques to get at the explainability challenge emerge. One promising technique is the use of Local-Interpretable-Model Agnostic Explanations, or LIME. LIME tries to identify which particular data sets a trained model relies on most to make a prediction. Another promising technique is the use of Generalized Additive Models, or GAMs. These use single feature models additively and therefore limit interactions between features, and so changes in predictions cane be determined as features are added.

Yet another area we should think about more is the "detection problem," which is where we might find it very hard to even detect when there's malicious use of an AI system—which could be anything from a terrorist to a criminal situation. With other weapons systems, like nuclear weapons, we have fairly robust detection systems. It's hard to set off a nuclear explosion in the world without anybody knowing because you have seismic tests, radioactivity monitoring, and other things. With AI systems, not so much, which leads to an important question: How do we even know when an AI system is being deployed?

There are several critical questions like this that still need a fair amount of technical work, where we must make progress, instead of everybody just running away and focusing on the upsides of applications for business and economic benefits.

The silver lining of all this is that groups and entities are emerging and starting to work on many of these challenges. A great example is the Partnership on AI. If you look at the agenda for the Partnership, you'll see a lot of these questions are being examined, about bias, about safety, and about these kinds of existential threat questions. Another great example is the work that Sam Altman, Jack Clarke and others at OpenAI are doing, which aims to make sure all of society benefits from AI.

Right now, the entities and groups that are making the most progress on these questions have tended to be places that have been able to attract the AI superstars, which, even in 2018, tends to be a relatively small group. That will hopefully diffuse over time. We've also seen some relative concentrations of talent go to places that have massive computing power and capacity, as well as places that have unique access to lots of data, because we know these techniques benefit from those resources. The question is, in a world in which there's a tendency for more progress to go to where the superstars are, and where the data is available, and where the computer capacity is available, how do you make sure this continues to be widely available to everybody?

MARTIN FORD: What do you think about the existential concerns? Elon Musk and Nick Bostrom talk about the control problem or the alignment problem. One scenario is where we could have a fast takeoff with recursive improvement, and then we've got a superintelligent machine that gets away from us. Is that something we should be worried about at this point?

JAMES MANYIKA: Yes, somebody should be worrying about those questions—but not everybody, partly because I think the time frame for a super intelligent machine is so far away, and because the probability of that is fairly low. But again, in a Pascal-wager like sense, somebody should be thinking about those questions, but I wouldn't get society all whipped up about the existential questions, at least not yet.

I like the fact that a smart philosopher like Nick Bostrom is thinking about it, I just don't think that it should be a huge concern for society as a whole just yet.

MARTIN FORD: That's also my thinking. If a few think tanks want to focus on these concerns, that seems like a great idea. But it would be hard to justify investing massive governmental resources at this point. And we probably wouldn't want politicians delving into this stuff in any case.

JAMES MANYIKA: No, it shouldn't be a political issue, but I also disagree with people who say that there is zero probability that this could happen and say that no-one should worry about it.

The vast majority of us shouldn't be worried about it. I think that we should be more worried about these more specific questions that are here now, such as safety, use and misuse, explainability, bias, and the economic and workforce effects questions and related transitions. Those are the bigger, more real questions that are going to impact society beginning now and running over the next few decades.

MARTIN FORD: In terms of those concerns, do you think there's a place for regulation? Should governments step in and regulate certain aspects of AI, or should we rely on industry to figure it out for themselves?

JAMES MANYIKA: I don't know what form regulation should take, but somebody should be thinking about regulation in this new environment. I don't think that we've got any of the tools in place, any of the right regulatory frameworks in place at all right now.

So, my simple answer would be yes, somebody should be thinking about what the regulation of AI should look like. But I think the regulation shouldn't start with the view that its goal is to stop AI and put back the lid on a Pandora's box, or hold back the deployment of these technologies and try and turn the clock back.

I think that would be misguided because first of all, the genie is out of the bottle; but also, more importantly, there's enormous societal and economic benefit from these technologies. We can talk more about our overall productivity challenge, which is something these AI systems can help with. We also have societal "moonshot" challenges that AI systems can help with.

So, if regulation is intended to slow things down or stop the development of AI then I think that's wrong, but if regulation is intended to think about questions of safety, questions of privacy, questions of transparency, questions around the wide availability of these techniques so that everybody can benefit from them—then I think those are the right things that AI regulation should be thinking about.

MARTIN FORD: Let's move on to the economic and business aspects of this. I know the McKinsey Global Institute has put out several important reports on the impact of AI on work and labor.

I've written quite a lot on this, and my last book makes the argument that we're really on the leading edge of a major disruption that could have a huge impact on labor markets. What's your view? I know there are quite a few economists who feel this issue is being overhyped.

JAMES MANYIKA: No, it is not overhyped. I think we're on the cusp and we're about to enter a new industrial revolution. I think these technologies are going to have an enormous, transformative and positive impact on businesses, because of their efficiency, their impact on innovation, their impact on being able to make predictions and to find new solutions to problems, and in some case go beyond human cognitive capabilities. The impact of AI on business to me, based on our research at MGI, is for the businesses undoubtedly positive.

The impact on the economy is also going to be quite transformational too, mostly because this is going to lead to productivity gains, and productivity is the engine of economic growth. This will all take place at a time when we're going to have aging and other effects that will create headwinds for economic growth. AI and automation systems, along with other technologies, are going to have this transformational and much-needed effect on productivity, which in the long term leads to economic growth. These systems can also significantly accelerate innovation and R&D, which leads to new products and services and even business models that will transform the economy.

I'm also quite positive about the impact on society in the sense of being able to solve the societal "moonshot" challenges I hinted at before. This could a new project or application that yields new insights into a societal challenge or proposes a radical solution or leads to the development of a breakthrough technology. This could be in healthcare, climate science, humanitarian crises or in discovering new materials. This is another area that my colleagues and I are researching where it's clear that AI techniques from image classification to natural language processing and object identification can make a big contribution in many of these domains.

Having said all of that, if you say AI is good for business, good for economic growth, and helps tackle societal moonshots, then the big question is—what about work? I think this is a much more mixed and complicated story. But I think if I were to summarize my thoughts about jobs, I would say there will be jobs lost, but also jobs gained.

MARTIN FORD: So, you believe the net impact will be positive, even though a lot of jobs will be lost?

JAMES MANYIKA: While there will be jobs lost, there'll also be jobs gained. In the "jobs gained" side of the story, jobs will come from the economic growth itself, and from the resulting dynamism. There's always going to be demand for work, and there are mechanisms, through productivity and economic growth, that lead to the growth of jobs and the creation of new jobs. In addition, there are multiple drivers of demand for work that are relatively assured in the near- to mid-term, these include, again, rising prosperity around the world as more people enter the consuming class and so on. Another thing which will occur is something called "jobs changed," and that's because these technologies are going to complement work in lots of interesting ways, even when we don't fully replace people doing that work.

We've seen versions of these three ideas of jobs lost, jobs gained, and jobs changed before with previous eras of automation. The real debate is, what are the relative magnitudes of all those things, and where do we end up? Are we going to have more jobs lost than jobs gained? That's an interesting debate.

Our research at MGI suggests that we will come out ahead, that there will be more jobs gained than jobs lost; this of course is based on a set of assumptions around a few key factors. Because it's impossible to make predictions, we have developed scenarios around the multiple factors involved, and in our midpoint scenarios we come out ahead. The interesting question is, even in a world with enough jobs, what will be the key workforce issues to grapple with, including the effect on things like wages, and the workforce transitions involved? The jobs and wages picture is more complicated than the effect on business and the economy, in terms of growth, which as I said, is clearly positive.

MARTIN FORD: Before we talk about jobs and wages, let me focus on your first point: the positive impact on business. If I were an economist, I would immediately point out that if you look at the productivity figures recently, they're really not that great—we are not seeing any increases in productivity yet in terms of the macroeconomic data. In fact, productivity has been pretty underwhelming, relative to other periods. Are you arguing that there's just a lag before things will take off?

JAMES MANYIKA: We at MGI recently put out a report on this. There are a lot of reasons why productivity growth is sluggish, one reason being that in the last 10 years we've had the lowest capital intensity period in about 70 years.

We know that capital investment, and capital intensity, are part of the things that you need to drive productivity growth. We also know the critical role of demand—most economists, including here at MGI, have often looked at the supply-side effects of productivity, and not as much at the demand side. We know that when you've got a huge slowdown in demand you can be as efficient as you want in production, and measured productivity still won't be great. That's because the productivity measurement has a numerator and a denominator: the numerator involves growth in value-added output, which requires that output is being soaked up by demand. So, if demand is lagging for whatever reason, that hurts growth in output, which brings down productivity growth, regardless of what technological advances there may have been.

MARTIN FORD: That's an important point. If advancing technology increases inequality and holds down wages, so it effectively takes money out of the pockets of average consumers, then that could dampen down demand further.

JAMES MANYIKA: Oh, absolutely. The demand point is absolutely critical, especially when you've got advanced economies, where anywhere between 55% and 70% of the demand in those economies is driven by consumer and household spending. You need people earning enough to be able to consume the output of everything being produced. Demand is a big part of the story, but I think there is also the technology lag story that you mentioned.

To your original question, I had the pleasure between 1999 and 2003 to work with one of the academic advisors of the McKinsey Global Institute, Bob Solow, the Nobel laureate. We were looking at the last productivity paradox back in the late 1990s. In the late '80s, Bob had made the observation that became known as The Solow Paradox, that you could see computers everywhere except in the productivity numbers. That paradox was finally resolved in the late '90s, when we had enough demand to drive productivity growth, but more importantly, when we had very large sectors of the economy—retail, wholesale, and others—finally adopting the technologies of the day: client-server architectures, ERP systems. This transformed their business processes and drove productivity growth in very large sectors in the economy, which finally had a big enough effect to move the national productivity needle.

Now if you fast-forward to where we are today, we may be seeing something similar in the sense that if you look at the current wave of digital technologies, whether we're talking about cloud computing, e-commerce, or electronic payments, we can see them everywhere, we all carry them in our pockets, and yet productivity growth has been very sluggish for several years now. But if you actually systematically measure how digitized the economy is today, looking at the current wave of digital technologies, the surprising answer is: not so much, actually, in terms of assets, processes, and how people work with technology. And we are not even talking about AI yet or the next wave of technologies with these assessments of digitization.

What you find is that the most digitized sectors—on a relative basis—are sectors like the tech sector itself, media and maybe financial services. And those sectors are actually relatively small in the grand scheme of things, measuring as a share of GDP or as a share of employment, whereas the very large sectors are, relatively speaking, not that digitized.

Take a sector like retail and keep in mind that retail is one of the largest sectors. We all get excited by the prospect of e-commerce and what Amazon is doing. But the amount of retail that is now done through e-commerce is only about 10%, and Amazon is a large portion of that 10%. But retail is a very large sector with many, many small- and medium-sized businesses. That already tells you that even in retail, one of the large sectors which we'd think of as highly digitized, in reality, it turns out we really haven't yet made much widespread progress yet.

So, we may be going through another round of the Solow paradox. Until we get these very large sectors highly digitized and using these technologies across business processes, we won't see enough to move the national needle on productivity.

MARTIN FORD: So, you're saying that globally we haven't even started to see to the impact of AI and advanced forms of automation yet?

JAMES MANYIKA: Not yet. And that gets to another point worth making: we're actually going to need productivity growth even more than we can imagine, and AI, automation and all these digital technologies are going to be critical to driving productivity growth and economic growth.

To explain why, let's look at the last 50 years of economic growth, and you look at that for the G20 countries (which make up a little more than 90% of global GDP), the average economic GDP growth over the last 50 years where we have the data, so between 1964 and 2014, was 3.5%. This was the average GDP growth across those countries. If you do classic growth decomposition and growth accounting work, it shows that GDP and economic growth comes from two things: one is productivity growth, and the other is expansions in the labor supply.

Of the 3.5% of average GDP growth we've had in the last 50 years, 1.7% has come from expansions in the labor supply, and the other 1.8% has come from productivity growth over those 50 years. If you look to the next 50 years, the growth from expansions in the labor supply is going to come crashing down from the 1.7% that it's been the last 50 years to about 0.3%, because of aging and other demographic effects.

So that means that in the next 50 years we're going to rely even more than we have in the past 50 years on productivity growth. And unless we get big gains in productivity, we're going to have a downdraft in economic growth. If we think productivity growth matters right now for our current growth, which it does, it's going to matter even more for the next 50 years if we still want economic growth and prosperity.

MARTIN FORD: This is kind of touching on the economist Robert Gordon's argument that may be there's not going to be much economic growth in the future.[1]

JAMES MANYIKA: While Bob Gordon's saying there may not be economic growth, he's also questioning whether we're going to have big enough innovations, comparable to electrification and other things like that, to really drive economic growth. He's skeptical that there's going to be anything as big as electricity and some of the other technologies of the past.

MARTIN FORD: But hopefully AI is going to be that next thing?

JAMES MANYIKA: We hope it will be! It is certainly a general-purpose technology like electricity, and in that sense should benefit multiple activities and sectors of the economy.

MARTIN FORD: I want to talk more about The McKinsey Global Institute's reports on what's happening to work and wages. Could you go into a bit more detail about the various reports you've generated and your overall findings? What methodology do you use to figure out if a particular job is likely to be automated and what percentage of jobs are at risk?

---

1 Robert Gordon's 2017 book The Rise and Fall of American Growth, offers a very pessimistic view of future economic growth in the United States.

JAMES MANYIKA: Let's take this in three parts: "jobs lost," "jobs changed," and then "jobs gained," because there's something to be said about each of these pathways.

In terms of "jobs lost," there's been lots of research and reports, and it's become a cottage industry speculating on the jobs question. At MGI the approach we've taken we think is a little bit different in two ways. One is that we've conducted a task-based decomposition, and so we've started with tasks, as opposed to starting with whole occupations. We've looked at something like over 2,000 tasks and activities using a variety of sources, including the O*NET dataset, and other datasets that we've got by looking at tasks. Then, the Bureau of Labor Statistics in the US tracks about 800 occupations; so, we mapped those tasks into the actual occupations.

We've also looked at 18 different kinds of capabilities required to perform these tasks, and by capabilities, I'm talking everything from cognitive capabilities to sensory capabilities, to physical motor skills that are required to fulfill these tasks. We've then tried to understand to what extent technologies are now available to automate and perform those same capabilities, which then we can map back to our tasks and show what tasks machines can perform. We've looked at what we've called "currently demonstrated technology," and what we're distinguishing there is technology that has actually been demonstrated, either in a lab or in an actual product, not just something that's hypothetical. By looking at these "currently demonstrated technologies," we can provide a view into the next decade and a half or so, given typical adoption and diffusion rates.

By looking at all this, we have concluded that on a task level in the US economy, roughly about 50% of activities—not jobs, but tasks, and it's important to emphasize this—that people do now are, in principle, automatable.

MARTIN FORD: You're saying that half of what workers do could conceivably be automated right now, based on technology we already have?

JAMES MANYIKA: Right now, it is technically feasible to automate 50% of activities based on currently demonstrated technologies. But there are also separate questions, like how do those automatable activities then map into whole occupations?

So, when we then map back into occupations, we actually find that only about 10% of occupations have more than 90% of their constituent tasks automatable.

Remember this is a task number, not a jobs number. We also find that something like 60% of occupations have about a third of their constituent activities automatable—this mix of course varies by occupation. This 60-30 already tells you that many more occupations will be complemented or augmented by technologies than will be replaced. This leads to the "jobs changed" phenomena I mentioned earlier.

MARTIN FORD: I recall that when your report was published, the press put a very positive spin on it—suggesting that since only a portion of most jobs will be impacted, we don't need to worry about job losses. But if you had three workers, and a third of each of their work was automated, couldn't that lead to consolidation, where those three workers become two workers?

JAMES MANYIKA: Absolutely, that's where I was going to go next. This is a task composition argument. It might give you modest numbers initially, but then you start to realize that work could be reconfigured in lots of interesting ways.

For instance, you can combine and consolidate. Maybe the tipping point is not that you need all of the tasks in an occupation to be automatable; rather, maybe when you get close to say, 70% of the tasks being automatable, you may then say, "Let's just consolidate and reorganize the work and workflow altogether." So, the initial math may begin with modest numbers, but when you reorganize and consolidate the work, the number of impacted jobs start to get bigger.

However, there is yet another set of considerations that we've looked at in our research at MGI which we think have been missing in some of the other assessments on the automation question. Everything that we have described so far is simply asking the technical feasibility question, which gives you those 50% numbers, but that is really only the first of about five questions you need to ask.

The second question is around the cost of developing and deploying those technologies. Obviously, just because something's technically feasible, doesn't mean it will happen.

Look at electric cars. It's been demonstrated we could build electric cars, and in fact that was a feasible thing to do more than 50 years ago, but when did they actually show up? When the costs of buying it, maintaining it, charging it, etc., became reasonable enough that consumers wanted to buy them and companies want to deploy them. That's only happened very recently.

So, the cost of deployment is clearly an important consideration and will vary a lot, depending on whether you're talking about systems that are replacing physical work, versus systems that are replacing cognitive work. Typically, when you're replacing cognitive work, it's mostly software and a standard computing platform, so the marginal cost economics can come down pretty fast, so that doesn't cost very much.

If you're replacing physical work, on the other hand, then you need to build a physical machine with moving parts; and the economics of those things, while they'll come down, they're not going to come down as fast as where things are just software. So, the cost of deployment is the second important consideration, which then starts to slow down deployment rates that might initially be suggested by simply looking at technical feasibility.

The third consideration is labor-market demand dynamics, taking into account labor quality and quantity, as well as the wages associated with that. Let me illustrate this by thinking in terms of two different kinds of jobs. We'll look at an accountant, and we'll look at a gardener. First let's see how these considerations could play out in these occupations.

First, it is technically easier to automate large portions of what the accountant does, mostly data analysis, data gathering, and so forth, whereas it's still technically harder to automate what a gardener does, which is mostly physical work in a highly unstructured environment. Things in these kinds of environments aren't quite lined up exactly where you want them to be—as they would be in a factory, for example, and there's unforeseen obstacles that can be in the way. So, the degree of technical difficulty of automating those tasks, our first question, is already far higher than your accountant.

Then we get to the second consideration: the cost of deploying the system, which goes back to the argument I just made. In the case of the accountant, this requires software with near zero-marginal cost economics running on a standard computing platform. With the gardener, it's a physical machine with many moving parts. The cost economics of deploying a physical machine is always going to be—even as costs come down, and they are coming down for robotic machines—more expensive than the software to automate an accountant.

Now to our third key consideration, that is the quantity and quality of labor, and the wage dynamics. Here again it favors an automating the accountant, rather than automating the gardener. Why? Because we pay a gardener, on average in the United States, something like $8 an hour; whereas we pay an accountant something like $30 an hour. The incentive to automate the accountant is already far higher than the incentive to automate the gardener. As we work our way through this, we start to realize that it may very well be that some of these low-wage jobs may actually be harder to automate, from both a technical and economic perspective.

MARTIN FORD: This sounds like really bad news for university graduates.

JAMES MANYIKA: Not so fast. Often the distinction that's made is high wage versus low wage; or high skill versus low skill. But I really don't know if that's a useful distinction.

The point I want to make is that the activities likely to be automated don't line up neatly with traditional conceptions of wages structures or skills requirements. If the work that's being done looks like mostly data collection, data analysis, or physical work in a highly structured environment, then much of that work is likely to be automated, whether it's traditionally been high wage or low wage, high skill or low skill. On the other hand, activities that are very difficult to automate also cut across wage structures and skills requirements, including tasks that require judgment or managing people, or physical work in highly unstructured and unexpected environments. So many traditionally low wage and high wage jobs are exposed to automation, depending on the activities, but also many other traditionally low wage and high wages jobs may be protected from automation.

I want to make sure we cover all the different factors at play here, as well. The fourth key consideration has to do with benefits including and beyond labor substitution. There are going to be some areas where you're automating, but it's not because you're trying to save money on labor, it is because you're actually getting a better result or even a superhuman outcome. Those are places where you're getting better perception or predictions that you couldn't get with human capabilities. Eventually, autonomous vehicles will likely be an example of this, once they reach the point where they are safer and commit fewer errors than humans driving. When you start to go beyond human capabilities and see performance improvements, that can really speed up the business case for deployment and adoption.

The fifth consideration could be called societal norms, which is a broad term for the potential regulatory factors and societal acceptance factors we may encounter.

A great example of this can be seen in driverless vehicles. Today, we already fully accept the fact that most commercial planes are only being piloted by an actual pilot less than 7% of the time. The rest of the time, the plane is flying itself. The reason no-one really cares about the pilot situation, even if it goes down to 1%, is because no-one can see inside the cockpit. The door is closed, and we're sitting on a plane. We know there's a pilot in there, but whether we know that they're flying or not doesn't matter because we can't see. Whereas with a driverless car, what often freaks people out is the fact that you can actually look in the driver's seat and there's no-one there; the car's moving on its own.

There's a lot of research going on now looking at people's social acceptance or comfort with interacting with machines. Places like MIT are looking at social acceptance across different age groups, across different social settings, and across different countries. For example, in places like Japan, having a physical machine in a social environment is a bit more acceptable than in some other countries. We also know that, for example, different age groups are more or less accepting of machines, and it can vary depending on different environments or settings. If we move to a medical setting, with a doctor who goes into the back room to use a machine, out of view, and then just comes back with your diagnosis—is that okay? Most of us would accept that situation, because we don't actually know what happened in the back room with the doctor. But if a screen wheels into your room and a diagnosis just pops up without a human there to talk you through it, would we be comfortable with that? Most of us probably wouldn't be. So, we know that social settings affect social acceptance, and that this is going to also affect where see these technologies adopted and applied in the future.

MARTIN FORD: But at the end of the day, what does this mean for jobs across the board?

JAMES MANYIKA: Well, the point is that as you work your way through these five key considerations, you start to realize that the pace and extent of automation, and indeed the scope of the jobs that are going to decline, is actually a more deeply nuanced picture that's likely to vary from occupation to occupation and place to place.

In our last report at MGI, which considered the factors I just described, and in particular considered wages, costs and feasibility, we developed a number of scenarios. Our midpoint scenario suggests that as many as 400 million jobs could be lost globally by 2030. This is an alarmingly large number, but as a share of the global labor force that is about 15%. It will be higher, though, in advanced countries than in developing countries, given labor-market dynamics, especially wages, that we've been discussing.

However, all these scenarios are obviously contingent on whether the technology accelerates even faster, which it could. If it did, then our assumption about "currently demonstrated technology" would be out of the window. Further, if the costs of deploying come down even faster than we anticipate, that would also change things. That's why we've got these wide ranges in the scenarios that we've actually built for how many jobs would be lost.

MARTIN FORD: What about the "jobs gained" aspect?

JAMES MANYIKA: The "jobs gained" side of things is interesting because we know that whenever there's a growing and dynamic economy, there will be growth in jobs and demand for work. This has been the history of economic growth for the last 200 years, where you've got vibrant, growing economies with a dynamic private sector.

If we look ahead to the next 20 years or so, there are some relatively assured drivers of demand for work. One of them is rising global prosperity as more people around the work enter the consuming class and demand products and services. Another is aging; and we know that aging is going to create a lot of demand for certain kinds of work that will lead to growth in a whole host of jobs and occupations. Now there's a separate question as to whether those will turn into well-paying jobs or not, but we know that the demand for care work and other things is going to go up.

At MGI we've also looked at other catalysts, like whether we're going to ramp up adaptation for climate change, retrofitting our systems and our infrastructure—which could drive demand for work above and beyond current course and speed. We also know that if societies like the United States and others finally get their act together to look at infrastructure growth, and make investments in infrastructure, then that's also going to drive demand for work. So, one place where work's going to come from is a growing economy and these specific drivers of demand for work.

Another whole set of jobs are going to come from the fact that we're actually going to invent new occupations that didn't previously exist. One of the fun analyses we did at MGI—and this was prompted by one of our academic advisors, Dick Cooper at Harvard—was to look at the Bureau of Labor Statistics. This typically tracks about 800 occupations, and there's always a line at the bottom called "Other." This bucket of occupations called "Other" typically reflects occupations that in the current measurement period have not yet been defined and didn't exist, so the Bureau doesn't have a category for them. Now, if you had looked at the Labor Statistics list in 1995, a web designer would have been in the "Other" category because it hadn't been imagined previously, and so it hadn't been classified. What's interesting is that the "Other" category is the fastest-growing occupational category because we're constantly inventing occupations that didn't exist before.

MARTIN FORD: This is an argument that I hear pretty often. For example, just 10-years ago, jobs that involve social media did not exist.

JAMES MANYIKA: Exactly! If you look at 10-year periods in the United States, at least 8% to 9% of jobs are jobs that didn't exist in the prior period—because we've created them and invented them. That's going to be another source of jobs, and we can't even imagine what those will be, but we know they'll be there. Some people have speculated that category will include new types of designers, and people who trouble shoot and manage machines and robots. This undefined, new set of jobs will be another driver of work.

When we've looked at the kind of the jobs gained, and considered these different dynamics, then unless the economy tanks and there's massive stagnation, the numbers of jobs gained are large enough to more than make up for the jobs lost. Unless, of course, some of variables change catastrophically underneath us, such as a significant acceleration in the development and adoption of these technologies, or we end up with massive economic stagnation. Any combination of those things and then yes, we'll end up with more jobs lost than jobs gained.

MARTIN FORD: Ok, but if you look at the employment statistics, aren't most workers employed in pretty traditional areas, such as cashiers, truck drivers, nurses, teachers, doctors or office workers? These are all job categories that were here 100 years ago, and that's still where the vast majority of the workforce is employed.

JAMES MANYIKA: Yes, the economy is still made up of a large chunk of those occupations. While some of these will decline, few will disappear entirely and certainly not as quickly as some are predicting. Actually, one of the things that we've looked at is where, over the last 200 years, we've seen the most massive job declines. For example, we studied what happened to manufacturing in the United States, and the shift from agriculture to industrialization. We looked at 20 different massive job declines in different countries and what happened in each, compared to the range of scenarios for job declines due to automation and AI. It turned out the ranges that we anticipate now are not out of the norm, at least in the next 20 years anyway. Now beyond that, who knows? Even with some very extreme assumptions, we're still well within the ranges of shifts that we have seen historically.

The big question, at least in the next 20 or so years, is whether there will be enough work for everybody. As we discussed, at MGI we conclude there will be enough work for everybody, unless we get to those very extreme assumptions. The other important question we must ask ourselves is how big are the scale of transitions that we'll see between those occupations that are declining, and those occupations that are be growing? What level of movement will we see from one occupation to another, and how much will the workplace need to adjust and adapt to machines complementing people as opposed to people losing their jobs?

Based on our research, we're not convinced that on our current course and speed we're well set up to manage those transitions in terms of skilling, educating, and on-the-job training. We actually worry more about that question of transition than about the "Will there be enough work?" question.

MARTIN FORD: So, there really is the potential for a severe skill mismatch scenario going forward?

JAMES MANYIKA: Yes, skill mismatches is a big one. Sectoral and occupation changes, where people have to move from one occupation to another, and adapt to higher or lower skill, or just different skills.

When you look at the transition in terms of sectoral and geographic locational questions, say in the United States, there will be enough work, but then you go down to the next level to look at the likely locations for that work, and you see the potential for geographic locational mismatches, where some places look like they'll be more in a hole than other places. These kinds of transitions are quite substantial, and it's not quite clear if we're ready for them.

The impact on wages is another important question. If you look at the likely occupational shifts, so many of the occupations that are likely to decline have tended to be the middle-wage occupations like accountants. Many well-paying occupations have involved data analysis in one form or another. They have also involved physical work in highly structured environments, like manufacturing. And so that's where many of the occupations that are going to decline sit on the wage spectrum. Whereas many of the occupations that are going to grow—like the care work we just talked about—are occupations that, at today's current wage structures, don't pay as well. These occupational mix shifts will likely cause a serious wage issue. We will need to either change the market mechanisms for how these wage dynamics work or develop some other mechanisms that shape the way these wages are structured.

The other reason to worry about the wage question comes from a deeper examination of the narrative that many of us as technologists have been saying so far. When we say, "No, don't worry about it. We're not going to replace jobs, machines are going to complement what people do," I think this is true, our own MGI analysis suggests that 60% of occupations will only have about a third of their activities automated by machines, which means people will be working alongside machines.

But if we examine this phenomenon with wages in mind, it's not so clear-cut because we know that when people are complemented by machines, you can have a range of outcomes. We know that, for example, if a highly skilled worker is complemented by a machine, and the machine does what it does best, and the human is still doing highly value-added work to complement the machine, that's great. The wages for that work are probably going to go up, productivity will go up and it'll all work out wonderfully well all round, which is a great outcome.

However, we could also have the other end of the spectrum, where if the person's being complemented by a machine—even if the machine is only 30% of the work, but the machine is doing all the value-added portion of that work—then what's left over for the human being is deskilled or less complex. That can lead to lower wages because now many more people can do those tasks that previously required specialized skills, or required a certification. That means that what you've done by introducing machines into that occupation could potentially put pressure on wages in that occupation.

297

This idea of complementing work has this wide range of potential outcomes, and we tend just to celebrate the one end of the result spectrum, and not talk as much about the other, deskilled, end of the spectrum. This by the way also increases the challenge of reskilling on an ongoing basis as people work alongside ever evolving and increasingly capable machines.

MARTIN FORD: A good example of that is the impact of GPS on London taxi drivers.

JAMES MANYIKA: Yes, that's a great example of where the labor-supplied limiting portion was really "the Knowledge" of all the streets and shortcuts in the minds of the London taxi drivers. When you devalue that skill because of GPS systems, what's left over is just the driving, and many more people can drive and get you from A to B.

Another example here, in an old form of deskilling, is to think about call center operators. It used to be that your call center person actually had to know what they were talking about often at a technical level in order to be helpful to you. Today, however, organizations embedded that knowledge into the script that they read. What's left over for the most part is just someone who can read a script. They don't really need to know the technical details, at least not as much as before; they just need to be able to follow and read the script, unless they get to a real corner case, where they can escalate to a deep expert.

There are many examples of service work and service technician work, whether it's through the call center, or even people physically showing up to done on-site repairs, where some portions of that work are going through this massive deskilling—because the knowledge is embedded in either technology, or scripts, or some other way to encapsulate the knowledge required to solve the problem. In the end, what's left over is something much more deskilled.

MARTIN FORD: So, it sounds like overall, you're more concerned about the impact on wages than outright unemployment?

JAMES MANYIKA: Of course you always worry about unemployment, because you can always have this corner-case scenario that could play out, which results in a game over for us as far as employment is concerned. But I worry more about these workforce transition issues, such as skills shifts, occupational shifts and how will we support people through these transitions.

I also worry about the wage effects, unless we evolve how we value work in our labor markets. In a sense this problem has been around for a while. We all say that we value people who look after our children, and we value teachers; but we've never quite reflected that in the wage structure for those occupations, and this discrepancy could soon get much bigger, because many of the occupations that are likely to grow are going to look like that.

MARTIN FORD: As you noted earlier, that can feed back into the consumer-demand problem, which in itself dampens down productivity and growth.

JAMES MANYIKA: Absolutely. That would create a vicious cycle that further hurts demand for work. And we need to move quickly. The reason why the reskilling and on-the-job training portions are a really important thing is, first of all, because those skills are changing pretty rapidly, and people are going to need to adapt pretty rapidly.

We already have a problem. We have pointed this out in our research that if you look across most advanced economies at how much these countries spend on on-the-job training, the level of on-the-job training has been declining in the last 20 to 30 years. Given that on-the-job training is going to be a big deal in near the future, this is a real issue.

The other measure you can also look at is what is typically called "active labor-market supports." These are things that are separate from on-the-job training and are instead the kind of support you provide workers when they're being displaced, as they transition from one occupation to another. This is one of the things I think we screwed up in the last round of globalization.

With globalization, one can argue all day along about how globalization was great for productivity, economic growth, for consumer choice, and for products. All true, except when you look at the question of globalization through the worker lens; then it's problematic. The thing that didn't happen effectively was providing support for the workers who were displaced. Even though we know the pain of globalization was highly localized in specific places and sectors, they were still significant enough and really affected many real people and communities. If you and your 9 friends worked in apparel manufacturing in the US in 2000, a decade later only 3 of those jobs still exist, and the same is true if you and your 9 friends worked in a textile mill. Take Webster County in Mississippi where one third of jobs were lost due to what happened to apparel manufacturing, which was a major part of that community. We can say this will probably work out at an overall level, but that isn't very comforting if you're one of the workers in these particularly hard-hit communities.

If we say that we're going to need to support both workers who have been, and those who are going to be, dislocated through these work transitions and will need to go from one job to another, or one occupation to another, or one skill-set to another, then we're starting from behind. So, the worker transition challenges are a really big deal.

MARTIN FORD: You're making the point that we're going to need to support workers, whether they're unemployed or they're transitioning. Do you think a universal basic income is potentially a good idea for doing that?

JAMES MANYIKA: I'm conflicted about the idea of universal basic income in the following sense. I like the fact that we're discussing it, because it's an acknowledgment that we may have a wage and income issue, and it's provoking a debate in the world.

My issue with it is that I think it misses the wider role that work plays. Work is a complicated thing because while work provides income, it also does a whole bunch of other stuff. It provides meaning, dignity, self-respect, purpose, community and social effects, and more. By going to a UBI-based society, while that may solve the wage question, it won't necessarily solve these other aspects of what work brings. And, I think we should remember that there will still be lots of work to be done.

One of the quotes that really sticks with me and I find quite fascinating is from President Lyndon B. Johnson's Blue-Ribbon Commission on "Technology, Automation, and Economic Progress," which incidentally included Bob Solow. One of the report's conclusions is that "The basic fact is that technology eliminates jobs, not work."

MARTIN FORD: There's always work to be done, but it might not be valued by the labor market.

JAMES MANYIKA: It doesn't always show up in our labor markets. Just think about care work, which in most societies tends to be done by women and is often unpaid. How do we reflect the value of that care work in our labor markets and discussions on wages and incomes? The work will be there. It's just whether it's paid work, or recognized as work, and compensated in that way.

I like the fact that UBI is provoking the conversation about wages and income, but I'm not sure it solves the work question as effectively as other things might do. I prefer to consider concepts like conditional transfers, or some other way to make sure that we are linking wages to some kind of activity that reflects initiative, purpose, dignity, and other important factors. These questions of purpose, meaning and dignity may in the end be what defines us.

JAMES MANYIKA *is a senior partner at McKinsey & Company and chairman of the McKinsey Global Institute (MGI). James also serves on McKinsey's Board of Directors. Based in Silicon Valley for over 20 years, James has worked with the chief executives and founders of many of the world's leading technology companies on a variety of issues. At MGI, James has led research on technology, the digital economy, as well as growth, productivity, and globalization. He has published a book on AI and robotics, another on global economic trends as well as numerous articles and reports that have appeared in business media and academic journals.*

James was appointed by President Obama as vice chair of the Global Development Council at the White House (2012-16) and by Commerce Secretaries to the US Commerce Department's Digital Economy Board of Advisors and the National Innovation Advisory Board. He serves on the boards of the Council on Foreign Relations, John D. and Catherine T. MacArthur Foundation, Hewlett Foundation, and Markle Foundation.

He also serves on academic advisory boards including the Oxford Internet Institute, MIT's Initiative on the Digital Economy. He is on the standing committee for the Stanford-based 100 Year Study on Artificial Intelligence, a member of the AIIndex.org team, and a fellow at DeepMind.

James was on the engineering faculty at Oxford University and a member of the Programming Research Group and the Robotics Research Lab, a fellow of Balliol College, Oxford, a visiting scientist at NASA Jet Propulsion Labs, and a faculty exchange fellow at MIT. A Rhodes Scholar, James received his DPhil, MSc, and MA from Oxford in Robotics, Mathematics, and Computer Science, and a BSc in electrical engineering from University of Zimbabwe as an Anglo-American scholar.

JAMES MANYIKA

> **“** It's not clear to me that you get to the accuracy levels you need for driving in Manhattan simply by adding more data to these big data-driven systems. You might get to 99.99% accuracy, but if you do the numbers on that, that's much worse than humans.

GARY MARCUS

FOUNDER AND CEO, GEOMETRIC INTELLIGENCE (ACQUIRED BY UBER)
PROFESSOR OF PSYCHOLOGY AND NEURAL SCIENCE, NYU

Gary Marcus was Founder and CEO of Geometric Intelligence, a machine learning company acquired by Uber, and is a professor of psychology and neural science at New York University, as well as the author and editor of several books, including The Future of the Brain *and the bestseller* Guitar Zero. *Much of Gary's research has focused on understanding how children learn and assimilate language. His current work is on how insights from the human mind can inform the field of artificial intelligence.*

MARTIN FORD: You wrote a book, *Kluge*, about how the brain is an imperfect organ; presumably, then, you don't think the route to AGI is to try to perfectly copy the human brain?

GARY MARCUS: No, we don't need to replicate the human brain and all of its inefficiencies. There are some things that people do much better than current machines, and you want to learn from those, but there are lots of things you don't want to copy.

I'm not committed to how much like a person an AGI system will look. However, humans are currently the only system that we know of that can make inferences and plans over very broad ranges of data and discuss them in a very efficient way, so it pays to look into how people are doing that.

The first book that I wrote, published in 2001, was titled *The Algebraic Mind*, and it compared neural networks with humans. I explored what it would take to make neural networks better, and I think those arguments are still very relevant today.

The next book I wrote was called *The Birth of the Mind*, and was about understanding how genes can build the innate structures in our mind. It comes from the Noam Chomsky and Steven Pinker tradition of believing that there are important things built into the mind. In the book, I tried to understand what innateness might mean in terms of molecular biology and developmental neuroscience. Again, I think the ideas there are quite relevant today.

In 2008 I published *Kluge: The Haphazard Evolution of the Human Mind*. For those who may not know, "kluge" is an old engineer's term for a clumsy solution to a problem. In that book, I argued that in many ways the human mind was actually something like that. I examined discussions about whether humans are optimal—to which I think they're clearly not—and tried to understand from an evolutionary perspective why we're not optimal.

MARTIN FORD: That's because evolution has to work from an existing framework and build from there, right? It can't go back and redesign everything from scratch.

GARY MARCUS: Exactly. A lot of the book was about our memory structure, and how that compares to other systems. For example, when you compare our auditory systems to what's theoretically possible, we come very close to optimal. If you compare our eyes to the theoretical optimum, we're again close—given the right conditions, you can see a single photon of light, and that's amazing. Our memory, however, is not optimal.

You could very quickly upload the complete works of Shakespeare to a computer, or in fact, most of what's been written ever, and a computer won't forget any of it. Our memories are nowhere near theoretically optimal in terms of their capacity or in terms of the stability of the memory that you store. Our memories tend to blur together over time. If you park in the same space every day you can't remember where you parked today, because you can't keep today's memory distinct from yesterday's memory. A computer would never have trouble with that.

The argument I made in the book was that we could examine and understand why humanity had such crummy memories, in terms of what our ancestors needed from their memory. It was mostly broad statistical summaries like: "there's more food up the mountain than down the mountain." I don't need to remember what individual days I derived those memory traces from, I just need the general trend that it's more fertile up the mountain as opposed to down the mountain.

Vertebrates evolved that kind of memory—instead of what computers use, which is a location-addressable memory where every single location in the memory is assigned to a particular stable function. That's what allows you to store essentially infinite information on a computer without having the problem of blurring things together. Humans went down a different path in the evolutionary chain, and it would be very costly in terms of the number of genes that we would need to change in order to just rebuild the system from scratch around location-addressable memory.

It's actually possible to build hybrids. Google is a hybrid, as it has location-addressable memory underneath and then cue-addressable memory, which is what we have, on top. That's a much better system. Google can take reminder cues as we can, but then it has a master map of where everything is, so it serves up the right answer instead of arbitrarily distorting the answer.

MARTIN FORD: Could you explain that in more detail?

GARY MARCUS: Cue-addressable memory is where memories are triggered or aided by other factors. There are crazy versions of this like posture-dependent memory. This is where if you learned something standing up then you'll remember it better if you try to recall it standing up than if you're lying down. The most notorious one is state-dependent memory. For example, if you study for an exam while you're stoned, you might actually be better off being stoned when you take the exam. I don't suggest doing that...the point is that the state and the cues around you influence what you remember.

On the other hand, you can't say, "I want memory location 317" or "the thing I learned on March 17, 1997." As a human, you can't pull things out the way a computer could. A computer has these indexes that are actually like a set of post-office boxes, and what is put in box number 972 stays there indefinitely, unless you deliberately tamper with it.

It doesn't even appear that our brain has a handle on this. The brain does not have an internal addressing system to know where individual memories are stored. Instead, it seems like the brain does something more like an auction. It says, "Is there anything out there that can give me information about what I should be doing in a car on a sunny day?" What you get back is a set of relevant memories without knowing, at least consciously, where they are physically stored in the brain.

The problem is sometimes they blur together, and that leads for example, to problems with eyewitness testimonies. You can't actually keep the state of what happened at a particular moment, separate from what you thought about later, or what you saw on television or read in the newspaper. All these things blur together because they're not distinctly stored.

MARTIN FORD: That's interesting.

GARY MARCUS: The first central claim of my book *Kluge* was that there are basically two kinds of memory and that humans got stuck with the one that's less useful. I further argued that once we have that in our evolutionary history, it becomes astonishingly unlikely that you're going to start from scratch, so you just build on top of that. This is like Stephen Jay Gould's famous arguments about the panda's thumb.

Once you have that kind of memory, other things come with it, such as confirmation bias. Confirmation bias is where you remember facts that are consistent with your theory better than facts that are inconsistent with your theory. A computer doesn't need to do that. A computer can search for everything that matches a zip code or everything that doesn't match a zip code. It can use NOT operators. Using a computer, I can search for everybody that is male and over 40 in my zip code, or equally everybody that doesn't match those criteria. The human brain, using cue-addressable memory, can only search for matches within data. Everything else is much harder.

If I have a theory then I can find material that matches my theory, but anything that doesn't match doesn't come to mind as easily. I can't systematically search for it. That's confirmation bias.

Another example is the focusing illusion, where I ask you two questions in one of two orders. I either ask you how happy are you with your marriage and then how happy are you with your life, or in the other order. If I ask you first how happy you are with your marriage, that influences how you think about your life in general. You should be able to keep the two things completely separate.

MARTIN FORD: That sounds like Daniel Kahneman's anchoring theory, where he talks about how you can give people a random number, and then that number will influence their guess about anything.

GARY MARCUS: Yes, it's a variation. If I asked you when the Magna Carta was signed, after first asking you to look at the last three digits on a dollar bill, those three digits on the dollar bill anchor your memory.

MARTIN FORD: Your career trajectory is quite different from a lot of other people in the field of AI. Your early work focused on understanding human language and the way children learn it, and more recently you co-founded a startup company and helped launch Uber's AI labs.

GARY MARCUS: I feel a bit like Joseph Conrad (1857-1924), who spoke Polish but wrote in English. While he wasn't a native speaker of English, he had a lot of insights into the workings of it. In the same way, I think of myself as not a native speaker of machine learning or AI, but as someone who is coming to AI from the cognitive sciences and has fresh insights.

I did a lot of computer programming throughout my childhood and thought a lot about artificial intelligence, but I went to graduate school more interested in the cognitive sciences than artificial intelligence. During my time at graduate school, I studied with the cognitive scientist Steven Pinker, where we looked at how children learn the past tense within a language and then examined that using the precursors to deep learning that we had at the time, namely multi-layer and two-layer perceptrons.

In 1986, David Rumelhart and James L. McClelland published a paper titled *Parallel Distributed Processing: explorations in the microstructure of cognition*, which showed that a neural network could learn the past tense of English. Pinker and I looked at the paper in some detail, and although it was true that you could get a neural network to overregularize and say things like "goed" or "breaked" like kids do, all of the facts about when and how they made those errors were actually quite different. In response to the paper, we hypothesized that kids use a hybrid of both rules and neural networks.

MARTIN FORD: You're talking about irregular word endings, where kids will sometimes make them regular by mistake.

GARY MARCUS: Right, kids sometimes regularize irregular verbs. I once did an automated machine-driven analysis of 11,000 utterances of kids talking to their parents with past-tense verbs. In my study, I was looking at when kids made these overregularization errors and plotting the time course of the errors and which verbs were more vulnerable to these errors.

The argument that we made was that children seem to have a rule for the regulars. For example, they add -ed, but at the same time, they also had something of an associative memory, which you might think of nowadays as a neural network, to do the irregular verbs. The idea is if you're inflecting the verb "sing" as "sang" in the past tense, you might be just using your memory for that. If your memory understands "sing" and "sang," it'll help you to remember "ring" and "rang."

However, if you inflect a word that doesn't sound like anything you've heard before, like to "rouge," which would be to apply rouge to your face, then the word doesn't need to sound like anything you've heard before. You'll still know to add -ed to it. You'd say, "Diane rouged her face yesterday."

The point of that was that while neural networks are very good at things that work by similarity, they're very weak at things where you don't have a similarity but where you still understand the rule. That was 1992, 25 years later and that basic point still persists today. Most neural networks still have the problem that they're very data-driven, and they don't induce a high level of abstraction relative to what they've been trained on.

Neural networks are able to capture a lot of the garden-variety cases, but if you think about a long-tail distribution, they're very weak at the tail. Here's an example from a captioning system: a system might be able to tell you that a particular image is of a group of kids playing frisbee, simply because there are a lot of pictures that are like that, but if you show it a parking sign covered with stickers then it might say it's a refrigerator filled with food and drinks. That was an actual Google captioning result. That's because there aren't that many examples of parking signs covered with stickers in the database, so the system performs miserably.

That key problem of neural networks not being able to generalize well outside of some core situations has been something that's interested me for my entire career. From my point of view, it's something that the machine learning field has still not really come to grips with.

MARTIN FORD: Understanding human language and learning is clearly one of the pillars of your research. I was wondering if you could delve into some real-life experiments that you've undertaken?

GARY MARCUS: During my years of studying this from the perspective of understanding human generalization, I did research with children, adults, and ultimately with babies in 1999, all of which pointed to humans being very good at abstraction.

The experiment with babies showed that seven-month-olds could hear two minutes of an artificial grammar and recognize the rules of sentences constructed by that grammar. Babies would listen to sentences like "la ta ta" and "ga na na" for two minutes with A-B-B grammar and would then notice that "wo fe wo" had a different grammar (an A-B-A grammar) as opposed to "wo fe fe" that had the same grammar as the other sentences that they'd been trained on.

This was measured by how long they would look. We found that they would look longer if we changed the grammar. That experiment really nailed that from very early on in life babies have an ability to recognize pretty deep abstractions in the language domain. Another researcher later showed that newborns could do the same thing.

MARTIN FORD: I know that you have a great interest in IBM's Watson, and that it drew you back into the field of AI. Could you talk about why Watson reignited your interest in artificial intelligence?

GARY MARCUS: I was skeptical about Watson, so I was surprised when it first won at Jeopardy in 2011. As a scientist, I've trained myself to pay attention to the things that I get wrong, and I thought natural language understanding was too hard for a contemporary AI to do. Watson should not be able to beat a human in Jeopardy, and yet it did. That made me start thinking about AI again

I eventually figured out that the reason Watson won is because it was actually a narrower AI problem than it first appeared to be. That's almost always the answer. In Watson's case it's because about 95% of the answers in Jeopardy turn out to be the titles of Wikipedia pages. Instead of understanding language, reasoning about it and so forth, it was mostly doing information retrieval from a restricted set, namely the pages that are Wikipedia titles. It was actually not as hard of a problem as it looked like to the untutored eye, but it was interesting enough that it got me to think about AI again.

Around the same time, I started writing for *The New Yorker*, where I was producing a lot of pieces about neuroscience, linguistics, psychology, and also AI. In my pieces, I was trying to use what I knew about cognitive science and everything around that—how the mind and language work, how children's minds develop, etc.—in order to give me a better understanding of AI and the mistakes people were making.

Around the same time, I starting writing and thinking a lot more about AI. One was a critical piece on one of Ray Kurzweil's books. Another was about self-driving cars and how they would make a decision if an out-of-control school bus were hurtling toward them. Another, very prescient, piece criticized deep learning, saying that I think, as a community, we should understand it as one tool among many, not as a complete solution to AI. When I wrote that piece five years ago, I said that I didn't think deep learning would be able to do things like abstraction and causal reasoning, and if you look carefully, you'll see that deep learning is still struggling with exactly that set of problems.

MARTIN FORD: Let's talk about the company you started in 2014, Geometric Intelligence. I know that was eventually bought by Uber, shortly after which you moved to Uber and became the head of their AI labs. Can you take us through that journey?

GARY MARCUS: Back in January 2014 it occurred to me that instead of writing about AI I should actually try to start a company of my own. I recruited some great people, including my friend Zoubin Ghahramani, who is one of the best machine learning people in the world, and I spent the next couple of years running a machine learning company. I learned a lot about machine learning and we built on some ideas of how to generalize better. That became our company's core intellectual property. We spent a lot of time trying to make algorithms learn more efficiently from data.

Deep learning is incredibly greedy in terms of the amount of data that it needs in order to solve a problem. That works well in artificial worlds, such as the game of Go, but it doesn't work that well over in the real world, where data is often expensive or difficult to obtain. We spent a lot of our time trying to do better in that area and had some nice results. For example, we could learn arbitrary tasks like the MNIST character recognition task with half as much data as deep learning.

Word got around, and eventually, we sold to Uber in December 2016. This entire process taught me quite a bit about machine learning, including its strengths and weaknesses. I worked briefly at Uber, helping with the launch of Uber AI labs, and then moved on. Since then, I've been researching into how AI and medicine can be combined, and also thinking a lot about robotics.

In January of 2018, I wrote two papers[1] as well as a couple of pieces on Medium. One strand of that was about deep learning and how although it's very popular and our best tool for AI at the moment, it's not going to get us to AGI (artificial general intelligence). The second piece was about innateness, saying that, at least in biology, systems start with a lot of inherent structure, whether you're talking about the heart, the kidney, or the brain. The brain's initial structure is important for how we go about understanding the world.

---

1 https://arxiv.org/abs/1801.00631

People talk about Nature versus Nurture, but it's really Nature and Nurture working together. Nature is what constructs the learning mechanisms that allow us to make use of our experience in interesting ways.

MARTIN FORD: That's something that's demonstrated by experiments with very young babies. They haven't had time to learn anything, but they can still do essential things like recognize faces.

GARY MARCUS: That's right. My research with eight-month-olds also bears that out, and a recent paper in *Science* suggests that children are able to do logical reasoning after just the first year of life. Keep in mind that innate doesn't mean exactly at birth. My ability to grow a beard is not something I began at birth, it was timed to hormones and puberty. A lot of the human brain actually develops outside the womb, but relatively early in life.

If you look at precocial species like horses, they can walk almost right away after being born, and they have fairly sophisticated vision and obstacle detection. Some of those mechanisms for humans get wired up in the first year of life. You'll often hear people say that a baby learns to walk, but I don't think that's actually the case. There's certainly some learning and calibration of muscle forces and so on, but some of it is maturation. A head containing a fully developed human brain would be too big to pass through the birth canal.

MARTIN FORD: Even if you had an innate ability to walk, you'd have to wait for the muscles to develop before you could put it into operation.

GARY MARCUS: Right, and those aren't fully developed either. We come out not quite fully hatched, and I think that confuses people. A lot of what's going on in the first few months is still pretty much genetically controlled. It's not about learning per se.

Look at a baby ibex. After a couple of days, it can scramble down the side of a mountain. It doesn't learn that by trial-and-error—if it falls off the side of a mountain then it's dead—yet it can do spectacular feats of navigation and motor control.

I think our genomes wire a very rich first draft of how our brains should operate, then there's lots of learning on top of that. Some of that first draft is, of course, about making the learning mechanisms themselves.

People in AI often try to build things with as little prior knowledge as they can get away with, and I think that's foolish. There's actually lots of knowledge about the world that's been gathered by scientists and ordinary people that we should be building into our AI systems, instead of insisting, for no really good reason, that we should start from scratch.

MARTIN FORD: Any innateness that exists in the brain has to be the result of evolution, so with an AI you could either hardcode that innateness, or perhaps you could use an evolutionary algorithm to generate it automatically.

GARY MARCUS: The problem with that idea is that evolution is pretty slow and inefficient. It works over trillions of organisms and billions of years to get great results. It's not clear that you'd get far enough with evolution in a lab in a reasonable timeframe.

One way to think about this problem is that the first 900 million years of evolution were not that exciting. Mostly you had different versions of bacteria, which is not that exciting. No offense to the bacteria.

Then suddenly things pick up and you get vertebrates, then mammals, then primates, and finally, you get us. The reason that the pace of evolution increased is because it's like having more subroutines and more library code in your programming. The more subroutines you have, the quicker you can build more complicated things on top of that. It's one thing to build a human on top of a primate brain with 100 or 1,000 important genetic changes, but you wouldn't be able to make a similar leap from bacteria to a human brain.

People working on evolutionary neural networks often start too close to the bone. They're trying to evolve individual neurons and connections between them, when my belief is that in the biological evolution of, say, humans, you already had very sophisticated sets of genetic routines. Essentially, you've got cascades of genes on which to operate and people haven't really figured out how to do that in the evolutionary programming context.

I think they will eventually, but partly because of prejudice they haven't so far. The prejudice is, "I want to start from scratch in my lab and show that I can be God by creating this in seven days." That's ridiculous; it's not going to happen.

315

MARTIN FORD: If you were going to build this innateness into an AI system, do you have a sense of what that would look like?

GARY MARCUS: There are two parts to it. One is functionally what it should do, and the other is mechanically how you should do it.

At the functional level, I have some clear proposals drawing from my own work, and that of Elizabeth Spelke at Harvard. I laid this out in a paper that I wrote early in 2018, where I talked about ten different things that would be required[2]. I won't go into them in depth here, but things like symbol manipulation and the ability to represent abstract variables, which computer programs are based on; operations over those variables, which is what computer programs are; a type-token distinction, recognizing this bottle as opposed to bottles in general; causality; spatial translation or translation invariance; the knowledge that objects tend to move on paths that are connected in space and time; the realization that there are sets of things, places, and so on.

If you had things like that, then you could learn about what particular kinds of objects do when they're in particular kinds of places and they're manipulated by particular kinds of agents. That would be better than just learning everything from pixels, which is a very popular but I think ultimately inadequate idea that we are seeing in the field right now.

What we see at the moment is people doing deep reinforcement learning over pixels of, for example, the Atari game *Breakout*, and while you get results that look impressive, they're incredibly fragile.

DeepMind trained an AI to play Breakout, and when you watch it, it looks like it's doing great. It's supposedly learned the concept of breaking through the wall and trapping the ball at the top so it can ricochet across a lot of blocks. However, if you were to move the paddle three pixels up, the whole system breaks because it doesn't really know what a wall is or what a ricochet is. It's really just learned contingencies, and it's interpolating between the contingencies that it's memorized. The programs are not learning the abstraction that you need, and this is the problem with doing everything from pixels and very low-level representations.

---

2 https://arxiv.org/abs/1801.05667

MARTIN FORD: It needs a higher level of abstraction to understand objects and concepts.

GARY MARCUS: Exactly. You may also need to actually build in certain notions. like "object." One way to think about it is like the ability to learn to process color. You don't start with black-and-white vision and eventually learn that there is color. It starts by having two different color-receptor pigments that are sensitive to particular parts of the spectrum. Then, from there, you can learn about particular colors. You need some piece to be innate before you can do the rest. Maybe in a similar way, you might need to have innately the notion that there's an object, and maybe the constraint that objects don't just randomly appear and disappear.

Imagine a world in which there was a Star Trek transporter, and anything could appear at any place at any moment. You'd never be able to learn from that. What allows us to learn about the world is the fact that objects do move on paths that are connected in space and time, and over a billion years of evolution that might have been wired in as a way of getting you off the ground faster.

MARTIN FORD: Let's talk about the future. What do you see as the main hurdles to getting to AGI, and can we get there with current tools?

GARY MARCUS: I see deep learning as a useful tool for doing pattern classification, which is one problem that any intelligent agent needs to do. We should either keep it around for that, or replace it with something that does similar work more efficiently, which I do think is possible.

At the same time, there are other kinds of things that intelligent agents need to do that deep learning is not currently very good at. It's not very good at abstract inference, and it's not a very good tool for language, except things like translation where you don't need real comprehension, or at least not to do approximate translation. It's also not very good at handling situations that it hasn't seen before and where it has relatively incomplete information. We therefore need to supplement deep learning with other tools.

More generally, there's a lot of knowledge that humans have about the world that can be codified symbolically, either through math or sentences in a language. We really want to bring that symbolic information together with the other information that's more perceptual.

Psychologists talk about the relationship between top-down information and bottom-up information. If you look at an image, light falls on your retina and that's bottom-up information, but you also use your knowledge of the world and your experience of how things behave to add top-down information to your interpretation of the image.

Deep learning systems currently focus on bottom-up information. They can interpret the pixels of an image, but don't then have any knowledge of the object the image contains.

An example of this recently was the *Adversarial Patch* paper[3]. In the paper, they show how you can fool a deep learning system by adding a sticker to an image. They take a photo of a banana that is recognized with great confidence by a deep learning system and then add a sticker that looks like a psychedelic toaster next to the banana in the photo. Any human looking at it would say it was a banana with a funny looking sticker next to it, but the deep learning system immediately says, with great confidence, that it's now a picture of a toaster.

The deep learning system is just trying to say what the most salient thing in the image is, and the high-contrast psychedelic toaster grabs its attention and it ignores the perfectly clear banana.

This is an example of how deep learning systems are only getting the bottom-up information, which is what your occipital cortex does. It's not capturing at all what your frontal cortex does when it reasons about what's really going on.

To get to AGI, we need to be able to capture both sides of that equation. Another way to put it is that humans have all kinds of common-sense reasoning, and that has to be part of the solution. It's not well captured by deep learning. In my view, we need to bring together symbol manipulation, which has a strong history in AI, with deep learning. They have been treated separately for too long, and it's time to bring them together.

MARTIN FORD: If you had to point to one company or project that's going on now that is the closest to being on the path to AGI, who would you point to?

---

3 https://arxiv.org/pdf/1712.09665.pdf

GARY MARCUS: I'm very excited about Project Mosaic at the Allen Institute for AI. They're taking a second crack at the problem Doug Lenat was trying to solve, which was how you take human knowledge and put it in computable form. This is not about answering questions like where was Barack Obama born—computers actually represent that information pretty well and can extract it from available data.

There's a lot of information, though, that's not written anywhere, for example, toasters are smaller than cars. The likelihood is that no one says that on Wikipedia, but we know it to be true and that allows us to make inferences. If I said, "Gary got run over by a toaster," you would think that's weird because a toaster's not that big an object, but "run over by a car" makes sense.

MARTIN FORD: So this is in the area of symbolic logic?

GARY MARCUS: Well, there are two related questions. One question is, how do you get that knowledge at all? The other is, do you want symbolic logic as a way to manipulate that?

My best guess is that symbolic logic is actually pretty useful for it, and we shouldn't throw it out the window. I'm open to somebody finding another way to deal with it, but I don't see any ways in which people have dealt with it well, and I don't see how we can build systems that really understand language without having some of that common sense. This is because every time I say a sentence to you, there's some common-sense knowledge that goes into your understanding of that sentence.

If I tell you I'm going to ride my bicycle from New York to Boston, I don't have to tell you that I'm not going to fly through the air, go underwater, or take a detour to California. You can figure all that stuff out for yourself. It's not in the literal sentence, but it's in your knowledge about humans that they like to take efficient routes.

You, as a human, can make a lot of inferences. There's no way you can understand my sentences without filling in those inferences, where you're effectively reading between the lines. We read an enormous amount between the lines, but for that whole transaction to work there has to be shared common sense, and we don't have machines that have that shared common sense yet.

The biggest project to do that was Doug Lenat's *Cyc*, which started around 1984 and by most accounts, it didn't work very effectively. It was developed 30 years ago in a closed form. Nowadays we know much more about machine learning, and the Allen Institute for AI is committed to doing things in open-source ways in which the community can participate. We know more about big data now than we did back in the 1980s, but it's still a very difficult problem. The important thing is that they're confronting it when everybody else is hiding from it.

MARTIN FORD: What do you think the timeframe is for AGI?

GARY MARCUS: I don't know. I know most of the reasons why it's not here now and the things that need to be solved, but I don't think you can put a single date on that. What I think is that you need a confidence interval—as a statistician would describe it—around it.

I might tell you that I think it'll come between 2030 if we're phenomenally lucky and more likely 2050, or in the worst case 2130. The point is that it's very hard to give an exact date. There are lots of things we just don't know. I always think about how Bill Gates wrote the book *The Road Ahead* in 1994, and even he didn't really realize that the internet was going to change things as it did. My point is that there could be all kinds of things that we're just not anticipating.

Right now, machines are weak at intelligence, but we don't know what people are going to invent next. There's a lot of money going into the field, which could move things along, or alternatively it could be much harder than we think that it is. We just really don't know.

MARTIN FORD: That's still a fairly aggressive time frame. You're suggesting as soon as 12 years away or as far away as 112 years.

GARY MARCUS: And those figures could of course be wrong. Another way to look at it is while we've made a lot of progress on narrow intelligence, we haven't made nearly as much progress so far on general intelligence, AGI.

Apple's Siri, which began life in 2010, doesn't work that much differently from ELIZA, an early natural language computer program created in 1964, which matched templates in order to give an illusion of understanding language that it didn't really.

A lot of my optimism comes from how many people are working at the problem and how much money businesses are investing to try and solve it.

MARTIN FORD: It definitely is a massive change in terms of AI not being something just done as a research project at a university. Now AI is central to the business models of big companies like Google and Facebook.

GARY MARCUS: The amount of money being spent on AI far eclipses anything before, although there certainly was a lot of money spent in the 1960s and early 1970s before the first so-called AI Winter. It's also important to acknowledge that money is not a guaranteed solution to the problems of AI, but is very likely a prerequisite.

MARTIN FORD: Let's focus on a prediction for a much narrower technology: the self-driving car.

When are we going to be able to call for something like an Uber that's driven by nothing but an AI, and that can pick you up at a random location and then take you to a destination that you specify?

GARY MARCUS: It's at least a decade away, and probably more.

MARTIN FORD: You're almost getting into the same territory as your AGI prediction.

GARY MARCUS: That's right, and for the principal reason that if you're talking about driving in a very heavy metropolitan location like Manhattan or Mumbai, then the AI will face a lot of unpredictability. It's one thing to have a driverless car in Phoenix, where the weather is good and the population is a lot less densely packed. The problem in Manhattan is that anything goes at any moment, nobody is particularly well-behaved and everybody is aggressive, the chance of having unpredictable things occur is much higher.

Even simple road elements like barricades to protect people can cause issues for an AI. These are complex situations that humans deal with by using reasoning. Right now, driverless cars navigate by having highly detailed maps and things like LIDAR, but no real understanding of the motives and behavior of other drivers. Humans have an OK visual system, but a good understanding of what's out there and what they're doing when they're driving. Machines are trying to fake their way around that with big data, and it's not clear to me that you get to the accuracy levels you need for driving in Manhattan simply by adding more data to these big data-driven systems. You might get to 99.99% accuracy, but if you do the numbers on that, that's much worse than humans, and it's far too dangerous to have that scale on the road, especially on busy streets like in Manhattan.

MARTIN FORD: Maybe then there's a nearer term solution, where rather than a location of your choice, it takes you to a predefined location?

GARY MARCUS: There's a possibility that very soon we may well have that in Phoenix, or another limited location. If you can find a route where you never need to take a left turn, where humans are unlikely to be in the way, and the traffic is civilized, you might be able to do that. We already have monorails at airports that work in a similar way following a predefined path.

There's a continuum from super-controlled circumstances like the monorail at the airport where nobody should be on that track, to the Manhattan streets where anybody and anything could be there at any time. We also have other factors like the fact that weather is much more complicated than in Phoenix. We get everything. Sleet, slush, hail, leaves, things that fall off trucks; everything.

The more you go into an unbounded open-ended system, the more challenge there is and the more you need to be able to reason the way an AGI system does. It's still not as open-ended as AGI per se, but it starts to approach that, and that's why my numbers are not totally different.

MARTIN FORD: Let's talk about an area that I've focused on a lot: the economic and job market impact of AI.

Many people believe we're on the leading edge of a new Industrial Revolution; something that's going to completely change the way the labor market looks. Would you agree with that?

GARY MARCUS: I do agree with that, though on a slightly slower time frame. Driverless cars are harder than we thought, so paid drivers are safe for a while, but fast-food workers and cashiers are in deep trouble, and there's a lot of them in the workplace. I do think these fundamental changes are going to happen.

Some of them will be slow, but in the scale of, say, 100 years, if something takes an extra 20 years, it's nothing.

There is going to be a problem with AI robots and employment sometime in this century, whether it's 2030 or 2070. At some point we need to change how we structure our societies because we are going to get to a point where there's less employment available but still a working-age population.

There are counterarguments, like when most agricultural jobs disappeared they were just replaced by industrial jobs, but I don't find them to be compelling. The main issue we will face is scale and the way that once you have a solution, you can use it everywhere relatively cheaply.

Getting the first driverless car algorithm/database system that works might be 50 years of work and cost billions of dollars in research, but once we have them, people are going to roll them out at scale. As soon as we reach that point, millions of truck drivers are going to be put in a position where they could lose their jobs within a matter of years.

It's not clear that we are going to have new jobs appear that can replace existing jobs at the scale of the truck-driving industry. A lot of the new jobs that have arisen need fewer people. For example, a YouTube entrepreneur is a great job. You can make millions of dollars staying at home making videos. That's terrific, but maybe 1,000 people do that, not a million people and not enough to replace all the potentially lost truck driving jobs.

It's easy to come up with jobs that we will have that we didn't have before, but it's hard to come up with new industries that will employ large numbers of people in an era where you can build something like Instagram with 18 people.

MARTIN FORD: Probably something like half the current workforce is engaged in fundamentally predictable activities. What they're doing is encapsulated in the data and ultimately is going to be susceptible to machine learning over some time frame.

GARY MARCUS: True, but things like that that are pretty hard right now. AI systems just don't really understand the data as a natural language like humans do. For example, extricating information from medical records is something that's very hard for machines to do right now. It's predictable, and it's not that hard work, but doing it well with a machine is a while away. In the long run, though, I agree with you. Natural language understanding will get better and eventually those predictable jobs will go away.

MARTIN FORD: Given that you believe job loss to AI will happen at some point, would you support a basic income as a potential solution to that?

GARY MARCUS: I see no real alternative. We will get there, but it's a question of whether we get there peacefully through a universal agreement or whether there are riots on the street and people getting killed. I don't know the method, but I don't see any other ending.

MARTIN FORD: You could argue that technology is already having an impact of that sort. We do have an opioid epidemic in the US at the moment, and automation technology in factories has likely played a role in that in terms of middle-class job opportunities disappearing. Perhaps opioid use is tied to a perceived loss of dignity or even despair among some people, especially working-class men?

GARY MARCUS: I would be careful about making that assumption. It may be true, but I don't think the links are ironclad. A better analogy, in my opinion, is how a lot of people use their phones as an opioid, and that smartphones are the new opium of the people. We may be moving toward a world where a lot of people just hang out in virtual reality, and if the economics work they may be reasonably happy. I'm not sure where that's all going to go.

MARTIN FORD: There's a range of risks associated with AI that have been raised. People like Elon Musk have been especially vocal about existential threats. What do you think we should be worried about in terms of the impacts and risks of AI?

GARY MARCUS: We should be worrying about people using AI in malevolent ways. The real problem is what people might do with the power that AI holds as it becomes more embedded in the grid and more hackable. I'm not that worried about AI systems independently wanting to eat us for breakfast or turn us into paper clips. It's not completely impossible, but there's no real evidence that we're moving in that direction. There is evidence, though, that we're giving more and more power to those machines, and that we have no idea how to solve the cybersecurity threats in the near term.

MARTIN FORD: What about long-term threats, though? Elon Musk and Nick Bostrom are very concerned about the control problem with AI; the idea that there could be a recursive self-improvement cycle that could lead to an intelligence explosion. You can't completely discount that, right?

GARY MARCUS: I don't completely discount it, I'm not going to say the probability is zero but the probability of it happening anytime soon is pretty low. There was recently a video circulated of robots opening doorknobs, and that's about where they are in development.

We don't have AI systems that can robustly navigate our world at all, nor do we have robotic systems that know how to improve themselves, except in constrained ways like tailoring their motor control system to a particular function. This is not a current problem. I think it's fine to invest some money in the field and have some people think about those problems. My issue is that, as we saw with the 2016 US election, there are more pressing problems like using AI to generate and target fake news. That's a problem today.

MARTIN FORD: Earlier you said AGI is conceivable as early as 2030. If a system is genuinely intelligent, potentially superintelligent, do we need to make sure that its goals are aligned with what we want it to do?

GARY MARCUS: Yes, I think so. I will be surprised if we get there that quickly, but it's for that reason why I think that we should have some people thinking about these problems. I just don't think that they're our most pressing problems right now. Even when we do get to an AGI system, who's to say that the AGI system is going to have any interest whatsoever in meddling in human affairs?

We've gone from AI not being able to win at checkers about 60 years ago to being able to win at Go, which is a much harder game, in the last year. You could plot a game IQ, and make up a scale to say that game IQ has gone from 0 to 60 in 60 years. You could then do a similar thing for machine malevolence. Machine malevolence has not changed at all over that time. There's no correlation, there is zero machine malevolence. There was none, and there is none. It doesn't mean that it's impossible—I don't want to make the inductive argument that because it never happened, it never will—but there's no indication of it.

MARTIN FORD: It sounds to me like a threshold problem, though, you can't have machine malevolence until you have AGI.

GARY MARCUS: Possibly. Some of it has to do with motivational systems and you could try to construct an argument saying that AGI is a prerequisite for machine malevolence, but you couldn't say that it's a necessary and sufficient condition.

Here's a thought experiment. I can name a single genetic factor that will increase your chance of committing violent acts by a factor of 5. If you don't have it, your proclivity to violence is pretty low. Are machine's going to have this genetic factor, or not? The genetic factor, of course, is male versus female.

MARTIN FORD: Is that an argument for making AGI female?

GARY MARCUS: The gender is a proxy, it's not the real issue, but it is an argument for making AI nonviolent. We should have restrictions and regulations to reduce the chance of AI being violent or of coming up with ideas of its own about what it wants to do with us. These are hard and important questions, but they're much less straightforward than Elon's quotes might lead a lot of people to think.

MARTIN FORD: What he's doing in terms of making an investment in OpenAI doesn't sound like a bad thing, though. Somebody ought to be doing that work. It would be hard to justify having the government invest massive resources in working on AI control issues, but having private entities doing that seems positive.

GARY MARCUS: The US Department of Defense does spend some money on these things, as they should, but you have to have a risk portfolio. I'm more worried about certain kinds of bioterrorism than I am about these particular AI threats, and I'm more worried about cyber warfare, which is a real going concern.

There are two key questions here. One is, do you think that the probability of X is greater than 0? The answer is clearly yes. The other is, relative to the other risks that you might be concerned about, where would you rank this? To which I would say, these are somewhat unlikely scenarios, and there are other scenarios that are more likely.

MARTIN FORD: If at some point we succeed in building an AGI, do you think it would be conscious, or is it possible to have an intelligent zombie with no inner experience?

GARY MARCUS: I think it's the latter. I don't think that consciousness is a prerequisite. It might be an epiphenomenon in humans or maybe some other biological creatures. There's another thought experiment that says, could we have something that behaves just like me but isn't conscious? I think the answer is yes. We don't know for sure, because we don't have any independent measure of what consciousness is, so it's very hard to ground these arguments.

How would we tell if a machine was conscious? How do I know that you're conscious?

MARTIN FORD: Well, you can assume I am because we're the same species.

GARY MARCUS: I think that's a bad assumption. What if it turns out that consciousness is randomly distributed through our population to one-quarter of the people? What if it's just a gene? I have the supertaster gene that makes me sensitive to bitter compounds, but my wife doesn't. She looks like she's from the same species as me, but we differ in that property, and so maybe we differ in the consciousness property also? I'm kidding, but we can't really use an objective measure, here.

MARTIN FORD: It sounds like an unknowable problem.

GARY MARCUS: Maybe someone will come up with a cleverer answer, but so far, most of the academic research is focused on the part of consciousness we call awareness. At what point does your central neural system realize logically that certain information is available?

Research has shown that if you only see something for 100 milliseconds then you might not realize you'd seen it. If you see it for half a second, you're pretty sure you actually saw it. With that data we can start to build up a characterization of which neural circuits at which time frame contribute information that you can reflect on, and we can call that awareness. That we're making progress on, but not yet general consciousness.

MARTIN FORD: You clearly think AGI is achievable, but do you think it's inevitable? Do you think there is any probability that maybe we can never build an intelligent machine?

GARY MARCUS: It's almost inevitable. I think the primary things that would keep us from getting there are other extinction-level existential risks, such as getting hit by an asteroid, blowing ourselves up, or engineering a super-disease. We're continuously accumulating scientific knowledge, we're getting better at building software and hardware, and there's no principled reason why not to do it. I think it will almost certainly happen unless we reset the clock, which I can't rule out.

MARTIN FORD: What do you think about the international arms race toward advanced AI, particularly with countries like China?

GARY MARCUS: China has made AI a major center of its ambitions and been very public about it. The United States for a while had no response whatsoever, and I found that disturbing and upsetting.

MARTIN FORD: It does seem that China has many advantages, such as a much larger population and fewer privacy controls, which means more data.

GARY MARCUS: They're much more forward-thinking because they realize how important AI is, and they are investing in it as a nation.

MARTIN FORD: How do you feel about regulation of the field? Do you think that the government should get involved in regulating AI research?

GARY MARCUS: I do, but it's not clear to me what those regulations should be. I think a significant portion of AI funding should address those questions. They're hard questions.

For example, I don't love the idea of autonomous weapons, but to simply ban them outright is maybe naive and creates more problems, where some people have them, and others don't. What should those regulations be, and how should we enforce them? I'm afraid I don't have the answer.

MARTIN FORD: Do you believe that AI is going to be positive for humanity?

GARY MARCUS: Hopefully, but I don't think that is a given. The best way in which AI could help humanity is by accelerating scientific discovery in healthcare. Instead, AI research and implementation right now is mostly about ad placement.

AI has a lot of positive potential, but I don't think there's enough focus on that side of it. We do some, but not enough. I also understand that there are going to be risks, job losses, and social upheaval. I'm an optimist in a technical sense in that I do think AGI is achievable, but I would like to see a change in what we develop and how we prioritize those things. Right now, I'm not totally optimistic that we're heading in the right direction in terms of how we're using AI and how we're distributing it. I think there's serious work to be done there to make AI have the positive impact on humanity that it could.

GARY MARCUS is a professor of psychology and neural science at New York University. Much of Gary's research has focused on understanding how children learn and assimilate language, and how these findings might inform the field of artificial intelligence.

He is the author of several books, including The Birth of the Mind, Kluge: The Haphazard Construction of the Human Mind, and the bestselling Guitar Zero, in which he explores cognitive challenges involved as he learns to play the guitar. Gary has also contributed numerous articles on AI and brain science to The New Yorker and the New York Times. In 2014 he founded and served as CEO of Geometric Intelligence, a machine learning startup that was later acquired by Uber.

Gary is known for his criticism of deep learning and has written that current approaches may soon "hit a wall." He points out that the human mind is not a blank slate, but comes preconfigured with significant structure to enable learning. He believes that neural networks alone will not succeed in achieving more general intelligence, and that continued progress will require incorporating more innate cognitive structure into AI systems.

GARY MARCUS

66 *I'm thrilled that AI is actually out there in the world making a difference because I didn't think that it would happen in my lifetime—because it seemed the problems were so hard.*

BARBARA J. GROSZ

HIGGINS PROFESSOR OF NATURAL SCIENCES, HARVARD UNIVERSITY

Barbara J. Grosz is Higgins Professor of Natural Sciences at Harvard University. Over the course of her career, she has made ground-breaking contributions in artificial intelligence that have led to the foundational principles of dialogue processing that are important for personal assistants like Apple's Siri or Amazon's Alexa. In 1993, she became the first woman to serve as president of the Association for the Advancement of Artificial Intelligence.

MARTIN FORD: What initially drove you to be interested in artificial intelligence, and how did your career progress?

BARBARA GROSZ: My career was a series of happy accidents. I went to college thinking I would be a 7th-grade math teacher because my 7th-grade math teacher was the only person I had met in my first 18 years of life who thought that women, in general, could do mathematics, and he told me that I was quite good at math. My world really opened up though when I went to Cornell for college, as they had just started a computer science faculty.

At the time there was no undergraduate major in computer science anywhere in the US, but Cornell provided the opportunity to take a few classes. I started in numerical analysis, a rather mathematical area of computer science, and ended up going to Berkeley to graduate school, initially for a master's, then I moved into the PhD program.

I worked in what would come to be called computational science and then briefly in theoretical computer science. I decided that I liked the solutions in the mathematical areas of computer science, but not the problems. So when I needed a thesis topic, I talked with many people. Alan Kay said to me, "Listen. You have to do something ambitious for your thesis. Why don't you write a program that will read a children's story and tell it back from one of the character's points of view?" That's what spurred my interest in natural language processing and is the root of my becoming an AI researcher.

MARTIN FORD: Alan Kay? He invented the graphical user interface at Xerox PARC, right? That's where Steve Jobs got the idea for the Macintosh.

BARBARA GROSZ: Yes, right, Alan was a key player in that Xerox PARC work. I actually worked with him on developing a programming language called Smalltalk, which was an object-oriented language. Our goal was to build a system suitable for students [K-12] and learning. My children's story program was to be written in Smalltalk. Before the Smalltalk system was finished, though, I realized that children's stories were not just stories to be read and understood, but that they're meant to inculcate a culture, and that Alan's challenge to me was going to be really hard to meet.

During that time, the first group of speech-understanding systems were also being developed through DARPA projects, and the people at SRI International who were working on one of them said to me, "If you're willing to take the risk of working on children's stories, why don't you come work with us on a more objective kind of language, task-oriented dialogues, but using speech not text?" As a result, I got involved in the DARPA speech work, which was on systems that would assist people in getting tasks done, and that's really when I started to do AI research.

It was that work which led to my discovery of how dialogue among people, when they're working on a task together, has a structure that depends on the task structure—and that a dialogue is much more than just question-answer pairs. From that insight, I came to realize that as human beings we don't in general ever speak in a sequence of isolated utterances, but that there's always a larger structure, much like there is for a journal article, a newspaper article, a textbook, even for this book, and that we can model that structure. This was my first major contribution to natural-language processing and AI.

MARTIN FORD: You've touched on one of the natural language breakthroughs that you're most known for: an effort to somehow model a conversation. The idea that a conversation can be computed, and that there's some structure within a conversation that can be represented mathematically.

I assume that this has become very important, because we've seen a lot of progress in the field. Maybe you could talk about some of the work you've done there and how things have progressed. Has it astonished you where things are at now in terms of natural language processing, compared to where they were back when you started your research?

BARBARA GROSZ: It absolutely has astonished me. My early work was exactly in this area of how we might be able to build a computer system that could carry on a dialogue with a person fluently and in a way that seemed natural. One of the reasons I got connected to Alan Kay, and did that work with him, was because we shared an interest in building computer systems that would work with and adapt to people, rather than require people to adapt to them.

At the time that I took that work on, there was a lot of work in linguistics on syntax and on formal semantics in philosophy and linguistics, and on parsing algorithms in computer science. People knew there was more to language understanding than an individual sentence, and they knew that context mattered, but they had no formal tools, no mathematics, and no computational constructs to take that context into account in speech systems.

I said to people at the time that we couldn't afford to just hypothesize about what was going on, that we couldn't just carry on introspecting, that we had to get samples of how people actually carry on a dialogue when they're doing a task. As a result, I invented this approach, which later was dubbed the "The Wizard of Oz" approach by some psychologists. In this work, I sat two people—in this case, an expert and an apprentice—in two different rooms, and I had the expert explain to the apprentice how to get something done. It was by studying the dialogues that resulted from their working together that I recognized the structure in these dialogues and its dependence on task structure.

Later, I co-wrote a paper with Candy Sidner titled *Attention, Intentions, and the Structure of Discourse*. In that paper we argue that dialogues have a structure that is in part the language itself and is in part the intentional structure of why you're speaking, and what your purposes are when speaking. This intentional structure was a generalization of task structure. These structural aspects are then moderated by a model of the attentional state.

MARTIN FORD: Let's fast forward and talk about today. What's the biggest difference that you've seen?

BARBARA GROSZ: The biggest difference I see is going from speech systems that were essentially deaf, to today's systems that are incredibly good at processing speech. In the early days we really could not get much out of speech, and it proved very hard to get the right kinds of parses and meaning back then. We've also come a long way forward with how incredibly well today's technology can process individual utterances or sentences, which you can see in modern search engines and machine translation systems.

If you consider any of the systems that purport to carry on dialogues, however, the bottom line is they essentially don't work. They seem to do well if the dialogue system constrains the person to following a script, but people aren't very good at following a script. There are claims that these systems can carry on a dialogue with a person, but in truth, they really can't. For instance, the Barbie doll that supposedly can converse with a child is script-based and gets in trouble if the child responds in a way the designers didn't anticipate. I've argued that the mistakes it makes actually raise some serious ethical challenges.

Similar examples arise with all the phone personal assistant systems. For example, if you ask where the nearest emergency room is, you'll get an answer of the nearest hospital to wherever you are when you ask, but if you ask where you can go to get a sprained ankle treated, the system is likely to just take you to a web page that tells you how to treat a sprained ankle. That's not a problem for a sprained ankle, but if you're asking about a heart attack because you think someone's had one, it could actually lead to death. People would assume a system that can answer one of those questions you can answer the other.

A related problem arises with dialogue systems based on learning from data. Last summer (2017), I was given the Association for Computational Linguistics Lifetime Achievement Award and almost all the people listening to my talk at the conference work on deep learning based natural-language systems. I told them, "if you want to build a dialogue system, you have to recognize that Twitter is not a real dialogue." To build a dialogue system that can handle dialogues of the sort people actually engage in, you need to have real data of real people having real dialogues, and that's much harder to get than Twitter data.

MARTIN FORD: When you talk about going off script, it seems to me that this is the blurry line between pure language processing and real intelligence. The ability to go off script and deal with unpredictable situations is what true intelligence is all about; it's the difference between an automaton or robot and a person.

BARBARA GROSZ: You're exactly right, and that's exactly the problem. If you think about having a lot of data, that, with deep learning, enables you to, say, go from a sentence in one language to the same sentence in another language; or to go from a sentence with a question in it to an answer to that question; or from one sentence to a possible following sentence, there's no real understanding of what those sentences actually mean, so there's no way to work off script with them.

This problem links back to a philosophical idea that was elaborated in the 1960s by Paul Grice, J. L. Austin, and John Searle that language is action. For example, if I say to the computer, "The printer is broken," then what I don't want is for it to say back to me, "Thanks, fact recorded." What I actually want is for the system to do something that will get the printer fixed. For that to occur, the system needs to understand why I said something.

Current deep-learning based natural-language systems perform poorly on these kinds of sentences in general. The reasons are really deeply rooted. What we're seeing here, is that these systems are really good at statistical learning, pattern recognition and large-scale data analysis, but they don't go below the surface. They can't reason about the purposes behind what someone says. Put another way, they ignore the intentional structure component of dialogue. Deep-learning based systems more generally lack other hallmarks of intelligence: they cannot do counterfactual reasoning or common-sense reasoning.

You need all these capabilities to participate in a dialogue, unless you tightly constrain what a person says and does; but that makes it very hard for people to actually do what they want to do!

MARTIN FORD: What would you point to as being state-of-the-art right now? I was pretty astonished when I saw IBM Watson win at *Jeopardy!* I thought that was really remarkable. Was that as much of a breakthrough as it seemed to be, or would you point to something else as really being on the leading edge?

BARBARA GROSZ: I was impressed by Apple's Siri and by IBM's Watson; they were phenomenal achievements of engineering. I think that what is available today with natural language and speech systems is terrific. It's changing the way that we interact with computer systems, and it's enabling us to get a lot done. But these systems are nowhere near the human capacity for language, and you see that when you try to engage in a dialogue with them.

When Siri came out it in 2011, it took me about three questions to break the system. Where Watson makes mistakes is most interesting in that it shows us where it is not processing language like people do.

So yes, on the one hand, I think the progress in natural language and speech systems is phenomenal. We are far beyond what we could do in the '70s, partly because computers are way more powerful, and partly because there's a lot more data out there. I'm thrilled that AI is actually out in the world making a difference because I didn't think that it would happen in my lifetime—because it seemed the problems were so hard.

BARBARA J. GROSZ

MARTIN FORD: Really, you didn't think it would happen in your lifetime?

BARBARA GROSZ: Back in the 1970s? No, I didn't.

MARTIN FORD: I was certainly very taken aback by Watson and especially by the fact that it could handle, for example, puns, jokes, and very complex presentations of language.

BARBARA GROSZ: But just going back to "The Wizard of Oz" analogy, you look behind what's actually in those systems, and you realize they all have limitations. We're at a moment where it's really important to understand what these systems are good at and where they fail.

This is why I think it's very important for the field, and frankly for the world, to understand that we could make a lot more progress on AI systems that would be good for people in the world if we didn't aim to replace people, or build generalized artificial intelligence—but if we instead focus our understanding on what all these great capabilities are both good and not good for, and how to complement people with these systems, and these systems with the people.

MARTIN FORD: Let's focus on this idea of going off script and being able to really have a conversation. That relates directly to the Turing test, and I know you've done some additional work in that area. What do you think Turing's intentions were in coming up with that test? Is it a good test of machine intelligence?

BARBARA GROSZ: I remind people that Turing proposed his test in 1950, a time where people had new computing machines that they thought were amazing. Now of course, those systems could do nothing compared to what a smartphone can do today, but at the time many people wondered if these machines could think like a human thinks. Remember, Turing used "intelligence" and "thinking" similarly—he wasn't talking about intelligence like say, Nobel prize-winning science type of intelligence.

Turing was posing a very interesting philosophical question, and he made some conjectures about whether or not machines could exhibit a certain kind of behavior. The 1950s was also at a time where psychology was rooted in behaviorism, and so his test is not only an operational test but also a test where there would be no looking below the surface.

The Turing test is not a good test of intelligence. Frankly, I would probably fail the Turing test because I'm not very good at social banter. It's also not a good guide for what the field should aim to do. Turing was an amazingly smart person, but I've conjectured, somewhat seriously, that if he were alive today—and if he knew what we now know about how learning works, how the brain and language work, and how people develop intelligence and thinking, then he would have proposed a different test.

MARTIN FORD: I know that you've proposed some enhancements or even a replacement for the Turing test.

BARBARA GROSZ: Who knows what Turing would have proposed, but I have made a proposal that, given that we know that the development of human intelligence depends on social interaction, and that language capacity depends on social interaction, and that human activity in many setting is collaborative—then I recommend that we aim to build a system that is a good team partner, and works so well with us that we don't recognize that it isn't human. I mean, it's not that we're fooled into the idea that a laptop, robot, or phone is a human being, but that you don't keep wondering "Why did it do that?" when it makes a mistake that no human would.

I think that this is a better goal for the field, in part because it has several advantages over the Turing test. One advantage is that you can meet it incrementally—so if you pick a small enough arena in which to build a system, you can build a system that's intelligent in that arena, and it works well on that kind of task. We could find systems out there now that we would say are intelligent in that way—and of course children, as they develop, are intelligent in different limited ways, and then they get more and different kinds of smart in more varied kinds of ways.

With the Turing test, a system either succeeds or it fails, and there's no guide for how to incrementally improve its reasoning. For science to develop, you need to be able to make steps along the way. The test I proposed also recognizes that for the foreseeable future people and computer systems will have complementary abilities, and it builds on that insight rather than ignoring it.

I first proposed this test in a talk in Edinburgh on the occasion of the 100th anniversary of Turing's birth. I said given all the progress in computing and psychology, "We should think of new tests." I asked the attendees at that talk for their ideas, and in subsequent talks. To date, the main response has been that this test is a good one.

MARTIN FORD: I've always thought that once we really have machine intelligence, we'll just kind of know it when we see it. It'll just be somehow obvious, and maybe there's not a really explicit test that you can define. I'm not sure there's a single test for human intelligence. I mean, how do you know another human being is intelligent?

BARBARA GROSZ: That's a really good observation. If you think about what I said when I gave this example of "where's the nearest emergency room and where can I go to get a heart attack treated?", no human being you would consider intelligent would be able to answer one of those questions and not the other one.

There's a possibility that the person you asked might not be able to answer either question, say if you plonked them in some foreign city; but if they could answer one question, they could answer the other question. The point is, if you have a machine that answers both questions, then that seems intelligent to you. If you have a machine that answers only one and not the other question, then it doesn't seem so intelligent.

What you just said actually fits with the test that I proposed. If the AI system is going along and acting, as it were, as intelligently as you would expect another human to act, then you'd think it is intelligent. What happens right now with many AI systems, is that people think the AI system is smart and then it does something that takes them aback, and then they think it's completely stupid. At that point, the human wants to know why the AI system worked that way or didn't work the way they expected, and by the end they no longer think it's so smart.

By the way, the test that I proposed is not time-limited; in fact, it is actually supposed to be extended in time. Turing's test was also not supposed to have a time limit, but that characteristic has been frequently forgotten, in particular in various recent AI competitions.

MARTIN FORD: That seems silly. People aren't intelligent for only half an hour. It has to be for an indefinite time period to demonstrate true intelligence. I think there's something called the Loebner Prize where Turing tests are run under certain limited conditions each year.

BARBARA GROSZ: Right, and it proves what you say. It also makes clear what we learned very early on in the natural-language processing arena, which is that if you have only a fixed task with a fixed set of issues (and in this case, a fixed amount of time), then cheap hacks will always win over real intelligent processing, because you'll just design your AI system to the test!

MARTIN FORD: The other area that you have worked in is multi-agent systems, which sounds pretty esoteric. Could you talk a little about that and explain what that means?

BARBARA GROSZ: When Candy Sidner and I were developing the intentional model of discourse that I mentioned earlier, we first tried to build on the work of colleagues who were using AI models of planning developed for individual robots to formalize work in philosophy on speech act theory. When we tried to use those techniques in the context of dialogue, we found that they were inadequate. This discovery led us to the realization that teamwork or collaborative activity, or working together, cannot be characterized as simply the sum of individual plans.

After all, it's not as if you have a plan to do a certain set of actions and I have a plan to do a certain set of actions, and they just happen to fit together. At the time, because AI planning researchers often used examples involving building stacks of toy blocks, I used the particular example of one child having a stack of blue blocks and another child having a stack of red blocks, and they build a tower that has both red and blue blocks. But it's not that the child with the blue blocks has a plan with those blocks in spaces that just happen to match where the plan of the child with red blocks has empty spaces.

Sidner and I realized, at this point, that we had to come up with a new way of thinking about—and representing in a computer system—plans of multiple participants, whether people or computer agents or both. So that's how I got into multi-agent systems research.

The goal of work in this field is to think about computer agents being situated among other agents. In the 1980s, work in this area mostly concerned situations with multiple computer agents, either multiple robots or multiple software agents, and asked questions about competition and coordination.

BARBARA J. GROSZ

MARTIN FORD: Just to clarify: when you talk about a computer agent, what you mean is a program, a process that goes and performs some action or retrieves some information or does something.

BARBARA GROSZ: That's right. In general, a computer agent is a system able to act autonomously. Originally, most computer agents were robots, but for several decades AI research has involved software agents as well. Today there are computer agents that search and ones that compete in auctions, among many other tasks. So, an agent doesn't have to be a robot that's actually out there physically in the world.

For instance, Jeff Rosenheim had some really interesting work in the early years of multi-systems agents research, which considered situations like having a bunch of delivery robots, and they need to get things all over the city, and maybe if they exchanged packages they could do it more efficiently. He considered questions like whether they would tell the truth or lie about the tasks they actually had to do, because if an agent lied, it might come out ahead.

This whole area of multi-agent systems now addresses a wide range of situations and problems. Some work focuses on strategic reasoning; other on teamwork. And, I'm thrilled to say, more recently, much of it is now really looking at how computer agents can work with people, rather than just with other computer agents.

MARTIN FORD: Did this multi-agent work lead directly to your work in computational collaboration?

BARBARA GROSZ: Yes, one of the results of my work in multiple-agent systems was to develop the first computational model of collaboration.

We asked, what does it mean to collaborate? People take an overall task and divide it up, delegating tasks to different people and leaving to them figuring out the details. We make commitments to one another to do subtasks, and we (mostly) don't wander off and forget what we committed to doing.

In business, a common message is that one person doesn't try to do everything, but delegates tasks to other people depending on their expertise. This is the same in more informal collaborations.

I developed a model of collaboration that made these intuitions formal, in work with Sarit Kraus, and then generated many new research questions including how you decide who's capable of doing what, what happens if something goes wrong, and what's your obligation to the team. So, you don't just disappear or say, "Oh, I failed, Sorry. Hope you guys can do the task without me."

In 2011-2012 I had a year's sabbatical in California and I decided that I wanted to see if this work on collaboration could make a difference in the world. So, pretty much since then, I have been working in the healthcare arena developing new methods for healthcare coordination, working with Stanford pediatrician Lee Sanders. The particular medical setting is children who have complex medical conditions and see 12 or 15 doctors. In this context, we're asking: how can we provide systems that help those doctors share information and more successfully coordinate what they're doing.

MARTIN FORD: Would you say that health care is one the most promising areas for research for AI? It certainly seems like the part of the economy that most needs to be transformed and made more productive. I'd say we'd be much better off as a society if we could give transforming medicine a higher priority than having robots that flip hamburgers and produce cheaper fast food.

BARBARA GROSZ: Right, and healthcare is an area, along with education, where it's absolutely crucial that we focus on building systems that complement people, rather than systems that replace people.

MARTIN FORD: Let's talk about the future of artificial intelligence. What do you think about all of the focus right now on deep learning? I feel a normal person reads the press and could come away with the impression that AI and deep learning are synonymous. What would you point to, speaking of AI generally, as the things that are absolutely on the forefront?

BARBARA GROSZ: Deep learning is not deep in any philosophical sense. The name comes from there being many layers to the neural network. It isn't that deep learning is more intelligent in the sense of being a deeper "thinker" than other kinds of AI systems or learning. It functions well because it mathematically has more flexibility.

Deep learning is tremendously good for certain tasks, essentially ones that fit its end-to-end processing: a signal comes in and you get an answer out; but it is also limited by the data it gets. We see this limitation in systems that can recognize white males much better than other kinds of people because there are more white males in the training data. We see it also in machine translation that works very well for literal language, where it's had a lot of examples, but not for the kind of language you see in novels or anything that's literary or alliterative.

MARTIN FORD: Do you think there will be a backlash against all the hype surrounding deep learning when its limitations are more widely recognized?

BARBARA GROSZ: I have survived numerous AI Winters in the past and I've come away from them feeling both fearful and hopeful. I'm fearful that people, once they see the limitations of deep learning will say, "Oh, it doesn't really work." But I'm hopeful that, because deep learning is so powerful for so many things, and in so many areas, that there won't be an AI Winter around deep learning.

I do think, however, that to avoid an AI Winter for deep learning, people in the field need to put deep learning in its correct place, and be clear about its limitations.

I said at one point that "AI systems are best if they're designed with people in mind." Ece Kamar has noted that the data from which these deep learning systems learn, comes from people. Deep learning systems are trained by people. And these deep learning systems do better if there are people in the loop correcting them when they're getting something wrong. On the one hand, deep learning is very powerful, and it's enabled the development of a lot of fantastic things. But deep learning is not the answer to every AI question. It has, for instance, so far shown no usefulness for common sense reasoning!

MARTIN FORD: I think people are working on, for example, figuring out how to build a system so it can learn from a lot less data. Right now, systems do depend on enormous datasets in order to get them to work at all.

BARBARA GROSZ: Right, but notice the issue is not just how much data they need, but the diversity of the data.

I've been thinking about this recently; simply put, why does it matter? If I or you were building a system to work in New York City or San Francisco, that would be one thing. But these systems are being used by people around the world from different cultures, with different languages, and with different societal norms. Your data has to sample all of that space. And we don't have equal amounts of data for different groups. If we go to less data, we have to say something like (and I'm being a bit facetious here), "This is a system that works really well for white men, upper income."

MARTIN FORD: But is that just because the example you're using is facial recognition and they're feeding in photographs of white people mostly? If they expanded and had data from a more diverse population, then that would be fixed, right?

BARBARA GROSZ: Right, but that's just the easiest example I can give you. Let's take healthcare. Until only a few years ago, medical research was done only on males, and I'm not talking only about human males, I'm even talking about only male mice in basic biomedical research. Why? Because the females had hormones! If you're developing a new medicine, a related problem arises with young people versus old people as older people don't need the same dosages as young people. If most of your studies are on younger people, you again have a problem of biased data. The face data is an easy example, but the problem of data bias permeates everything.

MARTIN FORD: Of course, that's not a problem that's exclusive to AI; humans are subject to the same issues when confronted with flawed data. It's a bias in the data that results from past decisions that people doing research made.

BARBARA GROSZ: Right, but now look what's going on in some areas of medicine. The computer system can, "read all the papers" (more than a person could) and do certain kinds of information retrieval from them and extract results, and then do statistical analyses. But if most of the papers are on scientific work that was done only on male mice, or only on male humans, then the conclusions the system is coming to are limited.

We're also seeing this problem in the legal realm, with policing and fairness. So, as we build these systems, we have to think, "OK. What about how my data can be used?" Medicine is a place where I think it's really dangerous to not be careful about the limitations of the data that you're using.

MARTIN FORD: I want to talk about the path to AGI. I know you feel very strongly about building machines that work with people, but I can tell you from having done these interviews that a lot of your colleagues are very interested in building machines that are going to be independent, alien intelligences.

BARBARA GROSZ: They read too much science fiction!

MARTIN FORD: But just in terms of the technical path to true intelligence, I guess the first question is if you think that AGI is achievable? Maybe you think it can't be done at all. What are the technical hurdles ahead?

BARBARA GROSZ: The first thing I want to tell you is that in the late 1970s, as I was finishing my dissertation, I had this conversation with another student who said, "Good thing we don't care about making a lot of money, because AI will never amount to anything." I reflect on that prediction often, and I know I have no crystal ball about the future.

I don't think AGI is the right direction to go. I think the focus on AGI is actually ethically dangerous because it raises all sorts of issues of people not having jobs, and robots run amok. Those are fine issues to think about, but they are very far in the future. They're a distraction. The real point is we have any number of ethical issues right now, with the AI systems we have now, and I think it's unfortunate to distract attention from those because of scary futuristic scenarios.

Is AGI a worthwhile direction to go or not? You know, people have been wondering since at least *The Golem of Prague*, and *Frankenstein*, for many hundreds of years, if humanity could create something that is as smart as a human. I mean, you can't stop people from fantasizing and wondering, and I am not going to try, but I don't think that thinking about AGI is the best use of the resources we have, including our intelligence.

MARTIN FORD: What are the actual hurdles to AGI?

BARBARA GROSZ: I mentioned one hurdle, which is getting the wide range of data that would be needed and getting that data ethically because you're essentially being Big Brother and watching a lot of behavior and from that, taking a lot of data from a lot of people. I think that may be one of the biggest issues and biggest hurdles.

The second hurdle is that every AI system that exists today is an AI system with specialized abilities. Robots that can clean your house or systems that can answer questions about travel, or restaurants. To go from that kind of individualized intelligence to general intelligence that flexibly moves from one domain to another domain, and takes analogs from one domain to another, and can think not just about the present but also the future, those are really hard questions.

MARTIN FORD: One major concern is that AI is going to unleash a big economic disruption and that there might be a significant impact on jobs. That doesn't require AGI, just narrow AI systems that do specialized things well enough to displace workers or deskill jobs. Where do you fall on the spectrum of concern about the potential economic impact? How worried should we be?

BARBARA GROSZ: So yes, I am concerned, but I'm concerned in a somewhat different way from how many other people are concerned. The first thing I want to say is that it's not just an AI problem, but a wider technology problem. It's a problem where those of us who are technologists of various sorts are partially responsible, but the business world carries a lot of responsibility as well.

Here's an example. You used to call in to get customer service when something wasn't working, and you got to talk to a human being. Not all of those human customer service agents were good, but the ones who were good understood your problem and got you an answer.

Of course, human beings are expensive, so now they've been replaced in many customer service settings by computer systems. At one stage, companies got rid of more intelligent people and hired the cheaper people who could only follow a script, and that wasn't so good. But now, who needs a person who can only follow a script when you have a system? This approach makes for bad jobs, and it makes for bad customer service interactions.

When you think about AI and the increasingly intelligent systems, there are going to be more and more opportunities where you can think, "OK, we can replace the people." But it's problematic to do that if the system isn't fully capable of doing the task it's been assigned. It's also why I'm on the soapbox about building systems that complement people.

MARTIN FORD: I've written quite a lot about this, and I guess the point I would make is that this is very much at the intersection of technology and capitalism.

BARBARA GROSZ: Exactly!

MARTIN FORD: There is an inherent drive within capitalism to make more money by cutting costs and historically that has been a positive thing. My view is that we need to adapt capitalism so that it can continue to thrive, even if we are at an inflection point, where capital will really start to displace labor to an unprecedented extent.

BARBARA GROSZ: I'm with you entirely on that. I spoke about this recently at the American Academy of Arts and Sciences, and for me there are two key points.

My first point was that it's not a question of just what systems we can build but what systems we should build. As technologists, we have a choice about that, even in a capitalist system that will buy anything that saves money.

My second point was that we need to integrate ethics into the teaching of computer science, so students learn to think about this dimension of systems along with efficiency and elegance of code.

To the corporate and marketing people at this meeting, I gave the example of Volvo, who made a competitive advantage out of building cars that were safe. We need it to be a competitive advantage for companies to make systems that work well with people. But to do that is going to require engineers who don't just think about replacing people, but who work with social scientists and ethicists to figure out, "OK. I can put this kind of capability in, but what does it mean if I do that? How does it fit with people?"

We need to support building the kind of systems we should build, not just the systems that in the short-term look like they'll sell and save money.

MARTIN FORD: What about AI risks beyond the economic impact? What do you think we should be genuinely concerned about in terms of artificial intelligence, both in the near term and further out?

BARBARA GROSZ: From my perspective, there is a set of questions around the capabilities AI provides, the methods it has and what they can be used for, and the design of AI systems that go out in the world.

And there's a choice. Even with weapons, there's a choice. Are they fully autonomous? Where are the people in the loop? Even with cars, Elon Musk had a choice. He could have said that what Tesla cars had was driver-assist instead of saying he had a car with autopilot, because of course he doesn't have a car with autopilot. People get in trouble because they buy into the autopilot idea, trust it will work, and then have accidents.

So, we have a choice in what we put in the systems, what claims we make about the systems, and how we test, verify and set up the systems. Will there be a disaster? That depends on what choices we make.

Now is an absolutely crucial time for everyone involved in building systems that incorporate AI in some way—because those are not just AI systems: they're computer systems that have some AI involved. Everyone needs to sit down and have, as part of their design teams, people who are going to help them think more broadly about the unintended consequences of the systems they're building.

I mean, the law talks about unintended consequences, and computer scientists talk about side effects. It's time to stop, across technology development, as far as I'm concerned, saying, "Oh, I wonder if I can build a thing that does thus and such," and then build it and foist it on the world. We have to think about the long-range implications of the systems we're building. That's a societal problem.

I have gone from teaching a course on *Intelligent Systems: Design and Ethical Challenges* to now mounting an effort with colleagues at Harvard, which we call Embedded EthiCS, to integrate the teaching of ethics into every computer science course. I think that people who are designing systems, should not only be thinking about efficient algorithms and efficient code, but they should also be thinking about the ethical implications of the system.

MARTIN FORD: Do you think there's too much focus on existential threats? Elon Musk has set up OpenAI, which I think is an organization focused on working on this problem. Is that a good thing? Are these concerns something that we should take seriously, even though they may only be realized far in the future?

BARBARA GROSZ: Somebody could very easily put something very bad on a drone, and it could be very damaging. So yes, I'm in favor of people who are thinking about how they can design safe systems and what systems to build as well as how they can teach students to design programs that are more ethical. I would never say not to do that.

I do think that it's too extreme, however, as some people are saying, that we shouldn't be doing any more AI research or development until we have figured out how to avoid all such threats. It would be harmful to stop all of the wonderful ways in which AI can make the world a better place, because of perceived existential threats in the longer term.

I think we can continue to develop AI systems, but we have to be mindful of the ethical issues and to be honest about the capabilities and limitations of AI systems

MARTIN FORD: One phrase that you've used a lot is "we have a choice." Given your strong feeling that we should build systems that work with people, are you suggesting that these choices should be made primarily by computer scientists and engineers, or by entrepreneurs? Decisions like that are pretty heavily driven by the incentives in the market. Should these choices be made by society as a whole? Is there a place for regulation or government oversight?

BARBARA GROSZ: One thing I want to say is that even if you don't design the system to work with people, it's got to eventually work with people, so you'd better think about people. I mean, the Microsoft Tay bot and Facebook fake news disasters are examples of designers and systems where people didn't think enough about how they were releasing systems into the "wild," into a world that is full of people, not all of whom are trying to be helpful and agreeable. You can't ignore people!

So, I absolutely think there's room for legislation, there's room for policy, and there's room for regulation. One of the reasons I have this hobbyhorse about designing systems to work well with people is that I think if you get social scientists and ethicists in the room when you're thinking about your design, then you design better. As a result, the policies and the regulations will be needed only to do what you couldn't do by design as opposed to over-reacting or retrofitting badly designed systems. I think we'll always wind up with better systems if we design them to be the best systems they can be, and then the policy is on top of that.

MARTIN FORD: One concern that would be raised about regulation, within a country, or even in the West, is that there is an emerging competitive race with China. Is that something we should worry about, that the Chinese are going to leap ahead of us and set the pace, and that too much regulation might leave us at a disadvantage?

BARBARA GROSZ: There are two separate answers here right now. I know I sound like a broken record, but if we stop all AI research and development or severely restrict it, then the answer is yes.

If, however, we develop AI in a context which takes ethical reasoning and thinking into account as well as the efficiency of code then no, because we'll keep developing AI.

The one place where there's extraordinary danger is with weapons systems. A key issue is what would happen if we didn't build AI-driven weapons and an enemy did; but that topic is so large that it would take another hour conversation.

MARTIN FORD: To wind up, I wanted to ask you about women in the field. Is there any advice you would offer to women, or men, or to students just getting started? What would you want to say about the role of women in the field of AI and how things have evolved over the course of your career?

BARBARA GROSZ: The first thing I would say to everybody is that this field has some of the most interesting questions of any field in the world. The set of questions that AI raises has always required a combination of thinking analytically, thinking mathematically, thinking about people and behavior, and thinking about engineering. You get to explore all sorts of ways of thinking and all sorts of design. I'm sure other people think their fields are the most exciting, but I think it's even more exciting now for us in AI because we have much stronger tools: just look at our computing power. When I started in the field I had a colleague who'd knit a sweater waiting for a carriage return to echo!

Like all of computer science and all of technology, I think it's essential that we have the broadest spectrum of people involved in designing our AI systems. I mean not just women as well as men, I mean people from different cultures, people of different races, because that's who's going to use the systems. If you don't, you have two big dangers. One is the systems you design are only appropriate for certain populations, and the second is that you have work climates that aren't welcoming to the broadest spectrum of people and therefore benefit from only certain subpopulations. We've got to all work together.

As for my experience, there were almost no women involved in AI at the beginning, and my experience depended entirely on what the men with whom I worked were like. Some of my experiences were fantastic, and some were horrible. Every university, every company that has a group doing technology, should take on the responsibility of making sure the environments encourage women as well as men, and people from under-represented minorities because, in the end, we know that the more diverse the design team, the better the design.

ARCHITECTS OF INTELLIGENCE

BARBARA GROSZ is *Higgins Professor of Natural Sciences in the School of Engineering and Applied Sciences at Harvard University and a member of the External Faculty of Santa Fe Institute. She has made groundbreaking contributions to the field of artificial intelligence through pioneering research in natural language processing and in theories of multi-agent collaboration and their application to human-computer interaction. Her current research explores ways to use models developed in this research to improve health care coordination and science education.*

Barbara received an AB in mathematics from Cornell University, and a master's and PhD in computer science from the University of California, Berkeley. Her many awards and distinctions include election to the National Academy of Engineering, the American Philosophical Society, and the American Academy of Arts and Sciences, and as a fellow of the Association for the Advancement of Artificial Intelligence and the Association for Computing Machinery. She received the 2009 ACM/AAAI Allen Newell Award, the 2015 IJCAI Award for Research Excellence, and the 2017 Association for Computational Linguistics Lifetime Achievement Award. She is also known for her leadership of interdisciplinary institutions and contributions to the advancement of women in science.

BARBARA J. GROSZ

66 *The current machine learning concentration on deep learning and its non-transparent structures is a hang-up. They need to liberate themselves from this data-centric philosophy.*

JUDEA PEARL

PROFESSOR OF COMPUTER SCIENCE AND STATISTICS,
UNIVERSITY OF CALIFORNIA, LOS ANGELES
DIRECTOR OF THE COGNITIVE SYSTEMS LABORATORY

Judea Pearl is known internationally for his contributions to artificial intelligence, human reasoning, and philosophy of science. He is particularly well known in the AI field for his work on probabilistic (or Bayesian) techniques and causality. He is the author of more than 450 scientific papers and three landmark books: Heuristics *(1984),* Probabilistic Reasoning *(1988), and* Causality *(2000; 2009). His 2018 book,* The Book of Why, *makes his work on causation accessible to a general audience. In 2011, Judea received the Turing Award, which is the highest honor in the field of computer science and is often compared to the Nobel Prize.*

MARTIN FORD: You've had a long and decorated career. What path led you to get started in computer science and artificial intelligence?

JUDEA PEARL: I was born in Israel in 1936, in a town named Bnei Brak. I attribute a lot of my curiosity to my childhood and to my upbringing, both as part of Israeli society and as a lucky member of a generation that received a unique and inspiring education. My high-school and college teachers were top-notch scientists who had come from Germany in the 1930s, and they couldn't find a job in academia, so they taught in high schools. They knew they would never get back to academia, and they saw in us the embodiment of their academic and scientific dreams. My generation were beneficiaries of this educational experiment—growing up under the mentorship of great scientists who happened to be high-school teachers. I never excelled in school, I was not the best, or even second best, I was always third or fourth, but I always got very involved in each area taught. And we were taught in a chronological way, focusing on the inventor or scientist behind the invention or theorem. Because of this, we got the idea that science is not just a collection of facts, but a continuous human struggle with the uncertainties of nature. This added to my curiosity.

I didn't commit myself to science until I was in the army. I was a member of a Kibbutz and was about to spend my life there, but smart people told me that I would be happier if I utilized my mathematical skills. As such, they advised me to go and study electronics in Technion, the Israel Institute of Technology, which I did in 1956. I did not favor any particular specialization in college; but I enjoyed circuit synthesis and electromagnetic theory. I finished my undergraduate degree and got married in 1960. I came to the US with the idea of doing graduate work, getting my PhD, and going back.

MARTIN FORD: You mean you planned to go back to Israel?

JUDEA PEARL: Yes, my plan was to get a degree and come back to Israel. I first registered at the Brooklyn Polytechnic Institute (now part of NYU), which was one of the top schools in microwave communication at the time. However, I couldn't afford the tuition, I ended up employed at the David Sarnoff Research Center at the RCA laboratory in Princeton, New Jersey. There, I was a member of the computer memory group under Dr. Jan Rajchman, which was a hardware-oriented group. We, as well as everybody else in the country, were looking for different physical mechanisms that could serve as computer memory. This was because magnetic core memories became too slow, too bulky, and you had to string them manually.

People understood that the days of core memory were numbered, and everybody—IBM, Bell Labs, and RCA Laboratories—was looking for various phenomena that could serve as a mechanism to store digital information. Superconductivity was appealing at that time because of the speed and the ease of preparing the memory, even though it required cooling to liquid helium temperature. I was investigating circulating currents in superconductors, again for use in memory, and I discovered a few interesting phenomena there. There's even a Pearl vortex named after me, which is a turbulent current that spins around in superconducting films, and gives rise to a very interesting phenomenon that defies Faraday's law. It was an exciting time, both on the technological side and on the inspirational, scientific side.

Everyone was also inspired by the potential capabilities of computers in 1961 and 1962. No one had any doubt that eventually, computers would emulate most human intellectual tasks. Everyone was looking for tricks to accomplish those tasks, even the hardware people. We were constantly looking for ways of making associative memories, dealing with perception, object recognition, the encoding of visual scenes; all the tasks that we knew are important for general AI. The management at RCA also encouraged us to come up with inventions. I remember our boss Dr. Rajchman visiting us once a week and asking if we had any new patent disclosures.

Of course, all work on superconductivity stopped with the advent of semiconductors, which, at the time, we didn't believe would take off. We didn't believe that miniaturization technology would succeed as it did. We also didn't believe they could overcome the vulnerability problem where the memory would be wiped if the battery ran out. Obviously, they did, and semiconductor technology wiped out all its competitors. At that point, I was working for a company called Electronic Memories, and the rise of semiconductors left me without a job. That was how I came to academia, where I pursued my old dreams of doing pattern recognition and image encoding.

MARTIN FORD: Did you go directly to UCLA from Electronic Memories?

JUDEA PEARL: I tried to go to the University of Southern California, but they wouldn't hire me because I was too sure of myself. I wanted to teach software, even though I'd never programmed before, and the Dean threw me out of his office. I ended up at UCLA because they gave me a chance of doing the things that I wanted to do, and I slowly migrated into AI from pattern recognition, image encoding, and decision theory. The early days of AI were dominated by chess and other game-playing programs, and that enticed me in the beginning, because I saw there a metaphor for capturing human intuition. That was and remained my life dream, to capture human intuition on a machine.

In games, the intuition comes about in the way you evaluate the strength of a move. There was a big gap between what machines can do and what experts can do, and the challenge was to capture experts' evaluation in the machine. I ended up doing some analytical work and came up with a nice explanation of what heuristics is all about, and an automatic way of discovering heuristics, it is still in use today. I believe I was the first to show that alpha-beta search is optimal, as well other mathematical results about what makes one heuristic better than another. All of that work was compiled in my book, *Heuristics*, which came out in 1983. Then expert systems came to the scene, and people were excited about capturing different kinds of heuristics—not the heuristic of a chess master, but the intuition of highly-paid professionals, like a physician or a mineral explorer. The idea was to emulate professional performance on a computer system, either to replace or to assist the professional. I looked at expert systems as another challenge of capturing intuition.

MARTIN FORD: Just to clarify, expert systems are mostly based on rules, correct? If this is true, then do that, etc.

JUDEA PEARL: Correct, it was based on rules, and the goal was to capture the mode of operation of an expert, what makes an expert decide one way or the other while engaging in professional work.

What I did, was to replace it with a different paradigm. For example, instead of modeling a physician—the expert—we modeled the disease. You don't have to ask the expert what they do. Instead, you ask, what kind of symptoms you expect to see if you have malaria or if you have the flu; and what do you know about the disease? On the basis of this information, we built a diagnosis system that could examine a collection of symptoms and come out with the suspected disease. It also works for mineral exploration, for troubleshooting, or for any other expertise.

MARTIN FORD: Was this based on your work on heuristics, or are you referring now to Bayesian networks?

JUDEA PEARL: No, I left heuristics the moment my book published in 1983, and I started working on Bayesian networks and uncertainty management. There were many proposals at the time for managing uncertainties, but they didn't gel with the dictates of probability theory and decision theory, and I wanted to do it correctly and efficiently.

MARTIN FORD: Could you talk about your work on Bayesian networks? I know they are used in a lot of important applications today.

JUDEA PEARL: First, we need to understand the environment at the time. There was a tension between the scruffies and the neaties. The scruffies just wanted to build a system that works, not caring about guarantees or whether their methods comply with any theory or not. The neaties wanted to understand why it worked and make sure that they have performance guarantees of some kind.

MARTIN FORD: Just to clarify, these were nicknames for two groups of people with different attitudes.

JUDEA PEARL: Yes. We see the same tension today in the machine learning community, where some people like to get machines to do important jobs, regardless of whether they're doing it optimally or whether the system can explain itself, as long as the job is being done. The neaties would like to have explainability and transparency, systems that can explain themselves and systems that have performance guarantees.

Well, at that time, the scruffies were in command, and they still are today, because they have a good conduit to funders and to industry. Industry, however, is short-sighted and requires short-term success, which creates an imbalance in research emphasis. It was the same in the Bayesian network days; the scruffies were in command. I was among the few loners who advocated doing things correctly by the rules of probability theory. The problem was that probability theory, if you adhere to it in the traditional way, would require exponential time and exponential memory, and we couldn't afford these two resources.

I was looking for a way of doing it efficiently, and I was inspired by the work of David Rumelhart, a cognitive psychologist who examined how children read text so quickly and reliably. His proposal was to have a multi-layered system going from the pixel level to the semantic level, then the sentence level and the grammatical level, and they all shake hands and pass messages to each other. One level doesn't know what the other's doing; it's simply passing messages. Eventually, these messages converge on the correct answer when you read a word like "the car" and distinguish it from "the cat," depending on the context in the narrative.

I tried to simulate his architecture in probability theory, and I couldn't do it very well until I discovered that if you have a tree as a structure connecting the modules, then you do have this convergence property. You can propagate messages asynchronously, and eventually, the system relaxes to the correct answer. Then we went to a polytree, which is a fancier version of a tree, and eventually, in 1995, I published a paper about general Bayesian networks.

This architecture really caught us by surprise because it was very easy to program. A programmer didn't have to use a supervisor to oversee all the elements, all they had to do was to program what one variable does when it wakes up and decides to update its information. That variable then sends messages to its neighbors. The neighbors send messages to their neighbors, and so on. The system eventually relaxes to the correct answer.

The ease of programming was the feature that made Bayesian networks acceptable. It was also made acceptable by the idea that you can program the disease and not the physician—the domain, and not the professional that deals with the domain—that made the system transparent. The users of the system understood why the system provided one result or another, and they understood how to modify the system when things changed in the environment. You had the advantage of modularity, which you get when you model the way things work in nature.

It's something that we didn't realize at the time, mainly because we didn't realize the importance of modularity. When we did, I realized that it is causality that gives us this modularity, and when we lose causality, we lose modularity, and we enter into no-man's land. That means that we lose transparency, we lose reconfigurability, and other nice features that we like. By the time that I published my book on Bayesian networks in 1988, though, I already felt like an apostate because I knew already that the next step would be to model causality, and my love was already on a different endeavor.

MARTIN FORD: We always hear people saying that "correlation is not causation," and so you can never get causation from the data. Bayesian networks do not offer a way to understand causation, right?

JUDEA PEARL: No, Bayesian networks could work in either mode. It depends on what you think about when you construct it.

MARTIN FORD: The Bayesian idea is that you update probabilities based on new evidence so that your estimate should get more accurate over time. That's the basic concept that you've built into these networks, and you figured out a very efficient way to do that for a large number of probabilities. It's clear that this has become a really important idea in computer science and AI because it's used all over the place.

JUDEA PEARL: Using Bayes' rule is an old idea; doing it efficiently was the hard part. That's one of the things that I thought was necessary for machine learning. You can get evidence and use the Bayesian rule to update the system to improve its performance and improve the parameters. That's all part of the Bayesian scheme of updating knowledge using evidence, it is probabilistic, not causal knowledge, so it has limitations.

MARTIN FORD: But it's used quite frequently, for example, in voice recognition systems and all the devices that we're familiar with. Google uses it extensively for all kinds of things.

JUDEA PEARL: People tell me that every cellphone has a Bayesian network doing error correction to minimize transmission noise. Every cellphone has a Bayesian network and belief propagation, that's the name we gave to the message passing scheme. People also tell me that Siri has a Bayesian network in it, although Apple is too secretive about it, so I haven't been able to verify it.

Although Bayesian updating is one of the major components in machine learning today, there has been a shift from Bayesian networks to deep learning, which is less transparent. You allow the system itself to adjust the parameters without knowing the function that connects input and output. It's less transparent than Bayesian networks, which had the feature of modularity, and which we didn't realize was so important. When you model the disease, you actually model the cause and effect relationship of the disease, not the expert, and you get modularity. Once we realize that, the question begs itself: What is this ingredient that you and I call "cause and effect relationships"? Where does it reside, and how do you handle it? That was the next step for me.

MARTIN FORD: Let's talk about causation. You published a very famous book on Bayesian networks, and it was really that paper that led to Bayesian techniques becoming so popular in computer science. But before that book was even published, you were already starting to think about moving on to focus on causation?

JUDEA PEARL: Causation was part of the intuition that gave rise to Bayesian networks, even though the formal definition of Bayesian networks is purely probabilistic. You do diagnostics, you make predictions, and you don't deal with interventions. If you don't need interventions, you don't need causality—theoretically. You can do everything that a Bayesian network does with purely probabilistic terminology. However, in practice, people noticed that if you structure the network in the causal direction, things are much easier. The question was why.

Now we understand that we were craving for features of causality that we didn't even know come from causality. These were: modularity, reconfigurability, transferability, and more. By the time I looked into causality, I had realized that the mantra "correlation does not imply causation" is much more profound than we thought. You need to have causal assumptions before you can get causal conclusions, which you cannot get from data alone. Worse yet, even if you are willing to make causal assumptions, you cannot express them.

There was no language in science in which you can express a simple sentence like "mud does not cause rain," or "the rooster does not cause the sun to rise." You couldn't express it in mathematics, which means that even if you wanted to take it for granted that the rooster does not cause the sun to rise, you couldn't write it down, you couldn't combine it with data, and you couldn't combine it with other sentences of this kind.

In short, even if you agree to enrich the data with causal assumptions, you couldn't write down the assumptions. It required a whole new language. This realization was really a shock and a challenge for me because I grew up on statistics, and I believed that scientific wisdom lies in statistics. Statistics allows you to do induction, deduction, abduction, and model updating. And here I find the language of statistics crippled in hopeless helplessness. As a computer scientist, I was not scared because computer scientists invent languages to fit their needs. But what is the language that should be invented, and how do we marry this language with the language of data?

Statistics speaks a different language—the language of averages, of hypothesis testing, summarizing data and visualizing it from different perspectives. All of this is the language of data, and here comes another language, the language of cause and effect. How do we marry the two so that they can interact? How do we take assumptions about cause and effect, combine them with the data that I have, and then get conclusions that tell me how nature works? That was my challenge as a computer scientist and as a part-time philosopher. This is essentially the role of a philosopher, to capture human intuition and formalize it in a way that it can be programmed on a computer. Even though philosophers don't think about the computer, if you look closely at what they are doing, they are trying to formalize things as much as they can with the language available to them. The goal is to make it more explicable and more meaningful so that computer scientists can eventually program a machine to perform cognitive functions that puzzle philosophers.

MARTIN FORD: Did you invent the technical language or the diagrams that are used for describing causation?

JUDEA PEARL: No, I didn't invent that. The basic idea was conceived in 1920 by a geneticist named Sewall Wright, who was the first to write down a causal diagram with arrows and nodes, like a one-way city map. He fought all his life to justify the fact that you can get things out of this diagram that statisticians could not get from regression, association, or from correlation. His methods were primitive, but they proved the point that he could get things that the statisticians could not get.

What I did was to take Sewall Wright's diagrams seriously and invested into them all my computer science background, reformalized them, and exploited them to their utmost. I came up with a causal diagram as a means of encoding scientific knowledge and as a means of guiding machines in the task of figuring out cause-effect relationships in various sciences, from medicine, to education, to climate warming. These were all areas where scientists worry about what causes what, how nature transmits the information from cause to effect, what are the mechanisms involved, how do you control it, and how do you answer practical questions which involve cause-effect relationships.

This has been my life's challenge for the past 30 years. I published a book on that in 2000, with the second edition in 2009, called *Causality*. I co-authored a gentler introduction in 2015. And this year, I co-authored *The Book of Why*, which is a general audience book explaining the challenge in down-to-earth terms, so that people can understand causality even without knowing equations. Equations of course help to condense things and to focus on things, but you don't have to be a rocket scientist to read *The Book of Why*. You just have to follow the conceptual development of the basic ideas. In that book, I look at history from a causal lens perspective; I asked what conceptual breakthroughs made a difference in the way we think, rather than what experiments discovered one drug or another.

MARTIN FORD: I've been reading *The Book of Why* and I'm enjoying it. I think one of the main outcomes of your work is that causal models are now very important in the social and natural sciences. In fact, I just saw an article the other day, written by a quantum physicist who used causal models to prove something in quantum mechanics. So clearly your work has had a big impact in those areas.

JUDEA PEARL: I read that article. In fact, I put it on my next-to-read list because I couldn't quite understand the phenomena that they were so excited about.

MARTIN FORD: One of the main points I took away from *The Book of Why* is that, while natural and social scientists have really begun to use the tools of causation, you feel that the field of AI is lagging behind. You think AI researchers will have to start focusing on causation in order for the field to progress.

JUDEA PEARL: Correct. Causal modeling is not at the forefront of the current work in machine learning. Machine learning today is dominated by statisticians and the belief that you can learn everything from data. This data-centric philosophy is limited.

I call it curve fitting. It might sound derogatory, but I don't mean it in a derogatory way. I mean it in a descriptive sense that what people are doing in deep learning and neural networks is fitting very sophisticated functions to a bunch of points. These functions are very sophisticated, they have thousands of hills and valleys, they're intricate, and you cannot predict them in advance. But they're still just a matter of fitting functions to a cloud of points.

This philosophy has clear theoretical limitations, and I'm not talking about opinion, I'm talking about theoretical limitations. You cannot do counterfactuals, and you cannot think about actions that you've never seen before. I describe it in terms of three cognitive levels: seeing, intervening, and imagining. Imagining is the top level, and that level requires counterfactual reasoning: how would the world look like had I done things differently? For example, what would the world look like had Oswald not killed Kennedy, or had Hillary won the election? We think about those things and can communicate with those kinds of imaginary scenarios, and we are quite comfortable to engage in this "let's pretend" game.

The reason why we need this capability is to build new models of the world. Imagining a world that does not exist gives us the ability to come up with new theories, new inventions, and also to repair our old actions so as to assume responsibility, regret, and free will. All of this comes as part of our ability to generate worlds that do not exist but could exist, but still generate them widely, not wildly. We have rules for generating plausible counterfactuals that are not whimsical. They have their own inner structure, and once we understand this logic, we can build machines that imagine things, that assume responsibility for their actions, and understand ethics and compassion.

I'm not a futurist and I try not to talk about things that I don't understand, but I did some thinking, and I believe I understand how important counterfactuals are in all these cognitive tasks that people dream of which eventually will be implemented on a computer. I have a few basic sketches of how we can program free will, ethics, morality, and responsibility into machines, but these are in the realm of sketches. The basic thing is that we know today what it takes to interpret counterfactuals and understand cause and effect.

These are the mini-steps toward general AI, but there's a lot we can learn from these steps, and that's what I'm trying to get the machine learning community to understand. I want them to understand that deep learning is a mini-step toward general AI. We need to learn what we can from the way theoretical barriers were circumvented in causal reasoning, so that we can circumvent them in general AI.

MARTIN FORD: So, you're saying that deep learning is limited to analyzing data and that causation can never be derived from data alone. Since people are able to do causal reasoning, the human mind must have some built-in machinery that allows us to create causal models. It's not just about learning from data.

JUDEA PEARL: To create is one thing, but even if somebody creates it for us, our parents, our peers, our culture, we need to have the machinery to utilize it.

MARTIN FORD: Right. It sounds like a causal diagram, or a causal model is really just a hypothesis. Two people might have different causal models, and somewhere in our brain is some kind of machinery that allows us to continuously create these causal models internally, and that's what allows us to reason based on data.

JUDEA PEARL: We need to create them, to modify them, and to perturb them when the need arises. We used to believe that malaria is caused by bad air, now we don't. Now we believe it's caused by a mosquito called Anopheles. It makes a difference because if it is bad air, I will carry a breathing mask the next time I go to the swamp; and if it's an Anopheles mosquito, I'll carry a mosquito net. These competing theories make a big difference in how we act in the world. The way that we get from one hypothesis to another was by trial and error; I call it playful manipulation.

This is how a child learns causal structure, by playful manipulation, and this is how a scientist learns causal structure—playful manipulation. But we have to have the abilities and the template to store what we learn from this playful manipulation so we can use it, test it, and change it. Without the ability to store it in a parsimonious encoding, in some template in our mind, we cannot utilize it, nor can we change it or play around with it. That is the first thing that we have to learn; we have to program computers to accommodate and manage that template.

MARTIN FORD: So, you think that some sort of built-in template or structure should be built into an AI system so it can create causal models? DeepMind uses reinforcement learning, which is based on practice or trial and error. Perhaps that would be a way of discovering causal relationships?

JUDEA PEARL: It comes into it, but reinforcement learning has limitations, too. You can only learn actions that have been seen before. You cannot extrapolate to actions that you haven't seen, like raising taxes, increasing the minimum wage, or banning cigarettes. Cigarettes have never been banned before, yet we have machinery that allows us to stipulate, extrapolate, and imagine what could be the consequences of banning cigarettes.

MARTIN FORD: So, you believe that the capability to think causally is critical to achieving what you'd call strong AI or AGI, artificial general intelligence?

JUDEA PEARL: I have no doubt that it is essential. Whether it is sufficient, I'm not sure. However, causal reasoning doesn't solve every problem of general AI. It doesn't solve the object recognition problem, and it doesn't solve the language understanding problem. We basically solved the cause-effect puzzle, and we can learn a lot from these solutions so that we can help the other tasks circumvent their obstacles.

MARTIN FORD: Do you think that strong AI or AGI is feasible? Is that something you think will happen someday?

JUDEA PEARL: I have no doubt that it is feasible. But what does it mean for me to say no doubt? It means that I am strongly convinced it can be done because I haven't seen any theoretical impediment to strong AI.

MARTIN FORD: You said that way back around 1961, when you were at RCA, people were already thinking about this. What do you think of how things have progressed? Are you disappointed? What's your assessment of progress in artificial intelligence?

JUDEA PEARL: Things are progressing just fine. There were a few slowdowns, and there were a few hang-ups. The current machine learning concentration on deep learning and its non-transparent structures is such a hang-up. They need to liberate themselves from this data-centric philosophy. In general, the field has been progressing immensely, because of technology and because of the people that the field attracts. The smartest people in science.

MARTIN FORD: Most of the recent progress has been in deep learning. You seem somewhat critical of that. You've pointed out that it's like curve fitting and it's not transparent, but actually more of a black-box that just generates answers.

JUDEA PEARL: It's curve fitting, correct, it's harvesting low-hanging fruits.

MARTIN FORD: It's still done amazing things.

JUDEA PEARL: It's done amazing thing because we didn't realize there are so many low-hanging fruits.

MARTIN FORD: Looking to the future, do you think that neural networks are going to be very important?

JUDEA PEARL: Neural networks and reinforcement learning will all be essential components when properly utilized in causal modeling.

MARTIN FORD: So, you think it might be a hybrid system that incorporates not just neural networks, but other ideas from other areas of AI?

JUDEA PEARL: Absolutely. Even today, people are building hybrid systems when you have sparse data. There's a limit, however, to how much you can extrapolate or interpolate sparse data if you want to get cause-effect relationships. Even if you have infinite data, you can't tell the difference between A causes B and B causes A.

MARTIN FORD: If someday we have strong AI, do you think that a machine could be conscious, and have some kind of inner experience like a human being?

JUDEA PEARL: Of course, every machine has an inner experience. A machine has to have a blueprint of some of its software; it could not have a total mapping of its software. That would violate Turing's halting problem.

It's feasible, however, to have a rough blueprint of some of its important connections and important modules. The machine would have to have some encoding of its abilities, of its beliefs, and of its goals and desires. That is doable. In some sense, a machine already has an inner self, and more so in the future. Having a blueprint of your environment, how you act on and react to the environment, and answering counterfactual questions amount to having an inner self. Thinking: What if I had done things differently? What if I wasn't in love? All this involves manipulating your inner self.

MARTIN FORD: Do you think machines could have emotional experiences, that a future system might feel happy, or might suffer in some way?

JUDEA PEARL: That reminds me of *The Emotion Machine*, a book by Marvin Minsky. He talks about how easy it is to program emotion. You have chemicals floating in your body, and they have a purpose, of course. The chemical machine interferes with, and occasionally overrides the reasoning machine when urgencies develop. So, emotions are just a chemical priority-setting machine.

MARTIN FORD: I want to finish by asking you about some of the things that we should worry about as artificial intelligence progresses. Are there things we should be concerned about?

JUDEA PEARL: We have to worry about artificial intelligence. We have to understand what we build, and we have to understand that we are breeding a new species of intelligent animals.

At first, they are going to be domesticated, like our chickens and our dogs, but eventually, they will assume their own agency, and we have to be very cautious about this. I don't know how to be cautious without suppressing science and scientific curiosity. It's a difficult question, so I wouldn't want to enter into a debate about how we regulate AI research. But we should absolutely be cautious about the possibility that we are creating a new species of super-animals, or in the best case, a species of useful, but exploitable, human beings that do not demand legal rights or minimum wage.

JUDEA PEARL *was born in Tel Aviv and is a graduate of the Technion-Israel Institute of Technology. He came to the United States for postgraduate work in 1960, and the following year he received a master's degree in electrical engineering from Newark College of Engineering, now New Jersey Institute of Technology. In 1965, he simultaneously received a master's degree in physics from Rutgers University and a PhD from the Brooklyn Polytechnic Institute, now Polytechnic Institute of New York University. Until 1969, he held research positions at RCA David Sarnoff Research Laboratories in Princeton, New Jersey and Electronic Memories, Inc. Hawthorne, California.*

Judea joined the faculty of UCLA in 1969, where he is currently a professor of computer science and statistics and director of the Cognitive Systems Laboratory. He is known internationally for his contributions to artificial intelligence, human reasoning, and philosophy of science. He is the author of more than 450 scientific papers and three landmark books: Heuristics *(1984),* Probabilistic Reasoning *(1988), and* Causality *(2000; 2009).*

A member of the National Academy of Sciences, the National Academy of Engineering and a founding Fellow of the American Association for Artificial Intelligence, Judea is the recipient of numerous scientific prizes, including three awarded in 2011: the Association for Computing Machinery A.M. Turing Award for his fundamental contributions to artificial intelligence through the development of a calculus for probabilistic and causal reasoning, the David E. Rumelhart Prize for Contributions to the Theoretical Foundations of Human Cognition, and the Harvey Prize in Science and Technology from Technion—Israel Institute of Technology. Other honors include the 2001 London School of Economics Lakatos Award in Philosophy of Science for the best book in the philosophy of science, the 2003 ACM Allen Newell Award for "seminal contributions that extend to philosophy, psychology, medicine, statistics, econometrics, epidemiology and social science," and the 2008 Benjamin Franklin Medal for Computer and Cognitive Science from the Franklin Institute.

JUDEA PEARL

66 *We're all working together on trying to build really intelligent, flexible AI systems. We want those systems to be able to come into a new problem and use pieces of knowledge that they've developed from solving many other problems to all of a sudden be able to solve that new problem in a flexible way, which is essentially one of the hallmarks of human intelligence. The question is, how can we build that capability into computer systems?*

JEFFREY DEAN

GOOGLE SENIOR FELLOW, HEAD OF AI AND GOOGLE BRAIN

Jeff Dean joined Google in 1999, and has played a role in developing many of Google's core systems in areas like search, advertising, news and language translation, as well as in the design of the company's distributed computing architecture. In recent years, he has focused on AI and machine learning and worked on the development of TensorFlow, Google's widely-used open source software for deep learning. He currently guides Google's future path in AI as director of artificial intelligence and head of the Google Brain project.

MARTIN FORD: As the Director of AI at Google and head of Google Brain, what's your vision for AI research at Google?

JEFF DEAN: Overall, I view our role as to advance the state of the art in machine learning, to try and build more intelligent systems by developing new machine learning algorithms and techniques, and to build software and hardware infrastructure that allows us to make faster progress on these approaches and allow other people to also apply these approaches to problems they care about. TensorFlow is a good example of that.

Google Brain is one of several different research teams that we have within the Google AI research team, and some of those other teams have slightly different focuses. For instance, there's a large team focused on machine perception problems, and another team focused on natural language understanding. It's not really hard boundaries here; interests overlap across the teams, and we collaborate quite heavily across many of these teams for many of the projects that we're working on.

We do deep collaborations with the Google product teams sometimes. We've done collaborations in the past with our search ranking team to try to apply deep learning to some of the problems in search ranking and retrieval. We've also done collaborations with both the Google Translate and Gmail team, as well as many other teams throughout Google. The fourth area is researching new and interesting emerging areas, where we know machine learning will be a significantly new and important piece of solving problems in that domain.

We have quite a lot of work, for example, in the use of AI and machine learning for healthcare, and also AI and machine learning for robotics. Those are two examples, but we're also looking at earlier-stage things. We have 20 different areas where we think there's a real key aspect of some of the problems in that area that machine learning, or our particular kind of expertise, could really help with. So, my role is basically to try to have us be as ambitious as possible in all these different kinds of projects, and also to push us in new and interesting directions for the company.

MARTIN FORD: I know that DeepMind is heavily focused on AGI. Does that mean that the other artificial intelligence research at Google is geared toward more narrow and practical applications?

JEFF DEAN: That's correct that DeepMind is more focused on AGI, and I think they have a structured plan where they believe if they solve this and this and this, that may lead to AGI. That's not to say that the rest of Google AI doesn't think about it. A lot of researchers in the Google AI research organization are also focused on building new capabilities for generally intelligent systems, or AGI if you want to call it that. I would say that our path is a bit more organic. We do things that we know are important but that we can't do yet, and once we solve those, then we figure out what is the next set of problems that we want to solve that will give us new capabilities.

It's really a slightly different approach, but ultimately, we're all working together on trying to build really intelligent, flexible AI systems. We want those systems to be able to come into a new problem and use pieces of knowledge that they've developed from solving many other problems to all of a sudden be able to solve that new problem in a flexible way, which is essentially one of the hallmarks of human intelligence. The question is, how can we build that capability into computer systems?

MARTIN FORD: What was the path that led to you becoming interested in AI and then to your current role at Google?

JEFF DEAN: My dad got a computer when I was 9 that he assembled from a kit, and I learned to program on that through middle and high school. From there, I went on to do a double degree in Computer Science and Economics at the University of Minnesota. My senior thesis was on parallel training of neural networks, and this was back when neural networks were hot and exciting in the late 1980s and early 1990s. At that time, I liked the abstraction that they provided; it felt good.

I think a lot of other people felt the same way, but we just didn't have enough computational power. I felt like if we could get 60-times the speed on those 64-bit processor machines then we could actually do great things. It turns out that we needed more like a million-times the speed, but we have that now.

I then went to work for the World Health Organization for a year, doing statistical software for HIV and AIDS surveillance and forecasting. After that, I went to graduate school at the University of Washington, where I got a PhD in Computer Science, doing mostly compiler optimization work. I went on to work for DEC in Palo Alto in their industrial research lab, before joining a startup—I lived in Silicon Valley, and that was the thing to do!

Eventually, I ended up at Google back when it only employed around 25 people, and I've been here ever since. I've worked on a number of things at Google. The first thing I did here was working on our first advertising system. I then worked for many years on our search systems and features like the crawling system, query-serving system, the indexing system, and the ranking functions, etc. I then moved on to our infrastructure software, things like MapReduce, Bigtable and Spanner, and also our indexing systems.

In 2011, I started to work on more machine learning-oriented systems, because I started to get very interested in how we could apply the very large amounts of computation that we had to train very large and powerful neural nets.

MARTIN FORD: You're the head, and one of the founders, of Google Brain, which was one of the first real applications of deep learning and neural networks. Could you sketch out the story of Google Brain, and the role it plays at Google?

JEFF DEAN: Andrew Ng was a consultant in Google X for one day a week, and I bumped into him in the kitchen one day, and I said, "What are you up to?" He said, "Oh, I'm still figuring things out here, but at Stanford, my students are starting to look at how neural networks can be applied to different kinds of problems, and they're starting to work." I had experience with neural networks from doing my undergraduate thesis 20 years ago, so I said, "That's cool, I like neural networks. How are they working?" We started talking, and we came up with the relatively ambitious plan of trying to use as much computation as we could throw at the problem to try to train neural networks.

We tackled two problems: the first was the unsupervised learning of image data. Here, we took 10 million frames from random YouTube videos and tried to use unsupervised learning algorithms to see what would happen if we trained a very large network. Maybe you've seen the famous cat neuron visualization?

MARTIN FORD: Yes. I remember that got a lot of attention at the time.

JEFF DEAN: That was a sign that there was something interesting going on there when you trained these models at scale with large amounts of data.

MARTIN FORD: Just to emphasize, this was unsupervised learning, in the sense that it figured out the concept of a cat organically, from unstructured, unlabeled data?

JEFF DEAN: Correct. We gave it the raw images from a bunch of YouTube videos, and had an unsupervised algorithm that was trying to build a representation that would allow it to reconstruct those images from that compact representation. One of the things it learned to do was to discover a pattern that would fire if there was a cat of some sort in the center of the frame because that's a relatively common occurrence in YouTube videos, so that was pretty cool.

The other thing we did was to work with the speech recognition team on applying deep learning and deep neural networks to some of the problems in the speech recognition system. At first, we worked on the acoustic model, where you try to go from raw audio waveforms to a part-of-word sound, like "buh," or "fuh," or "ss"—the things that form words. It turned out we could use neural networks to do that much better than the previous system they were using.

That got very significant decreases in word error rate for the speech recognition system. We then just started to look and collaborate with other teams around Google about what kinds of interesting perception problems that it had in the speech space or in the image recognition or video processing space. We also started to build software systems to make it easy for people to apply these approaches to new problems, and where we could automatically map these large computations onto multiple computers in a relatively easy way that the programmer didn't have to specify. They'd just say, "Here's a big model and I want to train it, so please go off and use 100 computers for it." And that would happen. That was the first generation of software that we built to address these kinds of problems.

We then built the second generation, that is, TensorFlow, and we decided we would open source that system. We were really designing it for three objectives. One was to be really flexible, so we could try out lots of different research ideas in the machine learning space quickly. The second was to be able to scale and tackle problems where we had lots of data, and we wanted very large, computationally expensive models. The third was that we wanted to be able to go from a research idea to a production-serving system for a model that worked in the same sort of underlying software system. We open sourced that at the end of 2015, and since then it's had quite a lot of adoption externally. Now there's a large community of TensorFlow users across a range of companies, academic institutions, and both hobbyists and public users using it.

MARTIN FORD: Is TensorFlow going to become a feature of your cloud server so that your customers have access to machine learning?

JEFF DEAN: Yes, but there's a bit of nuance here. TensorFlow itself is an open source software package. We want our cloud to be the best place to run TensorFlow programs, but you can run them wherever you want. You can run them on your laptop, you can run them on a machine with GPU cards that you bought, you can run them on a Raspberry Pi, and on Android.

MARTIN FORD: Right, but on Google Cloud, you'll have tensor processors and the specialized hardware to optimize it?

JEFF DEAN: That's correct. In parallel with the TensorFlow software development, we've been working on designing custom processors for these kinds of machine learning applications. These processors are specialized for essentially low-precision linear algebra, which forms the core of all of these applications of deep learning that you've been seeing over the last 6 to 7 years.

The processors can train models very fast, and they can do it more power-efficiently. They can also be used for inference, where you actually have a trained model, and now you just want to apply it very quickly with high throughput for some production use, like Google Translate, or our speech recognition systems, or even Google Search.

We've also made the second-generation Tensor Processing Units (TPUs), available to cloud customers in several ways. One is under the covers in a few of our cloud products, but the other is they can just get a raw virtual machine with a cloud TPU device attached, and then they can run their own machine learning computations expressed in TensorFlow on that device.

MARTIN FORD: With all of this technology integrated into the cloud, are we getting close to the point where machine learning becomes available to everybody, like a utility?

JEFF DEAN: We have a variety of cloud products that are meant to appeal to different constituencies in this space. If you're fairly experienced with machine learning, then you can get a virtual machine with one of these TPU devices on it, and write your own TensorFlow programs to solve your particular problem in a very customizable way.

If you're not as much of an expert, we have a couple of other things. We have pre-trained models that you can use that require no machine learning expertise. You can just send us an image or a clip of audio, and we will tell you what's in that image. For instance, "that's a picture of a cat," or "people seem happy in the image," or "we extracted these words from the image." In the audio case, it's "we think this is what the people said in this audio clip." We also have translation models and video models. Those are very good if what you want is a general-purpose task, like reading the words in an image.

We also have a suite of AutoML products, which are essentially designed for people who may not have as much machine learning expertise, but want a customized solution for a particular problem they have. Imagine if you have a set of images of parts that are going down your assembly line and there are 100 kinds of parts, and you want to be able to identify what part it is from the pixels in an image. There, we can actually train you a custom model without you having to know any machine learning through this technique called AutoML. Essentially, it can repeatedly try lots and lots of machine learning experiments as a human-machine learning expert would, but without you having to be a machine learning expert. It does it in an automated way, and then we give you a very high-accuracy model for that particular problem, without you needing to have machine learning expertise.

I think that's really important because if you think about the world today, there are between 10,000 to 20,000 organizations in the world that have hired machine learning expertise in-house and are productively employing it. I'm making up that number, but it's roughly that order of magnitude. Then, if you think about all the organizations in the world that have data that could be used for machine learning, it's probably 10 million organizations that have some sort of machine learning problem.

Our aim is to make that approach much easier to use, so that you don't need a master's-level course on machine learning to do this. It's more at the level of someone who could write a database query. If users with that level of expertise were able to get a working machine learning model, that would be quite powerful. For example, every small city has lots of interesting data about how they should set their stop light timers. Right now, they don't really do that with machine learning, but they probably should.

MARTIN FORD: So, a democratization of AI is one of the goals that you're working toward. What about the route to general intelligence, what are some of the hurdles that you see there?

JEFF DEAN: One of the big problems with the use of machine learning today is that we typically find a problem we want to solve with machine learning, and then we collect a supervised training dataset. We then use that to train a model that's very good at that particular thing, but it can't do anything else.

If we really want generally intelligent systems, we want a single model that can do hundreds of thousands of things. Then, when the 100,001st thing comes along, it builds on the knowledge that it gained from solving the other things and develops new techniques that are effective at solving that new problem. That will have several advantages. One of them is that you get this incredible multitask benefit from using the wealth of your experience to solve new problems more quickly and better, because many problems share some aspects. It also means that you need much less data, or fewer observations, to learn to do a new thing.

Unscrewing one kind of jar lid is a lot like unscrewing another kind of jar lid, except for maybe a slightly different kind of turning mechanism. Solving this math problem is a lot like these other math problems, except with some sort of twist. I think that's the approach we really need to be taking in these things, and I think experimentation is a big part of this. So, how can systems learn from demonstrations of things? Supervised data is like that, but we're doing a bit of work in this space in robotics as well. We can have humans demonstrate a skill, and then robots can learn from video demonstrations of that skill and learn to pour things with relatively few examples of humans pouring things.

Another hurdle is that we need very large computational systems, because if we really want a single system that solves all of our machine learning problems, that's a lot of computation. Also, if we really want to try different approaches of this, then you need the turnaround time on those kinds of experiments to be very fast. Part of the reason we're investing in building large-scale machine learning accelerator hardware, like our TPUs, is that we believe that if you want these kinds of large, single, powerful models, it's really important that they have enough computational capability to do interesting things and allow us to make fast progress.

JEFFREY DEAN

MARTIN FORD: What about the risks that come along with AI? What are the things that we really need to be concerned about?

JEFF DEAN: Changes in the labor force are going to be significant things that governments and policymakers should really be paying attention to. It's very clear that even without significant further advances in what we can do, the fact that computers can now automate a lot of things that didn't use to be automatable even four or five years ago, is a pretty big change. It's not just one sector; it's an aspect that cuts across multiple different jobs and employment.

I was on a White House Office of Science and Technology Policy Committee, which was convened at the end of the Obama administration in 2016, and which brought together about 20 machine learning people and 20 economists. In this group, we discussed what kinds of impact this would have on the labor markets. It's definitely the kind of thing where you want governments to be paying attention and figuring out for people whose jobs change or shift, how can they acquire new skills or get new kinds of training that make them able to do things that are not at risk of automation? That's an important aspect that governments have a strong, clear role to play in.

MARTIN FORD: Do you think someday we may need a universal basic income?

JEFF DEAN: I don't know. It's very hard to predict because I think any time we've gone through technological change, that has happened; it's not like this is a new thing. The Industrial Revolution, the Agricultural Revolution, all these things have caused imbalance to society as a whole. What people do in terms of their daily jobs has shifted tremendously. I think this is going to be similar, in that entirely new kinds of things will be created that people will do, and it's somewhat hard to predict what those things will be.

So, I do think it's important that people be flexible and learn new things throughout their career. I think that's already true today. Whereas 50 years ago, you could go to school and then start a career and be in that career for many, many years, today you might work in one role for a few years and pick up some new skills, then do something a bit different. That kind of flexibility is, I think, important.

In terms of other kinds of risks, I'm not as worried about the Nick Bostrom superintelligence aspect. I do think that as computer scientists and machine learning researchers we have the opportunity and the ability to shape how we want machine learning systems to be integrated and used in our society.

We can make good choices there, or we can make some not so good choices. As long as we make good choices, where these things are actually used for the benefit of humanity, then it's going to be fantastic. We'll get better healthcare and we'll be able to discover all kinds of new scientific discoveries in collaboration with human scientists by generating new hypotheses automatically. Self-driving cars are clearly going to transform society in very positive ways, but at the same time, that is going to be a source of disruption in the labor markets. There are nuances to many of these developments that are important.

MARTIN FORD: One cartoon view of this is that a small team—maybe at Google—develops AGI, and that small group of people are not necessarily tied into these broader issues, then it turns out that these few people are making the decision for everyone. Do you think there is a place for regulation of some AI research or applications?

JEFF DEAN: It's possible. I think regulation has a role to play, but I want regulation to be informed by people with expertise in the field. I think sometimes regulation has a bit of a lag factor, as governments and policymakers catch-up to what is now possible. Knee-jerk reactions in terms of regulation or policymaking are probably not helpful, but informed dialog with people in the field is important as government figures out what role it wants to play in informing how things should play out.

In respect to the development of AGI, I think it's really important that we do this ethically and with sound decision-making. That's one reason that Google has put out a clear document of the principles by which we're approaching these sorts of issues[1]. Our AI principles document is a good example of the thought we're putting into not just the technical development of this, but the way in which we want to be guided in what kinds of problems we want to tackle with these approaches, how we will approach them, and what we will not do.

---

1 https://www.blog.google/technology/ai/ai-principles/

JEFFREY DEAN

JEFFREY DEAN *joined Google in 1999, and is currently a Google Senior Fellow in the Research Group, where he leads the Google Brain project and is the overall director of artificial intelligence research at the company.*

Jeff received a PhD in Computer Science from the University of Washington, working with Craig Chambers on whole-program optimization techniques for object-oriented languages in 1996. He received a BS, summa cum laude from the University of Minnesota in Computer Science & Economics in 1990. From 1996 to 1999, he worked for Digital Equipment Corporation's Western Research Lab in Palo Alto, where he worked on low-overhead profiling tools, design of profiling hardware for out-of-order microprocessors, and web-based information retrieval. From 1990 to 1991, Jeff worked for the World Health Organization's Global Programme on AIDS, developing software to do statistical modeling, forecasting, and analysis of the HIV pandemic.

In 2009, Jeff was elected to the National Academy of Engineering, and he was also named a Fellow of the Association for Computing Machinery (ACM) and a Fellow of the American Association for the Advancement of Sciences (AAAS).

His areas of interest include large-scale distributed systems, performance monitoring, compression techniques, information retrieval, application of machine learning to search and other related problems, microprocessor architecture, compiler optimizations, and development of new products that organize existing information in new and interesting ways.

> **❝** *Stopping progress by stopping technology is the wrong approach. [...] If you don't make progress technologically, someone else will, and their intent might be considerably less beneficial than yours.*

DAPHNE KOLLER

CEO AND FOUNDER, INSITRO
ADJUNCT PROFESSOR OF COMPUTER SCIENCE, STANFORD

Daphne Koller was the Rajeev Motwani Professor of Computer Science at Stanford University (where she is currently an Adjunct Professor) and is one of the founders of Coursera. She is focused on the potential benefits of AI in healthcare and worked as the Chief Computing Officer at Calico, an Alphabet subsidiary researching longevity. She is currently the Founder and CEO of insitro, a biotech startup using machine learning to research and develop new drugs.

MARTIN FORD: You've just started a new role as CEO and founder of insitro, a startup company focused on using machine learning for drug discovery. Could you tell me more about that?

DAPHNE KOLLER: We need a new solution in order to continue driving progress in drug research forward. The problem is that it is becoming consistently more challenging to develop new drugs: clinical trial success rates are around the mid-single-digit range; the pre-tax R&D cost to develop a new drug (once failures are incorporated) is estimated to be greater than $2.5B. The rate of return on drug development investment has been decreasing linearly year by year, and some analyses estimate that it will hit zero before 2020. One explanation for this is that drug development is now intrinsically harder: Many (perhaps most) of the "low-hanging fruit"—in other words, druggable targets that have a significant effect on a large population—have been discovered. If so, then the next phase of drug development will need to focus on drugs that are more specialized—whose effects may be context-specific, and which apply only to a subset of patients. Figuring out the appropriate patient population is often hard, making therapeutic development more challenging, and that leaves many diseases without effective treatment and lots of patients with unmet needs. Also, the reduced market size forces an amortization of high development costs over a much smaller base.

Our hope at insitro is that big data and machine learning, applied to drug discovery, can help make the process faster, cheaper, and more successful. To do that, we plan to leverage both cutting-edge machine learning techniques, as well as the latest innovations that have occurred in life sciences, which enable the creation of the large, high-quality data sets that may transform the capabilities of machine learning in this space. Seventeen years ago, when I first started to work in the area of machine learning for biology and health, a "large" dataset was a few dozen samples. Even five years ago, data sets with more than a few hundred samples were a rare exception. We now live in a different world. We have human cohort data sets (such as the UK Biobank), which contain large amounts of high-quality measurements—molecular as well as clinical—for hundreds of thousands of individuals. At the same time, a constellation of remarkable technologies allow us to construct, perturb, and observe biological model systems in the laboratory with unprecedented fidelity and throughput. Using these innovations, we plan to collect and use a range of very large data sets to train machine learning models that will help address key problems in the drug discovery and development process.

MARTIN FORD: It sounds like insitro is planning to do both wet-lab experimental work and high-end machine learning. These are not often done within a single company. Does that integration pose new challenges?

DAPHNE KOLLER: Absolutely. I think the biggest challenge is actually cultural, in getting scientists and data scientists to work together as equal partners. In many companies, one group sets the direction, and the other takes a back seat. At insitro, we really need to build a culture in which scientists, engineers, and data scientists work closely together to define problems, design experiments, analyze data, and derive insights that will lead us to new therapeutics. We believe that building this team and this culture well is as important to the success of our mission as the quality of the science or the machine learning that these different groups will create.

MARTIN FORD: How important is machine learning in the healthcare space?

DAPHNE KOLLER: When you look at the places where machine learning has made a difference, it's really been where we have an accumulation of large amounts of data and we have people who can think simultaneously about the problem domain and how machine learning can solve that.

You can now get large amounts of data from resources like the UK Biobank or All of Us, which gather a lot of information about people and enable you to start thinking about the health trajectories of actual humans. On the other side, we have amazing technologies like CRISPR, DNA synthesis, next-generation sequencing, and all sorts of other things that are all coming together at the same time to be able to create large datasets on a molecular level.

We are now in the position where we can begin to deconvolute what is to my mind the most complex system that we've seen: the biology of humans and other organisms. That is an unbelievable opportunity for science, and is going to require major developments on the machine learning side to figure out and create the kinds of interventions that we need to live longer, healthier lives.

MARTIN FORD: Let's talk about your own life; how did you get started in AI?

DAPHNE KOLLER: I was a PhD student at Stanford working in the area of probabilistic modeling. Nowadays it would look like AI, but it wasn't really known as artificial intelligence back then; in fact, probabilistic modeling was considered anathema to artificial intelligence, which was much more focused on logical reasoning at the time. Things changed, though, and AI expanded into a lot of other disciplines. In some ways, the field of AI grew to embrace my work rather than me choosing to go into AI.

I went to Berkeley as a postdoc, and there I started to really think about how what I was doing was relevant to actual problems that people cared about, as opposed to just being mathematically elegant. That was the first time I started to get into machine learning. I then returned to Stanford as faculty in 1995 where I started to work on areas relating to statistical modeling and machine learning. I began studying applied problems where machine learning could really make a difference.

I worked in computer vision, in robotics, and from 2000 on biology and health data. I also had an ongoing interest in technology-enabled education, which led to a lot of experimentation at Stanford into ways in which we could offer an enhanced learning experience. This was not only for students on campus, but also trying to offer courses to people who didn't have access to a Stanford education.

That whole process led to the launch of the first three Stanford MOOCs (Massive Open Online Courses) in 2011. That was a surprise to all of us because we didn't really try and market it in any concerted way. It was really much more of a viral spread of information about the free courses Stanford was offering. It had an unbelievable response where each of those courses had an enrollment of 100,000 people or more. That really was the turning point of, "we need to do something to deliver on the promise of this opportunity," and that's what led to the creation of Coursera.

MARTIN FORD: Before we jump into that I want talk more about your research. You focused on Bayesian networks and integrating probability into machine learning. Is that something that can be integrated with deep learning neural networks, or is that a totally separate or competing approach?

DAPHNE KOLLER: This is a subtle answer that has several aspects. Probabilistic models lie on a continuum between those that try to encode the domain structure in an interpretable way—a way that makes sense to humans—and those that just try to capture the statistical properties of the data. The deep learning models intersect with probabilistic models—some can be viewed as encoding a distribution. Most of them have elected to focus on maximizing the predictive accuracy of the model, often at the expense of interpretability. Interpretability and the ability to incorporate structure in the domain has a lot of advantages in cases where you really need to understand what the model does, for instance in medical applications. It's also a way of dealing effectively with scenarios where you don't have a lot of training data, and you need to make up for it with prior knowledge. On the other hand, the ability to not have any prior knowledge and just let the data speak for themselves also has a lot of advantages. It'd be nice if you could merge them somehow.

MARTIN FORD: Let's talk about Coursera. Was it a case of seeing the online classes that you and others taught at Stanford do really well, and deciding to start a company to continue that work?

DAPHNE KOLLER: We struggled trying to figure out what was the right way to take the next steps. Was it continuing this Stanford effort? Was it launching a nonprofit organization? Was it creating a company? We thought about it a fair bit and decided that creating a company was the right way to maximize the impact that we could have. So, in January of 2012, we started the company which is now called Coursera.

MARTIN FORD: Initially, there was enormous hype about MOOCs and that people all over the world were going to get a Stanford education on their phone. It seems to have evolved more along the lines of people that already have a college degree going to Coursera to get extra credentials. It hasn't disrupted undergraduate education in the way that some people predicted. Do you see that changing, going forward?

DAPHNE KOLLER: I think it's important to recognize that we never said this is going to put universities out of business. There were other people who said that, but we never endorsed that and we didn't think it was a good idea. In some ways, the typical Gartner hype cycle of MOOCs was compressed. People made these extreme comments, in 2012 it was, "MOOCs are going to put universities out of business," then 12 months later it was "universities are still here, so obviously MOOCs have failed." Both of those comments are ridiculous extremes of the hype cycle.

I think that we actually have done a lot for people who don't normally have access to that level of education. About 25% of Coursera learners don't have degrees, and about 40% of Coursera learners are in developing economies. If you look at the percentage of learners who say that their lives were significantly transformed by access to this experience, it is disproportionately those people with low socioeconomic status or from developing economies who report that level of benefit.

The benefit is there, but you're right that the large majority are the ones who have access to the internet and are aware that this possibility exists. I hope that over time, there is the ability to increase awareness and internet access so that larger numbers of people can get the benefit of these courses.

MARTIN FORD: There is a saying that we tend to overestimate what happens in the short term and underestimate in the long term. This sounds like a classic case of that.

DAPHNE KOLLER: I think that's exactly right. People thought we were going to transform higher education in two years. Universities have been around for 500 years, and evolve slowly. I do think, however, that even in the five years that we've been around there has been a fair amount of movement.

For instance, a lot of universities now have very robust online offerings, often at a considerably lower cost than on-campus courses. When we started, the very notion that a top university would have an online program of any kind was unheard of. Now, digital learning is embedded into the fabric of many top universities.

MARTIN FORD: I don't think Stanford is going to be disrupted over the next 10 years or so, but an education at the 3,000 or so less selective (and less well-known) colleges in the US is still very expensive. If an inexpensive and effective learning platform arose that gave you access to Stanford professors, then you begin to wonder why someone would enroll much less prestigious college when they could go to Stanford online.

DAPHNE KOLLER: I agree. I think that transformation is going to come first in the graduate education space, specifically professional master's degrees. There's still an important social component to the undergraduate experience: that's where you go to make new friends, move away from home, and possibly meet your life partner. For graduate education, however, it's usually employed adults with commitments: a job, a spouse, and a family. For most of them, to move and do a full-time college experience is actually a negative, and so that's where we'll see the transformation happen first.

Down the line, I think we might see people at those smaller colleges begin to wonder whether that's the best use of their time and money, especially those that are part-time students because they need to work for a living while they do their undergraduate degrees. I think that's where we're going to see an interesting transformation in a decade or so.

MARTIN FORD: How might the technology evolve? If you have huge numbers of people taking these courses, then that generates lots and lots of data. I assume that data is something that can be leveraged by machine learning and artificial intelligence. How do you see those technologies integrated into these courses in the future? Are they going to become more dynamic, more personalized, and so forth?

DAPHNE KOLLER: I think that's exactly right. When we started Coursera, the technology was limited in innovating on new pedagogy; it was mostly just taking what was already present in standard teaching and modularizing it. We made courses more interactive with exercises embedded in the course material, but it wasn't a distinctly different experience. As more data is gathered and learning becomes more sophisticated, you will certainly see more personalization. I believe that you will see something that looks more like a personalized tutor who keeps you motivated and helps you over the hard bits. All of these things are not that difficult to do with the amount of data that we have available now. That wasn't available when we started Coursera, where we didn't have the data and we just needed to get the platform off the ground.

MARTIN FORD: There's enormous hype focused on deep learning at the moment and people could easily get the impression that all of artificial intelligence is nothing but deep learning. However, there have recently been suggestions that progress in deep learning may soon "hit a wall" and that it will need to be replaced with another approach. How do you feel about that?

DAPHNE KOLLER: It's not about one silver bullet, but I don't think it needs to be thrown out. Deep learning was a very significant step forward, but is it the thing that's going to get us to full, human-level AI? I think there's at least one, probably more, big leaps that will need to occur before we get to human-level intelligence.

Partly, it has to do with end-to-end training, where you optimize the entire network for one particular task. It becomes really good at that task, but if you change the task, you have to train the network differently. In many cases, the entire architecture has to be different. Right now, we're focused on really deep and narrow vertical tasks. Those are exceedingly difficult tasks and we're making significant progress with them, but each vertical task doesn't translate to the one next to it. The thing that makes humans really special is that they're able to perform many of these tasks using the same "software," if you will. I don't think we're quite there with AI.

The other place where we're not quite there in terms of general intelligence is that the amount of data that's required to train one of these models is very, very large. A couple of hundred samples are not usually enough. Humans are really good at learning from very small amounts of data. I think it's because there's one architecture in our brain that serves all of the tasks that we have to deal with and we're really good at transferring general skills from one path to the other. For example, it probably takes five minutes to explain how to use a dishwasher to someone who's never used one before. For a robot, it's not going to be anywhere close to that. That's because humans have these generally transferable skills and ways of learning that we haven't been able to give to our artificial agents yet.

MARTIN FORD: What other hurdles are there in the path to AGI? You've talked about learning in different domains and being able to cross domains, but what about things like imagination, and being able to conceive new ideas? How do we get to that?

DAPHNE KOLLER: I think those things that I mentioned earlier are really central: being able to transfer skills from one domain to the other, being able to leverage that to learn from a very limited amount of training data, and so on. There's been some interesting progress on the path to imagination, but I think we're fairly far away.

For instance, consider GANs (Generative Adversarial Networks). They are great at creating new images that are different from the images that they've seen before, but these images are amalgams, if you will, of images that they were trained on. You don't have the computer inventing Impressionism, and that's something that would be quite different than anything that we've done before.

An even more subtle question is that of relating emotionally to other beings. I'm not sure that's even well defined, because as a human you can fake it. There are people who fake an emotional connection to others. So, the question is, if you can get a computer to fake it well enough, how do you know that's not real? That brings to mind the Turing test regarding consciousness, to which the answer is that we can never know for sure if another being is really conscious, or what that even means; if the behavior aligns with what we consider to be "conscious," we just take it on faith.

MARTIN FORD: That's a good question. In order to have true artificial general intelligence, does that imply consciousness or could you have a superintelligent zombie? Could you have a machine that's incredibly intelligent, but with nothing there in terms of an inner experience?

DAPHNE KOLLER: If you go back to Turing's hypothesis, which is what gave rise to the Turing test, he says that consciousness is unknowable. I don't know for a fact that you are conscious, I just take that on faith because you look like me and I feel like I'm conscious and because there's that surface similarity, I believe that you're conscious too.

His argument was that when we get to a certain level of performance in terms of behavior we will not be able to know whether an intelligent entity is conscious or not. If it's not a falsifiable hypothesis then it's not science, and you just have to take it on faith. There is an argument that says that we will never know because it is unknowable.

MARTIN FORD: I want to ask now about the future of artificial intelligence. What would you point to as a demonstration of things that are currently at the forefront of AI?

DAPHNE KOLLER: The whole deep learning framework has done an amazing job of addressing one of the key bottlenecks in machine learning, which is having to engineer a feature space that captures enough about the domain so that you can get very high performance, especially in contexts where you don't have a strong intuition for the domain. Prior to deep learning, in order to apply machine learning you had to spend months or even years tweaking the representation of the underlying data in order to achieve higher performance.

Now, with deep learning combined with the amount of data that we are able to bring to bear, you can really let the machine pick out those patterns for itself. That is remarkably powerful. It's important to recognize, though, that a lot of human insight is still required in constructing these models. It's there in a different place: in figuring out what the architecture of the model is that captures the fundamental aspects of a domain.

If you look at the kind of networks, for instance, that one applies to machine translation, they're very different to the architectures that you apply to computer vision, and a lot of human intuition went into designing those. It's still, as of today, important to have a human in the loop designing these models, and I'm not convinced yet by the efforts to get a computer to design those networks as well as a human can. You can certainly get a computer to tweak the architecture and modify certain parameters, but the overall architecture is still one that a human has designed. That being said, there are a couple of key advances that are changing this. The first is being able to train these models with very large amounts of data. The second is the end-to-end training that I mentioned earlier, where you define the task from beginning to end, and you train the entire architecture to optimize the goal that you actually care about.

This is transformative because the performance differential turns out to be quite dramatic. Both AlphaGo and AlphaZero are really good examples of that. The model there was trained to win in a game, and I think end-to-end training, combined with unlimited training data (which is available in that context) is what's driven a lot of the huge performance gains in those applications.

MARTIN FORD: Following these advances, how much longer will it be before we reach AGI, and how will we know when we're close to it?

DAPHNE KOLLER: There are a number of big leaps forward that need to happen in the technology to get us there, and those are stochastic events that you can't predict. Someone could have a brilliant idea next month or it could take 150 years. Predicting when a stochastic event is going to happen is a fool's errand.

MARTIN FORD: But if these breakthroughs take place, then it could happen quickly?

DAPHNE KOLLER: Even if the breakthrough happens, it's going to require a lot of engineering and work to make AGI a reality. Think back to those advances of deep learning and end-to-end training. The seeds of those were planted in the '50s and the ideas kept coming back up every decade or so. We've made continual progress over time, but there were years of engineering effort to get us to the current point. And we're still far from AGI.

I think it's unpredictable when the big step forward will come. We might not even recognize it when we see it at the first, second, or third time. For all we know, it might already have been made, and we just don't know it. There's still going to be decades of work after that discovery to really engineer this until the point that it works.

MARTIN FORD: Let's talk about some of the risks of AI, starting with economics. There is an idea that we're on the leading edge of something on the scale of a new industrial revolution, but I think a lot of economists actually disagree with that. Do you think that we are looking at a big disruption?

DAPHNE KOLLER: Yes, I think that we are looking at a big disruption on the economic side. The biggest risk/opportunity of this technology is that it will take a lot of jobs that are currently being done by humans and have those be taken over to a lesser or greater extent by machines. There are social obstacles to adoption in many cases, but as robust increased performance is demonstrated, it will follow the standard disruptive innovation cycle.

It is already happening to paralegals and cashiers at the supermarket, and it will soon happen to the people who stack the shelves. I think that all of that is going to be taken over in five or ten years by robots or intelligent agents. The question is to what extent can we carve out meaningful jobs around that for humans to do. You can identify those opportunities in some cases, and in others it's less clear.

MARTIN FORD: One of the disruptive technologies that people focus on is self-driving cars and trucks. What's your sense of when you'll be able to call a driverless Uber and it will take you to your destination.

DAPHNE KOLLER: I think that it'll be a gradual transition, where you might have a fallback human remote driver. I think that is where a lot of these companies are heading as an intermediate step to full autonomy.

You'll have a remote driver sitting in an office and controlling three or four vehicles at once. These vehicles would call for help when they get stuck in a situation that they simply don't recognize. With that safeguard in place, I would say probably within five years we'll have a self-driving service available in some places. Full autonomy is more of a social evolution than a technical evolution, and those are harder to predict.

MARTIN FORD: Agreed, but even so that's a big disruption coming quite soon in one industry with a lot of drivers losing their jobs. Do you think a universal basic income is a possible solution to this job loss?

DAPHNE KOLLER: It is just too early to make that decision. If you look back at some of the previous significant revolutions in history: The Agricultural Revolution, the Industrial Revolution, there were all the same predictions of massive workforce disruption and huge numbers of people being out of jobs. The world changed and those people found other jobs. It is too early to say that this one is going to be completely different to the others, because every disruption is surprising.

Before we focus on universal basic income, we need to be a lot more thoughtful and deliberate about education. The world in general, with a few exceptions, has underinvested in educating people for this new reality, and I think it's really important to consider the kind of skills that people will need in order to be successful moving forwards. If after doing that we still have no idea of how to keep the majority of the human population employed then that's when we need to think about a universal basic income.

MARTIN FORD: Let's move on to some of the other risks associated with artificial intelligence. There are two broad categories, the near-term risks, such as privacy issues, security, and the weaponization of drones and AI, and the long-term risks such as AGI and what that means.

DAPHNE KOLLER: I'd say that all of those short-term risks already exist without artificial intelligence. For instance, there are already many complex, critical systems today that enemies could hack into.

Our electricity grid is not artificially intelligent at this point, but it's a significant security risk for someone to hack into that. People can currently hack into your pacemaker—again, it's not an artificially intelligent system, but it's an electronic system with the opportunity for hacking. As for weapons, is it impossible for someone to hack into the nuclear response system of one of the major superpowers and cause a nuclear attack to take place? So yes, there are security risks to AI systems, but I don't know that they're qualitatively different to the same risks with older technologies.

MARTIN FORD: As the technology expands, though, doesn't that risk expand? Can you imagine a future where self-driving trucks deliver all our food to stores, and someone then hacks into those and brings them to a halt?

DAPHNE KOLLER: I agree, it's just that it's not a qualitative difference. It's an increasing risk that grows as we rely more on electronic solutions that, by virtue of being larger and more interconnected, have a greater risk for a single point of failure. We started with individual drivers delivering goods to stores. If you wanted to disrupt those, you'd have to disrupt every single driver. We then moved on to large shipping companies directing large numbers of trucks. Disrupt one of those and you disrupt a larger proportion of deliveries. AI-controlled driverless trucks are the next step. As you increase centralization you increase the risks of a single point of failure.

I'm not saying those systems aren't more of a risk, I'm just saying that to me AI doesn't seem qualitatively different in that regard. It's the same progression of increasing risk as we rely more and more on complex technologies with a single point of failure.

MARTIN FORD: Going back to the military and the weaponization of AI and robotics, there's a lot of concern about advanced commercial technologies being used in nefarious ways. I've also interviewed Stuart Russell, who made a video, Slaughterbots, about that subject. Are you concerned that this technology could be used in threatening ways?

DAPHNE KOLLER: Yes, I think it is possible that this technology can get into the hands of anyone, but of course that is true for other dangerous technologies as well. The ability to kill larger numbers of people using increasingly easier ways has been another aspect of human evolution. In the early days, you needed a knife, and you could kill one person at a time. Then you had guns, and you could kill five or six. Then you had assault rifles, and you could kill 40 or 50. Now you have the ability to create dirty bombs in ways that don't require a huge amount of technological know-how. If you think about biological weapons and the ability to edit and print genomes to the point where people can now create their own viruses, that's another way of killing a lot of people with an accessible modern technology.

So yes, the risks of misusing technology are there, but we need to think about them more broadly than just AI. I wouldn't say that stories of intelligent killer drones are more dangerous than someone synthesizing a version of smallpox and letting it loose. I don't think we currently have a solution for either of those scenarios, but the latter actually seems much more likely to kill a lot of people quickly.

MARTIN FORD: Let's move on to those long-term risks, and in particular AGI. There's the notion of a control problem where a superintelligence might set its own goals or implement the goals we set it in ways that we don't expect or that are harmful. How do you feel about that concern?

DAPHNE KOLLER: I think it is premature. In my opinion, there are several breakthroughs that need to happen before we are at that point, and too many unknowns before we can come to a conclusion. What nature of intelligence might be formed? Will it have an emotional component? What will determine its goals? Will it even want to interact with us humans, or will it just go off on its own?

There are just so many unknowns that it seems premature to start planning for it. I don't think it is on the horizon, and even once we get to that breakthrough point there's going to be years or decades of engineering work that needs to be done. This is not going to be an emergent phenomenon that we just wake up to one day. This is going to be an engineered system, and once we figure out what the key components are, that would be a good time to start thinking about how we modulate and structure them so as to get the best outcomes. Right now, it's just very ephemeral.

MARTIN FORD: There are already a number of think-tank organizations springing up, such as OpenAI. Do you think those are premature in terms of the resources being invested, or do you think it's a productive thing to start working on?

DAPHNE KOLLER: OpenAI does multiple things. A lot of what it does is to create open source AI tools to democratize access to a truly valuable technology. In that respect, I think it's a great thing. There's a lot of work being done at those organizations thinking about the other important risks of AI. For instance, at a recent machine learning conference (NIPS 2017) there was a very interesting talk about how machine learning takes implicit biases in our training data and amplifies them to the point that it becomes really horrifying in capturing the worst behaviors (e.g., racism or sexism). Those are things that are important for us to be thinking about today, because those are real risks and we need to come up with real solutions to ameliorate them. That's part of what these think tanks are doing.

That's very different from your question of how we build safeguards into an as-yet-non-existent technology that will prevent it from consciously trying to exterminate humans for reasons that are unclear at this point. Why would they even care about exterminating humans? It just seems too early to start worrying about that.

MARTIN FORD: Do you think there's a need for government regulation of AI?

DAPHNE KOLLER: Let's just say that I think the level of understanding that the government has of this technology is limited at best, and it's a bad idea for governments to regulate something that they don't understand.

AI is also a technology that is easy to use and already available to other governments that have access to a lot of resources and are not necessarily bound by the same ethical scruples as our government might be. I don't think regulating this technology is the right solution.

MARTIN FORD: There's a lot of focus in particular on China. In some ways, they have an advantage: they've got enormous amounts of data because their population is so large, and they don't have to worry so much about privacy. Are we at risk of falling behind there, and should we be worried?

DAPHNE KOLLER: I think the answer to that is yes, and I think it's important. If you're looking for a place for government intervention that would be beneficial, I would say it's in enabling technological advancements that could maintain competitiveness not only with China but also with other governments. That includes an investment in science. It includes an investment in education. It includes the ability to get access to data in a way that is privacy-respecting and enables progress to be made.

In the healthcare space that I'm interested in, there are things that one can do that would hugely ease the ability to make progress. For instance, if you talk to patients you'll find that most of them are happy to have their data used for research purposes to drive progress toward cures. They realize that even if it doesn't help them it can help others down the line, and they really want to do that. However, the legal and technological hoops that one needs to jump through before medical data is shared are so onerous right now that it just doesn't happen. That really slows down our progress towards the ability to aggregate data for multiple patients and to figure out likely cures for certain subpopulations, and so on.

This is a place where government-level policy change, as well as a change in societal norms, can make a difference. As an example of what I mean, look at the difference in organ donation rates between countries where there is an opt-in for organ donation versus countries where there's an opt-out. Both give equal amounts of control over whether a person's organs are going to be donated should they die, but the countries that have opt-out have a much higher organ donation rate than the countries that have opt-in. You create the expectation that people naturally opt in for something although you give them every opportunity to opt out. A similar system for data sharing would make it much more available and would make publishing new research much faster.

MARTIN FORD: Do you believe that the benefits of AI, machine learning, and all these technologies are going to outweigh these risks?

DAPHNE KOLLER: Yes, I do. I also think that stopping progress by stopping technology is the wrong approach. If you want to ameliorate risks, you need to be thoughtful about how to change societal norms and how to put in appropriate safeguards. Stopping technology is just not a feasible approach. If you don't make progress technologically, someone else will, and their intent might be considerably less beneficial than yours. We need to let technology progress and then think about the mechanisms to channel it towards good rather than bad.

DAPHNE KOLLER

DAPHNE KOLLER *was the Rajeev Motwani Professor of Computer Science at Stanford University. Daphne has made significant contributions to AI, especially in the field of Bayesian (probabilistic) machine learning and knowledge representation. In 2004, she was the recipient of a MacArthur Foundation fellowship for her work in this area.*

In 2012, Daphne, along with her Stanford colleague, Andrew Ng, founded the online education company Coursera. Daphne served as co-CEO and president of the company. Her current research focuses especially on the use of machine learning and data science in healthcare, and she had a role as Chief Computing Officer at Calico, a Google/Alphabet company that is reportedly working on increasing human longevity. Daphne is currently CEO and founder of insitro, a startup biotech company focused on using machine learning for drug discovery.

Daphne received her undergraduate and masters degrees at Hebrew University of Jerusalem in Israel and her PhD in computer science at Stanford in 1993. She has received numerous awards for her research and is a fellow of the Association for the Advancement of Artificial Intelligence. She was inaugurated into the National Academy of Engineering in 2011. In 2013, Daphne was named one of the world's 100 most influential people by Time *magazine.*

> " *I don't think, as other people might, that we don't know how to do [AGI] and we're waiting for some enormous breakthrough. I don't think that's the case, I think we do know how to do it, we just need to prove that.*

DAVID FERRUCCI

FOUNDER, ELEMENTAL COGNITION
DIRECTOR OF APPLIED AI, BRIDGEWATER ASSOCIATES

David Ferrucci built and led the IBM Watson team from its inception to its landmark success in 2011 when Watson defeated the greatest Jeopardy! players of all time. In 2015 he founded his own company, Elemental Cognition, focused on creating novel AI systems that dramatically accelerate a computer's ability to understand language.

MARTIN FORD: How did you become interested in computers? What's the path that led you to AI?

DAVID FERRUCCI: I started back before computers were an everyday term. My parents wanted me to become a medical doctor, and my dad hated the fact that I would be home during the school holidays without anything to do. In the summer of my junior year at high school, my dad looked in the paper and found a math class for me at a local college. It turned out that it was actually a programming class using BASIC on DEC computers. I thought it was phenomenal because you could give this machine instructions, and if you could articulate the procedure or the algorithm that you're going through in your head you could get the machine to do it for you. The machine could store the data AND the thought process. I imagined this was my way out! If I could get the machine to think and memorize everything for me, then I wouldn't have to do all of that work to become a doctor.

It got me interested in what it meant to store information, to reason over it, to think, and to systematize or to turn into an algorithm whatever process was going on in my brain. If I could just specify that in enough detail, then I could get the computer to do it, and that was enthralling. It was just a mind-altering realization.

I didn't know the words "artificial intelligence" at the time, but I got very interested in the whole notion of coordinated intelligence from a mathematical, algorithmic, and philosophical perspective. I believed that modeling human intelligence in the machine was possible. There was no reason to think that it wasn't.

MARTIN FORD: Did you follow that with computer science at college?

DAVID FERRUCCI: No, I had no idea about careers in computer science or AI, so I went to college and majored in biology to become a medical doctor. During my studies, I got my grandparents to buy me an Apple II computer, and I just started programming everything I could think of. I ended up programming a lot of software for my college, from graphing software for experimental lab work, to ecology simulation software, to analog-to-digital interfacing for lab equipment. This, of course, was before any of this stuff even existed, never mind being able to just download it form the internet. I decided to do as much computer science as I could in my last year of college, so I did a minor in it. I graduated with the top biology award and I was ready to go to medical school, when I decided it just wasn't for me.

Instead, I went to graduate school for computer science, and AI in particular. I decided that was what I was passionate about, and that's what I wanted to study. So, I did my master's at Rensselaer Polytechnic Institute (RPI) in New York, where I developed a semantic network system as part of my thesis. I called it COSMOS, which I am sure stood for something related to cognition and sounded cool, but I can't remember the precise expansion. COSMOS represented knowledge and language, and could perform limited forms of logical reasoning.

I was giving a presentation of COSMOS at a sort of industrial science fair at RPI in 1985 when some folks from the IBM Watson Research Center, who had just started their own AI project, saw me presenting and they asked me if I wanted a job. My original plan had been to stay on and get my PhD, but a few years before this I'd seen an ad in a magazine to become an IBM Research Fellow where you could research whatever you want with unlimited resources—that sounded like my dream job, so I'd cut that ad out and pinned it on my bulletin board. When these people from IBM's Research Center offered me that job, I took it.

So, in 1985 I started working on an AI project at IBM Research, but then a couple of years later, the 1980s' AI winter had hit, and IBM was going around canceling every project that was associated with AI. I was told that they would be able to put me to work on other projects, but I didn't want to work on other projects, I wanted to work on AI, so I decided to quit IBM. My dad was mad at me. He was already pissed I didn't become a doctor, then by some miracle I had gotten a good job anyway and now I was quitting two years later. That just did not sound like a good thing to him.

I went back to RPI and did my PhD on non-monotonic reasoning. I designed and built a medical expert system called CARE (Cardiac and Respiratory Expert) and just learned a lot more about AI during that period. To support my studies, I also worked on a government contract building an object-oriented circuit design system at RPI. After completing my PhD, I needed to look for work. My dad had gotten pretty sick and he lived down in Westchester, where IBM was also based. I wanted to be near him, so I called some people I knew from my earlier IBM days and ended up going back to IBM Research.

IBM was not an AI company at that point, but 15 years later, with Watson and other projects, I had helped to shape it in that direction. I never gave up my desire to work on AI, and I built a skilled team over the years and engaged in every opportunity to work in areas like language processing, text and multimedia analytics, and automatic question answering. By the time there was this interest in doing *Jeopardy!*, I was the only one in IBM who believed it could be done and had a team capable of doing it. With Watson's huge success, IBM was able to transform itself into an AI company.

MARTIN FORD: I don't want to focus much on your work with Watson, as that's already a very well-documented story. I'd like to talk about how you were thinking about AI, after you left IBM.

DAVID FERRUCCI: The way I think about AI is that there's perception—recognizing things, there's control—doing things, and there's knowing—building, developing, and understanding the conceptual models that provide the foundation of communication, and the development of theories and ideas.

One of the interesting things I learned working on the Watson project was that pure statistical approaches were limited in the "understanding" part, that's their ability to produce casual and consumable explanations for their predictions or their answers. Purely data-driven or statistical approaches to prediction are very powerful for perception tasks, such as pattern recognition, voice recognition, and image recognition, and control tasks, such as driverless cars and robotics, but in the knowledge space AI is struggling.

We've seen huge advances in voice and image recognition and in general, perception-related stuff. We've also seen huge advances in the control systems that you see driving drones and all kinds of robotic driverless cars. When it comes to fluently communicating with a computer based on what it has read and understood, we're not even close to there yet.

MARTIN FORD: More recently in 2015 you started a company called Elemental Cognition. Could you tell us more about that?

DAVID FERRUCCI: Elemental Cognition is an AI research venture that's trying to do real language understanding. It's trying to deal with that area of AI that we still have not cracked, which is, can we create an AI that reads, dialogs, and builds understanding?

A human being might read books and develop rich models of how the world works in their head, and then reason about it and fluently dialog about it and ask questions about it. We refine and compound our understanding through reading and dialoging. At Elemental Cognition, we want our AI to do that.

We want to look beyond the surface structure of language, beyond the patterns that appear in word frequencies, and get at the underlying meaning. From that, we want to be able to build the internal logical models that humans would create and use to reason and communicate. We want to ensure a system that produces a compatible intelligence. That compatible intelligence can autonomously learn and refine its understanding through human interaction, language, dialog, and other related experiences.

Thinking about what knowing and understanding means is a really interesting part of AI. It's not as easy as providing labeled data for doing image analysis, because what happens is that you and I could read the same thing, but we can come up with very different interpretations. We could argue about what it means to understand that thing. Today's systems do more text matching and looking at the statistical occurrences of words and phrases, as opposed to developing a layered and logical representation of the complex logic that is really behind the language.

MARTIN FORD: Let's pause to make sure people grasp the magnitude of this. There are lots of deep learning systems today that can do great pattern recognition and could, for example, find a cat in a picture and tell you there's a cat in the image. But there is no system in existence that really understands what a cat is, in the way that a person does.

DAVID FERRUCCI: Well yes, but you and I could also argue about what a cat is. That's the interesting part because it asks what does it mean to actually understand. Think about how much human energy goes into helping each other to develop shared understandings of things. It's essentially the job of anyone compiling or communicating information, any journalist, artist, manager, or politician. The job is to get other people to understand things the way they understand them. That's how we as a society can collaborate and advance rapidly.

That's a difficult problem because in the sciences we've developed formal languages that are completely unambiguous for the purposes of producing value. So, engineers use specification languages, while mathematicians and physicists use mathematics to communicate. When we write programs, we have unambiguous formal programming languages. When we talk, though, using natural language, which is where we're absolutely prolific and where our richest and most nuanced things happen, there it's very ambiguous and it's extremely contextual. If I take one sentence out of context, it can mean lots of different things.

It's not just the context in which the sentence is uttered, it's also what is in that person's mind. For you and I to confidently understand each other, it is not enough for me just to say things. You have to ask me questions, and we have to go back and forth and get in sync and align our understandings until we are satisfied that we have a similar model in our heads. That is because the language itself is not the information. The language is a vehicle through which we communicate the model in our heads. That model is independently developed and refined, and then we align them to communicate. This notion of "producing" an understanding is a rich, layered, highly contextual thing that is subjective and collaborative.

A great example was when my daughter was seven years old and doing some school work. She was reading a page in a science book about electricity. The book says that it's energy that's created in different ways, such as by water flowing over turbines. It ends by asking my daughter a simple question, "How is the electricity produced?" She looks back at the text, and she's doing text matching, saying well it says electricity is created and "created" is a synonym of "produced," and then it has this phrase, "by water flowing over turbines."

She comes to me and says, "I can answer this question by copying this phrase, but I have no understanding of what electricity is or how it is produced." She didn't understand it at all, even though she could get the question right by doing text matching. We then discussed it and she gained a richer understanding. That is more-or-less how most language AI works today—it doesn't understand. The difference is that my daughter knew she didn't understand. That is interesting. She expected much more from her underlying logical representation. I took that as a sign of intelligence, but I may be have been biased in this case. Ha!

It's one thing to look at the words in a passage and take a guess at the answer. It's another thing to understand something enough to be able to communicate a rich model of your understanding to someone and then discuss, probe, and get in sync to advance your understanding as a result.

MARTIN FORD: You're imagining a system that has a genuine understanding of concepts and that can converse and explain its reasoning. Isn't that human-level artificial intelligence or AGI?

DAVID FERRUCCI: When you can produce a system that can autonomously learn, in other words, it can read, understand, and build models then converse, explain, and summarize the models to a person that it's talking to, then you're approaching more of what I would call holistic intelligence.

As I said, I think there are three parts to a complete AI, perception, control, and knowing. A lot of the stuff that's going on with deep learning is remarkable regarding the progress that we're making on the perception and the control pieces, the real issue is the final piece. How do we do the understanding and the collaborative communication with humans so that we can create a shared intelligence? That's super powerful, because our main means for building, communicating, and compounding knowledge is through our language and building human-compatible models. That's the AI that I'm endeavoring to create with Elemental Cognition.

MARTIN FORD: Solving the understanding problem is one of the holy grails of AI. Once you have that, other things fall into place. For example, people talk about transfer learning or the ability to take what you know and apply it in another domain, and true understanding implies that. If you really understand something, you should be able to apply it somewhere else.

DAVID FERRUCCI: That's exactly right. One of the things that we're doing at Elemental Cognition is testing how a system understands and compounds the knowledge that it reads in even the simplest stories. If it reads a story about soccer, can it then apply that understanding to what's going on in a lacrosse game or a basketball game? How does it reuse its concepts? Can it produce analogous understandings and explanations for things, having learned one thing and then doing that reasoning by analogy and explaining it in a similar way?

What's tricky is that humans do both kinds of reasoning. They do what we might think of as statistical machine learning, where they process a lot of data points and then generalize the pattern and apply it. They produce something akin to a trendline in their head and intuit new answers by applying the trend. They might look at some pattern of values and when asked what is next, intuitively say the answer is 5. When people are doing that, they're doing more pattern matching and extrapolation. Of course, the generalization might be more complicated than a simple trend line, as it certainly can be with deep learning techniques.

But, when people sit down and say, "Let me explain to you why this makes sense to me—the answer is 5 because…," now they have more of a logical or causal model that they've built up in their head, and that becomes a very different kind of information that is ultimately much more powerful. It's much more powerful for communication, it's much more powerful for an explanation, and it's much more powerful for extension because now I could critique it and say, "Wait, I see where your reasoning is faulty," as opposed to saying "It's just my intuition based on past data. Trust me."

If all I have is inexplicable intuition, then how do I develop, how do I improve, and how do I extend my understanding of the world around me? That's the interesting dilemma I think we face when we contrast these two kinds of intelligences. One that is focused on building a model that is explicable, that you can inspect, debate, explain, and improve on, and one that says, "I count on it because it's right more often than it's wrong." Both are useful, but they're very different. Can you imagine a world where we give up agency to machines that cannot explain their reasoning? That sounds bad to me. Would you like to give agency up to humans that cannot explain their reasoning?

MARTIN FORD: Many people believe that deep learning, that second model that you describe, is enough to take us forward. It sounds like you think we also need other approaches.

DAVID FERRUCCI: I'm not a fanatic one way or the other. Deep learning and neural networks are powerful because they can find nonlinear, very complex functions in large volumes of data. By function, I mean if I want to predict your weight given your height, that could be a very simple function represented by a line. Predicting the weather is less likely to be represented by a simple linear relationship. The behavior of more complex systems is more likely represented by very complex functions over many variables (think curvy and even discontinuous and in many dimensions).

You can give a deep learning system huge amounts of raw data and have it find a complex function, but in the end, you're still just learning a function. You might further argue that every form of intelligence is essentially learning a function. But unless you endeavor to learn the function that outputs human intelligence itself (what would be the data for that?), then your system may very well produce answers whose reasons are inexplicable.

Imagine I have a machine called a neural network where if I load in enough data, it could find an arbitrarily complex function to map the input to the output. You would think, "Wow! Is there any problem it can't solve?" Maybe not, but now the issue becomes, do you have enough data to completely represent the phenomenon over all time? When we talk about knowing or understanding, we have first to say, what's the phenomenon?

If we're talking about identifying a cat in a picture, it's very clear what the phenomenon is, and we would get a bunch of labeled data, and we would train the neural network. If you say: "How do I produce an understanding of this content?", it's not even clear I can get humans to agree on what an understanding is. Novels and stories are complex, multilayered things, and even when there is enough agreement on the understanding, it's not written down enough for a system to learn the immensely complex function represented by the underlying phenomenon, which is human intelligence itself.

Theoretically, if you had the data you needed that mapped every kind of English story to its meaning, and there was enough there to learn the meaning mapping—to learn what the brain does given an arbitrary collection of sentences or stories—then could a neural network learn it? Maybe, but we don't have that data, we don't know how much data is required, and we don't know what it takes to learn it in terms of the complexity of the function a neural network could potentially learn. Humans can do it, but that's because the human brain is constantly interacting with other humans and it's prewired for doing this kind of thing.

I would never take a theoretical position that says, "I have a general function finder. I can do anything with it." At some levels, sure, but where's the data to produce the function that represents human understanding? I don't know.

The methodology for engaging and acquiring that information is something I don't know how to do with a neural network right now. I do have ideas on how to do that, and that doesn't mean I don't use neural networks and other machine learning techniques as part of that overarching architecture.

MARTIN FORD: You had a part in a documentary called *Do You Trust This Computer?* and you said "In three to five years, we'll have a computer system that can autonomously learn to understand and how to build understanding, not unlike the way a human mind works." That really struck me. That sounds like AGI, and yet you're giving it a three- to five-year time frame. Is that really what you're saying?

DAVID FERRUCCI: It's a very aggressive timeline, and I'm probably wrong about that, but I would still argue that it's something that we could see within the next decade or so. It's not going to be a 50- or a 100-year wait.

I think that we will see two paths. We will see the perception side and the control side continue to get better in leaps and bounds. That is going to have a dramatic impact on society, on the labor market, on national security, and on productivity, which is all going to be very significant, and that's not even addressing the understanding side.

I think that will lead to a greater opportunity for AI to engage humans, with things like Siri and Alexa engaging humans more and more in language and thinking tasks. It's through those ideas, and with architectures like we're building at Elemental Cognition, that we will start to be able to learn how to develop that understanding side.

My three- to five-year estimate was a way of saying, this is not something that we have no idea how to do. This is something we do have an idea how to do, and it's a matter of investing in the right approach and putting in the engineering necessary to achieve it. I would make a different estimate if it was something I thought was possible, but that I had no idea how to get there.

However long the wait is depends a lot on where the investment goes. A lot of the investment today is going into the pure statistical machine learning stuff because it's so short-term and so hot. There are just a lot of low-hanging fruit returns. One of the things I'm doing is getting investment for another technology that I think we need in order to develop that understanding side. It all depends on how the investment gets applied and over what time frame. I don't think, as other people might, that we don't know how to do it and we're waiting for some enormous breakthrough. I don't think that's the case, I think we do know how to do it, we just need to prove that.

MARTIN FORD: Would you describe Elemental Cognition as an AGI company?

DAVID FERRUCCI: It's fair to say we're focused on building a natural intelligence with the ability to autonomously learn, read, and understand, and we're achieving our goals for fluently dialoging with humans in that way.

MARTIN FORD: The only other company I'm aware of that is also focused on that problem is DeepMind, but I'm struck by how different your approach is. DeepMind is focused on deep reinforcement learning through games and simulated environments, whereas what I hear from you is that the path to intelligence is through language.

DAVID FERRUCCI: Let's restate the goal a little bit. Our goal is to produce an intelligence that is anchored in logic, language and reason because we want to produce a compatible human intelligence. In other words, we want to produce something that can process language the way humans process language, can learn through language, and can deliver knowledge fluently through language and reason. This is very specifically the goal.

We do use a variety of machine learning techniques. We use neural networks to do a variety of different things. The neural networks, however, do not alone solve the understanding problem. In other words, it's not an end-to-end solution. We also use continuous dialog, formal reasoning, and formal logic representations. For things that we can learn efficiently with neural networks, we do. For the things we can't, we find other ways to acquire and model that information.

MARTIN FORD: Are you also working on unsupervised learning? Most AI that we have today is trained with labeled data, and I think real progress will probably require getting these systems to learn the way that a person does, organically from the environment.

DAVID FERRUCCI: We do both. We do corpus and large corpus analysis, which is unsupervised. We do unsupervised learning from large corpora, but we also do supervised learning from annotated content as well.

MARTIN FORD: Let's talk about the future implications of AI. Do you think there is the potential for a big economic disruption in the near future, where a lot of jobs are going to be deskilled or to disappear?

DAVID FERRUCCI: I think it's definitely something that we need to pay attention to. I don't know if it'll be more dramatic than in previous examples of when a new technology has rolled in, like in the Industrial Revolution, but I think this AI revolution will be significant and comparable to the industrial revolution.

I think there will be displacements and there will be the need to transition the workforce, but I don't think it's going to be catastrophic. There's going to be some pain in that transition, but in the end, my guess is that it's likely to create more jobs. I think that's also what has happened historically. Some people might get caught in that and they have to retrain; that certainly happens, but it doesn't mean there'll be fewer jobs overall.

MARTIN FORD: Do you think there's likely to be a skill mismatch problem? For instance, if a lot of the new jobs created are for robotics engineers, deep learning experts, and so forth?

DAVID FERRUCCI: Certainly, those jobs will get created, and there'll be a skills mismatch, but I think other jobs will be created as well where there'll be greater opportunities just for refocusing and saying, "What do we want humans doing if machines are doing these other things?" There are tremendous opportunities in healthcare and caregiving, where things like human contact are important.

The future we envision at Elemental Cognition has human and machine intelligence tightly and fluently collaborating. We think of it as thought-partnership. Through thought-partnership with machines that can learn, reason, and communicate, humans can do more because they don't need as much training and as much skill to get access to knowledge and to apply it effectively. In that collaboration, we are also training the computer to be smarter and more understanding of the way we think.

Look at all the data that people are giving away for free today, that data has value. Every interaction you have with a computer has value because that computer's getting smarter. So, to what extent do we start paying for that, and paying for that more regularly? We want computers to interact in ways that are more compatible with humans, so why aren't we paying humans to help us achieve that? I think the economics of the human-machine collaboration is interesting in and of itself, but there will be big transitions. Driverless cars are inevitable, and there are quite a few people who have decent blue-collar jobs driving, and I think that'll evolve. I don't know if that will be a trend, but that will certainly be a transition.

MARTIN FORD: How do you feel about the risks of superintelligence that Elon Musk and Nick Bostrom have both been talking about?

DAVID FERRUCCI: I think there's a lot of cause to be concerned anytime you give a machine leverage. That's when you put it in control over something that can amplify an error or the effect of a bad actor. For instance, if I put machines in control of the electrical grid, over weapon systems, or over the driverless car network, then any mistake there can be amplified into a significant disaster. If there's a cybersecurity problem or an evil actor hacks the system, it's going to amplify the impact of the error or the hack. That's what we should be super concerned about. As we're putting machines in control of more and more things like transportation systems, food systems, and national security systems, we need to be super careful. This doesn't have anything specifically to do with AI, only that you must design those systems with concern about error cases and cybersecurity.

The other thing that people like Nick Bostrom talk about is how the machine might develop its own goals and decide it's going to lay waste to the human race to achieve its goals. That's something I'm less concerned about because there are fewer incentives for machines to react like that. You'd have to program the computer to do something like that.

Nick Bostrom talks about the idea that you could give the machine a benign goal but because it's smart enough it will find a complex plan that will have unintended circumstances when it executes that plan. My response to that is simple, why would you do that? I mean, you don't give a machine that has to make paper clips leverage over the electrical grid, it comes back to thoughtful design and design for security. There are many other human problems I would put higher on the list of concerns than the notion that an AI would suddenly come up with its own desires and goals, and/or plan to sacrifice the human race to make more paper clips.

MARTIN FORD: What do you think about the regulation of AI, is there a need for that?

DAVID FERRUCCI: The idea of regulation is something we do have to pay attention to. As an industry, we have to decide broadly who's liable for what when we have machines making decisions that affect our lives. That's the case whether it's in health care, policymaking, or any of the other fields. Are we, as individuals who are affected by decisions that are made by machines, entitled to an explanation that we can understand?

In some sense, we already face these kinds of things today. For example, in healthcare we're sometimes given explanations that say, "We think you should do this and we highly recommend it because 90% of the time this is what happens." They're giving you a statistical average rather than particulars about an individual patient. Should you be satisfied with that? Can you request an explanation as to why they're recommending that treatment based on this individual patient? It's not about the probabilities, it's about the possibilities for an individual case. It raises very interesting questions.

That is one area where governments will need to step in and say, "Where does the liability fall and what are we owed as individuals who are potential subjects of machine decision-making?"

The other area, which we talked a little bit about, was, what are the criteria when you design systems that have dramatic leverage, where negative effects like errors or hacking can be dramatically amplified and have broad human societal impact? You don't want to slow down the advancement of technology, but at the same time, you don't want to be too casual about the controls around deploying systems like that.

Another area for regulation that's a little dicey is the labor market. Do you slow things down and say, "you can't put machines in this job because we want to protect the labor market"? I think there's something to be said for helping society transition smoothly and avoiding dramatic impacts, but at the same time, you don't want to slow down our advance as a society over time.

MARTIN FORD: Since you departed IBM, they've built a big business unit around Watson and are trying to commercialize that with mixed results. What do you think of IBM's experience and the challenges they've faced, and does that relate to your concern about building machines that can explain themselves?

DAVID FERRUCCI: I'm many miles away from what's going on there nowadays, but my sense of that from a business perspective, is that they seized Watson as a brand to help them get into the AI business, and I think it's given them that opportunity. When I was at IBM, they were doing all kinds of AI technology, it was very spread out throughout the company in different areas. I think that when Watson won the *Jeopardy!* competition and demonstrated to the public a really palpable AI capability, all that excitement and momentum helped IBM to organize and integrate all their technology under a single brand. That demonstration gave them the ability to position themselves well, both internally and externally.

With regard to the businesses, I think IBM is in a unique place regarding the way they can capitalize on this kind of AI. It's very different than the consumer space. IBM can approach the market broadly through business intelligence, data analytics, and optimization. And they can deliver targeted value, for example in healthcare applications.

It's tough to measure how successful they've been because it depends on what you count as AI and where you are in the business strategy. We will see how it plays out. As far as the consumer mindshare these days it seems to me like Siri and Amazon's Alexa are in the limelight. Whether or not they're providing good value on the business side is a question I can't answer.

MARTIN FORD: There are concerns that China may have an advantage given that they have a larger population, more data, and fewer concerns about privacy. Is that something we should worry about? Do we need more industrial policy in the United States in order to be more competitive?

DAVID FERRUCCI: I think that there is a bit of an arms race in the sense that these things will affect productivity, the labor markets, national security, and consumer markets, so it matters a lot. To stay competitive as a nation you do have to invest in AI to give a broad portfolio. You don't want to put all your eggs in one basket. You have to attract and maintain talent to stay competitive, so I think there's no question that national boundaries create a certain competition because of how much it affects competitive economics and security.

The challenging balancing act is how do you remain competitive there and at the same time, think carefully about controls, regulation, and other kinds of impacts, such as privacy. Those are tough issues, and I think one of the things that the world's going to need is more thoughtful and knowledgeable leaders in this space who can help set policy and make some of those calls. That's a very important service, and the more knowledgeable you are, the better, because if you look under the hood, this is not simple stuff. There's a lot of tough questions, a lot of technology issues to make choices on. Maybe you need AI for that!

MARTIN FORD: Given these risks and concerns, are you optimistic with regard to the future of artificial intelligence?

DAVID FERRUCCI: Ultimately, I'm an optimist. I think it's our destiny to pursue this kind of thing. Step back to what interested me when I first started on my path in AI: Understanding human intelligence; understanding it in a mathematical and systematic way; understanding what the limitations are, how to enhance it, how to grow it, and how to apply it. The computer provides us with a vehicle through which we can experiment with the very nature of intelligence. You can't say no to that. We associate our sense of self with our intelligence, and so how do we not do everything we can to understand it better, to apply it more effectively, and to understand its strengths and its weaknesses? It's more our destiny than anything else. It's the fundamental exploration—how do our minds work?

It's funny because we think about how humanity wants to explore space and beyond to find other intelligences, when in fact, we have one growing right next to us. What does it even mean? What's the very nature of intelligence? Even if we were to find another species, we'll know more about what to expect and what's both possible and impossible as we explore the very fundamental nature of intelligence. It's our destiny to cope with this, and I think that ultimately, it will dramatically enhance our creativity and our standard of living in ways we can't even begin to imagine today.

There is this existential risk, and I think it's going to impact a change in how we think about ourselves, and what we consider unique about being human. Coming to grips with that is going to be a very interesting question. For any given task, we can get a machine that does it better, so where does our self-esteem go? Where does our sense of self go? Does it fall back into empathy, emotion, understanding, and things that might be more spiritual in nature? I don't know, but these are the interesting questions as we begin to understand intelligence in a more objective way. You can't escape it.

DAVID FERRUCCI

DAVID FERRUCCI *is the award-winning AI researcher who built and led the IBM Watson team from its inception in 2006 to its landmark success in 2011 when Watson defeated the greatest* Jeopardy! *players of all time.*

In 2013, David joined Bridgewater Associates as Director of Applied AI. His nearly 30 years in AI and his passion to see computers fluently think, learn, and communicate inspired him to found Elemental Cognition LLC in 2015 in partnership with Bridgewater. Elemental Cognition is focused on creating novel AI systems that dramatically accelerate automated language understanding and intelligent dialog.

David graduated from Manhattan College, with a BS degree in biology and from Rensselaer Polytechnic Institute with a PhD degree in computer science specializing in knowledge representation and reasoning. He has over 50 patents and has published papers in the areas of AI, automated reasoning, NLP, intelligent systems architectures, automatic story generation, and automatic question-answering.

David was awarded the title of IBM Fellow (fewer than 100 of 450,000 hold this technical distinction) and has won many awards for his work creating UIMA and Watson, including the Chicago Mercantile Exchange's Innovation Award and the AAAI Feigenbaum Prize.

> *We don't have anything anywhere near as good as an insect, so I'm not afraid of superintelligence showing up anytime soon.*

RODNEY BROOKS

CHAIRMAN, RETHINK ROBOTICS

Rodney Brooks is widely recognized as one of the world's foremost roboticists. Rodney co-founded iRobot Corporation, an industry leader in both consumer robotics (primarily the Roomba vacuum cleaner) and military robots, such as those used to defuse bombs in the Iraq war (iRobot divested its military robotics division in 2016). In 2008, Rodney co-founded a new company, Rethink Robotics, focused on building flexible, collaborative manufacturing robots that can safely work alongside human workers.

MARTIN FORD: While at MIT, you started the iRobot company, which is now one of the world's biggest distributors of commercial robots. How did that come about?

RODNEY BROOKS: I started iRobot back in 1990 with Colin Angle and Helen Greiner. At iRobot we had a run of 14 failed business models and didn't get a successful one until 2002, at which point we hit on two business models that worked in the same year. The first one was robots for the military. They were deployed in Afghanistan to go into caves to see what was in them. Then, during the Afghanistan and Iraq conflicts, around 6,500 of them were used to deal with roadside bombs.

At the same time in 2002, we launched the Roomba, which was a vacuum cleaning robot. In 2017, the company recorded full-year revenue of $884 million and has, since launch, shipped over 20 million units. I think it's fair to say the Roomba is the most successful robot ever in terms of numbers shipped, and that was really based on the insect-level intelligence that I had started developing at MIT around 1984.

When I left MIT in 2010, I stepped down completely and started a company, Rethink Robotics, where we build robots that are used in factories throughout the world. We've shipped thousands of them to date. They're different from conventional industrial robots in that they're safe to be with, they don't have to be caged, and you can show them what you want them to do.

In the latest version of the software we use, *Intera 5*, when you show the robots what you want them to do, they actually write a program. It's a graphical program that represents behavior trees, which you can then manipulate if you want, but you don't have to. Since its launch, more sophisticated companies wanted to be able to get in and tweak exactly what the robot was doing after it had been shown what to do, but you don't have to know what the underlying representation is. These robots use force feedback, they use vision, and they operate in real environments with real people around them 24 hours a day, seven days a week, 365 days a year, all over the world. I think certainly they are the most advanced artificial intelligence robots currently in mass deployment.

MARTIN FORD: How did you come to be at the forefront of robotics and AI? Where does your story begin?

RODNEY BROOKS

RODNEY BROOKS: I grew up in Adelaide, South Australia, and in 1962 my mother found two American *How and Why Wonder Books*. One was called *Electricity* and the other, *Robots and Electronic Brains*. I was hooked, and I spent the rest of my childhood using what I'd learned from the books to explore and try to build intelligent computers, and ultimately robots.

I did an undergraduate degree in mathematics and started a PhD in artificial intelligence in Australia but realized there was a little problem in that there were no computer science departments or artificial intelligence researchers in the country. I applied to the three places that I'd heard of that did artificial intelligence, MIT (Massachusetts Institute of Technology), Carnegie Mellon (Pittsburgh, USA), and Stanford University. I got rejected by MIT but got accepted to Carnegie Mellon and Stanford, starting in 1977. I chose Stanford because it was closer to Australia.

My PhD at Stanford was on computer vision with Tom Binford. Following on from that, I was at Carnegie Mellon for a postdoc, then onto another postdoc at MIT, finally ending back at Stanford in 1983 as a member of the tenure-track faculty. In 1984 I moved back to MIT as a member of the faculty, where I stayed for 26 years.

While at MIT as a postdoc, I started working more on intelligent robots. By the time I moved back to MIT in 1984 I realized just how little progress we'd made in modeling robot perception. I got inspired by insects with a hundred thousand neurons outperforming any robot we had by fantastic amounts. I then started to try and model intelligence on insect intelligence, and that's what I did for the first few years.

I then ran the Artificial Intelligence Lab at MIT that Marvin Minsky had founded. Over time, that merged with the Laboratory of Computer Science and formed CSAIL, the Computer Science and Artificial Intelligence Lab, which is, today, still the largest lab at MIT.

MARTIN FORD: Looking back, what would you say is the highlight of your career with either robots or AI?

RODNEY BROOKS: The thing I'm proudest of was in March 2011 when the earthquake hit Japan and the tidal wave knocked out the Fukushima Nuclear Power Plant. About a week after it happened, we got word that the Japanese authorities were really having problems in that they couldn't get any robots into the plant to figure out what was going on. I was still on the board of iRobot at that time, and we shipped six robots in 48 hours to the Fukushima site and trained up the power company tech team. As a result, they acknowledged that the shutdown of the reactors relied on our robots being able to do things for them that they on their own were unable to do.

MARTIN FORD: I remember that story about Japan. It was a bit surprising because Japan is generally perceived as being on the very leading edge of robotics, and yet they had to turn to you to get working robots.

RODNEY BROOKS: I think there's a real lesson there. The real lesson is that the press hyped up things about them being far more advanced than they really are. Everyone thought Japan had incredible robotic capabilities, and this was led by an automobile company or two, when really what they had was great videos and nothing about reality.

Our robots had been in war zones for nine years being used in the thousands every day. They weren't glamorous, and the AI capability would be dismissed as being almost nothing, but that's the reality of what's real and what is applicable today. I spend a large part of my life telling people that they are being delusional when they see videos and think that great things are around the corner, or that there will be mass unemployment tomorrow due to robots taking over all of our jobs.

At Rethink Robotics, I say, if there was no lab demo 30 years ago, then it's too early to think that we could make it into a practical product now. That's how long it takes from a lab demo to a practical product. It's certainly true of autonomous driving; everyone's really excited about autonomous driving now. People forget that the first automobile that drove autonomously on a freeway at over 55 miles an hour for 10 miles was in 1987 near Munich. The first time a car drove across the US, hands off the wheel, feet off the pedals coast to coast, was *No Hands Across America* in 1995. Are we going to see mass-produced self-driving cars tomorrow? No. It takes a long, long, long time to develop something like this, and I think people are still overestimating how quickly this technology will be deployed.

MARTIN FORD: It sounds to me like you don't really buy into the Kurzweil Law of Accelerating Returns. The idea that everything is moving faster and faster. I get the feeling that you think things are moving at the same pace?

RODNEY BROOKS

RODNEY BROOKS: Deep learning has been fantastic, and people who are outside the field of it come in and say, wow. We're used to exponentials because we had exponentials in Moore's Law, but Moore's Law is slowing down because you can no longer halve the feature size. What it's leading to though is a renaissance of computer architecture. For 50 years, you couldn't afford to do anything out of the ordinary because the other guys would overtake you, just because of Moore's Law. Now we're starting to see a flourishing of computer architecture and I think it's a golden era for computer architecture because of the end of Moore's Law. That gets back to Ray Kurzweil and people who saw those exponentials and think that everything is exponential.

Certain things are exponential, but not everything. If you read Gordon Moore's 1965 paper, *The Future of Integrated Electronics*, where Moore's Law originated from, the last part was devoted to what the law doesn't apply to. Moore said it doesn't apply to power storage, for example, where it's not about the information abstraction of zeroes and ones, it's about bulk properties.

Take green tech as an example. A decade ago, venture capitalists in Silicon Valley got burned because they thought Moore's Law was everywhere, and that it would apply to green tech. No, that's not how it works. Green tech relies on bulk, it relies on energy, it's not something that is halve-able physically and you still have the same information content.

Getting back to deep learning, people think because one thing happened and then another thing happened, it's just going to get better and better. For deep learning, the fundamental algorithm of backpropagation was developed in the 1980s, and those people eventually got it to work fantastically after 30 years of work. It was largely written off in the 1980s and the 1990s for lack of progress, but there were 100 other things that were also written off at the same time. No one predicted which one out of those 100 things would pop. It happened to be that backpropagation came together with a few extra things, such as clamping, more layers, and a lot more computation, and provided something great. You could never have predicted that backpropagation and not one of those 99 other things were going to pop through. It was by no means inevitable.

Deep learning has had great success, and it will have more success, but it won't go on forever providing more or greater success. It has limits. Ray Kurzweil is not going to be uploading his consciousness any time soon. It's not how biological systems work. Deep learning will do some things, but biological systems rely on hundreds of algorithms, not just one algorithm. We will need hundreds more algorithms before we can make that progress, and we cannot predict when they will pop. Whenever I see Kurzweil I remind him that he is going to die.

MARTIN FORD: That's mean.

RODNEY BROOKS: I'm going to die too. I have no doubt about it, but he doesn't like to have it pointed out because he's one of these techno-religion people. There are different versions of techno religion. There are the life extension companies being started by the billionaires in Silicon Valley, then there's the upload yourself to a computer person like Ray Kurzweil. I think that probably for a few more centuries, we're still mortal.

MARTIN FORD: I tend to agree with that. You mentioned self-driving cars, let me just ask you specifically how fast you see that moving? Google supposedly has real cars with nobody inside them on the road now in Arizona.

RODNEY BROOKS: I haven't seen the details of that yet, but it has taken a lot longer than anyone thought. Both Mountain View (California) and Phoenix (Arizona) are different sorts of cities to much of the rest of the US. We may see some demos there, but it's going to be a few years before there is a practical mobility-as-a-service operation that turns out to be anything like profitable. By profitable, I mean making money almost at the rate at which Uber is losing money, which was $4.5 billion last year.

MARTIN FORD: The general thought is that since Uber loses money on every ride, if they can't go autonomous it's not a sustainable business model.

RODNEY BROOKS: I just saw a story this morning, saying that the median hourly wage of an Uber driver is $3.37, so they're still losing money. That's not a big margin to get rid of and replace with those expensive sensors required for autonomous driving. We haven't even figured out what the practical solution is for self-driving cars. The Google cars have piles of expensive sensors on the roof, and Tesla tried and failed with just built-in cameras. We will no doubt see some impressive demonstrations and they will be cooked. We saw that with robots from Japan, those demonstrations were cooked, very, very cooked.

RODNEY BROOKS

MARTIN FORD: You mean faked?

RODNEY BROOKS: Not faked, but there's a lot behind the curtain that you don't see. You infer, or you make generalizations about what's going on, but it's just not true. There's a team of people behind those demonstrations, and there will be teams of people behind the self-driving demonstrations in Phoenix for a long time, which is a long way from it being real.

Also, a place like Phoenix is different from where I live in Cambridge, Massachusetts, where it's all cluttered one-way streets. This raises questions, such as where does the driving service pick you up in my neighborhood? Does it pick you up in the middle of the road? Does it pull into a bus lane? It's usually going to be blocking the road, so it's got to be fast, people will be tooting horns at them, and so on. It's going to be a while before fully autonomous systems can operate in that world, so I think even in Phoenix we're going to see designated pickup and drop-off places for a long time, they won't be able to just slot nicely into the existing road network.

We've started to see Uber rolling out designated pick-up spots for their services. They now have a new system, which they were trying in San Francisco and Boston and has now expanded to six cities, where you can stand in line at an Uber rank with other people getting cold and wet waiting for their cars. We're imagining self-driving cars are going to be just like the cars of today except with no driver. No, there's going to be transformations of how they're used.

Our cities got transformed by cars when they first came along, and we're going to need a transformation of our cities for this technology. It's not going to be just like today but with no drivers in the cars. That takes a long time, and it doesn't matter how much of a fanboy you are in Silicon Valley, it isn't going to happen quickly.

MARTIN FORD: Let's speculate. How long will it take to have something like what we have with Uber today, a mass driverless product where you could be in Manhattan or San Francisco and it will pick you up somewhere and take you to another place you specify?

RODNEY BROOKS: It's going to come in steps. The first step may be that you walk to a designated pick-up place and they're there. It's like when you pick up a Zipcar (an American car-sharing company scheme) today, there are designated parking spots for Zipcars. That will come earlier than the service that I currently get from an Uber where they pull up and double park right outside my house. At some point, I don't know whether it is going to be in my lifetime, we'll see a lot of self-driving cars moving around our regular cities but it's going to be decades in the making and there's going to be transformations required, but we haven't quite figured out yet what they're going to be.

For instance, if you're going to have self-driving cars everywhere, how do you refuel them or recharge them? Where do they go to recharge? Who plugs them in? Well, some startups have started to think about how fleet management systems for electric self-driving cars might work. They will still require someone to do the maintenance and the normal daily operations. A whole bunch of infrastructure like that would have to come about for autonomous vehicles to be a mass product, and it's going to take a while.

MARTIN FORD: I've had other estimates more in the range of five years until something roughly the equivalent to Uber is ready. I take it that you think that's totally unrealistic?

RODNEY BROOKS: Yes, that's totally unrealistic. We might get to see certain aspects of it, but not the equivalent. It's going to be different, and there's a whole bunch of new companies and new operations that have to support it that haven't happened yet. Let's start with the fundamentals. How are you going to get in the car? How's it going to know who you are? How do you tell if you've changed your mind when you're driving and you want to go to a different location? Probably with speech, Amazon Alexa and Google Home have shown us how good speech recognition is, so I think we will expect the speech to work.

Let's look at the regulatory system. What can you tell the car to do? What can you tell the car to do if you don't have a driver's license? What can a 12-year-old, who's been put in the car by their parents to go to soccer practice, tell the car to do? Does the car take voice commands from 12-year-olds, or does it not listen to them? There's an incredible number of practical and regulatory problems that people have not been talking about that remain to be solved. At the moment, you can put a 12-year-old in a taxi and it will take him somewhere. That isn't going to happen for a long time with self-driving cars.

MARTIN FORD: Let's go back to one of your earlier comments on your previous research into insects. That's interesting because I've often thought that insects are very good biological robots. I know you're no longer a researcher yourself, but I was wondering what's currently happening in terms of building a robot or an intelligence that begins to approach what an insect is capable of, and how does that influence our steps toward superintelligence?

RODNEY BROOKS: Simply put, we don't have anything anywhere near as good as an insect, so I'm not afraid of superintelligence showing up anytime soon. We can't replicate the learning capabilities of insects using only a small number of unsupervised examples. We can't achieve the resilience of the insect in being able to adapt in the world. We certainly can't replicate the mechanics of an insect, which are amazing. No one has anything that approaches an insect's level of intent. We have great models that can look at something and classify it and even put a label on it in certain cases, but that's so much different to even the intelligence of an insect.

MARTIN FORD: Think back to the '90s and the time you started iRobot, do you think since then robotics has met or even exceeded your expectations, or has it been disappointing?

RODNEY BROOKS: When I came to the United States in 1977, I was really interested in robots and ended up working on computer vision. There were three mobile robots in the world at that point. One of those robots was at Stanford, where Hans Moravec would run experiments to get the robot to move 60 feet across a large room in six hours, another one was at NASA's Jet Propulsion Laboratory (JPL), and the last was at the Laboratory for Analysis and Architecture of Systems (LAAS) in Toulouse, France.

There were three mobile robots in the world. iRobot now ships millions of mobile robots per year, so from the point of view of how far that's come, I'm pretty happy. We made it big and we've moved a long, long way. The only reason that those advances in robotics haven't been a bigger story is because in that same time frame we've gone from room-size mainframe computers to having billions of smartphones throughout the world.

MARTIN FORD: Moving on from insects, I know you've been working on creating robotic hands. There have been some amazing videos of robotic hands from various teams. Can you let me know how that field is progressing?

RODNEY BROOKS: Yes, I wanted to differentiate that mobile commercial robot work that I was doing at iRobot from what I was doing with my students at MIT, so my research at MIT changed from insects to humanoids and as a result, I started to work there with robot arms. That work is progressing slowly. There are various exciting things happening in lab demos, but they're focusing on one particular task, which is very different from the more general way in which we operate.

MARTIN FORD: Is that slow progress due to a hardware or a software problem, and is it the mechanics of it or just the control?

RODNEY BROOKS: It's everything. There are a whole bunch of things that you have to make progress on in parallel. You have to make progress on the mechanics, on the materials that form the skin, on the sensors embedded throughout the hand, and on the algorithms to control it, and all those things have to happen at once. You can't race ahead with one pathway without the others alongside it.

Let me give you an example to drive this home. You've probably seen those plastic grabber toys that have a handle at one end that you squeeze to open a little hand at the other end. You can use them to grab hard-to-reach stuff, or to reach a light bulb that you can't quite get to on your own.

That really primitive hand can do fantastic manipulation beyond what any robot can currently do, but it's an amazingly primitive piece of plastic junk that you're using to do that manipulation with. That's the clincher, you are doing the manipulation. Often, you'll see videos of a new robot hand that a researcher has designed, and it's a person holding the robot hand and moving it around to do a task. They could do the same task with this little plastic grabber toy, it's the human doing it. If it was that simple, we could attach this grabber toy to the end of a robot arm and have it perform the task—a human can do it with this toy at the end of their arm, why can't a robot? There's something dramatic missing.

MARTIN FORD: I have seen reports that deep learning and reinforcement learning is being used to have robots learn to do things by practicing or even just by watching YouTube videos. What's your view on this?

RODNEY BROOKS: Remember they're lab demos. DeepMind has a group using our robots and they've recently published some interesting force feedback work with robots attaching clips to things, but each of these is painstakingly worked on by a team of really smart researchers for months. It's nowhere near the same as a human. If you take any person and show them something to do dexterously, they can do it immediately. We are nowhere close to anything like that from a robot's perspective.

I recently built some IKEA furniture and I've heard people say this would be a great robot test. Give them an IKEA kit, give them the instructions that come with it, and have them make it. I must have done 200 different dexterous sorts of tasks while building that furniture. Let's say we took my robots, that we sell in the thousands and are state of the art and have more sensors in them than any other robot that is sold today, and we tried to replicate that. If we worked for a few months in a very restricted environment we might get a coarse demonstration of one of those 200 tasks that I just knew and did. Again, it's imagination running wild here to think a robot could soon do all of those tasks, the reality is very different.

MARTIN FORD: What is the reality? Thinking 5 to 10 years ahead, what are we going to see in the field of robotics and artificial intelligence? What kinds of breakthroughs should we realistically expect?

RODNEY BROOKS: You can never expect breakthroughs. I expect 10 years from now the hot thing will not be deep learning, there'll be a new hot thing driving progress.

Deep learning has been a wonderful technology for us. It is what enables the speech systems for Amazon Echo and Google Home, and that's a fantastic step forward. I know deep learning is going to enable other steps forward too, but something will come along to replace it.

MARTIN FORD: When you say deep learning, do you mean by that neural networks using backpropagation?

RODNEY BROOKS: Yes, but with lots of layers.

MARTIN FORD: Maybe then the next thing will still be neural networks but with a different algorithm or Bayesian networks?

RODNEY BROOKS: It might be, or it might be something very different, that's what we don't know. I guarantee, though, that within 10 years there'll be a new hot topic that people will be exploiting for applications, and it will make certain other technologies suddenly pop. I don't know what they will be, but in a 10-year time frame we're certainly going to see that happen.

It's impossible to predict what's going to work and why, but you can in a predictable way say something about market pull, and market pull is going to come from a few different megatrends that are currently taking place.

For example, the ratio of elderly retired people to working-age people is changing dramatically. Depending on whose numbers you look at, the ratio is changing from something like nine working-age people to every one retired person (9:1) to two working-age people to every retired person (2:1). There are a lot more elderly people in the world. It depends on the country and other factors, but that means there will be a market pull toward helping the elderly get things done as they get frailer. We're already seeing this in Japan at robotics trade shows, where there are a lot of lab demos of robots helping the elderly to do simple tasks, such as getting into and out of bed, getting into and out of the bathroom, just simple daily things. Those things currently require one-to-one human help, but as that ratio of working-age to elderly changes, there isn't going to be the labor force to fulfil that need. That's going to pull robotics into helping the elderly.

MARTIN FORD: I agree that that elder care segment is a massive opportunity for the robotics and AI industry, but it does seem very challenging in terms of the dexterity that's required to really assist an elderly person in taking care of themselves.

RODNEY BROOKS: It is not going to be a simple substitution of a robotic system for a person, but there is going to be a demand so there will be motivated people working on trying to come up with solutions because it is going to be an incredible market.

I think we will also see a pull for construction work because we are urbanizing the world at an incredible rate. Many of the techniques that we use in construction were invented by the Romans, there's room for a little technological update in some of those.

MARTIN FORD: Do you think that would be construction robots or would it be construction scale 3D printing?

RODNEY BROOKS: 3D printing may come in for aspects of it. It's not going to be printing the whole building, but certainly we might see printed pre-formed components. We'll be able to manufacture a lot more parts off-site, which will in turn lead to innovation in delivering, lifting, and moving those parts. There's room for a lot of innovation there.

Agriculture is another industry that will potentially see robotics and AI innovation, particularly with climate change disrupting our food chain. People are already talking about urban farming, bringing farming out of a field and into a factory. This is something where machine learning can be very helpful. We have the computation power now to close a loop around every seed we need to grow and to provide it with the exact nutrients and conditions that it needs without having to worry about the actual weather outside. I think climate change is going to drive automation of farming in a different way than it has so far.

MARTIN FORD: What about real household consumer robots? The example people always give is the robot that would bring you a beer. It sounds like that might still be some way off.

RODNEY BROOKS: Colin Angle, the CEO of iRobot, who co-founded it with me in 1990, has been talking about that for 28 years now. I think that I'm still going to be going to the fridge myself for a while.

MARTIN FORD: Do you think that there will ever be a genuinely ubiquitous consumer robot, one that saturates the consumer market by doing something that people find absolutely indispensable?

RODNEY BROOKS: Is Roomba indispensable? No, but it does something of value at a low enough cost that people are willing to pay for it. It's not quite indispensable, it's a convenience level.

MARTIN FORD: When do we get there for a robot that can do more than move around and vacuum floors? A robot that has sufficient dexterity to perform some basic tasks?

RODNEY BROOKS: I wish I knew! I think no one knows. Everyone's saying robots are coming to take over the world, yet we can't even answer the question of when one will bring us a beer.

MARTIN FORD: I saw an article recently with the CEO of Boeing, Dennis Muilenburg, saying that they're going to have autonomous drone taxis flying people around within the next decade, what do you think of his projection?

RODNEY BROOKS: I will compare that to saying that we're going to have flying cars. Flying cars that you can drive around in and then just take off have been a dream for a long time, but I don't think it's going to happen.

I think the former CEO of Uber, Travis Kalanick, claimed that they were going to have flying Ubers deployed autonomously in 2020. It's not going to happen. That's not to say that I don't think we'll have some form of autonomous personal transport. We already have helicopters and other machines that can reliably go from place to place without someone flying them. I think it's more about the economics of it that will determine when that happens, but I don't have an answer to when that will be.

MARTIN FORD: What about artificial general intelligence? Do you think it is achievable and, if so, in what timeframe do you think we have a 50% chance of achieving it?

RODNEY BROOKS: Yes, I think it is achievable. My guess on that is the year 2200, but it's just a guess.

MARTIN FORD: Tell me about the path to get there. What are the hurdles we'll face?

RODNEY BROOKS: We already talked about the hurdle of dexterity. The ability to navigate and manipulate the world is important in understanding the world, but there's a much wider context to the world than just the physical. For example, there isn't a single robot or AI system out there that knows that today is a different day to yesterday, apart from a nominal digit on a calendar. There is no experiential memory, no understanding of being in the world from day to day, and no understanding of long-term goals and making incremental progress toward them. Any AI program in the world today is an idiot savant living in a sea of now. It's given something, and it responds.

The AlphaGo program or chess-playing programs don't know what a game is, they don't know about playing a game, they don't know that humans exist, they don't know any of that. Surely, though, if an AGI is equivalent to a human, it's got to have that full awareness.

As far back as 50 years ago people worked on research projects around those things. There was a whole community that I was a part of in the 1980s through the 1990s working on the simulation of adaptive behavior. We haven't made much progress since then, and we can't point to how it's going to be done. No one's currently working on it, and the people that claim to be advancing AGI are actually re-doing the same things that John McCarthy talked about in the 1960s, and they are making about as much progress.

It's a hard problem. It doesn't mean you don't make progress on the way in a lot of technologies, but some things just take hundreds of years to achieve. We think that we're the golden people at the critical time. Lots of people have thought that at lots of times, it doesn't make it true for us right now and I see no evidence of it.

MARTIN FORD: There are concerns that we will fall behind China in the race to advanced artificial intelligence. They have a larger population, and therefore more data, and they don't have as strict privacy concerns to hold back what they can do in AI. Do you think that we are entering a new AI arms race?

RODNEY BROOKS: You're correct, there is going to be a race. There's been a race between companies, and there will be a race between countries.

MARTIN FORD: Do you view it as a big danger for the West if a country like China gets a substantial lead in AI?

RODNEY BROOKS: I don't think it's as simple as that. We will see uneven deployment of AI technologies. I think we are seeing this already in China in their deployment of facial recognition in ways that we would not like to see here in the US. As for new AI chips, this is not something that a country like the US can afford to even begin to fall behind with. However, to not fall behind would require leadership that we do not currently have.

We've seen policies saying that we need more coal miners, while science budgets are cut, including places like the National Institute of Standards and Technology. It's craziness, it's delusional, it's backward thinking, and it's destructive.

MARTIN FORD: Let's talk about some of the risks or potential dangers associated with AI and robotics. Let's start with the economic question. Many people believe we are on the cusp of a big disruption on the scale of a new Industrial Revolution. Do you buy into that? Is there going to be a big impact on the job market and the economy?

RODNEY BROOKS: Yes, but not in the way people talk about. I don't think it's AI per se. I think it's the digitalization of the world and the creation of new digital pathways in the world. The example I like to use is toll roads. In the US, we've largely gotten rid of human toll takers on toll roads and toll bridges. It's not particularly done with AI but it's done because there's a whole bunch of digital pathways that have been built up in our society over the last 30 years.

One of the things that allowed us to get rid of toll takers is the tag that you can put on your windscreen that gives a digital signature to your car. Another advance that made it practical to get rid of all the human toll lanes is computer vision, where there is an AI system with some deep learning that can take a snapshot of the license plate and read it reliably. It's not just at the toll gate, though. There are other digital chains that have happened to get us to this point. You are able to go to a website and register the tag in your car and the particular serial code that belongs to you, and also provide your license number so that there's a backup.

There's also digital banking that allows a third party to regularly bill your credit card without them ever touching your physical credit card. In the old days you had to have the physical credit card, now it's become a digital chain. There's also the side effect for the companies that run the toll booth, that they no longer need trucks to collect the money and take it to the bank because they have this digital supply chain.

There's a whole set of digital pieces that came together to automate that service and remove the human toll taker. AI was a small, but necessary piece in there, but it wasn't that overnight that person was replaced by an AI system. It's those incremental digital pathways that enable the change in labor markets, it's not a simple one-for-one replacement.

MARTIN FORD: Do you think those digital chains will disrupt a lot of those grass roots service jobs?

RODNEY BROOKS: Digital chains can do a lot of things but they can't do everything. What they leave behind are things that we typically don't value very much but are necessary to keep our society running, like helping the elderly in the restroom, or getting them in and out of showers. It's not just those kinds of tasks—look at teaching. In the US, we've failed to give schoolteachers the recognition or the wages they deserve, and I don't know how we're going to change our society to value this important work, and make it economically worthwhile. As some jobs are lost to automation, how do we recognize and celebrate those other jobs that are not?

MARTIN FORD: It sounds like you're not suggesting that mass unemployment will happen, but that jobs will change. I think one thing that will happen is that a lot of desirable jobs are going to disappear. Think of the white-collar job where you're sitting in front of a computer and you're doing something predictable and routine, cranking out the same report again and again. It's a very desirable high-paying job that people go to college to get and that job is going to be threatened, but the maid cleaning the hotel room is going to be safe.

RODNEY BROOKS: I don't deny that, but what I do deny is when people say, oh that's AI and robots doing that. As I say, I think this is more down to digitalization.

MARTIN FORD: I agree, but it's also true that AI is going to be deployed on that platform, so things may move even faster.

RODNEY BROOKS: Yes, it certainly makes it easier to deploy AI given that platform. The other worry, of course, is that the platform is built on totally insecure components that can get hacked by anyone.

MARTIN FORD: Let's move on to that security question. What are the things that we really should worry about, aside from the economic disruption? What are the real risks, such as security, that you think are legitimate and that we should be concerned with?

RODNEY BROOKS: Security is the big one. I worry about the security of these digital chains and the privacy that we have all given up willingly in return for a certain ease of use. We've already seen the weaponization of social platforms. Rather than worry about a self-aware AI doing something willful or bad, it's much more likely that we're going to see bad stuff happen from human actors figuring out how to exploit the weaknesses in these digital chains, whether they be nation states, criminal enterprises, or even lone hackers in their bedrooms.

MARTIN FORD: What about the literal weaponization of robots and drones? Stuart Russell, one of the interviewees in this book, made a quite terrifying film called *Slaughterbots* about those concerns.

RODNEY BROOKS: I think that kind of thing is very possible today because it doesn't rely on AI. *Slaughterbots* was a knee-jerk reaction saying that robots and war are a bad combination. There's another reaction that I have. It always seemed to me that a robot could afford to shoot second. A 19-year-old kid just out of high school in a foreign country in the dark of night with guns going off around them can't afford to shoot second.

There's an argument that keeping AI out of the military will make the problem go away. I think you need to instead think about what it is you don't want to happen and legislate about that rather than the particular technology that is used. A lot of these things could be built without AI.

As an example, when we go to the Moon next, it will rely heavily on AI and machine learning, but in the '60s we got there and back without either of those. It's the action itself that we need to think about, not which particular technology is being used to perform that action. It's naive to legislate against a technology and it doesn't take into account the good things that you can do with it, like have the system shoot second, not shoot first.

MARTIN FORD: What about the AGI control problem and Elon Musk's comments about summoning the demon? Is that something that we should be having conversations about at this point?

RODNEY BROOKS: In 1789 when the people of Paris saw hot-air balloons for the first time, they were worried about those people's souls getting sucked out from up high. That's the same level of understanding that's going on here with AGI. We don't have a clue what it would look like.

I wrote an essay on *The Seven Deadly Sins of Predicting the Future of AI*[1], and they are all wrapped up in this stuff. It's not going to be a case of having exactly the same world as it is today, but with an AI super intelligence in the middle of it. It's going

---

1 https://rodneybrooks.com/the-seven-deadly-sins-of-predicting-the-future-of-ai/

to come very gradually over time. We have no clue at all about what the world or that AI system are going to be like. Predicting an AI future is just a power game for isolated academics who live in a bubble away from the real world. That's not to say that these technologies aren't coming, but we won't know what they will look like before they arrive.

MARTIN FORD: When these technology breakthroughs do arrive, do you think there's a place for regulation of them?

RODNEY BROOKS: As I said earlier, the place where regulation is required is on what these systems are and are not allowed to do, not on the technologies that underlie them. Should we stop research today on optical computers because they let you perform matrix multiplication much faster, so you could apply greater deep learning much more quickly? No, that's crazy. Are self-driving delivery trucks allowed to double park in congested areas of San Francisco? That seems to be a good thing to regulate, not what the technology is.

MARTIN FORD: Taking all of this into account, I assume that you're an optimist overall? You continue to work on this so you must believe that the benefits of all this are going to outweigh any risks.

RODNEY BROOKS: Yes, absolutely. We have overpopulated the world, so we have to go this way to survive. I'm very worried about the standard of living dropping because there's not enough labor as I get older. I'm worried about security and privacy, to name two more. All of these are real and present dangers, and we can see the contours of what they look like.

The Hollywood idea of AGIs taking over is way in the future, and we have no clue even how to think about that. We should be worried about the real dangers and the real risks that we are facing right now.

RODNEY BROOKS *is a robotics entrepreneur who holds a PhD in Computer Science from Stanford University. He's currently the Chairman and CTO of Rethink Robotics. For a decade between 1997 and 2007, Rodney was the Director of the MIT Artificial Intelligence Laboratory and later the MIT Computer Science and Artificial Intelligence Laboratory (CSAIL).*

He's a fellow to several organizations, including The Association for the Advancement of Artificial Intelligence (AAAI), where he is a founding fellow. So far in his career he's won a number of awards for his work within the field, including the Computers and Thought Award, the IEEE Inaba Technical Award for Innovation Leading to Production, the Robotics Industry Association's Engelberger Robotics Award for Leadership and the IEEE Robotics and Automation Award.

Rodney even starred as himself in the 1997 Error Morris movie, Fast, Cheap and Out of Control. *A movie named after one of his papers, and which currently holds a 91% Rotten Tomatoes score.*

RODNEY BROOKS

> ❝ *I am not nearly as concerned about super intelligence*
> *enslaving humanity as I am around people using the*
> *technology to do harm.*

CYNTHIA BREAZEAL

DIRECTOR OF THE PERSONAL ROBOTS GROUP, MIT MEDIA LABORATORY
FOUNDER, JIBO, INC.

Cynthia Breazeal is the Director of the Personal Robotics Group at the MIT Media Lab, as well as the founder of Jibo, Inc. She is a pioneer of social robotics and human-robot interaction. In 2000 she designed Kismet, the world's first social robot, as part of her doctoral research at MIT. Jibo was featured on the cover of TIME magazine, recognized as Best Inventions 2017. At the Media Lab, she has developed a variety of technologies focused on human-machine social interaction, including the development of new algorithms, understanding the psychology of human-robot interaction, as well as new social robot designs for applications in early childhood learning, home AI and personal robots, aging, healthcare and wellness, and more.

MARTIN FORD: Do you have a sense of when personal robots will become a true mass consumer product, so that we'll all want one in the same way we have a television set or a smartphone?

CYNTHIA BREAZEAL: Yes, I actually think we're already starting to see it. Back in 2014, when I was raising funds for my startup Jibo, a social robot for the home, everybody thought that our competitor was the smartphone, that the technology in the home that people were going to use to interact and control everything with was going to be a touchscreen. That Christmas, Amazon announced Alexa, and now we know that these VUI (Voice User Interface) assistants are actually the machines that people will use in their homes. It's opened up the whole opportunity space because you can see that people are willing to use voice devices because it's easy and it's convenient.

Back in 2014, most people interacting with AI at a consumer level were those with Siri or Google Assistant on their phones. Now, only four years later you've got everyone from young children to 98-year-olds talking to their voice-enabled AI smart devices. The type of people who are interacting with AI is fundamentally different now than it was even back in 2014. So, are the current talking speakers and devices going to be where it ends? Of course not. We're in the primordial age of this new way of interacting with ambient AIs that coexist with us. A lot of the data and evidence that we have gathered even through Jibo shows very clearly that this deeper collaborative social-emotional, personalized, proactive engagement supports the human experience in such a deeper way.

We're starting with these transactional VUI AIs who get the weather or the news, but you can see how that's going to grow and change into critical domains of real value for families, like extending education from the school to the home, scaling affordable healthcare from the healthcare institutions to the home, allowing people to age in place, and so on. When you're talking about those huge societal challenges, it's about a new kind of intelligent machine that can collaboratively engage you over an extended longitudinal relationship and personalize, grow, and change with you. That's what a social robot's about, and that's clearly where this is all going to go, and right now I think we're at the beginning.

MARTIN FORD: There are real risks and concerns associated with this kind of technology, though. People worry about the developmental impact on children if they're interacting with Alexa too much, or take a dystopian view of robots being used as companions for elderly people. How do you address those concerns?

CYNTHIA BREAZEAL: Let's just say there's the science that needs to be done, and there's the fact of what these machines do now. Those present a design opportunity and challenge to create these technologies in a way that is both ethical and beneficial and supports our human values. Those machines don't really exist yet. So yes, you can have dystopian conversations about what may happen 20 to 50 years from now, but the problem to be solved at this moment is: we have these societal challenges, and we have a range of technologies that have to be designed in the context of human support systems. The technologies alone are not the solution, they have to support our human support systems, and they have to make sense in the lives of everyday people. The work to be done is to understand how to do that in the right way.

So yes, of course there will always be critics and people wringing their hands and thinking, "oh my god, what could happen," and you need that dialog. You need those people being able to throw up the flares to say watch out for this, watch out for that. In a way, we're living in a society where the alternative is unaffordable; you can't afford the help. These technologies have the opportunity for scalable, affordable, effective, personalized support and services. That's the opportunity, and people do need help. Going without help is not a solution, so we've got to figure out how to do it.

There needs to be a real dialog and a real collaboration with the people who are trying to create solutions that are going to make a difference in people's lives—you can't just critique it. At the end of the day, everybody ultimately wants the same thing; people building the systems don't want a dystopian future.

MARTIN FORD: Can you talk a bit more about Jibo and your vision for where you see that going? Do you anticipate that Jibo will eventually evolve into a robot that runs around the house doing useful things, or is it intended to be focused more on the social side?

CYNTHIA BREAZEAL: I think there's going to be a whole bunch of different kinds of robots, and Jibo is the first of its kind that's out there and is leading the way. We're going to see other companies with other types of robots. Jibo is meant to be a platform that has extensible skills, but other robots may be more specialized. There'll be those kinds of robots, but there's also going to be physical assistance robots. A great example is the Toyota Research Institute, who are looking at mobile dexterous robots to provide physical support for elderly people, but they completely acknowledge those robots also need to have social and emotional skills.

In terms of what comes into people's homes, it's going to depend on what the value proposition is. If you're a person aging in place, you're probably going to want a different robot than parents of a child who want that child to learn a second language. In the end, it's all going to be based on what the value proposition is and what role that robot has in your home, including all the other factors like the price point. This is an area that's going to continue to grow and expand, and these systems are going to be in homes, in schools, in hospitals, and in institutions.

MARTIN FORD: How did you become interested in robotics?

CYNTHIA BREAZEAL: I grew up in Livermore, California, which has two National Labs. Both my parents worked in those as computer scientists, so I was really bought up in a home where engineering and computer science were seen as a really great career path with a lot of opportunities. I also had toys like Lego, because my parents valued those kinds of constructive media.

When I was growing up, there wasn't nearly as much around for kids to do with computers as there is now, but I could go into the National Labs where they would have various activities for kids to do—I remember the punch cards! Because of my parents, I was able to get into computers at a much earlier age than a lot of my peers and, not surprisingly my parents were some of the first people to bring home personal computers.

The first *Star Wars* movie came out when I was around 10 years old, and that was the first epiphany moment that set me on my particular career trajectory. I remember just being fascinated by the robots. It was the first time I had seen robots that were presented as full-fledged and collaborative characters, not just drones or automatons but mechanical beings who had emotions and relationships with each other and people. It really wasn't just about the amazing things they could do; it was also around the human interpersonal connection they also formed with those around them that really struck that emotional chord. Because of that film, I grew up with this attitude that robots could be like that and I think that's shaped a lot of what my research has been about.

CYNTHIA BREAZEAL

MARTIN FORD: Rodney Brooks, who is also interviewed in this book, was your doctoral adviser at MIT. How did that influence your career path?

CYNTHIA BREAZEAL: At the time I decided that what I really wanted to do when I grew up was to be an astronaut mission specialist, so I knew I needed to get a PhD in a relevant field, and so I decided that mine was going to be space robotics. I applied to a bunch of graduate schools and one of the schools I was admitted to was MIT. I went to a visit week at MIT and I remember my first experience in Rodney Brooks' mobile robot lab.

I remember walking into his lab and seeing all these insect-inspired robots that were completely autonomous going around doing a variety of different tasks depending on what the graduate students were working on. For me that was the *Star Wars* moment all over again. I remember thinking if there were ever going to be robots like I saw in *Star Wars*, it was going to happen in a lab like that. That's where it was going to begin, and quite possibly in that very lab, and I decided I had to be there and that's really what clinched the deal for me.

So, I went to MIT for graduate school, where Rodney Brooks was my academic adviser. Back then, Rod's philosophy was always a very biologically inspired philosophy to intelligence, which was not typical for the overall field. During the course of my graduate degree, I started reading a lot of literature on intelligence, not just on AI and computational methods, but natural forms of intelligence and models of intelligence. The deep interplay between psychology and what we can learn from ethology and other forms of intelligence and machine intelligence has always been a thread and a theme of my work.

At that time, Rodney Brooks was working on small-legged robots and he wrote a paper, *Fast, Cheap and Out of Control: A Robot Invasion of the Solar System*, where instead of sending up one or two very large, very expensive rovers, he was advocating for sending many, many small autonomous rovers, and if you did that then you could actually explore Mars and other kinds of celestial bodies much more easily. That was a very influential paper, and my master's thesis was actually developing the first primordial planetary Micro-Rover-inspired robots. I had the opportunity as a graduate student to work with JPL (the Jet Propulsion Laboratory), and I like to think that some of that research contributed to Sojourner and Pathfinder.

Years later, I was finishing up my master's thesis and about to embark on my doctoral work when Rod went on sabbatical. When he came back he pronounced that we were going to do humanoids. This came as a shock because we all thought it was going to go from insects to reptiles, and maybe to mammals. We thought we were going to be developing up the evolutionary chain of intelligence, so to speak, but Rod insisted it had to be humanoids. It's because when he was in Asia, particularly in Japan, they were already developing humanoids and he saw that. I was one of the senior graduate students at that time, so I stepped up to lead the effort on developing these humanoid robots to explore theories of embodied cognition. That hypothesis was about the nature of physical embodiment having a very strong constraint and influence on the nature of intelligence a machine can have or learn to develop.

The next step occurred literally on the date that NASA landed the Sojourner Mars Pathfinder rover on July 5th, 1997. On that day, I was working on my doctorate on a very different topic and I remember thinking at that moment, here we are in this field where we're sending robots to explore the oceans and volcanoes, because the value proposition of autonomy was that machines can do tasks that are far too dull, dirty, and dangerous for people. The rover was really about the autonomy allowing people to do work in hazardous environments apart from people, and that's why you needed them. We could land a robot on Mars, but they weren't in our homes.

It was from that moment that I started thinking quite a lot about how we in academia were developing these amazing autonomous robots for experts, but nobody was really embracing the scientific challenge of designing intelligent robots and researching the nature of intelligent robots that you need in order to have them coexist with people in society—from children to seniors, and everyone in between. It's like how computers used to be huge and very expensive devices that experts used, and then there was a shift to thinking about a computer on every desk in every home. This was that moment in autonomous robotics.

We already recognized that when people interacted with or talked about autonomous robots, they would anthropomorphize them. They would engage their social thinking mechanisms to try to make sense of them, so the hypothesis was that the social, interpersonal interface would be the universal interface. Up to that time, the focus on the nature of intelligence of machines was more around how do you engage and manipulate the physical inanimate world. This was now a complete shift to thinking about building a robot that can actually collaborate, communicate, and interact with people in a way that's natural for people. That's a very different kind of intelligence. If you look at human intelligence we have all these different kinds of intelligences, and social and emotional intelligence are a profoundly important, and of course underlies how we collaborate and how we live in social groups and how we coexist, empathize, and harmonize. At the time, no one was really working on that.

At this point I was quite far into my PhD, but I walked into Rod's office on that day, and I said, "I have to change everything I'm doing about my PhD. My PhD has got to be about robots and the lives of everyday people; it's got to be about robots being socially and emotionally intelligent." To his credit, Rod understood that this was a really important way to think about these problems and that it was going to be key to having robots become part of our everyday lives, so he let me go for it.

From that point, I built a whole new robot, Kismet, which is recognized as the world's first social robot.

MARTIN FORD: I know Kismet is now in the MIT museum.

CYNTHIA BREAZEAL: Kismet was really the beginning of it. It's the robot that started this field of the interpersonal human-robot social interaction, collaboration, and partnership, much more akin to the droids in *Star Wars*. I knew I could not build an autonomous robot that could rival adult social and emotional intelligence because we are the most socially and emotionally sophisticated species on the planet. The question was what kind of entity can I model, because I'm coming from a lab where we're very biologically inspired, and the only entities that exhibit this behavior are living things, mainly people. So, I thought the place to start looking at this was the infant-caregiver relationship and looking at where does our sociability originate and how does that develop over time? Kismet was modeling that nonverbal, emotive communication at the infant stage, because if a baby cannot form its emotional bond with its caregiver, the baby can't survive. The caregiver has to sacrifice and do many things in order to care for an infant.

Part of our survival mechanism is to be able to form this emotional connection and to have enough sociability there that the caregiver—the mother, the father, or whoever—is compelled to treat the newborn or young infant as a fully-fledged social and emotional being. Those interactions are critical to us actually developing true social and emotional intelligence, it's a whole bootstrapping process. That's another moment of just acknowledging that even human beings, with all of our evolutionary endowments, don't develop these capabilities if we don't grow up in the right kind of social environment.

It became a really important intersection of not only what you program in and endow an AI robot with, you have to also think deeply about the social learning and how you create the behaviors in the entity so that people will treat it as a social, emotionally responsive entity that they can empathize with and form that connection with. It's from those interactions that you can develop and grow and go through another developmental trajectory to develop full adult social and emotional adult intelligence.

That was always the philosophy, which is why Kismet was modeled to be not like a baby literally, but instead being altricial. I remember reading a lot of animation literature too, which raised questions like, how do you design something that pulls on those social, emotive, nurturing instincts within people so people would interact with Kismet in a subconscious way and nurture it naturally? Because of the way the robot was designed, every aspect about its quality of movement, its appearance, and its vocal quality was all about trying to create the right social environment that would allow the robot to engage, interact, and eventually be able to learn and develop.

In the early 2000s, a lot of the work was in understanding the mechanics of interpersonal interaction and how people really communicate, not just verbally but importantly nonverbally. A huge part of human communication is nonverbal, and a lot of our social judgments of trustworthiness and affiliation, etc., are heavily influenced by our nonverbal interaction.

When you look at voice assistants today, the interaction is very transactional; it feels a lot like playing chess. I say something, the machine says something, I say something, the machine says something, and so on. When you look at human interpersonal interaction, developmental psychology literature talks about the "dance of communication." The way we communicate is constantly mutually adapted and regulated between the participants; it's a subtle, nuanced dance. First, I'm influencing the listener, and while I'm talking and gesturing the listener is proving me nonverbal cues in dynamic relation to my own. All the while, their cues are influencing me and shaping my inferences about how the interaction is going, and vice versa. We're a dynamically coupled, collaborative duo. That's what human interaction and human communication really is, and a lot of the early work was trying to capture that dynamic and appreciating how critical the nonverbal aspects were as well as the linguistic side of it.

The next phase was to actually create an autonomous robot that could collaborate with people in this interpersonal way, still pushing on the social and emotional intelligence and the theory of other minds, now to do cooperative activities. In AI we have this habit of thinking that just because there's a competence that's easy for us as humans to do because we've evolved to do it, then it must not be that hard, but actually, we are the most socially and emotionally sophisticated species on the planet. Building social and emotional intelligence into machines is very, very hard.

MARTIN FORD: And also, very computationally challenging?

CYNTHIA BREAZEAL: Right. Arguably more so than a lot of other capabilities, like vision or manipulation, when we think about how sophisticated we are. The machine has to dovetail its intelligence and behavior with our own. It has to be able to infer and predict our thoughts, intents, beliefs, desires, etc. from context. What we do, what we say. Our pattern of behavior over time. What if you can build a machine that can engage people in this partnership where it doesn't have to be about physical work or physical assistance, but instead is about assistance and support in the social and emotional domains? We started looking at new applications for robots that these intelligent machines could have a profound impact on, like education, behavior change, wellness, coaching, aging... but people hadn't even thought about yet because they're so hung up on the physical aspect of physical work.

When you start to look at areas where social and emotional support is known to be really important, these are often areas of growth and transformation of the human themselves. If the task of the robot isn't just to get a thing built, what if the thing you're actually trying to help improve or build is the person themselves? Education is a great example. If you can learn something new, you are transformed. You are able to do things that you could not do otherwise, and you have opportunities now available to you that you didn't have otherwise. Aging in place or managing chronic disease are other examples. If you can stay healthier, your life is transformed because you're going to be able to do things and access opportunities you would not have been able to do otherwise.

Social robots broaden the relevance and application of huge areas of social significance beyond manufacturing and autonomous cars. Part of my life's work is trying to show people that you have physical competence in one dimension but orthogonal to that, which is critically important, is the ability for these machines to interact, engage, and support people in a way that unlocks our human potential. In order to do that, you need to be able to engage people and all of our ways of thinking and understanding the world around us. We are a profoundly social and emotional species, and it's really critical to engage and support those other aspects of human intelligence in order to unlock human potential. The work within the social robotics community has been focused on those huge impact areas.

We're now just recently starting to see that an appreciation of robots or AI that work collaboratively with people is actually really important. For a long, long time human-AI or human-robot collaboration was not a widely adopted problem that people thought we had to figure out, but now I think that's changed.

Now that we're seeing the proliferation of AI impacting so many aspects of our society, people are appreciating that this field of AI and robotics is no longer just a computer science or engineering endeavor. The technology has come into society in a way that we have to think much more holistically around the societal integration and impact of these technologies.

Look at a robot like Baxter, built by Rethink Robotics. It's a manufacturing robot that's designed to collaborate with humans on the assembly line, not to be roped off far from people but to work shoulder-to-shoulder with them. In order to do that, Baxter has got a face so that coworkers can anticipate, predict, and understand what the robot's likely to do next. Its design is supporting our theory of mind so that we can collaborate with it. We can read those nonverbal cues in order to make those assessments and predictions, and so the robot has to support that human way of understanding so that we can dovetail our actions and our mental states with those of the machine, and vice versa. I would say Baxter is a social robot; it just happens to be a manufacturing social robot. I think we'll have broad genres of robots that will be social, which means they're able to collaborate with people, but they may do a wide variety of tasks from education and healthcare to manufacturing and driving, and any other tasks. I see it as a critical kind of intelligence for any machine that is meant to coexist with human beings in a human-centered way that dovetails with the way we think and the way we behave. It doesn't matter what the physical task or capabilities of the machine are; if it's collaborative it is also a social robot.

We're seeing a wide variety of robots being designed today. They're still going into the oceans and on manufacturing lines, but now we're also seeing these other kinds of robots coming in to human spaces in education and therapeutic applications for autism, for instance. It's worth remembering, though, that the social aspect is also really hard. There's still a long way to go in improving and enhancing the social and emotional collaborative intelligence of this kind of technology. Over time, we'll see combinations of the social, emotional intelligence with the physical intelligence, I think that's just logical.

MARTIN FORD: I want to ask you about progress toward human-level AI or AGI. First of all, do you think it's a realistic objective?

CYNTHIA BREAZEAL: I think the question actually is, what is the real-world impact we want to achieve? I think there is the scientific question and challenge of wanting to understand human intelligence, and one way of trying to understand human intelligence is to model it and to put it in technologies that can be manifested in the world, and trying to understand how well the behavior and capabilities of these systems mirror what people do.

Then, there's the real-world application question of what value are these systems supposed to be bringing to people? For me, the question has always been about how you design these intelligent machines that dovetail with people—with the way we behave, the way we make decisions, and the way we experience the world—so that by working together with these machines we can build a better life and a better world. Do these robots have to be exactly human to do that? I don't think so. We already have a lot of people. The question is what's the synergy, what's the complementarity, what's the augmentation that allows us to extend our human capabilities in terms of what we do that allows us to really have greater impact in the world.

That's my own personal interest and passion; understanding how you design for the complementary partnership. It doesn't mean I have to build robots that are exactly human. In fact, I feel I have already got the human part of the team, and now I'm trying to figure out how to build the robot part of the team that can actually enhance the human part of the team. As we do these things, we have to think about what people need in order to be able to live fulfilling lives and feel that there's upward mobility and that they and their families can flourish and live with dignity. So, however we design and apply these machines needs to be done in a way that supports both our ethical and human values. People need to feel that they can contribute to their community. You don't want machines that do everything because that's not going to allow for human flourishing. If the goal is human flourishing, that gives some pretty important constraints in terms of what is the nature of that relationship and that collaboration to make that happen.

MARTIN FORD: What are some of the breakthroughs that need to take place in order to reach AGI?

CYNTHIA BREAZEAL: What we know how to do today is to build special-purpose AI that, with sufficient human expertise, we can craft, and hone, and polish so that it can exceed human intelligence with narrow domains. Those AIs, however, can't do multiple things that require fundamentally different kinds of intelligence. We don't know how to build a machine that can develop in the same way as a child and grow and expand its intelligence in an ongoing way.

We have had some recent breakthroughs with deep learning, which is a supervised learning method. People learn in all kinds of ways, though. We haven't seen the same breakthrough in machines that can learn from real-time experience. People can learn from very few examples and generalize. We don't know how to build machines that can do that. We don't know how to build machines that have human-level common sense. We can build machines that can have knowledge and information within domains, but we don't know how to do the kind of common sense we all take for granted. We don't know how to build a machine with deep emotional intelligence. We don't know how to build a machine that has a deep theory of mind. The list goes on. There's a lot of science to be done, and in the process of trying to figure these things out we're going to come to a deeper appreciation and understanding of how we are intelligent.

MARTIN FORD: Let's talk about some of the potential downsides, the risks and the things we should legitimately worry about.

CYNTHIA BREAZEAL: The real risks right now that I see have to do with people with nefarious intents using these technologies to hurt people. I am not nearly as concerned about superintelligence enslaving humanity as I am around people using the technology to do harm. AI is a tool, and you can apply it to both benefit and help people, but also to hurt people or to privilege one group of people over others. There's a lot of legitimate concern around privacy and security because that's tied to our freedom. There is a lot of concern around democracy and what do you do when we have fake news and bots proliferating falsehoods, and people are struggling to understand what's true and to have a common ground. Those are very real risks. There are real risks around autonomous weapons. There's also a question of a growing AI gap where AI exacerbates the divide instead of closing it. We need to start working on making AI far more democratized and inclusive so we have a future where AI can truly benefit everyone, not just a few.

MARTIN FORD: But are superintelligence and the alignment or control problem ultimately real concerns, even if they lie far in the future?

CYNTHIA BREAZEAL: Well, you have to then really get down to the brass tacks of what do you mean by super intelligence, because it could mean a lot of different things. If it is a superintelligence, why are we assuming the same evolutionary forces that drove the creation of our motivations and drives would be anything like those of the super intelligence? A lot of the fear I hear is basically mapping onto AI our human baggage that we evolved with to survive in a hostile complex world with competitive others. Why assume that a super intelligence is going to be saddled with the same machinery? It's not human, so why would it be?

What are the practical driving forces to create that? Who's going to build it and why? Who's going to invest the time and effort and money? Will it be universities or will it be corporations? You've got to think about the practicalities of what are the societal and economic drivers that would lead to the creation of something like that. It's going to require enormous amounts of talent and funding and people in order to do that instead of working on something else important.

MARTIN FORD: There is definitely a lot of interest. People like Demis Hassabis at DeepMind, are definitely interested in building AGI, or at least getting much closer to it. It's their stated goal.

CYNTHIA BREAZEAL: People may be interested in building it, but where are the resources, time, and talent coming from at massive scale? My question is, what are the actual societal driving conditions and forces that would lead to the investment necessary to create that versus what we see now? I'm just asking a very practical question. Think about what the path is given the amount of investment it's going to take to get there. What is the driver that's going to lead to that? I don't see the motivation of agencies or entities to fund what it's going to take to achieve real superhuman AGI right now.

MARTIN FORD: One potential driver of interest and investment might be the perceived AI arms race with China, and perhaps other countries as well. AI does have applications in the military and security space, so is that a concern?

CYNTHIA BREAZEAL: I think we're always going to be in a race with other countries around technology and resources, that's just the way it is. That doesn't necessitate leading to general-purpose intelligence; everything you've just said wouldn't necessarily require general intelligence, they could be broader, more flexible, but still more bounded AI.

All I'm pushing on is that there's the general super intelligence thing versus what the driving forces are right now by the entities that can fuel the work and the people and the talent to work on those problems. I see much more reason and rationale for the more domained aspects of AI versus the true general super intelligence. Certainly, within academia and research, people are absolutely very interested in creating that and people will continue to work on it. But when you get to the brass tacks of resources and time, talent, and patience for a very long-term commitment to do that, it's not obvious to me who's going to push that forward in a very practical sense just by the nature of who's going to provide those resources. I don't see that yet.

MARTIN FORD: What do you think about the potential impact on the job market? Are we on the leading edge of a new Industrial Revolution? Is there potential for a massive impact on employment or on the economy?

CYNTHIA BREAZEAL: AI is a powerful tool that can accelerate technology-driven change. It's something that right now very few people know how to design, and very few entities have the expertise and resources to be able to deploy it. We're living in a time where there is a growing social-economic divide, where I feel that one of my biggest concerns is whether AI is going to be applied to close that divide or exacerbate it. If only a few people know how to develop it, design with it, and can apply it to the problems they care about, you've got a hell of a lot of people in the world who aren't going to be able to really benefit from that.

One solution to democratizing the benefit of AI to everyone is through education. Right now, I have put significant effort in trying to address things like K-12 AI. Today's children are growing up with AI; they're no longer digital natives, they are now AI natives. They're growing up in a time when they will have always been able to interact with intelligent machines, so it's imperative these not be black box systems to them. Today's children need to start to be educated about these technologies, to be able to create things with these technologies, and in doing that, grow up with an attitude of empowerment so that they can apply these technologies and solve problems that matter to them and their community on a global scale. In an increasingly AI-powered society, we need an AI-literate society. This is something that has to happen, and from the industry standpoint, there's already a shortage of highly qualified people with this level of expertise, you can't hire these people fast enough. People's fears about AI can be manipulated because they don't understand it.

Even from that standpoint, I think there's a lot of stakeholder interest from the current organizations in wanting to open the tent and be much more inclusive to a much broader diversity of people who can develop that expertise and that understanding. Just like you can have early math and early literacy, I think you can have early AI. It's about understanding what's the level of curriculum, the sophistication of concepts and hands-on activities and communities so that students can grow up with more levels of sophistication about understanding AI and making stuff with AI. They don't have to wait until university to be able to get access to this stuff. We need to have a much broader diversity of people able to understand and apply these technologies to problems that matter to them.

MARTIN FORD: You seem to be focusing on people headed toward professional or technical careers, but most people are not college graduates. There could be a huge impact on jobs like driving a truck or working in a fast food restaurant, for example. Do we need policies to address that?

CYNTHIA BREAZEAL: I think clearly there's going to be disruption, and I think that right now, the big one people talk about is autonomous vehicles. There's disruption, and the problem is that those people whose jobs either change or get displaced need to be trained so that they can continue to be competitive in the workforce.

AI can also be applied to retrain people in an affordable, scalable way to keep our workforce vibrant. AI education can be developed for vocational programs. For me, one of the big AI application areas that we should be focusing on is AI education and personalized education systems. A lot of people can't afford to have a personal tutor or to go to an institution to get educated. If you could leverage AI to make access to those skills, knowledge, and capabilities much more scalable and affordable, then you're going to have way more people who are going to be much more agile and resilient over their lifetime. To me, that just argues that we need to double down and really think about the role of AI in empowering people and helping our citizens to be resilient and adaptive to the reality of jobs that continue to be changing.

MARTIN FORD: How do you feel about regulation of the AI field? Is that something you would support going forward?

CYNTHIA BREAZEAL: In my particular research field it's still pretty early. We need to understand it more before you could come up with any policies or regulations that would be sensible for social robots. I do feel that the dialogs that are happening right now around AI are absolutely important ones to have, because we're starting to see some major unintended consequences. We need to have a serious ongoing dialog to figure these things out, and we get down to privacy, security and all of these things, which are critically important.

For me, it really just gets down to the specifics. I think we're going to start with a few high-impact areas, and then maybe from that experience we will be able to think more broadly about what the right thing to do is. You're obviously trying to balance the ability to ensure human values and civil rights are supported with these technologies, as well as wanting to support innovation to open up opportunities. It's always that balancing act, and so, to me, it gets down to the specifics of how you walk that line so that you achieve both of those goals.

CYNTHIA BREAZEAL

CYNTHIA BREAZEAL *is an Associate Professor of Media Arts and Sciences at the Massachusetts Institute of Technology where she founded and directs the Personal Robots Group at the Media Lab. She is also founder of Jibo, Inc. She is a pioneer of social robotics and human robot interaction. She authored the book* Designing Sociable Robots, *and she has published over 200 peer-reviewed articles in journals and conferences on the topics of social robotics, human-robot interaction, autonomous robotics, artificial intelligence, and robot learning. She serves on several editorial boards in the areas of autonomous robots, affective computing, entertainment technology and multi-agent systems. She is also an Overseer at the Museum of Science, Boston.*

Her research focuses on developing the principles, techniques, and technologies for personal robots that are socially intelligent, interact and communicate with people in human-centric terms, work with humans as peers, and learn from people as an apprentice. She has developed some of the world's most famous robotic creatures, ranging from small hexapod robots, to embedding robotic technologies into familiar everyday artifacts, to creating highly expressive humanoid robots and robot characters.

Cynthia is recognized as a prominent global innovator, designer and entrepreneur. She is a recipient of the National Academy of Engineering's Gilbreth Lecture Award and an ONR Young Investigator Award. She has received Technology Review's *TR100/35 Award, and* TIME *magazine's Best Inventions of 2008 and 2017. She has received numerous design awards, including being named a finalist in the National Design Awards in Communication. In 2014 she was recognized as an entrepreneur as* Fortune Magazine's *Most Promising Women Entrepreneurs, and she was also a recipient of the L'Oréal USA Women in Digital NEXT Generation Award. The same year, she received the 2014 George R. Stibitz Computer and Communications Pioneer Award for seminal contributions to the development of social robotics and human-robot interaction.*

66 *If we could just get something at the level of the mind of a one-and-a-half-year-old into the robotic hardware that we already have, that would be incredibly useful as a technology.*

JOSHUA TENENBAUM

PROFESSOR OF COMPUTATIONAL COGNITIVE SCIENCE, MIT

Josh Tenenbaum is Professor of Computational Cognitive Science in the Department of Brain and Cognitive Sciences at the Massachusetts Institute of Technology. He studies learning and reasoning in humans and machines, with the twin goals of understanding human intelligence in computational terms and bringing artificial intelligence closer to human-level capacities. He describes his research as an attempt to "reverse engineer the human mind" and to answer the question "How do humans learn so much from so little?"

MARTIN FORD: Let's begin by talking about AGI or human-level AI. Do you consider that to be feasible and something that we will ultimately achieve?

JOSH TENENBAUM: Let's be concrete about what we mean by that. Do you mean something like an android robot, similar to C-3PO or Commander Data?

MARTIN FORD: Not necessarily in terms of being able to walk around and manipulate things physically, but an intelligence that can clearly pass a Turing test with no time limit. Something you could have a wide-ranging conversation with for hours, so that you'd be convinced that it's genuinely intelligent.

JOSH TENENBAUM: Yes, I think it's completely possible. Whether or when we will build it is hard to know, because that all depends on choices that we make as individuals in society. It's definitely possible, though—our brains and our existence prove that you can have machines that do this.

MARTIN FORD: What does progress toward AGI look like? What are the most important hurdles that you think we would need to overcome to reach that point?

JOSH TENENBAUM: One question is whether it's possible, but the other question is what version of it is most interesting or desirable? That has a lot to do with what is likely to happen sooner, because we can decide which versions of AGI are interesting and desirable and we can pursue those. I'm not actively working on machines that will do what you're saying—that will just be a disembodied language system that you can talk to for hours. I think it's exactly right to say that the system must reach the heights of human intelligence to have that kind of conversation. What we mean by intelligence is inextricably linked to our linguistic ability—our ability to communicate and to express our thoughts to others, and to ourselves, using the tools of language.

Language is absolutely at the heart of human intelligence, but I think that we have to start with the earlier stages of intelligence that are there before language, but that language builds on. If I was to sketch out a high-level roadmap to building some form of AGI of the sort you're talking about, I would say you could roughly divide it into three stages corresponding to three rough stages of human cognitive development.

The first stage, is basically the first year and a half of a child's life, which is building all the intelligence we have prior to really being linguistic creatures. The main achievement is to develop a common-sense understanding of the physical world and other people's actions. What we call intuitive physics, intuitive psychology: goals, plans, tools, and the concepts around those. The second stage, from about one and a half to three, is to use that foundation to build language, to really understand how phrases work, and to be able to construct sentences. Then, there's the third stage, from the age of three and up, which is now you've built language, use language to build and learn everything else.

So, when you talk about an AGI system that can pass a Turing test, and that you could have conversations with for hours, I would agree that reflects in some sense the height of human intelligence. However, my view is that it's most interesting and valuable to get there by going through these other stages. Both because that's how we're going to understand the construction of human intelligence, and because I think if we're using human intelligence and its development as a guide and an inspiration for AI, then that's the way to do it.

MARTIN FORD: Very often, we think about AGI in binary terms: either we've got true human-level intelligence, or else it's just narrow AI of the type that we have now. I think that what you are saying is that there might be a big middle ground there, is that right?

JOSH TENENBAUM: Yes. For example, in talks, I often show videos of 18-month-old humans doing remarkably intelligent things, and it's very clear to me that if we could build a robot that had the intelligence of a one-and-a-half-year-old, I would call that a kind of AGI. It's not adult-human level, but one and a half-year-olds have a flexible general-purpose understanding of the world that they live in, which is not the same world that adults live in.

You and I live in a world that extends backward in time thousands of years to the earliest recorded human history, and we can imagine hundreds of years forward into the future. We live in a world that includes many different cultures that we understand because we've heard about them and we've read about them. The typical one-and-a-half-year-old doesn't live in that world, because we only have access to that world through language. And yet, in the world that they live in, in the world of their immediate spatial and temporal environment, they do have a flexible, general-purpose, common-sense intelligence. That, to me, is the first thing to understand, and if we could build a robot that had that level of intelligence, it would be amazing.

If you look at today's robots, robotics on the hardware side is making great progress. Basic control algorithms allow robots to walk around. You only have to think about Boston Dynamics, which was founded by Mark Raibert. Have you heard about them?

MARTIN FORD: Yeah. I've seen the videos of their robots walking and opening doors and so forth.

JOSH TENENBAUM: That stuff is real, that's biologically inspired. Mark Raibert always wanted to understand legged locomotion in animals, as well as in humans, and he was part of a field that built engineering models of how biological systems walked. He also understood that the best way to test those models was to build real robots and to see how biological legged locomotion worked. He realized that in order to test that idea, he needed the resources of a company to actually make those things. So, that's what led to Boston Dynamics.

At this point, whether it's Boston Dynamics or other robots, such as Rodney Brooks' work with the Baxter Robots, we've seen these robots do impressive things with their bodies, like pick up objects and open doors, yet their minds and brains hardly exist at all. The Boston Dynamics robots are mostly steered by a human with a joystick, and the human mind is setting their high-level goals and plans. If we could just get something at the level of the mind of a one-and-a-half-year-old into the robotic hardware that we already have, that would be incredibly useful as a technology.

MARTIN FORD: Who would you point to as being at the absolute forefront of progress toward AGI now? Is DeepMind the primary candidate, or are there other initiatives out there that you think are demonstrating remarkable progress?

JOSH TENENBAUM: Well, I think we're at the forefront, but everybody does what they do because they think it's the right approach. That being said, I have a lot of respect for what DeepMind is doing. They certainly do a lot of cool things and get a lot of well-deserved attention for what they're doing, motivated by trying to build AGI. But I do have a different view than they do about the right way to approach more human-like AI.

DeepMind is a big company, and they represent a diversity of opinion, but in general, their center of gravity is on building systems that are trying to learn everything from scratch, which is just not the way humans work. Humans, like other animals, are born with a lot of structure in our brains just like in our bodies, and my approach is to be more inspired by human cognitive development in that way.

There are some people within DeepMind who think similarly, but the focus of what the company has been doing, and really the ethos of deep learning, is that we should learn as much as we can from scratch, and that's the basis for building the most robust AI systems. That's something that I just think is not true. I think that's a story that people tell themselves, and I think it's not the way biology works.

MARTIN FORD: It seems clear that you believe there's a lot of synergy between AI and neuroscience. How did your interest in the two fields evolve?

JOSH TENENBAUM: Both of my parents were deeply interested in things that related to intelligence and AI. My father, Jay Tenenbaum—often known as Marty, was an early AI researcher. He was an MIT undergraduate and one of Stanford's first PhDs in AI after John McCarthy went to set up the AI lab effort there. He was an early leader in computer vision and one of the founders of AAAI, the professional organization for AI in America. He also ran an early industry AI lab. Essentially, as a child I lived through the previous big wave of excitement in AI in the late 1970s and 1980s, which allowed me to go to AI conferences as a kid.

We grew up in the Bay Area, and one-time my father took us to Southern California because there was an Apple AI conference taking place, and this was in the Apple II era. I remember that Apple had bought out Disneyland for the evening for all of the attendees of the big AI conference. So, we flew down for the day just to be able to go on Pirates of the Caribbean 13 times in a row, which, looking back, tells you something about just how big AI was even then.

It's hyped now, but it was the same back then. There were startups, there were big companies, and AI was going to change the world. Of course, that time-period didn't lead to the kinds of successes that were promised in the short term. My dad was also for a while director of the Schlumberger Palo Alto Research Lab, a major industry AI lab. I hung out around there as a kid and through that, I got to meet many great AI leaders. At the same time, my mother Bonnie Tenenbaum was a teacher and got a PhD in education. She was very interested in kids' learning and intelligence from that perspective and she would expose me to various puzzles and brainteasers—things that were not too different from some of the problems we work on now in the AI field.

I was always interested in thinking and intelligence while I was growing up, and so when I was looking at college, I thought I would major in philosophy or physics. I wound up as a physics major, but I never thought of myself as a physicist. I took psychology and philosophy classes, and I was interested in neural networks, which were at the peak of their first wave in 1989 when I was at college. Back then, it seemed that if you wanted to study the brain or the mind, you had to learn how to apply math to the world, which is what people advertise physics as being about, so physics seemed like a generally good thing to do.

I really got into the field in a serious way after taking a class on neural networks in my sophomore year in college, which would have been 1991. During that time, my dad introduced me to a friend and colleague of his at Stanford named Roger Shepard, who was one of the great cognitive psychologists of all time. Although he's long retired, he was one of the people who pioneered the scientific and mathematical study of mental processes through the 1960s, '70s, and '80s, when I worked with him. I wound up getting a summer job with him programming some neural network implementations of a theory that Roger had been working on. The theory was of how humans, and many other organisms, solve the basic problem of generalization, which turned out to be an incredibly deep problem.

Philosophers have thought about this for hundreds, if not thousands, of years. Plato and Aristotle considered this, as did Hume, Mill, and Compton, not to mention many 20th century philosophers of science. The basic problem is, how do we go beyond specific experiences to general truths? Or from the past to the future? In the case that Roger Shepard was thinking about, he was working on the basic mathematics of how might an organism, having experienced a certain stimulus to have some good or negative consequence, figure out which other things in the world are likely to have that same consequence?

Roger had introduced some mathematics based on Bayesian statistics for solving that problem, which was a very elegant formulation of the general theory of how organisms could generalize from experience and he was looking to neural networks to try to take that theory and implement it in a more scalable way. Somehow, I wound up working with him on this project. Through that, I was exposed to both neural networks, as well as to Bayesian analyses of cognition early on, and you can view most of my career since then as working through those same ideas and methods. I was just very lucky to have been exposed to exciting ideas from great thinkers and people who wanted to work with me from an early age, and then that led to me going into graduate school in the field.

I ended up going to graduate school at MIT—in the same department that I am now a professor in. After my PhD, Roger was very supportive of me and helped to bring me to Stanford, where I spent a couple of years as an assistant professor in psychology before I moved back to MIT and Brain and Cognitive Science, where I am now. A key feature of this route is that I came to AI from the natural science side, thinking about how human minds and brains work, or biological intelligence more generally. I was trying to understand human intelligence in mathematical, computational, and engineering terms.

I describe what I do as "reverse engineering the mind," and what that means is trying to approach the basic science of how intelligence works in the human mind as an engineer. The goal is to understand and to build models in the language and with the technical tools of engineering. We view the mind as an incredible machine that has been engineered through various processes, such as both biological and cultural evolution, learning, and development, and is developed to solve problems. If we approach it like an engineer to try to understand what problems it has been designed to solve and how it solves them, then we think that it is the best way that we can formulate our science.

MARTIN FORD: If you were advising a younger person who was considering a career in AI research, would you say that studying brain science and human cognition are important? Do you think that there is too much emphasis put on pure computer science?

JOSH TENENBAUM: I always saw these two things as being two sides of the same coin; it just made sense to me. I was interested in computer programming, and I was interested in the idea that you could program an intelligent machine. But I was just always more animated by what is clearly one of the biggest scientific and even philosophical questions of all time. The idea that it could be linked up and have a common purpose with building intelligent machines was the most exciting idea, as well as being a promising one.

My background training is not especially in biology, but more like what you might call psychology or cognitive science. More about the software of the mind, rather than the hardware of the brain, although the only reasonable scientific view is to see those as being deeply connected because, of course, they are. That's partly what led me to MIT, where we have this department of Brain and Cognitive Science. In the mid-1980s, it used to be called the Department of Psychology, but it was always a very biologically grounded psychology department.

To me, the most interesting and biggest questions are the scientific ones. The engineering side is a way toward building more intelligent machines, but to me the value of that is as a proof of concept that our scientific models are doing the work they're supposed to be doing. It's a very important test, a sanity check, and rigor check because there are so many models on the scientific side that may fit a data set that somebody collected on human behavior or neural data, but if those models don't solve the problem that the brain and the mind must solve, then they probably aren't right.

To me it's always been an important source of constraint that we want our models of how the brain and mind work to actually fit with all of the data that we have on the scientific side, but also to actually be implementable as engineering models that take the same kind of inputs that come into the brain and gives the same kind of outputs. That is also going to lead to all sorts of applications and payoffs. If we can understand how intelligence works in the mind and brain in engineering terms, then that is one direct route for translating the insights from neuroscience and cognitive science into various kinds of AI technologies.

More generally, I think that if you approach science like an engineer, and you say the point of neuroscience and cognitive science is not just to collect a bunch of data, but to understand the basic principles—the engineering principle by which brains and minds work—then that's a certain viewpoint on how to do the science, but then your insights are directly translatable into useful ideas for AI.

If you look at the history of the field, I think it's not unreasonable to say that many, if not most, of the best, interesting, new, and original ideas in artificial intelligence came from people who were trying to understand how human intelligence works. That includes the basic mathematics of what we now call deep learning and reinforcement learning, but also much further back to Boole as one of the inventors of mathematical logic, or Laplace in his work on probability theory. In more recent times, Judea Pearl, in particular, was fundamentally interested in understanding the mathematics of cognition and the way people reason under uncertainty and that led to his seminal work on Bayesian networks for probabilistic inference and causal modeling in AI.

MARTIN FORD: You described your work as an attempt to "reverse engineer the mind." Tell me about your actual methodology for attempting that. How are you going about it? I know you do a lot of work with children.

JOSH TENENBAUM: In the first part of my career, the big question that I would always start from and come back to was the question of, how do we get so much from so little? How do humans learn concepts not from hundreds or thousands of examples, as machine learning systems have always been built for, but from just one example?

You can see that in adults, but you can also see that in children when they are learning the meaning of a word. Children can often learn a new word from seeing just one example of that word used in the right context, whether it's a word like a noun that refers to an object, or a verb that refers to an action. You can show a young child their first giraffe, and now they know what a giraffe looks like; you can show them a new gesture or dance move, or how you use a new tool, and right away they've got it; they may not be able to make that move themselves, or use that tool, but they start to grasp what's going on.

Or think about learning causality, for example. We learn in basic statistics classes that correlation and causation are not the same thing, and correlation doesn't always imply causation. You can take a dataset, and you can measure that the two variables are correlated, but it doesn't mean that one causes the other. It could be that A causes B, B causes A, or some third variable causes both.

The fact that correlation doesn't uniquely imply causation is often cited to show how difficult it is to take observational data and infer the underlying causal structure of the world, and yet humans do this. In fact, we solve a much harder version of this problem. Even young children can often infer a new causal relation from just one or a few examples—they don't even need to see enough data to detect a statistically significant correlation. Think about the first time you saw a smartphone, whether it was an iPhone or some other device with a touchscreen where somebody swipes their finger across a little glass panel, and suddenly something lights up or moves. You had never seen anything like that before, but you only need to see that once or a couple of times to understand that there's this new causal relation, and then that's just your first step into learning how to control it and to get all sorts of useful things done. Even a very young child can learn this new causal relation between moving your finger in a certain way and a screen lighting up, and that is how all sorts of other possibilities of action open to you.

These problems of how we make a generalization from just one or a few examples are what I started working on with Roger Shepard when I was just an undergraduate. Early on, we used these ideas from Bayesian statistics, Bayesian inference, and Bayesian networks, to use the mathematics of probability theory to formulate how people's mental models of the causal structure of the world might work.

It turns out that tools that were developed by mathematicians, physicists, and statisticians to make inferences from very sparse data in a statistical setting were being deployed in the 1990s in machine learning and AI, and it revolutionized the field. It was part of the move from an earlier symbolic paradigm for AI to a more statistical paradigm. To me, that was a very, very powerful way to think about how our minds were able to make inferences from sparse data.

In the last ten years or so, our interests have turned more to where these mental models come from. We're looking at the minds and brains of babies and young children, and really trying to understand the most basic kind of learning processes that build our basic common-sense understanding of the world. For the first ten years or so of my career, so from the late 1990s until the late 2000s, we made a lot of progress modeling individual aspects of cognition using these Bayesian models, such as certain aspects of perception, causal reasoning, how people judge similarity, how people learn the meanings of words, and how people make certain kinds of plans, decisions, or understand other people's decisions, and so on.

However, it seemed like we still didn't really have a handle on what intelligence is really about—a flexible, general-purpose intelligence that allows you to do all of those things that you can do. 10 years ago in cognitive science, we had a bunch of really satisfying models of individual cognitive capacities using this mathematics of ways people made inferences from sparse data, but we didn't have a unifying theory. We had tools, but we didn't have any kind of model of common sense.

If you look at machine learning and AI technologies, and this is as true now as it was ten years ago, we were increasingly getting machine systems that did remarkable things that we used to think only humans could do. In that sense, we had real AI, in the sense of these AI technologies, but we didn't have any real AI. We still don't have any real AI in the sense of the original vision of the founders of the field, of what I think you might refer to as AGI—machines that have that same kind of flexible, general-purpose, common sense intelligence that every human uses to solve problems for themselves. But we are starting to lay the foundations for that now.

MARTIN FORD: Is AGI something that you're focused on?

JOSH TENENBAUM: Yes, in the last few years general-purpose intelligence has really been what I've been interested in. I'm trying to understand what that would be like, and how we could capture that in engineering terms. I've been heavily influenced by a few colleagues like Susan Carey, and Elizabeth Spelke, who are both professors at Harvard now, who studied these questions in babies and young children. I believe that's where we ought to look for this, it's what all our intelligence starts with and it's where our deepest and most interesting forms of learning happen.

Elizabeth Spelke is one of the most important people that anybody in AI should know if they're going to look to humans. She has very famously shown that from the age of two to three months, babies already understand certain basic things about the world, like how it's made from physical objects in three dimensions that don't wink in and out of existence. It's what we typically call object permanence. It used to be thought that that was something that kids came to and learned by the time they were one year old, but Spelke and others have shown that in many ways our brains are born already prepared to understand the world in terms of physical objects, and in terms of what we call intentional agents.

MARTIN FORD: There's a debate over the importance of innate structure in AI. Is this evidence that that kind of structure is very important?

JOSH TENENBAUM: The idea that you could build machine intelligence by looking at how humans grow into intelligence—a machine that starts as a baby and learns like a child—was famously introduced by Alan Turing in the same paper where he introduced the Turing test, so it could really be the oldest good idea in AI. Back in 1950, this was Turing's only suggestion on how you might build a machine that would pass a Turing test because back then nobody knew how to do that. Turing suggested that instead of trying to build a machine brain that was like an adult, we might build a child brain and then teach it the way we teach children.

In making his proposal, Turing was effectively taking a position on the nature-nurture question. His thinking was that children's brains presumably start off much simpler than adults' brains. He said, more or less, "Presumably a child's brain is something like a notebook when you buy it from the stationers: a rather little mechanism, and lots of blank sheets." So, building a child machine would be a sensible starting place on a scaling route to AI. Turing was probably right there. But he didn't know what we know now about the actual starting state of the human mind. What we now from the work of people like Elizabeth Spelke, Renee Baillargeon, Laura Schulz, Alison Gopnik, and Susan Carey is that babies start off with a lot more structure than we might have thought. We also know that the learning mechanisms that children have are a lot smarter and more sophisticated. So, in some sense, our current understanding from the scientific side is that the possibilities of both nature and nurture are more than we thought when the notion of AI was first proposed.

If you look at not just Turing's suggestions, but the way many AI people have since invoked that idea, you know that they are not looking at the real science of how babies' brains work, rather they're appealing to that intuitive, but incorrect, idea that babies' brains start off very simple, or that some kind of simple trial and error or unsupervised learning takes place. These are often ways that people in AI will talk about how children learn. Children do learn from trial and error, and they do learn in an unsupervised way, but it's much more sophisticated, especially the ways in which they learn from much less data and with much deeper kinds of understanding and explanatory frameworks. If you look at what machine learning usually means by trial and error learning or unsupervised learning, you're still talking about very data-hungry methods that learn relatively superficial kinds of patterns.

I've been inspired by the insights coming from cognitive scientists and developmental psychologists trying to explain and understand what we see and how we imagine things that we haven't seen, how we make plans and solve problems in the course of trying to make those things actually exist, and how learning is about taking these mental models that guide our explaining, our understanding, our planning, and our imagining and refining them, debugging them, and building new models. Our minds don't just find patterns in big data.

MARTIN FORD: Is this what you've been focusing on in your recent work with children?

JOSH TENENBAUM: Yes, I'm trying to understand the ways in which even young children are able to build models of the world in their heads from very sparse data. It's really fundamentally a different kind of approach than the one that most machine learning right now is working on. To me, just as Turing suggested, and just as many people in AI have realized, it's not the only way that you might think about building a human-like AI system, but it's the only way that we know works.

If you look at human children, they're the only scaling path to AI in the known universe that we know works. A scaling path that reliably, reproducibly, and robustly starts out knowing far less than a full adult human then develops into adult-human-level intelligence. If we could understand how humans learn, then that would certainly be a route to building much more real AI. It would also address some of the greatest scientific questions of all time that cut right to our identity, like what it means to be human.

MARTIN FORD: How does all of that thinking relate to the current overwhelming focus on deep learning? Clearly, deep neural networks have transformed AI, but lately I've been hearing more pushback against deep learning hype, and even some suggestions that we could be facing a new AI Winter. Is deep learning really the primary path forward, or is it just one tool in the toolbox?

JOSH TENENBAUM: What most people think of as deep learning is one tool in the toolbox, and a lot of deep learning people realize that too. The term "deep learning" has expanded beyond its original definition.

MARTIN FORD: I would define deep learning broadly as any approach using sophisticated neural networks with lots of layers, rather than using a very technical definition involving specific algorithms like backpropagation or gradient descent.

JOSH TENENBAUM: To me, the idea of using neural networks with lots of layers is also just one tool in the toolkit. What that's good at is problems of pattern recognition, and it has proven to be a practical, scalable route for it. Where that kind of deep learning has really had success is either in problems that are traditionally seen as pattern recognition problems, like speech recognition and object recognition, or problems that can be in some way coerced into or turned into pattern recognition problems.

Take Go for example. AI researchers have long believed that playing Go would require some kind of sophisticated pattern recognition, but they didn't necessarily understand that it could be solved using the same kind of pattern recognition approaches you would use for perception problems in vision and speech. However, now people have shown that you can take neural networks, the same kind that were developed in those more traditional pattern recognition domains, and you can use them as part of a solution to playing Go, as well as chess, or similar board games. I think those are interesting models because they use what we're calling deep learning here, but they don't just do that, they also use traditional game tree search and expected value calculations, and so on. AlphaGo is the most striking and best-known success of deep learning AI, and it's not even a pure deep learning system. It uses deep learning as part of a system for playing a game and searching a game tree.

That already represents the way that deep learning expands beyond deep neural networks, but still, the secret sauce that makes it work so well is a deep neural network and the methods of training it. Those methods are finding patterns in the structure of gameplay that go way beyond the patterns people were able to find in an automatic way before. If you look beyond any one task, like playing Go or playing chess, to the broader problems of intelligence, though, the idea that you're going to turn all of the intelligence into a pattern recognition problem is ridiculous, and I don't think any serious person can believe that. I mean maybe some people will say that, but that just seems crazy to me.

Every serious AI researcher has to think two things simultaneously. One is they have to recognize that deep learning and deep neural networks have contributed a huge amount to what we can do with pattern recognition, and that pattern recognition is going to be a part of probably any intelligent system's success. At the same time, you also have to recognize that intelligence goes way beyond pattern recognition in all the ways I was talking about. There are all these activities of modeling the world, such as explaining, understanding, imagining, planning, and building out new models, and deep neural networks don't really address that.

MARTIN FORD: Is that limitation one of the things you're addressing in your work?

JOSH TENENBAUM: Well, with my work I've been interested in finding the other kinds of engineering tools that we need to address the aspects of intelligence that go beyond pattern recognition. One of the approaches is to look to earlier waves of ideas in the field, including the ideas of graphical models and Bayesian networks, which were the big thing when I got into the field. Judea Pearl is probably the most important name associated with that era of the field.

Perhaps most important of all is the earliest wave, often called "symbolic AI," Many people will tell a story that in the early days of AI we thought intelligence was symbolic, but then we learned that was a terrible idea. It didn't work, because it was too brittle, couldn't handle noise and couldn't learn from experience. So we had to get statistical, and then we had to get neural. I think that's very much a false narrative. The early ideas that emphasize the power of symbolic reasoning and abstract languages expressed in formal systems were incredibly important and deeply right ideas. I think it's only now that we're in the position, as a field, and as a community, to try to understand how to bring together the best insights and the power of these different paradigms.

The three waves in the field of AI—the symbolic era, the probabilistic and causal era, and the neural networks era—are three of our best ideas on how to think about intelligence computationally. Each of these ideas has had their rise and fall, with each one contributing something, but neural networks have really had their biggest successes in the last few years. I've been interested in how we bring these ideas together. How do we combine the best of these ideas to build frameworks and languages for intelligent systems and for understanding human intelligence?

MARTIN FORD: Do you imagine a hybrid that would bring together neural networks and other more traditional approaches to build something comprehensive?

JOSH TENENBAUM: We don't just imagine it, we actually have it. Right now, the best examples of these hybrids go by the name of probabilistic programming. When I give talks or write papers, I often point to probabilistic programming as the general tool that I'm using in my work. It's one that some people know about. It's not nearly as broadly embraced to think about AI as neural networks are, but I think it's going to be increasingly recognized in its own form.

All these terms, like neural networks or probabilistic programming, are only vague terms that continually redefine themselves as the people working with these toolsets learn more about what works, what doesn't work, and what other things they need. When I talk about probabilistic programs, I sometimes like to say that they have about as much to do with probability as neural networks have to do with neurons. Namely, neural networks were inspired by early abstractions of how a neuron works, and the idea that if you wire neurons together into a network, whether it's biological or artificial, and you make that network complicated enough in certain ways, that it becomes very powerful. The core meaning of a neuron stays around, there are basic processing units that take linear combinations of their inputs and pass them through a non-linearity, but if you look at the ways in which people are using neural networks now, they go way beyond any kind of actual neuroscience inspiration. In fact, they bring ideas from probability and from symbolic programs into them. I would say probabilistic programs are just approaching that same kind of synthesis but coming from a different direction.

The idea of probabilistic programs starts from work that people did in the 1990s where they tried to build systematic languages for large-scale probabilistic reasoning. People realized that you needed to have tools that didn't just do probabilistic reasoning, but also had abstract, symbolic components that were more like earlier eras of AI, in order to capture real common-sense knowledge. It wasn't enough to work with numbers, you had to work with symbols. Real knowledge is not just about trading off numbers for other numbers, which is what you do in probability theory, it's about expressing abstract knowledge in symbolic forms, whether it's math, programming languages, or logic.

MARTIN FORD: So, this is the approach that you've been focusing on?

JOSH TENENBAUM: Yes, I was very lucky to work with students and postdocs in my group in the mid to late 2000s, especially Noah Goodman, Vikash Mansinghka, and Dan Roy, where we built a language that we called Church, named after Alonzo Church. It was an example of bringing together higher-order logic languages based on what we call the lambda calculus, which was Church's framework for universal computation. That's really the underlying formal basis of computer programming languages like Lisp and Scheme.

We took that formalism for representing abstract knowledge and used that to generalize patterns of probabilistic and causal reasoning. That turned out to be very influential for both myself and others in terms of thinking about how to build systems that had a common-sense reasoning capacity—systems that really reasoned and didn't just find patterns in data, and that could have abstractions that could generalize across many situations. We used these systems to capture, for example, people's intuitive theory of mind—how we understand other people's actions in terms of their beliefs and desires.

Using these tools of probabilistic programs over the last ten years, we were able to build for the first time reasonable, quantitative, predictive, and conceptually correct models of how humans, even young children, understand what other people are doing, and see people's actions not just as movements in the world, but rather as the expressions of rational plans. We were also able to look how people can work backward from seeing people move around in the world to figure out what they want and what they think, to infer their beliefs and desires. That's an example of core common-sense reasoning that even young babies engage in. It's part of how they really break into intelligence; they see other people doing something and they try to figure out why they are doing it and whether it's a good guide for what they should do. To us, these were some of the first really compelling applications of these ideas of probabilistic programs.

MARTIN FORD: Can these probabilistic methods be integrated with deep learning?

JOSH TENENBAUM: Yes, in the last couple of years, people have taken that same toolset and started to weave in neural networks. A key challenge for these probabilistic programs, as we were building them ten years ago and continue today, is that inference is difficult. You can write down probabilistic programs that capture people's mental models of the world, for example, their theory of mind or their intuitive physics, but actually getting these models to make inferences very fast from the data that you might infer is a hard challenge algorithmically. People have been turning to neural networks and other kinds of pattern recognition technology as a way of speeding up inference in these systems. In the same way, you could think of how AlphaGo uses deep learning to speed up inference and search in a game tree. It's still doing a search in the game tree, but it uses neural networks to make fast, quick, and intuitive guesses that guide its search.

Similarly, people are starting to use neural networks to find patterns in inference that can speed up inferences in these probabilistic programs. The machinery of neural networks and the machinery of probabilistic programs are increasingly coming to look a lot like each other. People are developing new kinds of AI programming languages that combine all these things, and you don't have to decide which to use. They're all part of a single language framework at this point.

MARTIN FORD: When I talked to Geoff Hinton, I suggested a hybrid approach to him, but he was very dismissive of that idea. I get the sense that people in the deep learning camp are perhaps thinking not just in terms of an organism learning over a lifetime, but in terms of evolution. The human brain evolved over a very long time, and in some earlier form or organism it must have been much closer to being a blank slate. So perhaps that offers support for the idea that any necessary structure might naturally emerge?

JOSH TENENBAUM: There's no question that human intelligence is very much the product of evolution, but by that, we also have to include biological evolution and cultural evolution too. A huge part of what we know, and how we know what we know, comes from culture. It's the accumulation of knowledge across multiple generations of humans in groups. There's no question that a baby who just grew up on a desert island with no other humans around would be a lot less intelligent. Well, they might be just as intelligent in some sense, but they would know a lot less than we know. They would also in a strict sense be less intelligent because a lot of the ways in which we are intelligent, our systems of thinking—whether it's mathematics, computer science, reasoning, or other systems of thought that we get through languages—are more generally the accumulation of many smart people over many generations.

It's very clear when we look at our bodies that biological evolution has built incredibly complex structures with amazing functions. There's no reason to think that the brain is any different. When we look at the brain, it's not as obvious what are the complex structures in the real neural networks that evolution has built, and it is not just a big blank slate mess of randomly wired connections.

I don't think any neuroscientist thinks that the brain is anything like a blank slate at this point. Real biological inspiration has to take seriously that at least in any one individual brain's lifetime, there's a huge amount of structure that's built in, and that structure includes both our most basic models for understanding the world, and also the learning algorithms that grow our models beyond that starting point.

Part of what we get genetically, as well as culturally, are ways of learning that are much more powerful, much more flexible, and much faster than the kinds of learning that we have in deep learning today. These methods allow us to learn from very few examples and to learn new things much more quickly. Anyone who looks and takes seriously the way real human babies' brains start and how children learn, has to think about that.

MARTIN FORD: Do you think deep learning could succeed at achieving more general intelligence by modeling an evolutionary approach?

JOSH TENENBAUM: Well, a number of people at DeepMind and others who follow the deep reinforcement learning ethos would say they're thinking about evolution in a more general sense, and that's also a part of learning. They'd say their blank slate systems are not trying to capture what a baby does, but rather what evolution has done over many generations.

I think that's a reasonable thing to say, but then my response to that would be to also look to biology for inspiration, which is to say, okay, fine, but look at how evolution actually works. It doesn't work by having a fixed network structure and doing gradient descent in it, which is the way today's deep learning algorithms work; rather evolution actually builds complex structures, and that structure building is essential for its power.

Evolution does a lot of architecture search; it designs machines. It builds very differently, structured machines across different species or over multiple generations. We can see this most obviously in bodies, but there's no reason to think it's any different in brains. The idea that evolution builds complex structures that have complex functions, and it does it by a process which is very different to gradient descent, but rather something more like search in the space of developmental programs, is very inspiring to me.

A lot of what we work on here is to think about how you view learning or evolution as something like search in a space of programs. The programs could be genetic programs, or they could be cognitive-level programs for thinking. The point is, it doesn't look like gradient descent in a big fixed network architecture. You could say, we're going to just do deep learning in neural networks, and say that's trying to capture what evolution does, and not what human babies do, but I don't think it's really what human babies or evolution does.

It is, however, a toolkit that has been highly optimized for, especially by the tech industry. People have shown you can do valuable things with big neural networks when you amplify them with GPUs and then with big distributed computing resources. All the advances that you see from DeepMind or Google AI, to name two, are essentially enabled by these resources, and a great program of integrated software and hardware engineering building them out specifically to optimize for deep learning. The point I'm making is that when you have a technology that Silicon Valley has invested a large amount of resources in optimizing for, it becomes very powerful. It makes sense for companies like Google to pursue that route to see where you can go with it. At the same time, I'm just saying when you look at how it works in biology, either in the lifetime of an individual human or over evolution, it really looks rather different from that.

MARTIN FORD: What do you think of the idea of a machine being conscious? Is that something that logically comes coupled with intelligence, or do you think that's something entirely separate?

JOSH TENENBAUM: That's a hard thing to discuss because the notion of consciousness means many different things to different people. There are philosophers, as well as cognitive scientists and neuroscientists who study it in a very serious and in-depth way, and there's no shared agreement on how to study it.

MARTIN FORD: Let me rephrase it, do you think that a machine could have some sort of inner experience? Is that possible or likely or even required for general intelligence?

JOSH TENENBAUM: The best way to answer that is to tease out two aspects of what we mean by consciousness. One is what people in philosophy have referred to as the sense of qualia or the sense of subjective experience that is very hard to capture in any kind of formal system. Think of the redness of red; we all know that red is one color and green is another color, and we also know that they feel different. We take for granted that other people when they see red, they not only call it red, but they experience subjectively the same thing we do. We know it's possible to build a machine that has those kinds of subjective experiences because we are machines and we have them. Whether we would have to do that, or whether we would be able to do that in the machines that we're trying to build right now, it's very hard to say.

There's another aspect of what we could call consciousness, which is what we might refer to as the sense of self. We experience the world in a certain kind of unitary way, and we experience ourselves being in it. It's much easier to say that those are essential to human-like intelligence. What I mean by this is that when we experience the world, we don't experience it in terms of tens of millions of cells firing.

One way to describe the state of your brain at any moment is at the level of what each neuron is doing, but that's not how we subjectively experience the world. We experience the world as consisting of objects, and all of our senses come together into a unitary understanding of those things. That's the way we experience the world, and we don't know how to link that level of experience to neurons. I think if we're going to build systems that are human-level intelligence, then they're going to have to have that kind of unitary experience of the world. It needs to be at the level of objects and agents, and not at the level of firings of neurons.

A key part of that is the sense of self—that I'm here, and that I'm not just my body. This is actually something that we're actively working on in research right now. I'm working with the philosopher Laurie Paul and a former student and colleague of mine, Tomer Ullman, on a paper which is tentatively called *Reverse Engineering the Self*.

MARTIN FORD: Along the same lines as reverse engineering the mind?

JOSH TENENBAUM: Yes, it's trying to take our reverse engineering approach and understand this one simple aspect of "self." I call it simple, but it's one small aspect of the big set of things you could mean by consciousness; to understand what is the basic sense of self that humans have, and what would it mean to build a machine this way. It's a really interesting question. AI people, especially those who are interested in AGI, will tell you that they are trying to build machines that think for themselves or learn for themselves, but you should ask, "What does that mean to build a machine that actually thinks for itself or learns for itself?" Can you do that unless it has a sense of self?

If we look at today's systems in AI, whether it's self-driving cars or systems like AlphaGo that in some sense are advertised as "learning for themselves." They don't actually have a self, that's not part of them. They don't really understand what they're doing, in the sense that I understand when I get into a car, and I'm in the car, and I'm driving somewhere. If I played Go, I would understand that I'm playing a game, and if I decide to learn Go, I've made a decision for myself. I might learn

Go by asking someone to teach me; I might practice with myself or with others. I might even decide I want to become a professional Go player and go to the Go Academy. Maybe I decide I'm really serious and I want to try to become one of the best in the world. When a human becomes a world-class Go player, that's how they do it. They make a bunch of decisions for themselves very much guided by their sense of self at many different time scales.

At the moment we don't have any notion like that in AI. We don't have systems that do anything for themselves, even at the high level. We don't have systems that have real goals the way a human has goals, rather we have systems that a human built to achieve their goals. I think it's absolutely essential that if we wanted to have systems that have human-like, human-level AI, they would have to do a lot of things for themselves that right now engineers are the ones doing, but I think it's possible that they could do that.

We're trying to understand in engineering terms what it is to make these large decisions for an agent for itself to set up the problems that it's trying to solve or the learning problems that it is trying to solve, all of which are currently being done by engineers. I think it's likely that we would have to have machines like that if they were going to be intelligent at the human level. I think it's also a real question of whether we want to do that, because don't have to do that. We can decide what level of selfness or autonomy we really want to give to our machine systems. They might well be able to do useful things for us without having the full sense of self that humans have. That might be an important decision for us to make. We might think that's the right way to go for technology and society.

MARTIN FORD: I want to ask you about some of the potential risks associated with AI. What should we really be concerned about, both in the relatively near term and in the longer term, with regard to the impact that artificial intelligence could have on society and the economy?

JOSH TENENBAUM: Some of the risks that people have advertised a lot are that we'll see some kind of singularity, or superintelligent machines that take over the world or have their own goals that are incompatible with human existence. It's possible that could happen in the far future, but I'm not especially worried about that, in part because of the things I was just talking about. We still don't know how to give machines any sense of self at all. The idea that they would decide for themselves to take over the world at our expense is something that is so far down the line, and there's a lot of steps between now and then.

Honestly, I'm a lot more worried about the shorter-term steps. I think between where we are right now, and any kind of human-level AGI, let alone super-human level, we are going to develop increasingly powerful algorithms, which can have all sorts of risks. These are algorithms that will be used by people for goals, some of which are good, and some of which are not good. Many of those not good goals are just people pursuing their own selfish ends, but some of them might actually be evil or bad actors. Like any technology, they can be used for good, but they can also be used for selfish purposes, and for evil or bad deeds. We should worry about those things because these are very powerful technologies, which are already being used in all of these ways, for example, in machine learning.

The near-term risks that we need to think about are the ones that everybody's talking about. I wish I had good ideas on how to think about those, but I don't. I think that the broader AI community increasingly realizes that they need to think about the near-term risks now, whether it's about privacy or human rights. Even topics like how AI or automation more generally is reshaping the economy and the job landscape. It's much bigger than AI, it's technology more broadly.

If we want to point to new challenges, I think one has to do with jobs, which is important. For pretty much all of human history, my understanding is that most people found some kind of livelihood, whether it was hunting and gathering, farming, working in a manufacturing plant, or whatever kind of business. You would spend the first part of your life learning some things, including a trade or skills that would then set up some kind of livelihood for you, which you could pursue until you died. You could develop a new skill set or change your line of work, but you didn't have to.

Now, what we're increasingly seeing is that technology is changing and has advanced to the point that many jobs and livelihoods change or come into existence or go out of existence on a faster time scale than an individual human adult work life. There was always technological change that made whole lines of work disappear, and others come to be, but it used to happen across generations. Now they're happening within generations, which puts a different kind of stress on the workforce.

More and more people will have to confront the fact that you can't just learn a certain set of skills and then use those to work for the rest of your life. You might have to be continually retraining yourself because technology is changing. It's not just more advanced, but it's advancing faster than it ever has. AI is part of that story, but it's much bigger than just AI. I think those are things that we as a society have to think about.

MARTIN FORD: Given that things could progress so rapidly, do you worry that a lot of people inevitably are going to be left behind? Is a universal basic income something that we should be giving serious consideration to?

JOSH TENENBAUM: We should think about a basic income, yes, but I don't think anything is inevitable. Humans are a resilient and flexible species. Yes, it might be that our abilities to learn and retrain ourselves have limitations to them. If technology keeps advancing, especially at this pace, it might be that we might have to do things like that. But again, we've seen that happen in previous eras of human history. It's just unfolded more slowly.

I think it would be fair to say that most of us who work for a living in the socio-economic bracket that you and I live in, where we're writers, scientists, or technologists, would find that if we went back thousands of years in human history, they would say "That's not work, that's just playing! If you're not laboring in the fields from dawn till dusk, you're not actually working." So, we don't know what the future of work is going to be like.

Just because it might change fundamentally, it doesn't mean that the idea that you would spend eight hours a day doing something economically valuable goes away. Whether we're going to have to have some kind of universal basic income, or just see the economy working in a different way, I don't know about that, and I'm certainly no expert on that, but I think that AI researchers should be part of that conversation.

Another conversation that's a much larger and much more urgent one is climate change. We don't know what the future of human-caused climate change is like, but we do know that AI researchers are increasingly contributing to it. Whether it's AI or Bitcoin mining, just look at what computers are being increasingly used for, and the massive and accelerating energy consumption.

I think we as AI researchers should think about the ways in which what we're doing is actually contributing to climate change, and ways we might contribute positively to solving some of those problems. I think that's an example of an urgent problem for society that AI researchers maybe don't think about too much, but they are increasingly part of the problem and maybe part of the solution.

There are also similar issues, like human rights and ways that AI technologies could be used to spy on people, but researchers could also use those technologies to help people figure out when they're being spied on. We can't, as researchers, prevent the things that we in our field invent from being used for bad purposes, but we can work harder to develop the good purposes, and also to develop and to use those technologies to push back against bad actors or uses. These are really moral issues that AI researchers need to be engaging in.

MARTIN FORD: Do you think there's a role for a regulation to help ensure that AI remains a positive force for society?

JOSH TENENBAUM: I think Silicon Valley can be very libertarian with their ethos that says we should break things and let other people pick up the pieces. Honestly, I wish that both governments and the tech industry were less far apart and hostile to each other, and saw more of a common purpose.

I am an optimist, and I do think that these different parties can and should be working more together, and that AI researchers can be one of the standard bearers for that kind of cooperation. I think we need it as a community, and not to mention as a society.

MARTIN FORD: Let me ask you to comment more specifically on the prospect for superintelligence and the alignment or control problem that Nick Bostrom has written about. I think his concern is that, while it might be a long time before superintelligence is achieved, it might take us even longer to work out how to maintain control of a superintelligent system, and that's what underlies his argument that we should be focusing on this issue now. How would you respond to that?

JOSH TENENBAUM: I think it's reasonable for people to be thinking about that. We think about that same thing. I wouldn't say that should be the overriding goal of our thinking, because while you could imagine some kind of superintelligence that would pose an existential risk to humanity, I just think we have other existential risks that are much more urgent. There are already ways that machine learning technologies and other kinds of AI technologies are contributing to big problems that are confronting us right now as a human species, and some of these grow to the level of existential risk.

I want to put that in context and say that people should be thinking about problems on all timescales. The issue of value alignment is difficult to address, and one of the challenges in addressing it right now is that we don't know what values are. Personally, I think that when AI safety researchers talk about value alignment, they have a very simplistic and maybe naive idea of what a value even is. In some of the work that we do in our computational cognitive science, we're actually trying to understand and to reverse engineer what are values to humans. What are moral principles, for example? These are not things that we understand in engineering terms.

We should think about these issues, but my approach is that we have to understand ourselves better before we can work on the technology side. We have to understand what actually our values are. How do we as humans come to learn them, and come to know them? What are the moral principles? How do those work in engineering terms? I think if we can understand that, that's an important part of understanding ourselves, and it's an important part of the cognitive science agenda.

It will be both useful and probably essential as machines not only become more intelligent but come to have more of an actual sense of self, where they become autonomous actors. It will be important for addressing these issues that you're talking about. I just think we're far from understanding how to address them, and how they work in natural intelligence.

We are also recognizing that there are nearer-term, really big risks and problems that are not of the AI value alignment sort, but are things like, what are we doing to our climate? How are governments or companies using AI technologies today to manipulate people?

Those are things we should worry about now. Parts of us should be thinking about how do we become good moral actors, and how do we do things that really make the world better and not worse. We should be engaging in things like that or climate change, which are current, or near-term risks that AI can make better or worse. As opposed to super intelligence value alignment, which we should also be thinking about, but I think more from a basic science perspective—what does it even mean to have a value?

AI researchers should work on all of these things. It's just that the value alignment questions are very basic research ones that are far from being put into practice or being needed to put into practice. We need to make sure that we don't lose sight of the real current moral issues that AI needs to be engaged with.

MARTIN FORD: Do you think that we'll succeed in making sure that the benefits of artificial intelligence outweigh the downsides?

JOSH TENENBAUM: I'm an optimist by nature, so my first response is to say yes, but we can't take it for granted. It's not just AI, but technology, whether it's smartphones or social media, is transforming our lives and changing how we interact with each other. It really is changing the nature of human experience. I'm not sure it's always for the better. It's hard to be optimistic when you see a family where everybody's just on their phones, or when you see some of the negative things that social media has led to.

I think it's important for us to realize, and to study, all the ways these technologies are doing crazy things to us! They are hacking our brains, our value systems, our reward systems, and our social interaction systems in a way that is pretty clearly not just positive. I think we need more active immediate research to try to understand this and to try to think about this. This is a place where I feel that we can't be guaranteed that the technology is leading us to a good outcome, and AI right now, with machine learning algorithms, are not necessarily on the side of good.

I'd like the community to think about that in a very active way. In the long term, yes, I'm optimistic that we will build the kinds of AI that are, on balance, forces for good, but I think this is really a key moment for all of us who work in this field to really be serious about this.

MARTIN FORD: Do you have any final thoughts, or is there anything I didn't ask about that you feel is important?

JOSH TENENBAUM: The questions that animate the work we're doing and that animate many of us in this field are questions that people have thought about for as long as people have thought about anything. What is the nature of intelligence? What are thoughts? What does it mean to be human? It's the most exciting thing that we have the opportunity to work on these questions now in ways that we can make both real engineering and real scientific progress on, and not simply consider as abstract philosophical questions.

When we think about building AI of any big sort, but especially AGI, if we see that as not just a technology and an engineering problem, but as one side of one of the biggest scientific questions that humanity has thought about ever. It's along the same line of thinking as, what is the nature of intelligence, or what are its origins in the universe? The idea to pursue that as part of that larger program is one that I think is tremendously exciting and that we should all be excited and inspired by. That means thinking about ways of making technology that makes us smarter, and doesn't make us stupider.

We have the opportunity to both understand more about what it means to be intelligent in a human way, and learn how to build technology that can make us smarter individually and collectively. It's super exciting to be able to do that, but it's also imperative that we take that seriously when we work on technology.

JOSHUA TENENBAUM

JOSH TENENBAUM *is Professor of Computational Cognitive Science in the Department of Brain and Cognitive Sciences at the Massachusetts Institute of Technology. He is also a member of the MIT Computer Science and Artificial Intelligence Laboratory (CSAIL), and the Center for Brains, Minds, and Machines (CBMM). Josh studies perception, learning and common-sense reasoning in humans and machines, with the twin goals of understanding human intelligence in computational terms and bringing artificial intelligence closer to human-level capabilities. Josh received his undergraduate degree in physics from Yale University in 1993, and his PhD from MIT in 1999. After a brief postdoc with the MIT AI Lab, he joined the Stanford University faculty as Assistant Professor of Psychology and (by courtesy) Computer Science. He returned to MIT as a faculty member in 2002.*

He and his students have published extensively in cognitive science, machine learning and other AI-related fields, and their papers have received awards at venues across the AI landscape, including leading conferences in computer vision, reinforcement learning and decision-making, robotics, uncertainty in AI, learning and development, cognitive modeling and neural information processing. They have introduced several widely used AI tools and frameworks, including models for nonlinear dimensionality reduction, probabilistic programming, and Bayesian approaches to unsupervised structure discovery and program induction. Individually, he is the recipient of the Howard Crosby Warren Medal from the Society of Experimental Psychologists, the Distinguished Scientific Award for Early Career Contribution to Psychology from the American Psychological Association, and the Troland Research Award from the National Academy of Sciences, and is a fellow of the Society of Experimental Psychologists and the Cognitive Science Society.

> **If you look at a question like, "Would an elephant fit through a doorway?", while most people can answer that question almost instantaneously, machines will struggle. What's easy for one is hard for the other, and vice versa. That is what I call the AI paradox.**

OREN ETZIONI

CEO, THE ALLEN INSTITUTE FOR ARTIFICIAL INTELLIGENCE

Oren Etzioni is the CEO of the Allen Institute for Artificial Intelligence, an independent organization established by Microsoft co-founder Paul Allen and dedicated to conducting high-impact research in artificial intelligence for the common good. Oren oversees a number of research initiatives, perhaps most notably Project Mosaic, a $125 million effort to build common sense into an artificial intelligence system—something that is generally considered to be one of the most difficult challenges in AI.

MARTIN FORD: Project Mosaic sounds very interesting. Could you tell me about that and the other projects that you're working on at the Allen Institute?

OREN ETZIONI: Project Mosaic is focused on endowing computers with common sense. A lot of the AI systems that humans have built, to date, are very good at narrow tasks. For example, humans have built AI systems that can play Go very well, but the room may be on fire, and the AI won't notice. These AI systems completely lack common sense, and that's something that we're trying to address with Mosaic.

Our over-arching mission at the Allen Institute for Artificial Intelligence is AI for the common good. We're investigating how you can use artificial intelligence to make the world a better place. Some of that is through basic research, while the rest has more of an engineering flavor.

A great example of this is a project called Semantic Scholar. In the Semantic Scholar project, we're looking at the problem of scientific search and scientific hypothesis generation. Because scientists are inundated with more and more publications, we realize that scientists, just like all of us when we're experiencing information overload, really need help in cutting through that clutter; and that's what Semantic Scholar does. It uses machine learning and natural language processing, along with various AI techniques, to help scientists figure out what they want to read and how to locate results within papers.

MARTIN FORD: Does Mosaic involve symbolic logic? I know there was an older project called *Cyc* that was a very labor-intensive process, where people would try to write down all the logical rules, such as how objects related, and I think it became kind of unwieldy. Is that the kind of thing you're doing with Mosaic?

OREN ETZIONI: The problem with the *Cyc* project is that, over 35 years in, it's really been a struggle for them, for exactly the reasons you said. But in our case, we're hoping to leverage more modern AI techniques—crowdsourcing, natural language processing, machine learning, and machine vision—in order to acquire knowledge in a different way.

With Mosaic, we're also starting with a very different point of view. *Cyc* started, if you will, inside out, where they said, "OK. We're going to build this repository of common-sense knowledge and do logical reasoning on top of it." Now, what we said in response is, "We're going to start by defining a benchmark, where we assess the common-sense abilities of any program." That benchmark then allows us to measure how much common sense a program has, and once we've defined that benchmark (which is not a trivial undertaking) we'll then build it and be able to measure our progress empirically and experimentally, which is something that *Cyc* was not able to do.

MARTIN FORD: So, you're planning to create some kind of objective test that can be used for common sense?

OREN ETZIONI: Exactly! Just the way the Turing test was meant to be a test for artificial intelligence or IQ, we're going to have a test for common sense for AI.

MARTIN FORD: You've also worked on systems that attempt to pass college examinations in biology or other subjects. Is that one of the things you're continuing to focus on?

OREN ETZIONI: One of Paul Allen's visionary and motivating examples, which he's investigated in various ways even prior to the Allen Institute for AI, was the idea of a program that could read a chapter in a textbook and then answer the questions in the back of that book. So, we formulated a related problem by saying, "Let's take standardized tests, and see to what extent we can build programs that score well on these standardized tests." And that's been part of our Aristo project in the context of science, and part of our Euclid project in the context of math problems.

For us it is very natural to start working on a problem by defining a benchmark task, and then continually improving performance on it. So, we've done that in these different areas.

MARTIN FORD: How is that progressing? Have you had successes there?

OREN ETZIONI: I would say the results have been mixed, to be frank. I would say that we're state of the art in both science and math tests. In the case of science, we ran a Kaggle competition, where we released the questions, and several thousand teams from all over the world joined. With this, we wanted to see whether we were missing anything, and we found that in fact our technology did quite a bit better than anything else out there, at least who participated in the test.

In the sense of being state of the art and having that be a focus for research, and publishing a series of papers and datasets, I think it's been very positive. What's negative is that our ability on these tests is still quite limited. We find that, when you have the full test, we're getting something like a D, not a very stellar grade. This is because these problems are quite hard, and often they also involve vision and natural language. But we also realized that a key problem that was blocking us was actually the lack of common sense. So, that's one of the things that led us to Project Mosaic.

What's really interesting here is that there's something I like to call the AI paradox, where things that are really hard for people—like playing World Championship-level Go—are quite easy for machines. On the other hand, there are things that are easy for a person to do, for example if you look at a question like, "Would an elephant fit through a doorway?", while most people can answer that question almost instantaneously, machines will struggle. What's easy for one is hard for the other, and vice versa. That is what I call the AI paradox.

Now, the standardized test writers, they want to take a particular concept like photosynthesis, or gravity, and have the student apply that concept in a particular context, so that they demonstrate their understanding. It turned out that representing something like photosynthesis, at a 6th grade level, and representing that to the machine is really quite easy, so we have an easy time doing that. But where the machine struggles is when it's time to applying the concept in a particular situation that requires language understanding and common-sense reasoning.

MARTIN FORD: So, you think your work on Mosaic could accelerate progress in other areas, by providing a foundation of common-sense understanding?

OREN ETZIONI: Yes. I mean, a typical question is. "If you have a plant in a dark room and you move it nearer the window, will the plant's leaves grow faster, slower or at the same rate?" A person can look at that question and understand that if you move a plant nearer to the window then there's more light, and that more light means the photosynthesis proceeds faster, and so the leaves are likely to grow faster. But it turns out that the computer really struggles with this—because the AI doesn't necessarily understand what you mean when you say, "What happens when you move a plant nearer the window."

These are some examples that indicate what led us to Project Mosaic, and what some of our struggles have been with things like Aristo and Euclid over the years.

MARTIN FORD: What led you to work in AI, and how did you end up working at the Allen Institute?

OREN ETZIONI: My foray into AI really started in high school when I read the book, *Gödel, Escher, Bach: An Eternal Golden Braid*. This book explored the themes of logician Kurt Gödel, the artist M. C. Escher, and the composer Johann Sebastian Bach, and expounded many of the concepts that are relatable to AI, such as mathematics and intelligence. This is where my fascination with AI began.

I then went to Harvard, for college, where they were just starting AI classes when I was a sophomore. So, I took my first AI class, and I was completely fascinated. They were not doing much in the way of AI at the time but, just a short subway ride away, I found myself at the MIT AI Lab and I remember that Marvin Minsky, the co-founder of MIT's AI lab, was teaching. And actually Douglas Hofstadter, the author of *Gödel, Escher, Bach*, was a visiting professor, so I attended Douglas's seminar and became even more enchanted with the field of AI.

I got a part-time job as a programmer at the MIT AI Lab and for somebody who was just starting their career, I was, as they say, over the moon. As a result, I decided to go to graduate school to study AI. Graduate school for me was at Carnegie Mellon University where I worked with Tom Mitchell, who is one of the founding fathers of the field of machine learning.

The next step in my career was when I became a faculty member at the University of Washington, where I studied many topics in AI. At the same time got involved in a number of AI-based start-ups, which I found to be very exciting. All of this resulted in me joining the Allen Institute of AI, and more specifically in 2013 Paul Allen's team reached out to me saying that they wanted me to launch an Institute for AI. So, in January 2014 we launched the Allen Institute for AI. Now fast forward to 2018 and here we are today.

MARTIN FORD: As the leader of one of Paul Allen's institutes, I assume you have a lot of contact with him. What would you say about his motivation and vision for the Allen Institute of AI?

OREN ETZIONI: I'm really lucky in that I've had a lot of contact with Paul over the years. When I was first contemplating this position, I read Paul's book *Idea Man*, which gave me a sense of both his intellect and his vision. While reading Paul's book, I realized that he's really operating in the tradition of the Medicis. He's a scientific philanthropist and has signed the Giving Pledge that was started by both Bill and Melinda Gates and Warren Buffett, where he's publicly dedicated most of his wealth to philanthropy. What drives him here is that he's been fascinated by AI and the questions around how we can imbue semantics and an understanding of text in machines since the 1970s.

Over the years, Paul and I have had many conversations and email exchanges, and Paul continues to help shape the vision of the institute, not just in terms of the financial support but in terms of the project choices, and the direction of the institute. Paul is still very much hands-on.

MARTIN FORD: Paul has also founded the Allen Institute of Brain Science. Given that the fields are related, is there some synergy between the two organizations? Do you collaborate or share information with the brain science researchers?

OREN ETZIONI: Yes, that's correct. So, way back in 2003, Paul started the Allen Institute of Brain Science. In our corner of the Allen Institutes, we call ourselves "AI2," partly because it's a bit kind of tongue-in-cheek as we're the Allen Institute of AI but also because we're the second Allen Institute.

But going back to Paul's scientific philanthropy, his strategy is to create a series of these Allen Institutes. There's a very close exchange of information between us all. But the methodologies that we use are really quite different, in that the Institute of Brain Science is really looking at the physical structure of the brain, while here at AI2 we're adopting a rather more classical-AI methodology for building software.

MARTIN FORD: So, at AI2 you're not necessarily trying to build AI by reverse-engineering the brain, you're actually taking more of a design approach, where you're building an architecture that's inspired by human intelligence?

OREN ETZIONI: That is exactly right. When we wanted to figure out flight, we ended up with airplanes, and now we've developed Boeing 747s, which are very different than birds in several ways. There are some of us within the AI field who think that it is quite likely that our artificial intelligence will be implemented very differently than human intelligence.

MARTIN FORD: There's enormous attention currently being given to deep learning and to neural networks. How do you feel about that? Do you think it's overhyped? Is deep learning likely to be the primary path forward in AI, or just one part of the story?

OREN ETZIONI: I guess my answer would be all of the above. There have been some very impressive achievements with deep learning, and we see that in machine translation, speech recognition, object detection, and facial recognition. When you have a lot of labeled data, and you have a lot of computer power, these models are great.

But at the same time, I do think that deep learning is overhyped because some people say that it's really putting us on a clear path towards artificial intelligence, possibly general artificial intelligence, and maybe even superintelligence. And there's this sense that that's all just around the corner. It reminds me of the metaphor of a kid who climbs up to the top of the tree and points at the moon, saying, "I'm on my way to the moon."

I think that in fact, we really have a long way to go and there are many unsolved problems. In that sense, deep learning is very much overhyped. I think the reality is that deep learning, and neural networks are particularly nice tools in our toolbox, but it's a tool that still leaves us with a number of problems like reasoning, background knowledge, common sense, and many others largely unsolved.

MARTIN FORD: I do get the sense from talking to some other people, that they have great faith in machine learning as the way forward. The idea seems to be that if we just have enough data, and we get better at learning—especially in areas like unsupervised learning—then common-sense reasoning will emerge organically. It sounds like you would not agree with that.

OREN ETZIONI: The notion of "emergent intelligence" was actually a term that Douglas Hofstadter, the cognitive scientist, talked about back in the day. Nowadays people talk about it in various contexts, with consciousness, and with common sense, but that's really not what we've seen. We do find that people, including myself, have all kinds of speculations about the future, but as a scientist, I like to base my conclusions on the specific data that we've seen. And what we've seen is people using deep learning as high-capacity statistical models. High capacity is just some jargon that means that the model keeps getting better and better the more data you throw at it.

Statistical models that at their core are based on matrices of numbers being multiplied, and added, and subtracted, and so on. They are a long way from something where you can see common sense or consciousness emerging. My feeling is that there's no data to support these claims and if such data appears, I'll be very excited, but I haven't seen it yet.

MARTIN FORD: What projects would you point to, in addition to what you're working on, that are really at the forefront? What are the most exciting things happening in AI? The places you'd look for the next big developments. Would that be AlphaGo, or are there other things going on?

OREN ETZIONI: Well, I think DeepMind is where some of the most exciting work is currently taking place.

I'm actually more excited about what they called AlphaZero, than AlphaGo, and so the fact that they were able to achieve excellent performance without hand-labeled examples, I think is quite exciting. At the same time, I think everybody in the community agrees that when you're dealing with board games, it's black and white, there's an evaluation function, it's a very limited realm. So, I would look to current work on robotics, and work on natural language processing to see some excitement. And I think that there's also some work in fields called "transfer learning," where people are trying to map from one task to the other.

I think Geoffrey Hinton is trying to develop a different approach to deep learning. I think at AI2, where we have 80 people who are looking at how do you put together the symbolic type of approaches and knowledge with the deep learning paradigm, I think that's also very exciting.

There's also "zero-shot learning," where people are trying to build programs that can learn when they see something even for the first time. And there is "one-shot learning" where a program sees a single example, and they're able to do things. I think that's exciting. Brenden Lake who's an assistant professor of Psychology and Data Science at NYU, is doing some work along those lines.

Tom Mitchell's work, with lifelong learning at CMU, is also very interesting—they're trying to build a system that looks more like a person: it doesn't just run through a dataset and build a model and then it's done. Instead, it continually operates and continually tries to learn, and then learn based on that, over a longer extended period of time.

MARTIN FORD: I know there's an emerging technique called "curriculum learning," where you start with easier things and then move to the harder things, in the same way a human student would.

OREN ETZIONI: Exactly. But if we just take a step back for a minute here, we can see that AI is a field that's rife with bombastic and overly grandiose misnomers. In the beginning, the field was called "artificial intelligence," and to me, that's not the best name. Then there's "human learning" and "machine learning," both of which sound very grandiose but actually, the set of techniques they use are often very limited. All these terms that we just talked about—and curricular learning is a great example—refer to approaches where we're simply trying to extend a relatively limited set of statistical techniques, and to start to take on more of the characteristics of human learning.

MARTIN FORD: Let's talk about the path toward artificial general intelligence. Do you believe it is achievable, and if so, do you think it's inevitable that we will ultimately get to AGI?

OREN ETZIONI: Yes. I'm a materialist, so I don't believe there's anything in our brain other than atoms and consequently, I think that thought is a form of computation and so I think that it's quite likely that over some period of time we'll figure out how to do it in a machine.

I do recognize that maybe we're just not smart enough to do that, even with the help of a computer, but my intuition is that we will likely achieve AGI. As for the time line though, we're very far from AGI because there are so many problems that need to be solved that we haven't even been able to define appropriately for the machine.

This is one of the subtlest things in the whole field. People see these amazing achievements, like a program that beats people in Go and they say, "Wow! Intelligence must be around the corner." But when you get to these more nuanced things like natural language, or reasoning over knowledge, it turns out that we don't even know, in some sense, the right questions to ask.

Pablo Picasso is famous for saying computers are useless. They answer questions rather than asking them. So, when we define a question rigorously, when we can define it mathematically or as a computational problem, we're really good at hammering away at that and figuring out the answer. But there are a lot of questions that we don't yet know how to formulate appropriately, such as how can we represent natural language inside a computer? Or, what is common sense?

MARTIN FORD: What are the primary hurdles we need to overcome to achieve AGI?

OREN ETZIONI: When I talk to people working in AI about these questions, such as when we might achieve AGI, one of the things that I really like is to identify is what I call canaries in the coal mine. In the same way that the coal miners put canaries in the mines to warn them of dangerous gases, I feel like there are certain stepping stones—and that if we achieved those, then AI would be in a very different world.

So, one of those stepping stones would be an AI program that can really handle multiple, very different tasks. An AI program that's able to both do language and vision, it's able to play board games and cross the street, it's able to walk and chew gum. Yes, that is a joke, but I think it is important for AI to have the ability to do much more complex things.

Another stepping stone is that it's very important that these systems be a lot more data-efficient. So, how many examples do you need to learn from? If you have an AI program that can really learn from a single example, that feels meaningful. For example, I can show you a new object, and you look at it, you're going to hold it in your hand, and you're thinking, "I've got it." Now, I can show you lots of different pictures of that object, or different versions of that object in different lighting conditions, partially obscured by something, and you'd still be able to say, "Yep, that's the same object." But machines can't do that off of a single example yet. That would be a real stepping stone to AGI for me.

Self-replication is another dramatic stepping stone towards AGI. Can we have an AI system that is physically embodied and that can make a copy of itself? That would be a huge canary in the coal mine because then that AI system could make lots of copies of itself. People have quite a laborious and involved process for making copies of themselves, and AI systems cannot. You can copy the software easily but not the hardware. Those are some of the major stepping stones to AGI that come to mind.

MARTIN FORD: And maybe the ability to use knowledge in a different domain would be a core capability. You gave the example of studying a chapter in a textbook. To be able to acquire that knowledge, and then not just answer questions about it, but actually be able to employ it in a real-world situation. That would seem to be at the heart of true intelligence.

OREN ETZIONI: I completely agree with you, and that question is only a step along the way. It's employment of AI in the real world, and also in unanticipated situations.

MARTIN FORD: I want to talk about the risks that are associated with AI, but before we do that, do you want to say more about what you view as some of the greatest benefits, some of the most promising areas where AI could be deployed?

OREN ETZIONI: There are two examples that stand out to me, the first being self-driving cars, where we have upwards of 35,000 deaths each year on US highways alone, we have in the order of a million accidents where people are injured, and studies have shown that we could cut a substantial fraction of that by using self-driving cars. I get very excited when I see how AI can directly translate to technologies that save lives.

The second example, which we're working on, is science—which has been such an engine of prosperity in economic growth, the improvement of medicine, and generally speaking for humanity. Yet despite these advancements, there are still so many challenges, whether it's Ebola, or cancer, or superbugs that are resistant to antibiotics. Scientists need help to solve these problems and just to move faster. With a project like Semantic Scholar, it has the potential to save people's lives by providing better medical outcomes and better medical research.

My colleague, Eric Horvitz, is one of the most thoughtful people on these topics. He has a great quote when he responds to people who are worried about AI taking lives. He says that actually, it's the absence of AI technology that is already killing people. The third-leading cause of death in American hospitals is physician error, and a lot of that could be prevented using AI. So, our failure to use AI is really what's costing lives.

MARTIN FORD: Since you mentioned self-driving cars, let me try to pin you down on a timeframe. Imagine you're in Manhattan, in some random location, and you call for a car. A self-driving car arrives with no one inside, and it's going to take you to some other random location. When do you think we will see that as a widely available consumer service?

OREN ETZIONI: I would say that is probably somewhere between 10 and 20 years away from today.

MARTIN FORD: Let's talk about the risks. I want to start with the one that I've written a lot about, which is the potential economic disruption, and the impact on the job market. I think it's quite possible that we're on the leading edge of a new industrial revolution, which might really have a transformative impact, and maybe will destroy or deskill a lot of jobs. What do you think about that?

OREN ETZIONI: I very much agree with you, in the sense that I have tried, as you have, not to get overly focused on the threats of superintelligence because we should have fewer imaginary problems and more real ones. But we have some very real problems and one of the most prominent of them, if not the most prominent, is jobs. There's a long-term trend towards the reduction of manufacturing jobs, and due to automation, computer automation, and AI-based automation, we now have the potential to substantially accelerate that timeline. So, I do think that there's a very real issue here.

One point that I would make, is that it's also the case that the demographics are working in our favor. The number of children we have as a species is getting smaller on average, and the number of us living longer is increasing, and society is aging—especially after the baby boom. So, for the next 20 years, I think we're going to be seeing increasing automation, but we're also going to be seeing the number of workers not growing as quickly as it did before. Another way that demographic factors work in our favor is that, while for the last two decades, more women were entering the workforce, and the percentage of female participation in the workforce was going up, this affect has now plateaued. In other words, women who want to be in the workforce are now already there. So again, I think that for the next 20 years we're not going to see the numbers of workers increasing. The risk of automation taking jobs away from people is still serious though I think.

MARTIN FORD: In the long run, what do you think of the idea of a universal basic income, as a way to adapt society to the economic consequences of automation?

OREN ETZIONI: I think that what we've already seen with agriculture, and with manufacturing, is clearly going to recur. Let's say we don't argue about the exact timing. It's very clear that, in the next 10 to 50 years, many jobs are either going to go away completely or those jobs are going to be radically transformed—they'll be done a lot more efficiently, with fewer people.

As you know, the number of people working in agriculture is much smaller than it was in the past, and the jobs involved in agriculture are now much more sophisticated. So, when that happens, we have this question: "What are the people going to do?" I don't necessarily know, but I do have one contribution to this conversation, which I wrote up as an article for *Wired* in February 2017 titled *Workers displaced by automation should try a new job: Caregiver.*[1]

In that *Wired* paper, I said some of the most vulnerable workers, in this economic situation that we're discussing here, are people who don't have a high-school degree or those who don't have a college degree. I don't think it's likely that we're going to be successful in the principle of coal miners to data miners, that we're going to give these people technical retraining, and that they'll somehow become part of the new economy very easily. I think that's a major challenge.

I also don't think that universal basic income, at least given the current climate, where we can't even achieve universal health care, or universal housing, is going to be easy either.

MARTIN FORD: It seems pretty clear that any viable solution to this problem will be a huge political challenge.

OREN ETZIONI: I don't know that there is a general solution or a silver bullet, but my contribution to the conversation is to think about jobs that are very strongly human focused. Think of the jobs providing emotional support: having coffee with somebody or being a companion who keeps somebody company. I think that those are the jobs that when we think about our elderly, when we think about our special-

---

1 https://www.wired.com/story/workers-displaced-by-automation-should-try-a-new-job-caregiver/

needs kids, when we think about various populations like that, those are the ones that we really want a person to engage with—rather than a robot.

If we want society to allocate resources toward those kinds of jobs, to give the people engaged in those jobs better compensation and greater dignity, then I think that there's room for people to take on those jobs. That said, there are many issues with my proposal, I don't think it's a panacea, but I do think it's a direction that's worth investing in.

MARTIN FORD: Beyond the job market impact, what other things do you think we genuinely should be concerned about in terms of artificial intelligence in the next decade or two?

OREN ETZIONI: Cybersecurity is already a huge concern, and it becomes much more so if we have AI. The other big concern for me is autonomous weapons, which is a scary proposition, particularly the ones that can make life-or-death decisions on their own. But what we just talked about, the risks to jobs—that is still the thing that we should be most concerned about, even more so than security and weapons.

MARTIN FORD: How about existential risk from AGI, and the alignment or control problem with regard to a superintelligence. Is that something that we should be worried about?

OREN ETZIONI: I think that it's great for a small number of philosophers and mathematicians to contemplate the existential threat, so I'm not dismissing it out of hand. At the same time, I don't think those are the primary things that we should be concerned about, nor do I think that there's that much that we can do at this point about that threat.

I think that one of the interesting things to consider is if a superintelligence emerges, it would be really nice to be able to communicate with it, to talk to it. The work that we're doing at AI2—and that other people are also doing— on natural language understanding, seems like a very valuable contribution to AI safety, at least as valuable as worrying about the alignment problem, which ultimately is just a technical problem having to do with reinforcement learning and objective functions.

So, I wouldn't say that we're underinvesting in being prepared for AI safety, and certainly some of the work that we're doing at AI2 is actually implicitly a key investment in AI safety.

MARTIN FORD: Any concluding thoughts?

OREN ETZIONI: Well, there's one other point I wanted to make that I think people often miss in the AI discussion, and that's the distinction between intelligence and autonomy.[2]

We naturally think that intelligence and autonomy go hand in hand. But you can have a highly intelligent system with essentially no autonomy, and the example of that is a calculator. A calculator is a trivial example, but something like AlphaGo that plays brilliant Go but won't play another game until somebody pushes a button: that's high intelligence and low autonomy.

You can also have high autonomy and low intelligence. My favorite kind of tongue-in-cheek example is a bunch of teenagers drinking on a Saturday night: that's high autonomy but low intelligence. But a real-world example, that we've all experienced would be a computer virus that can have low intelligence but quite a strong ability to bounce around computer networks. My point is that we should understand that the systems that we're building have these two dimensions to them, intelligence and autonomy, and that it's often the autonomy that is the scary part.

MARTIN FORD: Drones or robots that could decide to kill without a human in the loop to authorize that action is something that is really generating a lot of concern in the AI community.

OREN ETZIONI: Exactly, when they're autonomous and they can make life-and-death decisions on their own. Intelligence, on the other hand, could actually help save lives, by getting them more targeted, or by having them abort when the human cost is unacceptable, or when the wrong person or building is targeted.

I want to emphasize the fact that a lot of our worries about AI are really worries about autonomy, and I want to emphasize that autonomy is something that we can choose as a society to meter out.

---

2 https://www.wired.com/2014/12/ai-wont-exterminate-us-it-will-empower-us/

I like to think of "AI" as standing for "augmented intelligence," just as it is with systems like Semantic Scholar and like with self-driving cars. One of the reasons that I am an AI optimist, and feel so passionate about it, and the reason that I've dedicated my entire career to AI since high school, is that I see this tremendous potential to do good with AI.

MARTIN FORD: Is there a place for regulation, to address that issue of autonomy? Is that something that you would advocate?

OREN ETZIONI: Yes, I think that regulation is both inevitable and appropriate when it comes to powerful technologies. I would focus on regulating the applications of AI—so AI cars, AI clothes, AI toys, and AI in nuclear power plants, rather than the field itself. Note that the boundary between AI and software is quite murky!

We're in a global competition for AI, so I wouldn't rush to regulate AI per se. Of course, existing regulatory bodies like the National Safety Transportation Board are already looking at AI cars, and the recent Uber accident. I think that regulation is very appropriate and that it will happen and should happen.

OREN ETZIONI

OREN ETZIONI *is the CEO of the Allen Institute for Artificial Intelligence (abbreviated as AI2), an independent, non-profit research organization established by Microsoft co-founder Paul Allen in 2014. AI2, located in Seattle, employs over 80 researchers and engineers with the mission of "conducting high-impact research and engineering in the field of artificial intelligence, all for the common good."*

Oren received a bachelor's degree in computer science from Harvard in 1986. He then went on to obtain a PhD from Carnegie Mellon University in 1991. Prior to joining AI2, Oren was a professor at the University of Washington, where he co-authored over 100 technical papers. Oren is a fellow of the Association for the Advancement of Artificial Intelligence, and is also a successful serial entrepreneur, having founded or co-founded a number of technology startups that were acquired by larger firms such as eBay and Microsoft, Oren helped to pioneer meta-search (1994), online comparison shopping (1996), machine reading (2006), open information extraction (2007), and semantic search of the academic literature (2015).

> ❝ *AI is the best thing since sliced bread. We should embrace it wholeheartedly and understand the secrets of unlocking the human brain by embracing AI. We can't do it by ourselves.*

BRYAN JOHNSON

ENTREPRENEUR
FOUNDER, KERNEL & OS FUND

Bryan Johnson is the founder of Kernel, OS Fund, and Braintree. After the sale of Braintree to PayPal in 2013 for $800m, Johnson founded OS Fund in 2014 with $100m of those funds. His objective was to invest in entrepreneurs and companies that develop breakthrough discoveries in hard science to address our most pressing global problems. In 2016, Johnson founded Kernel with another $100m of his funds. Kernel is building brain-machine interfaces with the intention of providing humans with the option to radically enhance their cognition.

MARTIN FORD: Could you explain what Kernel is? How did it get started, and what is the long-term vision?

BRYAN JOHNSON: Most people start companies with a product in mind, and they build that given product. I started Kernel with a problem identified—we need to build better tools to read and write our neural code, to address disease and malfunction, to illuminate the mechanisms of intelligence, and to extend our cognition. Look at the tools we have to interface with our brain right now—we can get an image of our brain via an MRI scan, we can do bad recordings via EEG outside the scalp that don't really give us much, and we can implant an electrode to address a disease. Outside of that, our brain is largely inaccessible to the world outside of our five senses. I started Kernel with $100 million with the objective of figuring out what tools we can build. We've been on this quest for two years, and we still remain in stealth mode on purpose. We have a team of 30 people and we feel very good about where we're at. We're working very hard to build the next breakthroughs. I wish I could give you more details about where we're at in the world. We will have that out in time, but right now we're not ready.

MARTIN FORD: The articles I've read suggest that you're beginning with medical applications to help with conditions like epilepsy. My understanding is that you initially want to try an invasive approach that involves brain surgery, and you then want to leverage what you learn to eventually move to something that will enhance cognition, while hopefully being less invasive. Is that the case, or are you imagining that we're all going to have chips inserted into our brain at some point?

BRYAN JOHNSON: Having chips in our brain is one avenue that we've contemplated, but we've also started looking at every possible entry point in neuroscience because the key in this game is figuring out how to create a profitable business. Figuring out how to create an implantable chip is one option, but there are many other options, and we're looking at all of them.

MARTIN FORD: How did you come to the idea of starting Kernel and OS Fund? What route did your early career take to bring you to that point?

BRYAN JOHNSON: The starting point for my career was when I was 21, where I had just returned from my Mormon mission to Ecuador. I lived among and witnessed extreme poverty and suffering. During my two years of living among extreme poverty, the only question that was weighing on my mind was, what could I do that would create the most value for the greatest number of people in the world? I wasn't motivated by fame or money, I just wanted to do good in the world. I looked at all the options I could find, and none of them satisfied me. Because of that, I determined to become an entrepreneur, build a business, and retire by the age of 30. In my 21-year-old mind that made sense. I got lucky, and fourteen years later I sold my company Braintree for $800 million in cash to eBay in 2013.

By that point, I had also left Mormonism, which had defined my entire reality of what life was about, and when I left that I had to recreate myself from scratch. I was 35, fourteen years since my initial life decisions, and that drive to benefit humanity hadn't left me. I asked myself the question, what's the one single thing that I can do that will maximize the probability that the human race will survive. In that moment of observation, it wasn't clear to me that humans have what we need to survive ourselves and survive the challenges we face. I saw two answers to that question, and they were Kernel and the OS Fund.

The idea behind OS Fund is that most people in the world who manage or have money do not have scientific expertise, and therefore, they typically invest in things that they are more comfortable with, such as finance or transportation. That means that there is insufficient capital going to science-based endeavors. My observation was that if I could demonstrate as a non-scientist that I could invest in some of the hardest science in the world and be successful in doing this, I would create a model that others could follow. So, I invested $100 million in my OS Fund to do that, and five years in, we are in the top decile of performance among US firms. We've made 28 investments, and we've been able to demonstrate that we can successfully invest in these science-based entrepreneurs that are doing world-changing technology.

The second thing was Kernel. In the beginning, I talked to over 200 really smart people, asking them what they were doing in the world and why. From there, I'd ask them follow-on on questions to understand the entire assumptions stack of how they think, and the one thing that I walked away from is that the brain is the originator of all things, everything we do as humans stems from our brains. Everything we build, everything we're trying to become, and every problem we're trying to solve. It lives upstream from anything else, yet it was absent in anybody's focus. There were efforts, for example from DARPA and the Allen Brain Institute, but most were focused on specific medical applications or basic research in neuroscience. There was nobody in the world that I could identify that basically said, the brain is the most important thing in existence because everything sits downstream from the brain. It's a really simple observation, but it was a blind spot everywhere.

Our brain sits right behind our eyes, yet we focus on everything downstream from it. There is not an endeavor that is on a scale that's relevant, something that lets us read and write neural code to read and write our cognition. So, with Kernel, I set out to do for the brain what we did for the genome, which is to sequence a genome and then create a tool to write the genome. In 2018, we can read and edit the DNA—the software—that makes us humans, and I wanted to do the same thing for the brain, which is read and write our code.

There's a bunch of reasons why I want to be able to read and write the human brain. My fundamental belief behind all of this is that we need to radically up-level ourselves as a species. AI is moving very quickly, and what the future of AI holds is anyone's guess. The expert opinions are across the board. We don't know if AI is growing on a linear curve, an S curve, an exponential curve, or a punctuated equilibrium, but we do know that the promise of AI is up and to the right.

The rate of our improvement as humans is flat. People hear this and say that we're hugely improved over people 500 years ago, but we're not. Yes, we understand greater complexity, for example, more complex concepts in physics and mathematics, but our species generally is exactly the same as we were thousands of years ago. We have the same proclivities and we make the same mistakes. Even if you were to make the case that we are improving as a species, if you compare it to AI, humans are flatlining. If you just simply look at the graph and say AI is up and to the right, humans might be a little bit to the right. So the question is, how big is that delta going to be between AI and ourselves when we begin to feel incredibly uncomfortable? It's going to just run by us, and then what are we as a species? It is an important question to ask.

Another reason is based on the concept that we have this impending job crisis with AI. The most creative thing people are coming up with is universal basic income, which is basically waving the white flag and saying we can't cope and we need some money from the government. Nowhere in the conversation is radical human improvement discussed. We need to figure out how to not just nudge ourselves forward, but to make a radical transformation. What we need to do is acknowledge the reason that we need to improve ourselves radically is that we cannot imagine the future. We are constrained in our imagination to what we are familiar with.

If you were to take humans and put them back with Gutenberg and the printing press, and say, paint me a miraculous vision of what's possible, they wouldn't be able to do it. They would never have guessed at what's evolved like the internet or computers. The same is true of radical human enhancement. We don't know what's on the other side. What we do know is that is if we are to be relevant as a species, we must advance ourselves significantly.

One more reason is the idea that somehow AI became the biggest threat that we should all care about, which in my mind is just silly. The biggest thing I'm worried about is humans. We have always been our own biggest threat. Look at all of history, we have done awful things to each other. Yes, we've done remarkable things with our technology, but we have also inflicted tremendous harm on each other. So, in terms of asking is AI a risk, and should we prioritize that? I would say AI is the best thing since sliced bread. We should embrace it wholeheartedly and understand the secrets of unlocking the human brain by embracing AI. We can't do it by ourselves.

MARTIN FORD: There are a number of other companies in the same general space as Kernel. Elon Musk has Neuralink and I think both Facebook and DARPA are also working on something. Do you feel that there are direct competitors out there, or is Kernel unique in its approach?

BRYAN JOHNSON: DARPA has done a wonderful job. They have been looking at the brain for quite some time now, and they've been a galvanizer of success. Another visionary in the field is Paul Allen and the Allen Institute for Brain Science. The gap that I identified was not understanding that the brain matters, but identifying the brain as the primary entry point to everything in existence we care about. Then through that frame, creating the tools to read and write neural code. To read and write human.

I started Kernel, and then less than a year later both Elon Musk and Mark Zuckerberg did similar things. Elon started a company that was roughly in a similar vein as mine, a similar trajectory of trying to figure out how to re-write human to play well with AI, and then Facebook decided to do theirs focused on further engagement with their users within the Facebook experience. Though it's still to be determined whether Neuralink, Facebook, and Kernel will be successful over the next couple of years, at least there's a few of us going at it, which I think is an encouraging situation for the entire industry.

MARTIN FORD: Do you have a sense of how long all this could take? When do you imagine that there will be some sort of device, or chip that is readily available that will enhance human intelligence?

BRYAN JOHNSON: It really depends upon the modality. If it's implantable, there is a longer time frame, but if it's not invasive, then that is a shorter time frame. My guess on the time frame is that within 15 years neural interfaces will be as common as smartphones are today.

MARTIN FORD: That seems pretty aggressive.

BRYAN JOHNSON: When I say neural interfaces, I am not specifying the type. I am not saying that people have a chip implanted in their brain. I'm just saying that the user will be able to bring the brain online.

MARTIN FORD: What about the specific idea that you might be able to download information or knowledge directly into your brain? A simple interface is one thing. But to actually download information seems especially challenging because I don't believe we have any real understanding of how information is stored in the brain. So, the idea that you could take information from another source and inject it directly into your brain really seems like a strictly science-fiction concept.

BRYAN JOHNSON: I agree with that, I don't think anybody could intelligently speculate on that ability. We have demonstrated methods for enhanced learning or enhanced memory, but the ability to decode thoughts in the brain has not been demonstrated. It's impossible to give a date because we are inventing the technology as we speak.

MARTIN FORD: One of the things that I have written a lot about is the potential for a lot of jobs to be automated and the potential for rising unemployment and workforce inequality. I have advocated the idea of a basic income, but you're saying the problem would be better solved by enhancing the cognitive capabilities of people. I think there are a number of problems that come up there.

One is that it wouldn't address the issue that a large fraction of jobs is routine and predictable, and they will eventually be automated by specialized machines. Increasing the cognition of workers won't help them keep those jobs. Also, everyone has different levels of ability to begin with, and if you add some technology that enhances cognition, that might raise the floor, but it probably wouldn't make everyone equal. Therefore, many people might still fall below the threshold that would make them competitive.

Another point that is often raised with this kind of technology is that access to it is not going to be equal. Initially, it's going to only be accessible to wealthy people. Even if the devices get cheaper and more people can afford them, it seems certain that there would be different versions of this technology, with the better models only accessible to the wealthy. Is it possible that this technology could actually increase inequality, and maybe add to the problem rather than address it?

BRYAN JOHNSON: Two points about this. At the top of everybody's minds are questions around inequality, around the government owning your brain, around people hacking your brain, and around people controlling your thoughts. The moment people contemplate the possibility of interfacing with their brain, they immediately jump into loss mitigation mode—what's going to go wrong?

Then, different scenarios come to mind: Will things go wrong? Yes. Will people do bad things? Yes. That's part of the problem, humans always do those things. Will there be unintended consequences? Yes. Once you get past all these conversations, it opens up another area of contemplation. When we ask those questions, we assume that somehow humans are in this undisputed secure position on this planet and that we can forfeit all the considerations as a species, so we can optimize for equality and other things.

My fundamental premise is that we are at risk of going extinct by doing harm to ourselves, and by exterior factors. I'm coming to this conversation with the belief that whether we enhance ourselves is not a question of luxury. It's not like should we, or shouldn't we? Or what are the pros and cons? I'm saying that if humans do not enhance themselves, we will go extinct. By saying that, though, I'm not saying that we should be reckless, or not thoughtful, or that we should embrace inequality.

What I'm suggesting is that the first principle discussion of conversation is that it is an absolute necessity. Once we acknowledge that, then we can contemplate and say, "Now given this constraint, how do we best accommodate everyone's interest within society? How do we make sure that we march forward at a steady pace together? How do we ensure that we design into the system knowing that people are going to abuse it?" There is a famous quote that the internet was designed with criminals in mind, so the question is, how do we design neural interfaces knowing that people are going to abuse it? How do we design it knowing that the government is going to want to get into your brain? How do we do all of those things? That is a conversation that is not currently happening. People stop at this luxury argument, which I think is short-sighted, and one of the reasons why we're in trouble as a species.

MARTIN FORD: It sounds like you're making a practical argument that realistically we may have to accept more radical inequality. We may have to enhance a group of people so that they can solve the problems we face. Then after the problems are solved, we can turn our attention to making the system work for everyone. Is that what you're saying?

BRYAN JOHNSON: No, what I am suggesting is that we need to develop the technology. As a species we need to upgrade ourselves to be relevant in the face of artificial intelligence, and to avoid destroying ourselves as a species. We already possess the weaponry to destroy ourselves today, and we've been on the verge of doing that for decades.

Let me put it in a new frame. I think it's possible that in 2050, humans look back and they say, "oh my goodness, can you believe that humans in 2017 thought it was acceptable to maintain weapons that could annihilate the entire planet?" What I am suggesting is that there's a future of human existence that is more remarkable than we can even imagine. Right now, we're stuck in our current conception of reality, and we can't get past this contemplation that we might be able to create a future based on harmoniousness instead of competition, and that we might somehow have a sufficient amount of resources and a mindset for all of us to thrive together.

We immediately jump into the fact that we always strive to hurt one another. What I am suggesting is this is why we need enhancement to get past these limits and cognitive bias that we have. So, I am in favor of enhancing everybody at the same time. That puts a burden on the development of the technology, but that's what the burden needs to be.

MARTIN FORD: When you describe this, I get the sense that you're thinking in terms of not just enhancing intelligence, but also morality and ethical behavior and decision making. Do you think that there's potential for technology to make us more ethical and altruistic as well?

BRYAN JOHNSON: To be clear, I find that intelligence is such a limiting word in its conception. People associate intelligence with IQ, and I'm not doing that at all. I don't want to suggest only intelligence. When I talk about humans radically improving themselves, I mean in every possible realm. For example, let me paint a picture of what I think could happen to AI. AI is extremely good at performing logistical components of our society, an example being it will be a lot better at driving cars than humans. Give AI enough time, and it will be substantially better, and there will be fewer deaths on the road. We'll look back and say, "can you believe humans used to drive?" AI is a lot better at flying autopilot on an airplane; it's a lot better at playing Go and chess.

Imagine a scenario where we can develop AI to a point where AI largely runs the logistical aspects of everyone's lives: transportation, clothing, personal care, health—everything is automated. In that world, our brain is now freed from doing what it does for 80% of the day. It's free to pursue higher-order complexities. The question now is, what will we do? For example, what if studying physics and quantum theory produced the same reward system that watching the Kardashians does today? What if we found out that our brains could extend to four, five, or ten dimensions? What would we create? What would we do?

What I'm suggesting is the hardest concept in the entire world to grasp, because our brain convinces us that we are an all-seeing eye, that we understand all of the things around us, and that current reality is the only reality. What I am suggesting is that there is a future in cognitive enhancement that we can't even see, and that's what limits our imaginations to contemplate it. It's like going back in time and asking Gutenberg to imagine all the kinds of books that will be written. Since then, the literary world has flourished over the centuries. The same thing is true for neural enhancement, and so you start to get a scale of how gigantic a topic this is.

By traveling through this topic, we'll get into the constraints of our imagination, we'll get into human enhancement, people will have to address all their fears even to get to a point where they'd be open to thinking about this. They have to reconcile with AI, they have to figure out if AI is a good thing or a bad thing. If we did enhance ourselves, what would it look like? To squeeze this all into a topic is really hard, and that's why this stuff is so complex, but also so important. Yet, getting to a level where we can talk about this as a society is very hard, because you have to scaffold your way to all the different pieces we have to get someone who is willing to scaffold to these different layers, and that's the hardest part of this.

MARTIN FORD: Assuming you could actually build this technology, then how as a society do we talk about it and really wrestle with the implications, particularly in a democracy? Just look at what's happened with social media, where a lot of unintended and unanticipated problems have clearly developed. What we're talking about here could be an entirely new level of social interaction and interconnection, perhaps similar to today's social media, but greatly amplified. What would address that? How should we prepare for that problem?

BRYAN JOHNSON: The first question is, why would we expect anything different than what's happened with social media? It's entirely predictable that humans will use the tools they are given to pursue their own self-interests along the lines of making money, gaining status, respect, and an advantage over others. That's what humans do, and it's how we've wired to do, and it how we've always done it. That's what I am saying, we haven't improved ourselves. We're the same.

We would expect this to happen just like it did with social media; after all, humans are humans. We'll always be humans. What I'm suggesting is this is the reason why we enhance ourselves. We know what humans do with stuff, it's a very proven model. We have thousands and thousands of years of data to know what humans do with stuff. We need to go beyond humans, to something akin to humanity 3.0 or 4.0. We need to radically improve ourselves as a species beyond what we can imagine, but the issue is that we don't have the tools to that right now.

MARTIN FORD: Are you suggesting that all of this in some sense would have to be regulated? There's a possibility that as an individual, I might not want my morality to be enhanced. Perhaps I just want to enhance my intelligence, my speed, or something similar, so that I can profit from that without buying in to the other beneficial stuff that you perceive happening. Wouldn't you need some overall regulation or control of this to be sure that it's used in a way that benefits everyone?

BRYAN JOHNSON: May I adjust the framing of your question in two ways? First, your statement about regulation implicitly assumes that our government is the only group that can arbitrate interests. I do not agree with that assumption. The government is not the only group in the entire world that can regulate interests. We could potentially create self-sustaining communities of regulation; we do not have to rely on government. The creation of new regulating bodies or self-regulating bodies can emerge that keep the government from being the sole keeper of that.

Second, your statement on morals and ethics assumes that you as a human have the luxury to decide what morals and ethics you want. What I'm suggesting is that if you look back through history, almost every biological species that has ever existed on this earth for the four-plus billion years it has existed have gone extinct. Humans are in a tough spot, and we need to realize we're in a tough spot because we are not born in an inherent position of luxury. We need to make very serious contemplations, which does not mean that we're not going to have moral ethics; it does. It just means that it needs to be balanced to realize that we are in a tough spot.

For example, there's a couple of books that have come out, like *Factfulness: Ten Reasons We're Wrong About the World, and Why Things Are Better Than You Think*, by Hans Rosling, and Steven Pinker's *The Better Angels of Our Nature: Why Violence Has Declined*. Those books basically say that the world's not bad, and that although everyone says how terrible it is, all the data says it's getting better, and it's getting better faster. What they're not contemplating is that the future is dramatically different to the past. We've never had a form of intelligence in the form of AI that has progressed this fast. Humans have never had these types of tools that have been this destructive. We have not experienced this future before, and it's our very first time going through this.

That's why I don't buy the historical determinism argument that somehow because we've done well in the past, we're guaranteed to do well in the future. I would say that I'm equal parts optimistic about what the future can bring, but I'm also equal parts cautious. I'm cautionary in terms of acknowledging that in order for us to be successful in the future, we must achieve future literacy. We must also be able to start planning for, thinking about, and creating models for the future that enable us to become future literate.

If you look at us as a species now, we fly by the seat of our pants. We pay attention to things when they become a crisis and we can't plan ahead, and as humans, we know this. We typically do not get ahead in life if we don't plan for it, and as a species, we have no plan. So again, there are all these concepts that if we are hoping to survive in the future, what gives us confidence that we can do that? We don't plan for it, we don't think about it, and we don't look at anything else beyond individuals, individual states, companies, or countries. We've never done it before. How do we deal with that in a thoughtful way so that we can maintain the things we care about?

MARTIN FORD: Let's talk more generally about artificial intelligence. First of all, is there anything that you can talk about in terms of your portfolio companies and what they are doing?

BRYAN JOHNSON: The companies that I invested in are using AI to push science discovery forward. That's the one thing they all have in common, whether they're developing new drugs to cure disease, or finding new proteins for everything, for inputs into agriculture, for food, drugs, pharmaceuticals, or physical products. Whether these companies are designing microorganisms, like synthetic bio, or they're designing new materials, like true nanotech, they're all using some form of machine learning.

Machine learning is a tool that is enabling discovery faster and better than anything we've ever had before. A couple of months ago, Henry Kissinger wrote an open letter to *The Atlantic* saying that when he was aware of what AlphaGo did in chess and Go, he was worried about "strategically unprecedented moves." He literally sees the world as a board game because he was in politics in the cold-war era when the US and Russia were arch rivals, and we literally were, both in chess and as nation states. He saw that when you apply AI to chess and Go—and human geniuses have been playing those games for thousands of years—when we gave the game to AlphaGo within a matter of days, the AI came up with genius moves that we had never seen before.

So, sitting underneath our nose the entire time was undiscovered genius. We didn't know, and we couldn't see it ourselves, but AI showed it to us. Henry Kissinger saw that, and he said, that makes me scared. I see that, and I say that's the best thing in the entire world because AI has the ability to show us what we cannot see ourselves. This is a limitation when humans cannot imagine the future. We cannot imagine what radically enhancing ourselves means, we can't imagine what the possibilities are, but AI can fill this gap. That's why I think it's the best thing that could ever happen to us; it is absolutely critical for us to survive. The issue is that most people, of course, have accepted this narrative of fear from outspoken people who have talked about it, and I think it's terribly damaging that as a society that narrative is ongoing.

MARTIN FORD: There is a concern expressed by people like Elon Musk and Nick Bostrom, where they talk about the fast take-off scenario, and the control problem related to superintelligence. Their focus is on the fear that AI could get away from us. Is that something we should worry about? I have heard the case made that by enhancing cognitive capability we will be in a better position to control the AI. Is that a realistic view?

BRYAN JOHNSON: I'm appreciative of Nick Bostrom for being as thoughtful as he has been about the risks that AI presents. He started this whole discussion, and he's been fantastic in framing it. It is a good use of time to contemplate how we might anticipate undesired outcomes and work to fend those off, and I am very appreciative that he allocated his brain to do that.

Regarding Elon, I think the fear mongering that he has done is a negative in society, because in comparison it has not been as thorough and thoughtful as Nick's work. Elon has basically just taken it out to the world, and both created and inflicted fear among a class of people that can't comment intelligently on the topic, which I think is unfortunate. I also think we would be well suited as a species to be humbler in acknowledging our cognitive limitations and in contemplating how we might improve ourselves in every imaginable way. The fact that it is not our number one priority as a species demonstrates the humility we need.

MARTIN FORD: The other thing I wanted to ask you about is that there is a perceived race with other countries, and in particular China both in terms of AI, and potentially with the kind of neural interface technology you're working on with Kernel. What's your view on that? Could competition be positive since it will result in more knowledge? Is it a security issue? Should we pursue some sort of industrial policy to make sure that we don't fall behind?

BRYAN JOHNSON: It's how the world works currently. People are competitive, nation states are competitive, and everybody pursues their self-interest above the other. This is exactly how humans will behave, and I come back to the same observation every single time.

The future that I imagine for humans that paves the way for our success is one in which we are radically improved. Could it mean we live in harmoniousness, instead of a competition-based society? Maybe. Could it mean, something else? Maybe. Could it mean a rewiring of our ethics and morals so far that we won't even be able to recognize it from our viewpoint today? Maybe. What I am suggesting is we may need a level of imagination about our own potential and the potential of the entire human race to change this game, and I don't think this game we're playing now is going to end well.

MARTIN FORD: You've acknowledged that if the kinds of technologies that you are thinking about fell into the wrong hands, then that could pose a great risk. We'd need to address that globally, and that seems to present a coordination problem.

BRYAN JOHNSON: I totally agree, I think we absolutely need to focus on that possibility with the utmost attention and care. That's how human and nation states are going to behave based on historical data.

An equal part to that is that we need to extend our imagination to a point where we can alter that fundamental reality to where we may not have to assume that everyone's going to just work on their own interests and that people will do whatever they can to other people to achieve what they want. What I am suggesting is that calling into question those fundamentals is something we are not doing as a society. Our brain keeps us trapped in our current perception of what is reality because it's very hard to imagine that the future would be different to what we currently live in.

MARTIN FORD: You have discussed your concern that we might all become extinct, but overall, are you an optimist? Do you think that as a race we will rise to these challenges?

BRYAN JOHNSON: Yes, I would definitely say I'm an optimist. I'm absolutely bullish on humanity. The statements I make about the difficulties that we face are in order to create a proper assessment of our risk. I don't want us to have our heads in the sand. We have some very serious challenges as a species, and I think we need to reconsider how we approach these problems. That's one of the reasons why I founded OS Fund—we need to invent new ways to solve the problems at hand.

As you've heard me say many times now, I think we need to rethink the first principles on our existence as a human, and what we can become as a species. To that end, we need to prioritize our own improvement above everything else, and AI is absolutely essential for that. If we do that to a point where we can prioritize our improvement and get fully involved in AI, in a way that we both progress together, I think we can solve all the problems that we are facing, and I think we can create an existence that's far more magical and fantastic than anything we can imagine.

BRYAN JOHNSON *is founder of Kernel, OS Fund and Braintree.*

In 2016, he founded Kernel, investing $100M to build advanced neural interfaces to treat disease and dysfunction, illuminate the mechanisms of intelligence, and extend cognition. Kernel is on a mission to dramatically increase our quality of life as healthy lifespans extend. He believes that the future of humanity will be defined by the combination of human and artificial intelligence (HI+AI).

In 2014, Bryan invested $100M to start OS Fund, which invests in entrepreneurs commercializing breakthrough discoveries in genomics, synthetic biology, artificial intelligence, precision automation, and the development of new materials.

In 2007, Bryan founded Braintree (and acquired Venmo), which he sold to PayPal in 2013 for $800M. Bryan is an outdoor-adventure enthusiast, pilot, and the author of a children's book, Code 7.

BRYAN JOHNSON

When Will Human-Level AI be Achieved? Survey Results

As part of the conversations recorded in this book, I asked each participant to give me his or her best guess for a date when there would be at least a 50 percent probability that artificial general intelligence (or human-level AI) will have been achieved. The results of this very informal survey are shown below.

A number of the individuals I spoke with were reluctant to attempt a guess at a specific year. Many pointed out that the path to AGI is highly uncertain and that there are an unknown number of hurdles that will need to be surmounted. Despite my best persuasive efforts, five people declined to give a guess. Most of the remaining 18 preferred that their individual guess remain anonymous.

As I noted in the introduction, the guesses are neatly bracketed by two people willing to provide dates on the record: Ray Kurzweil at 2029 and Rodney Brooks at 2200.

Here are the 18 guesses:

2029 ....11 years from 2018
2036 ....18 years
2038 ....20 years
2040 ....22 years
2068 (3) .....50 years
2080 ....62 years
2088 ....70 years
2098 (2) .....80 years
2118 (3) .....100 years
2168 (2) .....150 years
2188 ....170 years
2200 ....182 years

Mean: 2099, 81 years from 2018

Nearly everyone I spoke to had quite a lot to say about the path to AGI, and many people—including those who declined to give specific guesses—also gave intervals for when it might be achieved, so the individual interviews offer a lot more insight into this fascinating topic.

It is worth noting that the average date of 2099 is quite pessimistic compared with other surveys that have been done. The *AI Impacts* website[1] shows results for a number of other surveys.

Most other surveys have generated results that cluster in the 2040 to 2050 range for human-level AI with a 50 percent probability. It's important to note that most of these surveys included many more participants and may, in some cases, have included people outside the field of AI research.

For what it's worth, the much smaller, but also very elite, group of people I spoke with does include several optimists, but taken as a whole, they see AGI as something that remains at least 50 years away, and perhaps 100 or more. If you want to see a true thinking machine, eat your vegetables.

---

1 https://aiimpacts.org/ai-timeline-surveys/

Acknowledgments

This book has truly been a team effort. Packt acquisitions editor Ben Renow-Clarke proposed this project to me in late 2017, and I immediately recognized the value of a book that would attempt to get inside the minds of the foremost researchers responsible for building the technology that will very likely reshape our world.

Over the past year, Ben has been instrumental in guiding and organizing the project, as well as editing the individual interviews. My role primarily centered on arranging and conducting the interviews. The massive undertaking of transcribing the audio recordings and then editing and structuring the interview text was handled by the very capable team at Packt. In addition to Ben, this includes Dominic Shakeshaft, Alex Sorrentino, Radhika Atitkar, Sandip Tadge, Amit Ramadas, Rajveer Samra, and Clare Bowyer for her work on the cover.

I am very grateful to the 23 individuals I interviewed, all of whom were very generous with their time, despite extraordinarily demanding schedules. I hope and believe that the time they invested in this project has produced a result that will be an inspiration for future AI researchers and entrepreneurs, as well as a significant contribution to the emerging discourse about artificial intelligence, how it will impact society, and what we need to do to ensure that impact is a positive one.

Finally, I thank my wife Xiaoxiao Zhao and my daughter Elaine for their patience and support as I worked to complete this project.

Index

C

D

`mapt.io`

Mapt is an online digital library that gives you full access to over 5,000 books and videos, as well as industry leading tools to help you plan your personal development and advance your career. For more information, please visit our website.

Why subscribe?

- Spend less time learning and more time coding with practical eBooks and Videos from over 4,000 industry professionals

- Learn better with Skill Plans built especially for you

- Get a free eBook or video every month

- Mapt is fully searchable

- Copy and paste, print, and bookmark content

Packt.com

Did you know that Packt offers eBook versions of every book published, with PDF and ePub files available? You can upgrade to the eBook version at `www.packt.com` and as a print book customer, you are entitled to a discount on the eBook copy. Get in touch with us at `service@packt.com` for more details.

At `www.packt.com`, you can also read a collection of free technical articles, sign up for a range of free newsletters, and receive exclusive discounts and offers on Packt books and eBooks.